CROSSING THE POMERIUM

CROSSING THE POMERIUM

The Boundaries of Political, Religious, and Military
Institutions from Caesar to Constantine

Michael Koortbojian

PRINCETON UNIVERSITY PRESS   PRINCETON & OXFORD

Copyright © 2020 by Princeton University Press

Published by Princeton University Press
41 William Street, Princeton, New Jersey 08540
6 Oxford Street, Woodstock, Oxfordshire OX20 1TR

press.princeton.edu

All Rights Reserved
ISBN 978-0-691-19503-2
ISBN (e-book) 978-0-691-19749-4

British Library Cataloging-in-Publication Data is available

Editorial: Rob Tempio and Matt Rohal
Production Editorial: Mark Bellis
Text and Jacket Design: Pamela L. Schnitter
Production: Erin Suydam
Publicity: Alyssa Sanford and Amy Stewart
Copyeditor: Cynthia Buck

Jacket image: Trajan's Column, Rome. Scene 91. Photo: K. Anger, Neg. D-DAI-ROM 89.559

This publication is made possible in part by a grant from the Barr Ferree Foundation Fund for Publications, Department of Art and Archaeology, Princeton University

This book has been composed in Stempel Garamond, and Palatino display

Printed on acid-free paper. ∞

Printed in the United States of America

1 3 5 7 9 10 8 6 4 2

CONTENTS

List of Illustrations	VII
Acknowledgments	XIII
Abbreviations	XV
Introduction: Antiquarian Reconstructions and Living Realities	1
1. Crossing the *Pomerium*: The Armed Ruler at Rome	10
2. Octavian's *Imperium Auspiciumque* in 43 BC and Their Late Republican Context	43
3. Roman Sacrifice and the *Ritus Militaris*	78
4. Constantine's Arch and His Military Image at Rome	123
Bibliography	169
Index of Ancient Texts	201
Index of Inscriptions	215
Index of Persons	217
Index of Works of Art	221
General Index	225

ILLUSTRATIONS

I. Crossing the *Pomerium*: The Armed Ruler at Rome

1. Cuirassed statue of Julius Caesar. Palazzo Senatorio, Rome. Photo: D-DAI-ROM 1932.409, Felbermeyer. — 15

2. Sacrifice relief. Musei Vaticani. Photo: Author. — 16

3. Republican cuirassed statue from Frascati. Glyptothek, Munich. Photo: Museum. — 17

4. *Denarius* with representation of the *toga picta*, Spanish mint, ca. 18 BC. *RIC* I^2, no. 99 = *BMC* I, no. 397 = Giard I, no. 1191. Photo: ANS 1944.100.39072. — 20

5. Statue of a Roman "general" from Tivoli. Museo Nazionale Romano, Palazzo Massimo alle Terme, Rome. Photo: D-DAI-ROM 32.412, Faraglia. — 21

6. Statue of a Roman "general" from Foruli. Museum, Chieti. Photo: D-DAI-ROM 67.841, Singer. — 21

7. Statue of Augustus from Prima Porta. Musei Vaticani. Photo: D-DAI-ROM 91.72, Anger. — 26

8. Portrait of Augustus from Lucus Feroniae. Antiquarium, Lucus Feroniae. Photo: D-DAI-ROM 62.574, Felbermeyer. — 28

9. *Aureus* depicting Augustus's Parthian arch, Spanish mint (Colonia Patricia?), ca. 18–17 BC. *RIC* I^2, no. 131 = *BMC* 427 = Giard I, no. 1228. Photo: © Trustees of the British Museum. — 38

ILLUSTRATIONS

II. Octavian's *Imperium Auspiciumque* in 43 BC and Their Late Republican Context

1. *Denarius* of Octavian [C. CAESAR. IMP], 43 BC. *RRC* 490/1. Photo: © Trustees of the British Museum. 72

2. *Aureus* of Octavian [C. CAESAR. COS. PONT AUG.] 43 BC. *RRC* 490/2. Photo: © Trustees of the British Museum. 76

3. *Aureus* of Octavian [CAESAR IIIVIR R.P.C.] 43–42 BC. *RRC* 497/1. Photo: © Trustees of the British Museum. 77

III. Roman Sacrifice and the *Ritus Militaris*

1. Panel relief of Marcus Aurelius sacrificing. Musei Capitolini, Rome. Photo: Malter MAL 510, courtesy of Arachne, Cologne. 80

2. Augustan tripod base depicting a *XVvir*. Louvre, Paris. Photo: Museum. 81

3. *Dupondius* of Domitian, AD 88. Giard III, no. 464 = *BMC* II, no. 430 = *RIC* II, no. 381. Photo: © Trustees of the British Museum. 82

4. Sacrifice (scene 86), Column of Trajan, Rome. Photo: D-DAI-ROM 89.552–553, Anger. 84

5. Sacrifice (scene 91), Column of Trajan, Rome. Photo: D-DAI-ROM 89.559, Anger. 84

6. Sacrifice (scene 99), Column of Trajan, Rome. Photo: D-DAI-ROM 89.573, Anger. 85

7. Sacrifice (scene 75), Column of Marcus Aurelius, Rome. Photo: D-DAI-ROM 41.2476, Felbermeyer. 86

8a/b. Tiberius sacrificing before the Capitoline temple. Silver cup from Boscoreale. Louvre, Paris. Photo: After *Monuments et Mémoirs Piot*, 1899. 91

9. Census/*lustratio* relief: "Altar of Domitius Ahenobarbus." Louvre, Paris. Photo: Museum, courtesy of Art Resource, New York. 96

ILLUSTRATIONS

10. *Suovetaurilia* (scene 103), Column of Trajan, Rome.
    Photo: D-DAI-ROM 89.582, Anger. ... 98
11. *Suovetaurilia* (scene 30), Column of Marcus Aurelius, Rome.
    Photo: D-DAI-ROM 89.248, Schlechter. ... 98
12. Sacrifice relief. Musei Vaticani. Photo: Author. ... 102
13. Altar from the Vicus Sandaliarius, Rome. Uffizi, Florence.
    Photo: D-DAI-ROM 65.2155, Koppermann. ... 103
14. *Extispicium* relief. Louvre, Paris. Photo: D-DAI-ROM 77.1757, Rossa. ... 104
15. Monument of Attalus Nonius. Museo Civico, Aesernia.
    Photo: CIL Berlin. ... 108
16. Altar of T. Flavius Felix from Eining. Photo: Heidelberg
    Epigraphische Datenbank. ... 109
17. General's sarcophagus. Villa Medici, Poggio a Caiano.
    Photo: G. Fittschen-Badura (Fitt 68-79-10), courtesy
    of Arachne, Cologne. ... 112
18. Antonine inscribed panel from Hadrian's Wall (Bridgeness).
    National Museum of Scotland, Edinburgh. Photo: Courtesy of
    Art Resource, New York. ... 113
19. Rinuccini sarcophagus. Staatliche Museen, Berlin.
    Photo: Museum (J. Laurentius). ... 114
20. Balbinus sarcophagus, Museo di Pretestato, Rome.
    Photo: D-DAI-ROM 72.482, Singer. ... 114
21. Hercules altar (drawing after *Mon. d. Inst.* VI/VII). Galleria
    Borghese, Rome. ... 116
22. Sacrifice to Hercules, Hadrianic roundel on the Arch of
    Constantine, Rome. Photo: D-DAI-ROM 32.66, Faraglia. ... 118
23. *Sestertius* of Septimius Severus, ca. AD 204. *RIC* IV.1, no. 761.
    Photo: © Trustees of the British Museum. ... 118
24. Sacrifice to Diana, Hadrianic roundel on the Arch of
    Constantine, Rome. Photo: D-DAI-ROM 32.45, Faraglia. ... 120

ILLUSTRATIONS

25. Detail: Small Hunt mosaic, Piazza Armerina. Photo: Courtesy of Art Resource, New York.   121

IV. Constantine's Arch and His Military Image at Rome

1. North face of Arch of Constantine, Rome. Photo: D-DAI-ROM 61.2297, Koppermann.   124
2. Detail: *Adlocutio*, Arch of Constantine, Rome. Photo: J. Bondono.   125
3. Detail: *Adventus*, Arch of Constantine, Rome. Photo: Courtesy of William Storage.   135
4. Gold medallion of Constantine. *RIC* VII, Trier, no. 469, AD 326. Photo: Museum, courtesy of J. Wienand.   138
5. *Aureus* of Constantine with three standards, *RIC* VI, Trier, no. 815, ca. AD 310–313. Photo: ANS 1944.100.6007.   142
6. *Denarius* of Trajan with three standards. *RIC* II, Rome, no. 294 = *BMC* 452, ca. 113–114. British Museum, London. Photo: © Trustees of the British Museum.   142
7. Detail: *Adlocutio*, Arch of Constantine, Rome. Photo: J. Bondono.   143
8. Detail: *Liberalitas*, Arch of Constantine, Rome. Photo: J. Bondono.   145
9. Calendar of AD 354: Roma. MS Barb. Lat. 2154, pt. B, fol. 2r. Biblioteca Apostolica Vaticana. Photo: Courtesy of the Biblioteca Apostolica Vaticana.   150
10. Calendar of AD 354: Gallus. MS Barb. Lat. 2154, pt. B, fol. 13r. Biblioteca Apostolica Vaticana. Photo: Courtesy of the Biblioteca Apostolica Vaticana.   151
11. Calendar of AD 354: Constantinus II. MS Barb. Lat 2154, pt. B, fol. 14r. Biblioteca Apostolica Vaticana. Photo: Courtesy of the Biblioteca Apostolica Vaticana.   152
12. The Four Tetrarchs, San Marco, Venice. Photo: D-DAI-ROM 68.5154, Singer.   153

ILLUSTRATIONS

13. Tetrarchic statue. Staatliche Museen, Museum für Byzantinische Kunst, Berlin (inv. 6128). Photo: Courtesy of Art Resource, New York. — 155

14. Statue of Constantine *loricatus*. Capitoline, Rome. Photo: D-DAI-ROM 67.1759, Singer. — 156

15. Constantine relief portrait from the passageway of the Arch of Constantine, Rome. Photo: D-DAI-ROM 35.612, Felbermeyer. — 157

16. Colossal Constantine portrait from the Forum of Trajan. Rome. Photo: Hannestad-06-A0032, courtesy of Arachne, Cologne. — 158

17. *Aureus* of Constantine. *RIC* VI, no. 151, Rome, AD 307 = *principi iuventutis*. Photo: © Trustees of the British Museum. — 159

18. *Aureus* of Constantine. *RIC* VI, 627, Trier, AD 306–307 = *principi iuventutis*. Photo: © Trustees of the British Museum. — 160

19. *Argenteus* of Constantine. *RIC* VI, 636, Trier, AD 306–307 = *virtus militum*. Photo: © Trustees of the British Museum. — 160

20. *Argenteus* of Constantine. *RIC* VI, 638, Trier, AD 306–307 = *virtus militum*. Photo: © Trustees of the British Museum. — 161

21. *Nummus* of Constantine. BM no. B2142 = Kent 1957, 454, AD 312 = *liberator orbis*. Rome. Photo: © Trustees of the British Museum. — 161

22. *Follis* of Constantine. *RIC* VI, no. 63, Alexandria, ca. AD 306–307 = *perpetuitas augg*. Photo: © Ashmolean Museum, University of Oxford. — 162

23. *Aureus* of Constantine. *RIC* VI, 284 (add.), Rome, ca. AD 312–313 = *ubique victores*. Photo: © Trustees of the British Museum. — 162

24. *Aes* of Constantine. *RIC* VII, no. 208A, Trier, ca. AD 318–319 = *victoriae latae princ perp*. Photo: © Trustees of the British Museum. — 163

25. Silver medallion of Constantine. *RIC* VII, 36, Ticinum, ca. AD 313–315? 321? Photo: Courtesy of Numismatica Ars Classica NAC AG (Auction 106, lot 1051). — 163

ACKNOWLEDGMENTS

Parts and versions of the material offered here were presented in lectures and seminars at Yale University (2005), the University of Pennsylvania (2014), Durham University (2014), Princeton University (2015), New York University (2015), and the Institute for Advanced Study (Princeton) (2017–2018). I am indebted to many colleagues for advice and assistance of various kinds, on those occasions and on others, including especially: Javier Arce, Hartwin Brandt, Matteo Cadario, Angelos Channiotis, Kathleen Coleman, Olivier Hekster, Ted Kaizer, Ann Kuttner, Daria Lanzuolo, Clemente Marconi, Michael Peachin, Greg Rowe, Amy Russell, William Storage, Andrew Wallace-Hadrill, and Johannes Wienand. Further, I am grateful to several individuals who read chapters and offered their critiques: Richard Brilliant, Christina Corsiglia, and Matthew Roller (chapter 1), Frederik Vervaet, Harriet Flower, and Corey Brennan (chapter 2), Tonio Hölscher (chapter 3), and Brent Shaw and Noel Lenski (chapter 4). And it was my very good fortune that Tonio Hölscher and Barbara Kellum agreed to read the entire manuscript for the press; they both generously corrected a variety of mistakes, alerted me to materials I might not otherwise have known, and forced me to sharpen the presentation of my ideas. All of these individuals have my most sincere gratitude for offering their wise advice, although they will realize that, in some instances, my stubbornness has prevailed.

As is the case with all scholarly endeavors, without the aid of libraries and librarians, practically nothing is possible. For their continued assistance I wish to acknowledge the staffs of the Marquand Library of Art and Archaeology at Princeton (especially Rebecca Friedman and Jessica Dağci), the Interlibrary Loan Office at Princeton's Firestone Library, and the Institute for Advanced Study's Historical Studies and Social Sciences Library. A sabbatical leave from

ACKNOWLEDGMENTS

my Princeton duties granted by the Dean of the Faculty and a membership at the Institute of Advanced Study were essential to this project's completion.

A word about footnotes, the bibliography, and translations is in order. I have endeavored to keep the notes, at times voluminous, as succinct as feasible (albeit failing, it must be admitted, in the case of chapter 1); *deo volente diabolo adiuvante*, this forestalls, as much as possible, their becoming miniature essays on differing interpretations. The bibliography is limited exclusively to works cited in the notes and includes at least some material that appeared up through 2018; to have done otherwise might have produced a second volume. The cited translations of Greek and Latin authors follow those of the Loeb editions, although occasionally I have modified them, sometimes substantially; translations of the epigraphic material are my own unless otherwise noted. And finally, it will be observed that I idiosyncratically cite Mommsen's *Staatsrecht* in the 1887–1888 (third) edition as well as in Girard's French translation of 1889–1896. I have done so, not only in deference to my numerous French colleagues whose work has, to such a great degree, paved the way for my own, but because this monumental work constitutes perhaps the most thoroughgoing attempt to interpret Mommsen's fundamental achievement.

Lastly, I am grateful for Rob Tempio, Matt Rohal, Mark Bellis, Cynthia Buck, and the staff at PUP—all of whom have shepherded this volume to publication.

PRINCETON, MAY 2019

ABBREVIATIONS

AA	*Archäologischer Anzeiger*
ActaArchArtiumPert	*Acta ad archaeologiam et artium historiam pertinenta*
ActaArchHung	*Acta archaeologica Academiae scientiarum Hungaricae*
ActaClDebrec	*Acta classica Universitatis scientiarum Debreceniensis*
AHR	*American Historical Review*
AJA	*American Journal of Archaeology*
AJAH	*American Journal of Ancient History*
AJN	*American Journal of Numismatics*
AJP	*American Journal of Philology*
ANRW	*Aufstieg und Niedergang der römischen Welt*
ArchCl	*Archeologia Classica*
ARG	*Archiv für Religionsgeschichte*
ARID	*Analecta Romana Instituti Danici, Roma*
ArtBull	*The Art Bulletin*
AttiMemAccPat	*Atti e Memorie dell'Accademia Patavina*
BABesch	*Bulletin antieke beschaving: Annual Papers on Classical Archaeology*
Bjb	*Bonner Jahrbücher des rheinischen Landesmuseums in Bonn und des Vereins von Altertumsfreunden im Rheinlande*
BMC	H. Mattingly, *Coinage of the Roman Empire in the British Museum*, vols. I–III., London, 1923–1936 (reprint, 1965–1966)

ABBREVIATIONS

BMonMusPont	*Bollettino dei monumenti, musei e gallerie Pontificie*
Bonner HAC	*Bonner Historia Augusta Colloquium*
BullComm	*Bullettino della Commissione archeologica comunale di Roma*
CAH XII	A. K. Bowman, P. Garnsey, and A. Cameron, eds., *The Cambridge Ancient History: The Crisis of Europe*, AD 193–337, Cambridge, 2005
CalifStClassAnt	*California Studies in Classical Antiquity*
CCG	*Cahiers du Centre Gustave Glotz*
Chiron	*Chiron: Mitteilungen der Kommission für alte Geschichte und Epigraphik des Deutschen Archäologischen Instituts*
CIL	*Corpus Inscriptionum Latinarum*, Berlin, 1861ff
CJ	*Classical Journal*
COSTANTINO I	*Costantino I: Enciclopedia costantiniana sulla figura e l'immagine dell'imperatore del cosiddetto editto di Milano 313–2013*, 3 vols., Rome, 2013
CP	*Classical Philology*
CQ	*Classical Quarterly*
CSEL	*Corpus Scriptorum Ecclesiasticorum Latinorum*
DialArch	*Dialoghi di Archeologia*
DOP	*Dumbarton Oaks Papers*
Droits	*Droits: Revue française de théorie juridique*
EJ	V. Ehrenberg and A. H. M. Jones, *Documents Illustrating the Reigns of Augustus and Tiberius*, 2nd ed., Oxford, 1955
FRH	T. J. Cornell, ed., *The Fragments of the Roman Historians*, 3 vols., Oxford, 2013
Giard	J.-B. Giard, *Monnaies de l'empire romain*, 2nd ed., 4 vols., Paris, 1988
Helbig[4]	W. Helbig, *Führer durch die öffentlichen Sammlungen klassischer Altertümer in Rom*, 4th ed., 4 vols., Tübingen, 1963–1972
HSCP	*Harvard Studies in Classical Philology*

ABBREVIATIONS

ILLRP	*Inscriptiones Latinae Liberae Rei Publicae*, ed. A. Degrassi, 2 vols., Florence, 1965
ILS	*Inscriptiones Latinae Selectae*, ed. H. Dessau, 5 vols., Berlin, 1892ff
Inscr. Ital.	*Inscriptiones Italicae*, vol. XIII, *Fasti et Elogiae*, ed. A. Degrassi, Rome, 1947
JdI	*Jahrbuch des Deutschen Archäologischen Instituts*
JECS	*Journal of Early Christian Studies*
JLA	*Journal of Late Antiquity*
JRA	*Journal of Roman Archaeology*
JRS	*Journal of Roman Studies*
JSAH	*Journal of the Society of Architectural Historians*
LSA	"Last Statues of Antiquity" database: http://laststatues.classics.ox.ac.uk/
LTUR	*Lexicon Topographicum Urbis Romae*, ed. E. M. Steinby, 5 vols., Rome, 1993–1999
MAAR	*Memoirs of the American Academy in Rome*
MedAnt	*Mediterraneo antico: Economie, società, cultura (Pisa)*
MededRom	*Mededelingen van het Nederlands instituut te Rome*
MEFRA	*Mélanges d'Archéologie et d'Histoire de l'École Française de Rome, Antiquité*
Métis	*Métis: Revue d'anthropologie du monde grec ancien*
Mon Ant	*Monumenti Antichi*
MH	*Museum Helveticum*
MRR	T.R.S. Broughton, *Magistrates of the Roman Republic* [1951], 3 vols., Atlanta, 1986
Pan. Lat.	C. E. V. Nixon and B. Saylor Rodgers, *In Praise of Later Roman Emperors: The Panegyrici Latini*, intro., trans., and historical commentary with the Latin text of R. A. B. Mynors, Berkeley, 1994
PAPhS	*Papers of the American Philosophical Society*
PBSR	*Papers of the British School at Rome*
PCPhS	*Proceedings of the Cambridge Philological Society*
Plattner-Ashby	S. B. Plattner and T. Ashby, *A Topographical Dictionary of Rome*, Oxford, 1926 (reprint ed., n.d.)

ABBREVIATIONS

PSAS	*Proceedings of the Society of Antiquaries of Scotland*
RA	*Revue Archéologique*
RE	*Real-Encyclopädie der klassischen Altertumswissenschaft*, ed. A. Pauly, G. Wissowa, and W. Kroll, Stuttgart, 1893ff
Rend Linc	*Rendiconti dell'Accademia nazionale dei Lincei, Classe di scienze morali, storiche e filologiche*
RendPontAccArch	*Rendiconti: Atti della Pontificia academia romana di archeologia*
RGDA	*Res Gestae Divi Augusti*
RhM	*Rheinisches Museum für Philologie*
RIC I²	C. H. V. Sutherland, *The Roman Imperial Coinage*, vol. I, *31 BC–AD 69*, 2nd, rev. ed., London, 1984
RIC II	H. Mattingly and E. A. Sydenham, *The Roman Imperial Coinage*, vol. II, *Vespasian to Hadrian*, London, 1926
RIC VI	C. H. V. Sutherland and R. A. G. Carson, *Roman Imperial Coinage*, vol. VI, *From Diocletian's Reform (AD 294) to the Death of Maximinus (AD 313)*, London, 1967
RIC VII	P. M. Bruun, *Roman Imperial Coinage*, vol. VII, *Constantine and Licinius, AD 313–337*, London, 1966
RIDA	*Revue internationale des droits de l'antiquité*
RM	*Römische Mitteilungen*
RRC	M. H. Crawford, *Roman Republican Coinage*, 2 vols., Cambridge, 1974
RS	M. H. Crawford, ed., *Roman Statutes*, 2 vols., London, 1996
ScAnt	*Scienze dell'Antichita: Storia, archeologia, antropologia (Rome)*
SchwMbll	*Schweizer Münzblätter*
SDHI	*Studia et Documenta Historiae et Iuris*
StClOr	*Studi classici e orientali*

ABBREVIATIONS

ThesCRA *Thesaurus Cultus et Rituum Antiquorum,*
 ed. V. Lambrinoudakis and J.-C. Balty, 5 vols.,
 Los Angeles, 2004
ZPE *Zeitschrift für Papyrologie und Epigraphik*
ZRG *Zeitschrift der Savigny-Stiftung für Rechtsgeschichte*

CROSSING THE POMERIUM

INTRODUCTION

Antiquarian Reconstructions and Living Realities

Roman antiquarians of the imperial age looked back across the centuries to imagine their city's beginnings. Historical sources were few, as well as late, and myths abounded concerning the topography of Romulus's foundation, the political and religious character of his undertaking, and the initial preparations for the Romans' establishment of their new settlement and the construction of its defensive walls. The accounts that had reputedly survived from the earliest Republican era were often contradictory, and hypotheses were enlisted to rationalize the fragmentary tales, to reconstruct a coherent if largely mythical story of the state's origin and its institutions, and to explain the evolution of the city's originating acts as the basis of what could be understood of its social and political development. So, for example, in the early second century AD, Plutarch attempted to provide a narrative:

> Romulus ... then set himself to building his city, after summoning from Tuscany men who prescribed all the details in accordance with certain sacred ordinances and writings, and taught them to him as in a religious rite. A circular trench was dug around what is now the Comitium, and in this were deposited first-fruits of all things the use of which was sanctioned by custom as good and by nature as necessary; and finally, every man brought a small portion of the soil of his native land, and these were cast in among the first-fruits and mingled with them. They call this trench, as they do the heavens, by the name of "mundus." Then, taking this as a center, they marked out the city in

INTRODUCTION

a circle round it. And the founder, having shod a plough with a brazen ploughshare, and having yoked to it a bull and a cow, himself drove a deep furrow round the boundary lines, while those who followed after him had to turn the clods, which the plough threw up, inwards towards the city, and suffer no clod to lie turned outwards. With this line they mark out the course of the wall, and it is called, by contraction, "*pomerium*," that is "*post murum*," behind or next the wall. And where they purposed to put in a gate, there they took the share out of the ground, lifted the plough over, and left a vacant space. And this is the reason why they regard all the wall as sacred except the gates; but if they held the gates sacred, it would not be possible, without religious scruples, to bring into and send out of the city things which are necessary, and yet unclean.[1]

Among the many things that might be said about this reconstruction, in the present context three stand out.[2]

First, by Plutarch's day, the details of Rome's early political topography and the loci of the significant acts of foundation had long been lost to the passage of time. For instance, his account of the *mundus*, and its location at the Comitium in the Forum Romanum, is contradicted by other sources that place it on the Palatine.[3] In this confusion one might rightly see a dim reflection of the conflicting priority in early Roman narratives of the city's two rival centers—the hilltop's early mythology and the valley's status—in what has been established as historical chronology. Similarly, the definition of the *pomerium* as well as its relationship to the initial plowing of the primordial furrow (*sulcus primigenius*) and the subsequently built walls were contested by other antiquarian reconstructions. And the homology between the circular form of the Comitium and that of the *pomerium*'s trench surrounding the city

---

[1] Plut. *Rom.* 11.1–3.
[2] The sources for the highly selective sketch that follows are provided in the succinct accounts in *LTUR*, s.v. *mundus* (Coarelli), *pomerium* (Andreussi), and *Roma Quadrata* (Coarelli), to which add the discussions of Simonelli 2001, De Sanctis 2007, Carlà 2015, Maccari 2015, Sisani 2016—all of which update the bibliography.
[3] Notably Festus 310L.

("in a circle")[4] is challenged by those accounts that set the *mundus* on the Palatine and connect it to the demarcation of the city known as *Roma Quadrata*.[5] This alternative vision of Rome's initial topography marked by the city's early institutions was still known to Tacitus, Plutarch's contemporary, according to whom the *pomerium* ran, in roughly squarish form,

> from the Forum Boarium, then, where the bronze bull which meets the view is explained by the animal's use in the plough, the furrow to mark out the town was cut so as to take in the great altar of Hercules. From that point, boundary-stones were interspersed at fixed intervals along the base of the Palatine Hill up to the altar of Consus, then to the old curiae, then again to the shrine of the Lares, and after that to the Forum Romanum.[6]

A second conspicuous aspect of Plutarch's account is his emphasis on the religious character of Rome's foundation. In addition to the explicitly Etruscan origin of the foundation ceremony, a civic act that took place on a day vouchsafed by positive auspices, there is Livy's specific claim for the *pomerium*'s status as a *locus auguratus*; thus, Jupiter had sanctioned the delimiting of the city, and the significance of the site where this was enacted had been duly transformed, the god's approval having been granted.[7] In this fashion, on religious grounds, the ancient Romans divorced their new city from the rural lands that surrounded it, and it is as a corollary of this division that the *pomerium* was held to mark the limit of the urban auspices.[8]

---

[4] Commentary in De Sanctis 2007, 510, n. 35; cf. Varro's use of *orbis* at *Ling.* 5.143, and De Sanctis's discussion at 507.

[5] *Quadrata Roma in Palatio ante templum Apollinis dicitur, ubi reposita sunt, quae solent boni ominis gratia in urbe condenda adhiberi, quia saxo †minitus† est initio in speciem quadratam. Eius loci Ennius (Ann. 157L) meminit cum ait et †quis est erat† Romae regnare quadratae* (Festus 310-12L).

[6] Tac. *Ann.* 12.24, with Cecamore 2002.

[7] *Die auspicato*: Varro *Ling.* 5.143. *Inaugurato*: Livy 1.44.4; cf. Festus 294L with Lindsay's integration: <*ponti*>*ficalis pomerium, id est l*<*ocum quem pontifex transit auspi*>*cato*; with assent, Simonelli 2001, 125, and Carlà 2015, 621.

[8] Gell. 13.14.1–3 (*pomerium . . . finem urbani auspicii*); Cic. *Phil.* 2.40.102 (*colonia auspicato deducta*); cf. Livy 5.52.15 (*quid alia quae auspicato agimus omnia fere intra pomerium?*).

INTRODUCTION

Third, as the city's new walls separated what was *intra pomerium* from *extra pomerium*, they divided what belonged to the new foundation from what did not by the imposition of public land that belonged to the city itself and could not "by any legal means be removed from public ownership."⁹ In this sense, as the *urbs* developed over time the *pomerium* marked the end of the *continentia aedificia*, the sprawl of construction that signaled not only the city's habitation but its social and cultural advancement from the primordial huts of the original Palatine settlement.

The walls' construction provoked exclusions as well as protections, especially given the city's profoundly sacral character, and chief among the former were those acts deemed the province of the god Mars (*imperium militiae*), which religious scruple did not allow within the city.¹⁰ Thus the *comitia centuriata* met in the Campus Martius, and the two temples dedicated to the god himself were consigned beyond the *pomerium*, one *in circo*, in the Circus Flaminius, the other *in clivo*, reportedly on the Via Appia.¹¹

༄

In all three of these ways (indeed, there were others), the Roman antiquarians explained to themselves the origins of their city and its often baffling institutions. The *pomerium*, as a fundamental feature of Rome's political topography, proved especially confounding, as we have already seen. Its religious role lived on, cultivated by those priesthoods—the augurs and the pontiffs—charged with its related rituals. But the realities that accompanied Rome's growth from the Romulean foundation to the *caput mundi* rendered much of the surviving lore that surrounded the city's mythic past incommensurate with early imperial life in the *urbs*. The sheer scale of the city challenged one's belief in so many of the stories about its formation and its growth; thus, in the age of Augustus, Dionysius of Halicarnassus attributed to Servius Tullius the first great enlargement of the city in the sixth century:

---

⁹ Frontin., *De Controversiis*: *eum dico lucum quem nec ordo nullo iure a populo poterit amovere* (Lachmann, 1848), I:17, trans. Campbell 2000, 67.
¹⁰ Gell. 15.27.5, with the commentary of De Sanctis 2007, 504.
¹¹ Mars *in circo*: *LTUR* III:226–29 (Zevi); *in clivo*: Ziolkowski 1992, 101–4.

This king was the last who enlarged the circuit of the city, by adding these two hills [the Viminal and the Esquiline] to the other five, after he had first consulted the auspices, as the law directed, and performed the other religious rites. Farther than this the building of the city has not yet progressed, since the gods, they say, have not permitted it; but all the inhabited places round it, which are many and large, are unprotected and without walls, and very easy to be taken by any enemies who may come. If anyone wishes to estimate the size of Rome by looking at these suburbs he will necessarily be misled for want of a definite clue by which to determine up to what point it is still the city and where it ceases to be the city; so closely is the city connected with the country, giving the beholder the impression of a city stretching out indefinitely.[12]

The late Republican jurist Alfenus was apparently of the same opinion; so, in the *Digest*, it is reported that:

According to Marcellus [a jurist of the late second century AD], "As Alfenus said, 'urbs' means that part of 'Roma' which was surrounded by the wall, 'Roma' however also covers the neighboring built-up area (*continentia aedificia*); for one can see from daily usage that Rome is not regarded as extending only as far as the wall, since we say that we are going to Rome even if we live outside the urbs."[13]

The ancient city was compacted by the influx of foreigners that accompanied Republican expansion, in Italy and then abroad, and this new density was attended by the topographical extension of its center. The enlargement of the *pomerium* continued, although this would wait for more than half a millennium after Tullius's, and our sources are contradictory about who

---

[12] Dion. Hal. 4.13.4, with the broader context presented in Champlin 1982 (= 1985); commentary in Panciera 1999.

[13] *Dig.* 50.16.87; discussion in Carlà 2015, 619.

INTRODUCTION

was responsible and when; indeed, a certain mystery still remains save for the epigraphically attested expansions under Claudius and Vespasian.[14]

Under the pressures consequent to the city's expansion, traditional religious practices would give way to new ones. In what follows, chapters 1, 2, and 4 address the vexed question of how commanders would leave and enter the city, and how this was subject to continuous reinterpretations in a tradition that held sway for nearly a millennium. Chapter 2 examines how, by late Republican times, commanders who would have been forced by religious scruple to return to Rome for the reenactment of religious rites were now granted new dispensation, often in the form of political and religious "fictions" (examples are discussed in chapters 2, 3, and 4) that would accommodate new priorities with new protocols. Similarly, amid the continual military campaigns of Rome's expanding empire, the practice of taking the auspices by the observation of the flight of birds would be reconceived and redesigned. Romulus's "high-flying birds" (the *genus altivolantum*), reported by Ennius, were a past practice; rather than await the signs of the birds in the heavens, the Romans, in their haste, now carried them into the field in cages, starved so as to ensure that the signs would be favorable. Thus, Cicero complained that they seemed hardly believable as the messengers of Jupiter ("how can there be anything divine about an auspice so forced and so extorted?"), and Cato the Elder lamented that many auguries and auspices had been entirely abandoned and lost.[15] In this as in other matters, for those who regarded themselves as the guardians of Roman tradition, contemporary change was hardly seen as social progress.

Even as fundamental an exercise as the annual enrollment of the army (the *dilectus*) was subject to change over time. According to Polybius, the selection had customarily taken place on the Capitol, when, on the day decided, all those

---

[14] Enlargement of the *pomerium*: see the materials cited in n. 2 above and add: Rodríguez-Almeida 1978–1979/1979–1980; Boatwright 1986; Chioffi 1992–1993; Giardina 1995; Lyasse 2005; Coarelli 2009.

[15] Enn. *Ann.* I.81 = Cic. *Div.* 1.107, with the extensive commentary of Linderski 2007b. Birds in cages: Cic. *Div.* 2.73 and 1.27–28 (the latter = Cato in *FRH* F132, with Cornell's commentary; cf. commentary of Schultz 2014, *ad loc.*) and discussion in Koortbojian 2013, 75–76, with fig. III.22.

ANTIQUARIAN RECONSTRUCTIONS

liable for military service were to arrive in Rome.[16] Yet this does not always appear to have been the case, especially in emergencies. Dionysius provides a curious account of an event that suggests how, in such dire circumstances as reputedly existed in 483 BC, when M. Fabius and L. Valerius were consuls, the pressures of war transformed this annual ritual. For in the previous year, wars in Italy had taken a dramatic toll, and the new consuls,

> having taken office, asked for the levying of fresh troops to replace those who had perished in the war against the Antiates, in order that the gaps in the various centuries might be filled; and having obtained a decree of the senate, they appointed a day on which all who were of military age must appear. Thereupon there was a great tumult throughout the city and seditious speeches were made by the poorest citizens, who refused either to comply with the decrees of the senate or to obey the authority of the consuls, since they had violated the promises made to them concerning the allotment of land. And going in great numbers to the tribunes, they charged them with treachery. . . . Most of the tribunes did not regard it as a suitable time, when a foreign war had arisen, to fan domestic hatreds into flame again; but one of them, named Gaius Maenius, declared that he would not betray the plebeians or permit the consuls to levy an army unless they should first appoint commissioners for fixing the boundaries of the public land, draw up the decree of the senate for its allotment, and lay it before the people. When the consuls opposed this and made the war they had on their hands an excuse for not granting anything he desired, the tribune replied that he would pay no heed to them, but would hinder the levy with all his power. And this he attempted to do; nevertheless, he could not prevail to the end. For the consuls, going outside the city, ordered their generals' chairs to be placed in the near-by field; and there they not only enrolled the troops, but also fined those who refused obedience to the laws, since it was not in their power to seize their persons. . . . And the tribune who opposed the levy was no longer able to

---

[16] *Dilectus*: Nicolet 1988, 96–105; Polyb. 6.19–21.

INTRODUCTION

do anything. For those who are invested with the tribunate possess no authority over anything outside the city, since their jurisdiction is limited to the city walls.[17]

Here we find an antiquarian reconstruction of events that seemingly provides contemporary practices with their aetiologies. In the reputed clash between civil and military demands, the consuls, choosing to prioritize the latter, established themselves outside of the city's religio-political boundary and asserted their *imperium*, in the military sphere—*militiae*. Yet Dionysius's presentation not only contradicts Polybius's (much earlier) account of the traditional site of the enrollment of troops but acknowledges the role of the *pomerium* as the division of *res civiles* from *res militares* and retrojects it to the earliest moments of the Republic. Similarly anachronistic is his report of the tribunes' powers at such an early date (so too, in part, is Livy's version), and the finer details implied are misunderstood (for example, the fact that the limitation on the consuls' powers of *coercitio* within the active sphere of the tribunes' jurisdiction extended to the first milestone and thus was in effect in the Campus).[18]

In Dionysius's report, as in many preserved in Livy, in Plutarch, and in others, the realities of later Roman life—political, religious, or military—colored the vision of the past and remade traditions to conform to modern circumstances and practices. By the imperial age, Roman life had not only adapted itself to what had been preserved of its past, but also reconceived that past so as to validate its present. Such stories—for the Romans, the matter of their "history"—form both the backdrop and the foundation of the four chapters that make up the present volume.

---

[17] Dion. Hal. 8.87.3–6. Promises of land distribution made by Sp. Cassius, *cos.* 486: Dion. Hal. 8.69.3–4; cf. the presentation of events in Livy 2.42.6–9, who focuses solely on the denial of the allotments.

[18] Anachronisms: Lintott 2003, 122; for Livy, see Botsford 1909, 270, n. 2. *Coercitio* and its relation to the tribunes' powers: Mommsen 1887–1888, I:136–61 = Mommsen 1889–1896, 156–85; Lintott 2003, 97–99, 125–27. Extent of the tribunes' jurisdiction: Livy 3.20.7; Dio 51.19.6; one mile: *RS* I: no. 24, line 20, with parallels offered in the commentary of Nicolet and Crawford; cf. Gaius, *Inst.* 4.104.

ANTIQUARIAN RECONSTRUCTIONS

꿇

The interpretations that mark the studies collected here took shape over the course of nearly two decades. In a variety of ways, they take up the aforementioned themes, along with others, as they focus on a particular set of historical perplexities. Their common thread is the Romans' continuing effort to abide by—indeed, to live up to—the tenets of the political, religious, and military traditions they had inherited even when the meaning and purpose of those traditions were difficult, if not occasionally impossible, for them to understand. The four studies that follow address, each in its own way, the question of what it meant for the Romans to leave the hallowed ground of their capital for war or to return to it afterwards—even, at times, while still in the midst of military campaigns. In all of these chapters, the relationship between civic life at Rome and military life beyond its boundaries is scrutinized, albeit from differing points of view and to different historical purpose. In each, the "crossing of the *pomerium*," whether into the city (*ad domum*) or away from it (*ad militiam*), provides, explicitly or implicitly, the crux of a historical interpretation of certain distinctly Roman endeavors.

1

Crossing the *Pomerium*: The Armed Ruler at Rome

The distinction that the Romans made between *urbs* and *agri*, between the city and what lay beyond, is well known to all. A staple of both Roman public and augural law, it depended on the Romans' sense of the two spheres in which legitimate authority and the public auspices were held to obtain—"at home" and "in the field," *domi* and *militiae*, the proper realms of laws and war.[1]

The *pomerium* constituted the divison. It was a limit—but a conceptual, not a physical one. It was constituted not by the city's walls, but by the act of inaugurating the place where those defensive structures were to be built. The Etruscan rite of plowing the primordial furrow (the *sulcus primigenius*), the establishment of the ditch known as the *fossa*, and then the actual building of the city walls all depended on the site's formal inauguration, a matter of augural law. In a sense, we might say that the walls not only divided the *urbs*

---

[1] *Domi militiaeque*: Cic. *Div.* 1.3; *Leg.* 3.6, 2.31; cf. *Rep.* 1.63; Livy 10.8.9; Sall. *Cat.* 29.3; 52.21; cf. *domi forisque*: Livy 3.31.1, 6.11.1; Sall. *Jug.* 8.5.3. Spheres of war and law: Richardson 1991. Holders of *imperium* had, broadly speaking, four competences: political administration (*ius agendi cum populo, ius referendi*), military command, *iurisdictio*, and *coercitio* (so Rüpke 1990, 41). From a narrowly technical perspective, however, it is often held that the sphere of *imperium* pertained only beyond the boundary of the *urbs*; within was the sphere of *iurisdictio*: Linderski 1986, 2204–5; Magdelain 2015, 227–28, stressing the pairing *imperium iudicumque* (Cic. *Leg. Agr.* 2.34, *Div.* 1.3, *Leg.* 3.6, 2.31; Livy 10.8.9; Sall. *Cat.* 29.3, 52.213).

from the *agri*, but monumentalized what the *pomerium* stood for as a legal and religious idea.²

Thus, we comprehend that the distinction between the *urbs Romae* and the outside world was juridical and religious rather than merely geographical.³ When leaving the city and crossing the *pomerium*, the exercise of *imperium* took on its most fundamental aspect as the urban auspices ceased to be valid.⁴ Commanders now assumed the military auspices so as to exercise that power granted by the people in the military sphere (*imperium militiae*); the inverse situation held when entering the city, where the military facet of *imperium* was surrendered and a properly civil aspect of power prevailed. It was a fundamental tenet of the Republican constitution that, as magistrates moved between the spheres *domi* and *militiae*, it was required that the power to command be renewed. One took the auspices to acknowledge the passing of this fundamental boundary in either direction in order to inquire of Jupiter if the *imperium* about to be exercised in action—in either sphere of that authority—was unobstructed and might legitimately proceed. The import of these rituals is clear: without religious sanction, the power to command (*imperium*), whether exercised "at home" or "in the field," lost its legal foundation. So one readily understands how, for Roman magistrates and commanders, to "cross the *pomerium*" was a highly significant act.⁵

---

² Sources, bibliography, and discussion in *LTUR* IV (1999): 96–105 (Andreussi); analysis in Catalano 1978, 480; cf. Magdelain 1968, 65 ("le boulevard intérieur des murs . . . comme limite des auspices urbains"). Cogent synopsis in Beard, North, and Price 1998, I:177–81.

³ Distinction between *auspicia urbana* and *militaria* and its correspondence to that between *imperium domi* and *militiae*: Catalano 1960, 302–3, 431, n. 147, and 1978, 481. On these concepts' dual nature: Mommsen 1887–1888, I:61–70, 90, 99–101 = 1889–1896, I:69–76, 103, 113–16, with Brennan 2000, I:12–14. Giovannini 1983 rejects the idea of the boundary as essentially geographical; followed by Liou-Gille 1993, who argues for its "valeur symbolique ancienne" and gives priority to the two spheres in which *auspicia* might be held; cf. Fiori 2014b, 310, on the auspices ("una differenziazione spaziale"). For the vexed question of religious prohibitions: Orlin 2002.

⁴ *Pomerium* as the limit of urban auspices: Gell. 13.14.1; cf. Cic. *ND* 2.11, and *Div.* 1.33, with commentary in Magdelain 1968, 47–48.

⁵ The *lex Cornelia* established that military authority was held by the proconsuls *quoad in urbem introisse*: Cic. *Fam.* 1.9.25; cf. Cic. *Pis.* 50, for some of this law's other provisions. The need to renew one's *imperium* upon "crossing the *pomerium*": Mommsen 1887–1888,

CHAPTER 1

Yet legal distinctions did not always correspond to lived realities. Two examples must suffice. First, by the later Republic, the *pomerium* no longer marked the actual boundary of the city and the inhabitants of "Rome" did not reside solely within its limits, nor even inside the first milestone, to which this boundary was extended; thus, the *pomerium* ceased, in any real sense, to be the division between *domi* and *militiae*.[6] Second, and perhaps more significant, violence—and, at times, war—encroached on the city, which became, as a consequence, the center of the military sphere. The literary evidence for this is abundant: one need only think of Livy's account of 211 BC, with Hannibal's troops at the city walls.[7] Indeed, the rise of the dictatorship as an institution (which, as shall become clear, plays a fundamental role in our problem) is traced in the sources to precisely such conditions, and these would have a profound effect on other institutions as well. Thus, despite the traditional distinction between *domi* and *militiae*, not only arms but those quintessential symbols of the exercise of *imperium* in the military sphere—the *fasces* bound with axes—were allowed to be carried within the *pomerium*; on some occasions, *imperium militiae* was to find its role "at home."[8]

So we recognize that the assumption, repeatedly voiced, that a corollary of the distinction between *domi* and *militiae* was that arms were not to be carried within the *pomerium* is mistaken: armed troops *did* cross the *pomerium* and appeared in Rome—in art as well as in life—during the Republic as well as under the Empire.[9] While the Republican sources are, admittedly, ambigu-

---

I:67–68 = 1889–1896, I:75–76; Linderski 1986; Brennan 2004, 41–42, citing the example of Cicero's denigration of the validity of Verres's *imperium* at *Ver.* 2.5.34; see also Dio 39.63.4, for the example of Pompey, who, by custom, was prevented in 54 BC, from entering the city while a *proconsul*; on the transformation of the prohibition in late Republican and Augustan times: Ferrary 2001b.

[6] Mommsen 1887–1888, I:61–70 = 1889–1896, I:69–80; Richardson 1991, 3, with bibliography.

[7] Livy 26.9.6–10.10, with Mommsen 1887–1888, I:132 = 1889–1896, I:151, and Versnel 1970, 192.

[8] *Fasces cum securibus*: Magdelain 1968, 62–63. The varied competences associated with the exercise of *imperium domi* and the ceremonial appearance of arms have obscured the fundamental distinction. For example, the levying of troops was considered a civil matter and was conducted *domi*; rituals such as the *transvectio equitum*, in which armed equestrians paraded, were a conventionally *civic* display; see Magdelain 1968, 43; evidence and earlier bibliography in Alföldi 1970, 5–8, 47–49.

[9] For this mistaken assumption and the belief that it might serve to distinguish the settings of works of art, see Kleiner 1983, with earlier bibliography, and, most recently, Parisi Presicce 2013,

ous, those of the imperial period make plain that this ancient legal distinction had lost both its relevance and its reality: for instance, the stationing of troops in the capital was a staple of early imperial organization, and already by the reign of Tiberius the accompaniment of the emperor by an armed guard at Rome was an established practice.[10] Moreover, we have the striking evidence of the monuments: for example, on the Chatsworth relief we find armed men burning tax records, and on the Arch of Constantine the emperor appears *paludatus* in the forum. Despite the evidence of such images, discussions of some monuments—such as the Cancelleria reliefs—still founder on the mistaken view that a ban on all things military remained a fundamental aspect of Rome's civic life throughout the Roman era; the corollary, explicit or merely implied, is that this should be determinate for representations as well as reality. As we shall see, this was hardly the case. Although Republican Rome distinguished the *urbs* both legally and religiously from what lay beyond the *pomerium*, its fundamental boundary, the disintegration of this essential division was merely one of the many Republican traditions whose demise would gradually define the advent of empire.[11]

All Roman imagery demands to be set in the context of those legal, political, and religious institutions that not merely shaped but defined it. Three examples that have long been regarded as representations of the *imperator* are examined in the pages that follow; the meaning of these images is—as we shall see—hardly self-evident, despite convention. What ensues is an attempt to sketch the broader institutional background that allows us to establish *what it meant* to be represented in this fashion *at Rome* and, in so doing, to

---

126. Much of the discussion has revolved around the interpretation of the "Tiberius cup" from Boscoreale: Kuttner 1995, 140–42.

[10] Tac. *Ann.* 1.7.5, with Millar 1992, 61. Troops in the city under the empire: Coulston 2000.

[11] The appearance of *paludati* in Rome on the Anaglypha Traiani, the Chatsworth relief, and the Arch of Constantine has been noted by Kuttner 1995, 31, 46–48. Cancelleria relief B: Ghedini 1986 and, more recently, Herzog 2001, both with extensive bibliography. In general, see Lahusen 1983, 51–53.

CHAPTER 1

demonstrate what was, for the Romans of the dawning imperial age, the very real significance of "crossing the *pomerium*" and entering the city under arms.

The Dictator's Prerogative and Caesar's Statue

A statue of Julius Caesar is attested by the elder Pliny, who tells us that "Caesar the dictator allowed a cuirassed statue to be dedicated to himself in his forum (*loricatus in foro suo*)."[12] The work was in all likelihood of bronze, and may well be reflected (it is demonstrably not replicated) by a clearly later statue, now in the Senator's Palace on the Capitoline (figure I.1). That statue, according to a reference in a letter of the younger Pliny, seems to have still been standing in *his* day.[13] So, as Caesar's statue attests, in the late Republic and throughout the first century, men could clearly be *represented* in armor within the *pomerium*. But what did this represent? And what did such representations *mean*? These are our questions.

The statue's fame in the younger Pliny's day was sufficient that mention of it needed no further topographical reference—something might simply be *ad statuam loricatam divi Iulii*.[14] Was this because it was unusual? Images of cuirassed warriors are to be found among the surviving monuments of the late Republican period—for example, the Vatican relief (figure I.2) long (and mistakenly) associated with the taking of vows (the *nuncupatio votorum*).[15] There is an important difference, however, both in genre and in cultural significance, between these reliefs and what constituted an honorific statue. In fact, while the *statua loricata* was to become a central element of the imperial

---

[12] Plin. *HN* 34.18.

[13] *Loricatus in foro suo*: discussion in Weinstock 1971, 87; Corbier 1997; D'Accinni 1943–1945. The Capitoline statue: Albertoni 1993. Stemmer 1978, cat. VI 3, with Taf. 48.1, dates the cuirass-type and its decoration to the Trajanic era, comparing the fragmentary torso from Trajan's forum (cat. Va 1, Taf. 45, 5–6); for the *cingulum* as a Trajanic attribute, see 128–29 and notes. Pliny: *Ep.* 8.6.13–14.

[14] Plin. *Ep.* 8.6.13–14; discussion in Corbier 1997.

[15] *Nuncupatio votorum*: Wissowa 1912, 382; Scheid 1990, 339–56. Vatican "*nuncupatio*" relief: Kaschnitz von Weinberg 1937, 189–90; Simon in Helbig⁴ 1963, I:803–4; Felletti Maj 1977, 191–92; Kleiner 1983, 298; Kuttner 1995, 136–42; Holliday 2002, 176–77, and fig. 96. There is, as I have come to realize, no compelling reason to associate this scene with the *nuncupatio* (as in Koortbojian 2010, 250); see my discussion in chapter 3 at n. 54.

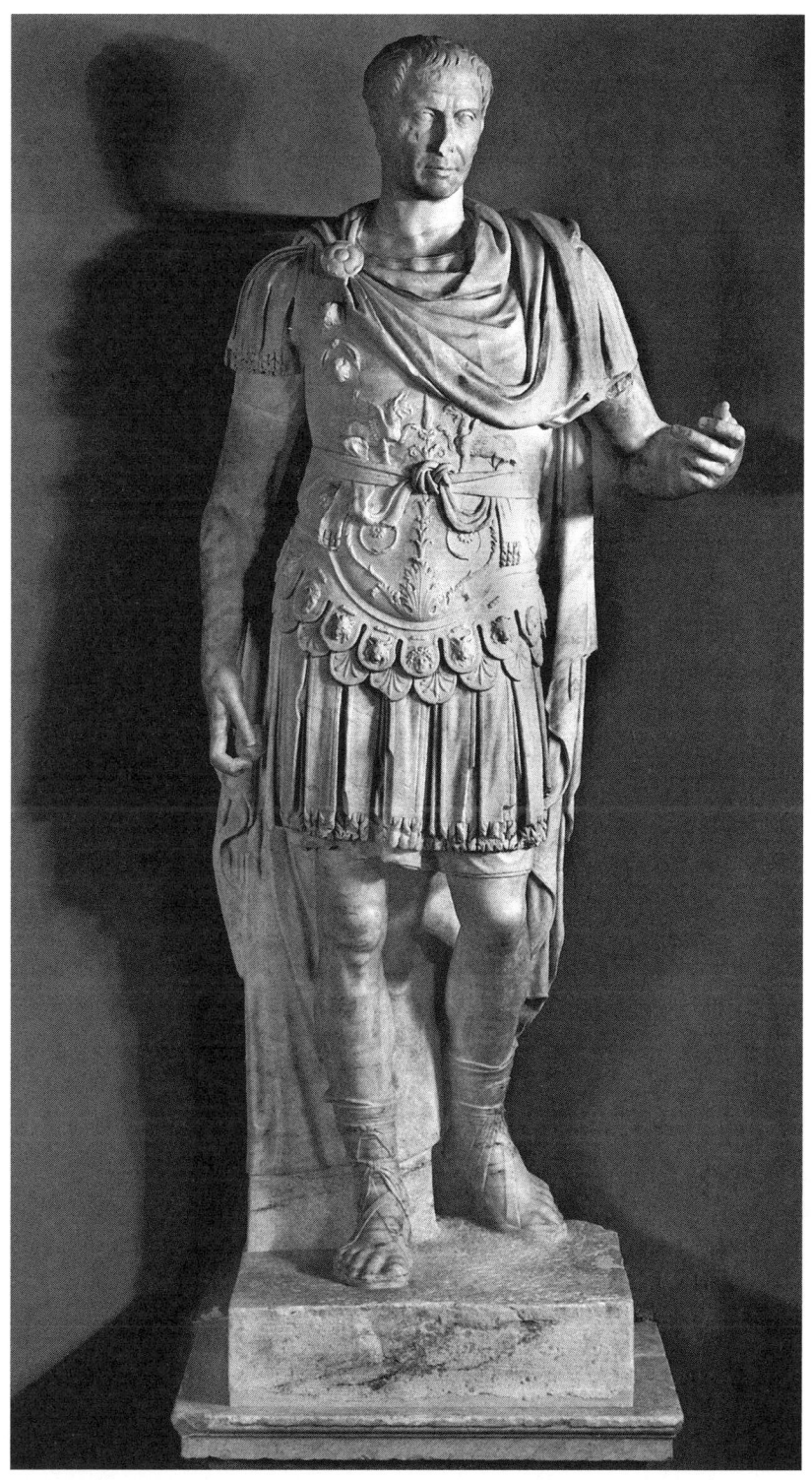

I.1 Cuirassed statue of Julius Caesar. Trajanic replica. Marble. Rome, Palazzo Senatorio.

CHAPTER 1

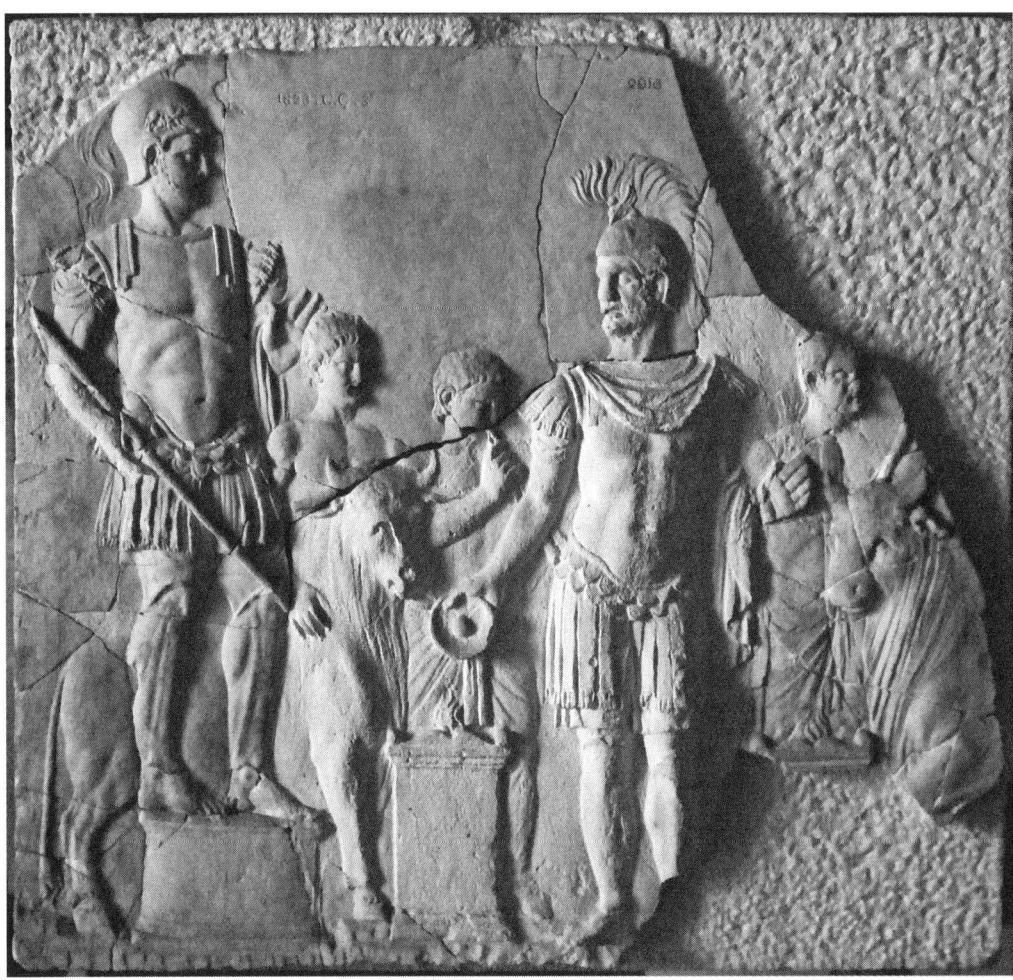

I.2 Sacrifice relief. Late Republican. Marble. Musei Vaticani.

statuary repertory, no other Republican examples of such a cuirassed statue survive from the city of Rome, physically or epigraphically, although several are known from elsewhere in Italy. For instance, a statue (figure I.3), now in Munich, was found at Frascati; others are known from the south, at Lecce and Brindisi; and there are a few whose date and provenance are uncertain, such as the late first-century statue now in Copenhagen (probably from somewhere near Rome).[16] Thus, it has been suggested by a number of scholars that such

---

[16] Munich *loricatus*: Felten 1971, 235–37, dated to the 40s BC, and considered an Italic copy of an original produced in Greece for a Greek context. Other examples: Lecce 4598 (= Stemmer 1978, 173, no. 243 = Vermeule 1959–1960, no. 98; see Simon 1991, 225 and n. 83, "early Augustan");

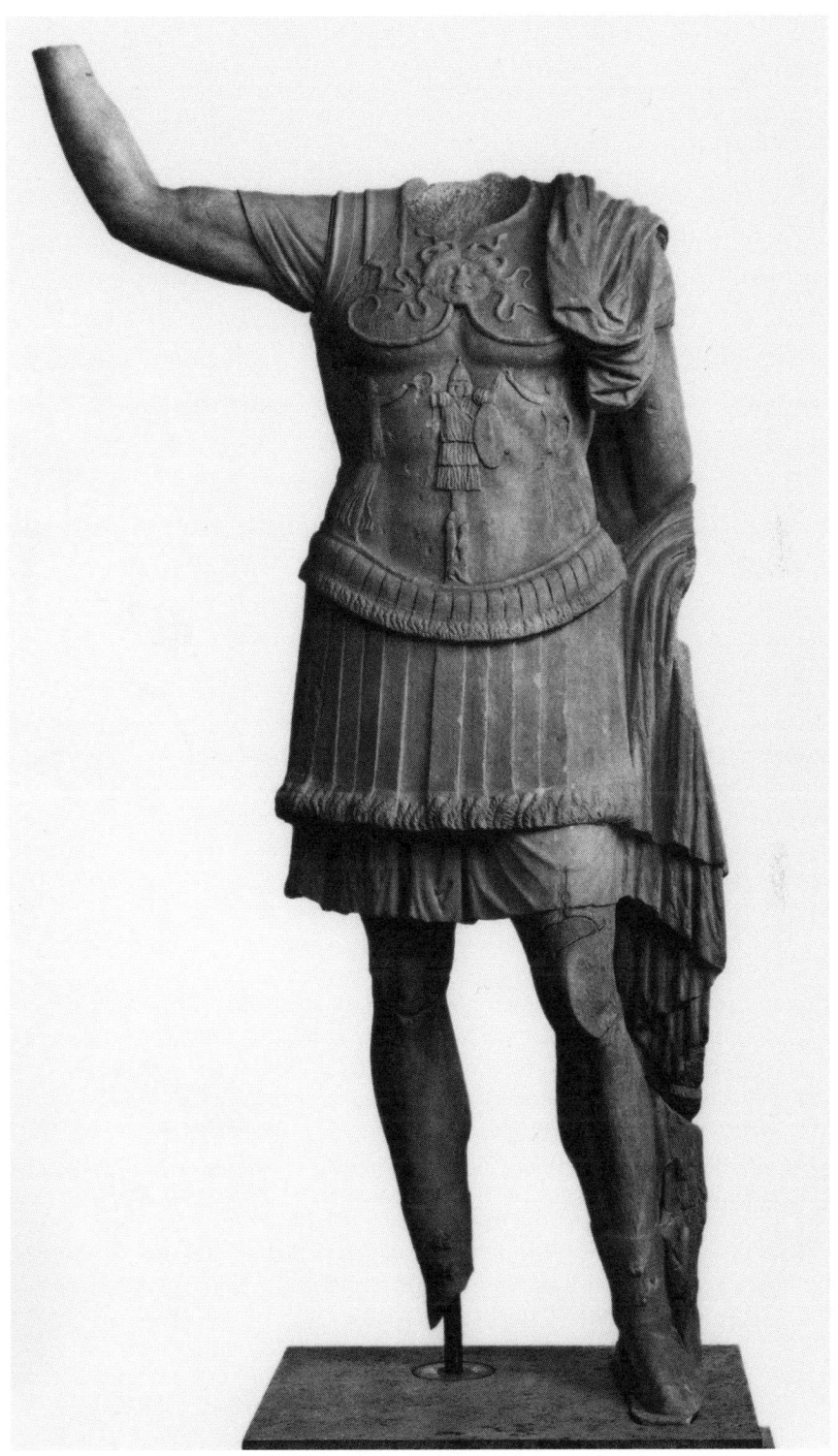

I.3 Cuirassed statue from Frascati. Late Republican. Marble. Munich, Glyptothek.

CHAPTER 1

an honorific cuirassed statue as Caesar's would have been an innovation in the capital—suggested, à propos of Caesar's statue, in large measure in response to the elder Pliny's comment that, contrary to Greek practice, it was the Roman way "to add a military breastplate."[17]

The sources, however, might seem to suggest that the *statua loricata* was an honor long familiar at Rome, although the matter is hardly clear. Much depends on our interpretation of the statue of Horatius Cocles, a work attested in the forum, at the Volcanal, and still standing in the time of the elder Pliny. Cicero mentions it, together with the statues of several other Republican worthies—the Decii, the Scipios, and Marcellus—and remarks that "their passion for military glory is shown in the fact that we see their statues usually in soldier's garb [*ornatu fere militari*]." But it is far from certain whether this refers to statues *loricatae*, as opposed to *paludatae*, or even arrayed in the *vestis triumphalis*—the sign of the highest military distinction. Moreover, the

---

Brindisi 144 (= Stemmer 1978, no. 87 = Vermeule 1959–1960, no. 19; see Simon 1991, 225 and n. 84 = ca. 40–30 BC). Cf. the survey in Niemeyer 1968, 48–49, who regarded the Munich statue as the oldest known from Italy. As Lahusen 1983, 52, points out, all the inscriptions that attest a *statua loricata* are from the second century AD; cf. Eck 1984, 144, who presumes that the practice was more widespread (the examples adduced are nevertheless of later imperial date); Stemmer 1978, 142 ("it was certainly not a common form of honorific statue"); Pekáry 1985, 97, who, following Niemeyer 1968 and Zanker 1981, believes (wrongly) that it was a widely established Republican type; Zanker 1981 discusses the Augustan statue of Holconius Rufus (after 2/1 BC). In short, the *loricata* seems to have still been relatively rare in mid-Augustan times.

[17] Plin. *HN* 34.18 (*Graeca res nihil velare, at contra Romana ac militaris thoraces addere*). Caesar's *loricata* as an innovation: Lahusen 1983, 51–52, claiming that "Caesar actually introduced the first official cuirassed statue in Rome"; followed by Jehne 1987, 209, n. 66; so too Sehlmeyer 1999, 230, as rare in the Republic; Stemmer 1978, 142–43, citing Cic. *Off.* 1.61 (see at n. 18 below) and, understanding this to refer to cuirassed statues, suggesting that it was not so rare; rebutted by Lahusen 1983, 52, n. 51; cf. Hausmann 1981, 518, n. 11a ("Das allgemeine Waffenverbot innerhalb des *Pomeriums* mochte der Errichtung von Panzerstatuen im Stadtgebiet Roms zunächst nicht förderlich sein; aber in den Landgemeinden (u.a. Tibur, Lanuvium) bestanden keine Hinderungsgründe. Die 'Erfinder' der Panzerstatue waren selbstverständlich die Römer nicht"). Felten 1971, 235, points out the absence of evidence for early cuirassed statues and, based on the surviving fragments of cuirassed statues associated with the hemicycles of the Forum of Augustus, suggests their relationship to the triumph (although, as we shall see, this seems unlikely for the *triumphatores* of the Republican period); cf. Rose 1997, 74, on their relative infrequency and mostly posthumous decree in early imperial times. In addition, it should be noted that, on the Belvedere Altar in the Vatican, Romulus(?) appears *loricatus* in a chariot, and we might conclude from this that in Augustan times the costume could be held to be of the greatest Roman antiquity (cf. n. 22 below).

late date of our sources, the early date assigned to Horatius (and, presumably, his statue: late sixth century BC), and the question of whether this was a statue honoring its subject in his lifetime or a long-posthumous recognition renders the question beyond definitive solution.[18]

What prompted Caesar's cuirassed statue? A survey of the repertory of honorific statues and a careful examination of Caesar's status offer an answer. Like all other honorific statues, the message of the costume in which Caesar was depicted was conveyed, not only by its *titulus*, but visually. What did the form itself symbolize?

We should recall that, in Republican times, successful commanders who held both *auspicia et imperium* had the right to triumph, and one might expect that their honorific statues would have shown them wearing the *vestis triumphalis*, the *toga picta*—although this (presumably painted) decoration does not survive on statues. Its only early appearance is on an Augustan coin (figure I.4), and it is not in evidence more regularly until its manifestation on the late Roman consular diptychs.[19] Those who did not qualify for this greatest of Roman honors might well have been presented *loricatus*.[20] But

---

[18] Horatius's statue: Livy 2.10.12; Gell. 4.5.1; Dion. Hal. 5.25.2; *De Viris Illust.* 11.2; Plut. *Publ.* 16.7; Plin. *HN* 34.22; Cic. *Off.* 1.61; commentary in Sehlmeyer 1999, 92–96, and Roller 2004, esp. 20–22, 34–35. *Paludatus = armatus*: Festus 298L; Cicero's *ornatu fere militari* (*Off.* 1.61) can hardly have meant *triumphali ornatu*, and his list of examples does not argue strongly in its favor, since the two Decii were not awarded a triumph. Cf. Cn. Cornelius Scipio Asina (*RE* 341, cos. 260, 254), triumph voted in 253 BC: *Inscr. Ital.* XIII.I, 77; P. Cornelius P. f. L. n. Scipio Africanus (*RE* 336, cos. 205, 194), triumphed in 201 BC: Livy 30.45.2, Polyb. 16.23; M. Claudius Marcellus M. f. M. n. (*RE* 220, cos. 222, 215, 214, 210 208), triumphed in 222 BC: *Inscr. Ital.* XIII.1, 79, and commentary at 54. Note the attempt to set up statues of the elder Scipio (*triumphali ornatu*), which Scipio refused: Livy 38.56.12 and Val. Max. 4.1.6. Cf. Fejfer 2008, 212, on the Pompeian statue of M. Holconius Rufus ("the earliest securely dated and identified statue of a private person in the cuirass that has been preserved in the west").

[19] *Vestis triumphalis*: Livy 5.41.2 (*augustissima vestis = toga picta*?); similarly, Festus 228L. Fittschen 1970, 544, notes that in imperial times the triumphal toga was probably the special preserve of the emperor himself; cf. Zanker 1979, 354, on the *statua triumphalis* ("höchste Ehrung"). Full discussion of the repertory of the *ornatus triumphalis* in Versnel 1970, ch. 2. *Toga picta* coin: *BMC* I, no. 397 = Giard, no. 1191 = *RIC* I², no. 99; discussion by Trillmich in *Kaiser Augustus* 1988, cat. 344. As Barbara Kellum has rightly pointed out to me, the absence of surviving evidence matching the *toga picta* coin is troubling; even the toga worn by Vel Saties in the François Tomb at Vulci, often adduced, differs; the statuary is surveyed in Goette 1990, the consular diptychs in Delbrueck 2009.

[20] Two problems, unresolvable, present themselves. First, according to Suetonius (*Aug.* 31.5), the statues that the emperor Augustus erected in the hemicycle of his forum were *statuae triumphales*,

CHAPTER 1

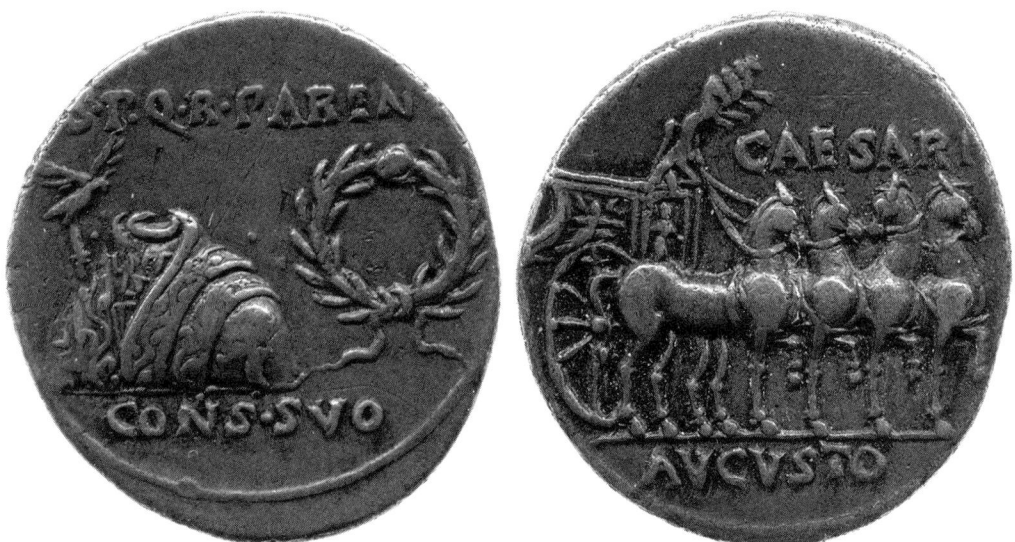

I.4 Representation of the *toga picta*, *denarius*, Spanish mint, ca. 18 BC. *RIC* I², no. 99 = *BMC* I, no. 397 = Giard I, no. 1191.

the use of the nude aggrandizing imagery so familiar from the "generals," from Tivoli (figure I.5) or Foruli (figure I.6), gives one pause, since this elevated visual rhetoric provided a dramatic alternative that was demonstrably employed outside Rome, quite probably on private land, as the origin of these statues suggests.[21] Indeed, the honorific statues that are attested or that survive from the late Republic imply the main reason for the rarity of the *statua*

---

but not all those attested as having been represented there (sc., Ap. Claudius Caecus and L. Albinius) had actually celebrated a triumph: Spannagel 1999, 326. Second, the *triumphatores* would have been depicted there, as the inscription for C. Marius (in the Arezzo text) shows: *veste triumphali, calceis patriciis* (*Inscr. Ital.* XIII.3, nos. 17 and 83). Was the surviving *loricatus* (torso) that is associated with the *summi viri* of Augustus's forum (Ungaro and Milella 1995, II: no. 16) the statuary form in which the two men who had not triumphed were commemorated? And if so, is this a *retrojection* of the use of the cuirass we find in the case of both Caesar's and Augustus's *statuae loricatae*? The problem is compounded by the thirteen fragmentary shoes—seemingly *mullei*, the animal-skin boots worn customarily (but apparently not only) with military costume (Rinaldi Tufi 1981, with Goette 1988)—that are similarly associated with the hemicycles.

[21] Similarly, Stemmer 1978, 142; cf. Zanker 1981 on Holoconius Rufus's statue (representing "provincial honors"), which he associates, confusingly, with those represented in "ideal nudity." The "generals" from Tivoli, Foruli, and Rome: Himmelmann 1989 and now Hallett 2005, ch. 4. Consider as well the appearance of men who had attained the rank of *tribunus militaris* and who appear on the early reliefs associated with the *liberti*: Kockel 1993, cat. nos. D1 (Mentana) and L9

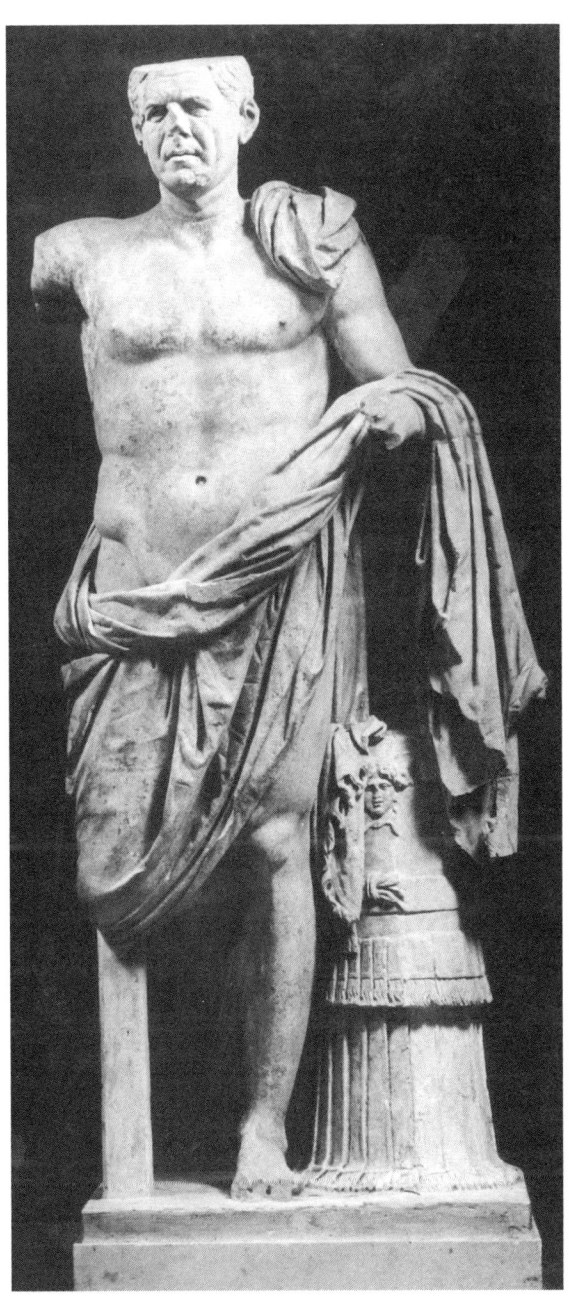 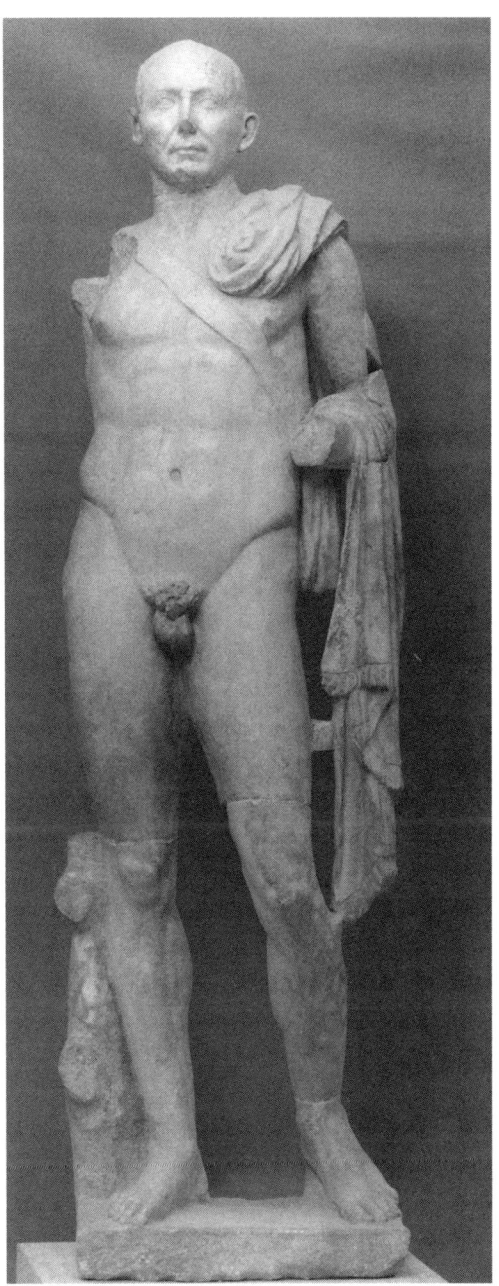

I.5 Statue of a Roman "general" from Tivoli. First century BC. Marble. Rome, Museo Nazionale Romano, Palazzo Massimo alle Terme.

I.6 Statue of a Roman "general" from Foruli. First century BC. Marble. Chieti, Museum.

CHAPTER 1

loricata: forms that conveyed greater distinction—literally (represented in the *toga picta*) or metaphorically (the nude statues)—were ready to hand and apparently widely employed. Thus, that Caesar should be presented *loricatus* was all the more unusual.[22]

Caesar's *cursus* dictated the *insignia* of office to which he was entitled, and it is hard to imagine his presentation in a form that failed to display those *insignia* commensurate with the highest of his honors. Caesar was nothing if not proud, and subsequent statues attested in the sources and the few surviving inscriptions, probably from statue bases, suggest as much. We recall that Caesar was consul for the first time in 59 BC; he was first appointed dictator in late 49, and for a second time, for the year, in 48. Although he had been acclaimed by his troops in Spain and awarded a triumph in 60, its celebration was blocked by Cato, and he did not triumph until 46, after Thapsus.[23] The unusual choice of a *statua loricata* suggests its date: *before* Caesar had the right to wear the triumphator's traditional garb, the *toga picta*, and *after* he had entered his second, year-long dictatorship in September 48, thus roughly late 48–47.[24] That we are told of Caesar's being granted the right, after 45, to wear

---

(Copenhagen), both nude with the *parazonium*, the former inscribed TR. MIL.; cat. J1 (Boston) and D2 (Rome), wearing the cuirass.

[22] Cf. Hausmann 1981, 518: the repertory of image-types for successful commanders, consuls, and proconsuls followed Hellenistic examples (cuirassed statues, both *equestres* and *pedestres*, and the "heroizing" type of the Tivoli General); cf. also the explanations for the "invention" of the *statua loricata* (nn. 16–17 above). The appearance of *loricati* on the tomb reliefs generally associated with Roman freedmen confirms the distinction between the cuirass and the triumphal costume (also noted by Stemmer 1978, 145); Weinstock 1971, 87, suggests that Romulus and Aeneas had been represented *loricatus*; cf. Spannagel 1999, 96–97, 132–33, on their appearance in this guise in the Forum Augustum, and 311, n. 337, along with n. 17 above, on their appearance on the Belvedere Altar.

[23] Inscribed bases: *ILS* 70 = *CIL* IX.2563 = *ILLRP* 406 (C. Iulio Caesari imperatori dictatori iterum pontifici maximo . . .); see Weinstock 1971, 105, n. 3, with the other examples, and the commentary in Raubitschek 1954. December 49 BC: Caes. *BCiv* 2.21.5; Dio 41.36.1–2. Anticipated in March 49 BC: Cic. *Att.* 9.15; cf. Gelzer 1968, 219, and 203, for the absence of the consuls, with the sources; Meier 1996, 385–87. The unusual procedure of Caesar's appointment: Brennan 2000, I:121. Second dictatorship, mid-September 48 BC, nominated dictator for one year: Gelzer 1968, 249, n. 2, with sources; further, 253. Celebration blocked: Gruen 1995, 89 and n. 21, with sources and bibliography. Caesar's first acclamation in Spain in 61 BC: Dio 44.41.3; App. *BCiv* 2.2.8. Caesar granted the *praenomen imperatoris* in 45 BC: Suet. *Iul.* 76.1; Dio 43.44.2, with Weinstock 1971, 104–6.

[24] Unqualified to wear the triumphator's *toga picta* before 46: similarly Itgenshorst 2004, 453 and n. 63. Second dictatorship: Dio 42.20.3.

triumphal dress and the laurel crown, not only at the games but when sacrificing, all but guarantees that the *statua loricata* belongs to a moment when a public display of honors more impressive was not yet his to make.[25] In fact, we know, thanks to a notice in Dio, that after Pharsalus (August 48) and the death of Pompey (28 September 48), on the occasion of Caesar's appointment to his second dictatorship, *eikones* were voted him by an appreciative, indeed fawning, senate; perhaps our statue was among them.[26]

Yet the cuirass was not the dictator's conventional mode of dress. One assumes that at Rome he wore the *toga praetexta* of the magistrates,[27] for the *insignia* of the dictator's powers were borne by the twenty-four lictors who accompanied him, brandishing—in contrast to the consuls—the *fasces* with their axes.[28] So, why the cuirass? At the close of 48 BC, the context is telling: Caesar was in Alexandria, and the situation at Rome was chaotic, with the city ruled by the equivalent of martial law under the command of Antony, whom

---

[25] At the games: Dio 43.43.1; sacrificing: App. *BCiv* 2.106; discussion in Weinstock 1971, 107–11. Weinstock's assertion that the statue of Caesar kept in the *cella* of the temple of Capitoline Jupiter and carried in the *pompa* of 45 BC depicted him in triumphal attire is, however, less than secure, despite the analogies with the honors for the elder Scipio (110 and n. 3).

[26] Statues decreed in later 48 BC, after Pharsalus: Dio 42.19.3, with Weinstock 1971, 41; see also Dio 42.20.1–3. The association of the statue dedicated on the Capitol (accompanied by *Oikoumene* and a chariot and labeled "Hemitheos": Dio 43.14.6) with the Via Cassia relief and its cuirassed *imperator* (notably by Weinstock 1971, 40–59) poses a relevant question about the appearance of Caesar *loricatus*. The award of the statue on the Capitol, if it was in fact decreed after Thapsus, would have *followed* that of the cuirassed figure in Caesar's forum. If it too depicted Caesar *loricatus* (as the Via Cassia relief is thought to do), its iconography might *not* be directly related to his triumph, since, like the *loricata* in his forum, the Capitol statue was decreed long after the award of his triumph (in 60 BC) and before its celebration; Caesar is said not to have seen it upon the arrival of his triumphal procession at the Capitol (Dio 43.21.1–2).

[27] Cf. Sehlmeyer 1999, 205–8, on the imagery of the equestrian statue of Sulla the dictator, set up in December 82 BC; cf. *RRC* 381, which shows the statue wearing the toga. Sehlmeyer suggests that "der zivilen Kleidung Sullas spricht dafür, daß Sullas Rolle als Ordnungsstifter herausgestellt werden sollte. Die absicht der Statue lag also eher darin, Grausamkeiten des Bürgerkrieges vergessen zu machen und die *dictatura rei publicae constituendae* vorzubereiten" (208).

[28] The *fasces* as *insignia imperii*: Livy 1.8.2, and cf. 1.17.6, 2.7.7; commentary and further examples in Staveley 1963, 459 and n. 3, and the full treatment of Schäfer 1989. Twenty-four *fasces*: Polyb. 3.87; Dion. Hal. 10.24.2; Plut. *Fab.* 4.2.; App. *BCiv* 1.100, with Staveley 1963, 459, n. 4. Dictatorship: Nicolet 2004. One might add that the dictator also sat on the *sella curulis* in public. According to Livy (4.41.11), the dictator's *auspicia* were superior to the consul's (Linderski 1986, 2181; *contra* Versnel 1970, 358, n. 2); whether his *imperium* was so is debated.

CHAPTER 1

Caesar had appointed as Master of the Horse. Soldiers protected the senate, and neither consuls nor praetors were appointed.[29] Antony prevailed, always girt with his sword and accompanied by an armed cohort.[30] Civil war may well have been settled, but its effects still pervaded the capital.

Under these circumstances, Caesar's image would have publicly acknowledged his authority as the sole supreme commander. Indeed, after 48 BC, he had engineered what has been recognized as the "dis-empowerment" (*Entmachtung*) of the consuls and the transformation of that magistracy into what was effectively a civil office: between 48 and 44, no consuls were prorogued to govern provinces and command troops, save for Caesar.[31] In 48, as dictator, he commanded both *domi et militiae*, and—more precisely—it was one of the central tenets of his extraordinary command that he was entitled to exercise his *imperium militiae* within the *pomerium*.[32] Despite his absence from Rome at the end of 48, the fact of his legal authority was not lost on his opponents in the senate, who feared his power and hoped for his clemency. Indeed, fears of the Sullan legacy, of proscriptions and summary executions, loomed large amid an aristocracy long torn by civil strife. Many aristocrats had sided with Pompey, and for them, both the memory of Caesar's professions of *clementia* and his supposed disdain for cruelty were no doubt the driving force behind the lavish new honors that were decreed—so as to ensure those memories' endurance.

---

[29] Dio 42.23–24.

[30] Dio 42.27.2, 42.29.3.

[31] Girardet 1990b, 91–93. The consuls of 49 BC, C. Claudius Marcellus and L. Cornelius Lentulus Crus, were assigned provinces *ex magistratu*, as had been Republican custom (despite the *lex Pompeia*, for which see nn. 56–57 below); of the five men other than Caesar who held the consulate between 48 and 45 BC, only two were allocated provinces—not prorogued, *ex magistratu*, but assigned as *privati* after a year's hiatus. P. Servilius Isauricus, *cos*. 48, was *procos*. in Asia, 46 (extended for 45); P. Vatinius, *cos*. 47, was *procos*. in Illyricum, 45.

[32] The dictator's powers: Dion. Hal. 5.70.1, 73.1 ("full authority over war and peace and every other matter"), and 5.70.4 ("having power superior to that of the consuls"); Livy 2.18.8–9 (single command in the field) and 6.38.3 (*summum imperium, summus civis*); cf. commentary in Lintott 2003, 18, 109–13. Not subject to *provocatio*, the dictator rules in the city by the standards of military authority: see Livy 6.16.3, with Oakley 1997, 534–35, and 6.16.5, on aspersions cast on A. Cornelius Cossus, who was said to have earned his triumph, *domi non militiae*. For the parallel to the temporary power of the triumphator, cf. the analysis in Versnel 1970, 191–92.

In this context, Caesar's *statua loricata* declared him *imperator*, but reminded both senate and people that, as dictator, he was legally entitled to "cross the *pomerium*" and wield those powers at Rome, to bear arms and employ his *imperium* within the city. Seen against the background of the events of 47–46—and particularly, the mutiny of his Gallic legions in Campania in early 47—the meaning of Caesar's *statua loricata* would have been clear to all. For whatever had been intended by the senate and people when they erected it—surely flattery—the armored statue not only declared Caesar *imperator* by signaling his famed prowess as a military commander, but also asserted his primacy as the sole if temporary leader of state and threatened that his well-known *clementia* had its limits. His *statua loricata* was the visible demonstration of his extraordinary status, legal and political, both *domi et militiae*, as an image and a reality. And in this regard it was the harbinger of a significant aspect of the Empire, yet to come. Thus, it heralded an entirely new sense of what it might mean for a leader of state "to cross the *pomerium*."[33]

The Image of Augustus's Imperium

Whether or not this interpretation of Caesar's statue is correct, the prerogatives of his status established a precedent for those of Augustus, and this prompts a second example—the famous statue from Prima Porta (figure I.7)—the original

---

[33] Renewal of proscriptions, a long-standing fear in both camps: Cic. *Att.* 8.9(a).2 and 8.13.1, with the comments of Jehne 1987, 249. Gallic mutiny: Chrissanthos 2001. Caesar on cruelty: Cic. *Att.* 9.16.1, quoting Caesar's letter: "You are right to infer of me (for I am well known to you) that there is nothing further from my nature than cruelty"; yet cf. Cic. *Att.* 10.4. Caesar's exercise of *iurisdictio* at Rome while dictator: Millar 1973, 60 = 2002, 258. *Clementia's* limits: Caesar's military imagery was subtly reiterated on the *denarius* of L. Aemilius Buca (*RRC* 480/6), on the reverse of which appear the rods of the *fasces*, crossed with the *caduceus*; in one quadrant appears the globe, and in another clasped hands. These most likely symbolize, respectively, *libertas*, *felicitas*, world dominion, and *concordia* (so Crawford at *RRC* I:494). An ax also appears, in the third quadrant, and in this context, cannot be the symbol of Caesar's pontificate (as it is, e.g., on *RRC* 456/1a, *pace* Crawford, who was followed here by Trillmich in *Kaiser Augustus* 1988, cat. 281), but must suggest that the DICT PERPETUO held his military powers both *domi* and *militiae*; the same conclusion was reached by Alföldi 1969, 2 ("Das Richtbeil des Diktators zuunterst ist eine Mahnung an Widerspenstige") and elaborated by Schäfer 1989, 223.

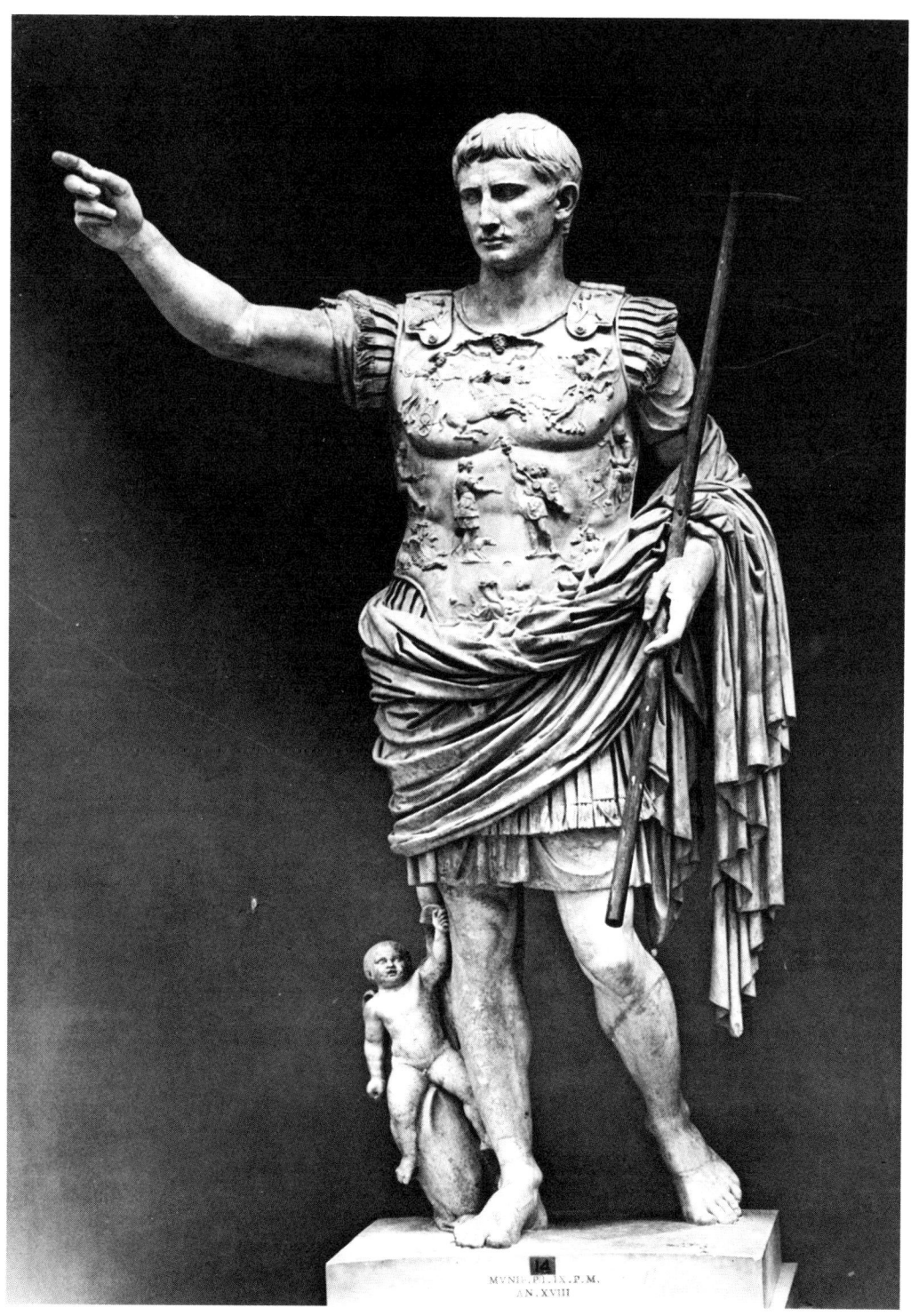

I.7 Statue of Augustus from Prima Porta. After 19 BC. Marble. Musei Vaticani.

of which was surely another monument in armor originally set up within the city of Rome. There can be little doubt that this statue is properly associated with the return of the Parthian standards, and that this is the significance of its figured breastplate—recent polemic notwithstanding. By contrast, what has received little attention, and what we should consider seriously, is why, in 19 BC, *this* statuary form should have been employed to represent Augustus at the moment of the Parthian success.[34]

Two questions require an answer. Was this statue-type, in 19, an innovation in Augustus's image repertory? That is, did this statue have a precedent other than Caesar's *statua loricata*? And what bearing did this statue-type have on this monument's meaning? While the literature devoted to this statue is voluminous, these are questions that, to the best of my knowledge, have not been adequately addressed.

With respect to precedent, three things must be recognized. First, the sources say relatively little about Augustus's statues. They record nothing in conjunction with the ovations of 40 and 36 BC, and there is no good reason to assume (as is so often done) that such celebrations were traditionally accompanied by the erection of honorific statuary.[35] Although physical evidence for other cuirassed statues of Augustus survives, all of these appear to have come from outside of Rome. Since three of the four known examples employed Prima Porta–type heads, and all three are dated later on the basis of style, these were quite likely intended to have been replicas of the Prima Porta statue itself. The exception is a head from Lucus Feroniae (figure I.8), which once

---

[34] Prima Porta statue: Pollini 1995 and 2012, with earlier bibliography. Polemic: Simpson 2005. The original statue's location is unknown, although suggestions abound: that it stood in the east (Ingholt 1969) has never found favor; that it stood on the Viminal Hill at the site of the *Gallinae Albae* (Kellum 1994, 223–24) seems equally unlikely. The imagery of the statue has nothing to do with the prophecy of the white hen (for which see Flory 1989), since Augustus's development of the Viminal with the construction of the Porticus Liviae did not commence until 15 BC, and it is hard to believe that such a significant honor would not have been erected in a *celeberrimus locus*. That it stood atop the Mausoleum (as some statues did: see Strabo 5.3.8), as advanced by Parisi Presicce 2013, 127 (following an argument of Stucchi), appears similarly untenable—for one thing, the breastplate's noted imagery would have been invisible!

[35] Statues: Lahusen 1984. Ovations of 40 BC: *Inscr. Ital.* XIII.I, 568 = *EJ*, 33; ovations of 36 BC: *Inscr. Ital.* XIII.I, 569 = *EJ*, 34. Lack of evidence for honorific statues: Wallace-Hadrill 1990; Itgenshorst 2004, 442, n. 25 ("the back-projection of a tradition introduced by Augustus").

CHAPTER 1

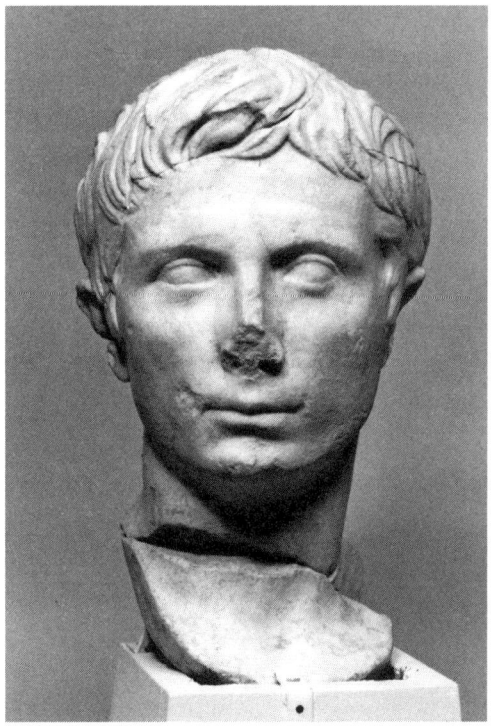

I.8 Portrait of Augustus. Early Augustan replica of an original from before 30 BC. Marble. Lucus Feroniae, Antiquarium.

formed part of a cuirassed statue and is thought to replicate a work earlier than the Prima Porta statue.[36] But is it evidence of an earlier *cuirassed* statue? It is virtually impossible to know what the *Urbild* for this Lucus Feroniae type was, since it was an essential aspect of the portrait system that early head-types were later replicated for differing contexts. Thus, the fact that the Lucus Feroniae head sat atop a cuirass-clad body is not in itself evidence of an early *statua loricata*.[37]

---

[36] Baltimore head: Boschung 1993, no. 75, late Augustan, Prima Porta type. Basel/Malibu head: Boschung 1993, no. 79, Caligulan, Prima Porta type. Boston head: Boschung 1993, no. 80, Caligulan, Prima Porta type. Lucus Feroniae head: Boschung 1993, no. 4, Octavianszeit, Lucus Feroniae type. On the portrait system's functioning: Pfanner 1989; Smith 1996; Pollini 1999, 728.

[37] Indeed, portrait studies focus on the typology of heads, not bodies, since the system of portrait replication did not attend to the original marriage of head and body central to the monu-

One further possibility exists. Dio reports that, ca. 27/25 BC, Agrippa erected statues of Augustus and himself at his new Pantheon. Apparently he had originally intended to display Augustus's statue together with those of Mars, Venus, and Divus Julius within, but in the face of Augustus's objection, Agrippa erected their statues (which are otherwise unspecified here) in the temple's porch.[38] Later, recording the prodigies of 22, Dio reports that during heavy rains, "many places were struck by thunderbolts, including the statues in the Pantheon, so that the spear actually fell from Augustus's hand."[39] The statue must have depicted Augustus *loricatus*. Given that statues inside the temple, among the gods, had been rejected, and that Dio refers to the two works erected in the porch explicitly as those of men (*andriantes*), it is unlikely that Augustus was depicted *in formam deorum*, the only other instance in which he might have brandished a spear. If Dio's report is to be trusted, here we find the *Augustan* precedent for the cuirassed statue from Prima Porta.[40]

This realization would address a second issue. Although the (presumably bronze) original of the Prima Porta statue must date, on account of its "Parthian" iconography, to ca. 20/19 BC, by general consensus the Prima Porta head-type should be dated ca. 27, in correspondence with the "constitutional settlement." Dependence on the cuirassed form of the reputed Pantheon statue would provide a plausible account for the contemporaneous creation of both the Prima Porta body- and head-type.

Third, and finally, what of the coinage? Does it provide evidence for an early cuirassed statue? The meaning of the silver coins associated with the Actium victory has been much debated, and many have seen these as depicting statues. While standing cuirassed figures are employed on these coins, they display distinctly differing poses, and there are no such statues attested

---

mental conceptions for which they were no doubt invented. Here my view is diametrically opposed to that espoused by Boschung 1993, 6–8 (followed by Smith 1996, 37), whose divorce of the *Urbilder* from particular monuments may well have been true for the high empire, when the mass production of imperial portraits was an established aspect of the machinery of state, but it is anachronistic for the earlier period, when no such system was yet in place.

[38] Dio 53.27.2–3.
[39] Dio 54.1.1.
[40] Broader context: Koortbojian 2013, 133–37; cf. Thomas 2017.

CHAPTER 1

in the sources for the period in which they are generally dated (ca. 32–31 to 29–27 BC), save for Dio's account of the Pantheon statue, to which they may, or may not, correspond. Thus, the coins offer little in the way of a solution to our problem.[41]

So it is impossible to know precisely when Augustus was, for the first time, represented by a *statua loricata*: either the original statue that bore the Prima Porta head-type (ca. 27 BC?) or the statue at the Pantheon (ca. 27–25) may have been the first: we simply don't know. What we do know is that *whenever* Augustus was first represented *loricatus*, it would have been Caesar's statue that provided the recent precedent for such a statue that vaunted, above all else, military authority.

But what did it mean for Augustus to be presented in this guise in 19 BC?[42] What were the alternatives that the statuary repertory offered? That repertory corresponded, *grosso modo*, to the *cursus*—as the famous inscription of Volusius Saturninus attests—and each of the repertory's forms signaled the attainment of ever-higher status, whether elective office or public honor, whether civic, military, or religious. Indeed, the richness of the repertory was required by such manifold and distinct honors, all the more so in the case of

---

[41] Silver coins: see, e.g., Liegle 1941, 325–26; Zanker 1973, 42 (but see the differing view in Zanker 1988, 53: "matching each of the *topoi* in Octavian's speech before the battle [of Actium] as it is recorded for us in Dio 50.24ff."); Trillmich in *Kaiser Augustus* 1988, 483–85. Cuirassed type: see, e.g., the coin series for the equestrian monument attested for 43 BC: Bergemann 1990, cat. L25, with earlier bibliography; cf. Stemmer 1978, 145. Summary of opinions: Gurval 1998, 47–52.

[42] It is generally held that the *statua loricata* was the symbol of *imperium* (see, e.g., Niemeyer 1968, 47–49); thus Pollini 1999, 729, dates the conception to 43 BC, when Octavian was first granted power, and associates this with the decree of the attested equestrian monument—on which see chapter 2. Further, Boschung 1993, 59, notes that the portraits on the earliest coins (ca. 43 BC) are both *widersprüchlich und summarisch*, and thus *do not* correspond with the earliest dated portrait-types (Beziers-Spoleto and Lucus Feroniae types, dated by Boschung to 44–40 BC). He sees the Lucus Feroniae type in the Voconius coins (*RRC* 526, 40 BC[?] or later) and those of Octavian and Balbus (*RRC* 518, 41 BC), and following Fittschen regards the Alcudia type reflected in the *Divos Iulius* coins of ca. 40–38 BC (Boschung 1993, 59–60 and notes). Do we infer from this not only that the equestrian monument decreed in 43 BC and depicted on the coins (*RRC* 490) represented a "projected monument," but that no portrait-type—that is, no public portrait statue—had yet been produced that might have been replicated on these early coins? Cf. Pollini 1999, 727, who says that the earliest coin portraits to conform to the portrait-types (Beziers-Spoleto type) are those of Livineius Regulus, minted in 42 BC (*RRC* 494, 3a and 25).

the emperor, since a freestanding statue might only visualize a single element of one's acquired titulature at a time.⁴³

The cuirassed image from Prima Porta surely cast Augustus as *imperator*, the traditional honorific, in 43 BC and directly associated with his person since he had adopted it as his *praenomen*, perhaps as early as 39—despite the greater glory of the "triple" triumph he had celebrated in 29 (13–15 August).⁴⁴ Two observations follow from this. First, it is generally acknowledged that the surviving imagery suggests the occurrence of a distinct change in Augustus's self-representation after 27, when the essentially Hellenistic pathos of the early portrait-types gave way to a more classicizing rendition of his features and a new emphasis on his role as a citizen.⁴⁵ The latter was patently not true, as the Prima Porta and the Pantheon statue, together with the coinage, suggest: in the mid-20s and after, Augustus's military position was still prominently advertised in Rome. And second, this prominence stood in direct contrast to a public claim of Augustus's full accomplishments. For, as we saw in the case of Caesar, the appearance of the successful *imperator*—one who had been granted the honor of a triumph—was traditionally in the costume of the triumphator, which was worn not only in the rite itself but at the games and at funerals.⁴⁶

So none of these martial images acknowledges Augustus as triumphator; why? In the case of the Prima Porta statue in particular, Augustus's depiction on this occasion in the triumphal *ornatus* was surely deemed inappropriate, as

---

⁴³ Volusius Saturninus: Koortbojian 2013, 58–60 and note 22, with bibliography. Statue repertory: cf. Simon 1991, 206, who merely draws the contrast with the togate-types; further, Koortbojian 2008. Statues' singular reference: Zanker 1979, 360.

⁴⁴ Cuirass = *imperator*, assumed yet unargued by, e.g., Pollini 1995, 264–65 and n. 22; Hölscher in *Kaiser Augustus* 1988, 386–87. *Praenomen imperatoris*: evidence surveyed in Simpson 1998, dating its assumption to 39–38 BC; Combès 1966, 134–35, for 40 BC (*Fasti triumphales Barberiniani*); Syme 1979, 368, for 38 BC. Hickson 1991, 132 (following Syme 1979, 372): "By assuming the name *Imperator*, Augustus made this image a permanent personal possession." The period from 43 onward is surveyed in detail in Girardet 1990a.

⁴⁵ Cf. Zanker 1979, 358, on the difference between the coin imagery after Actium (military) and the coinage (and statuary: Corinth) after 27 BC (*meist capite velato erscheint*); Boschung 1993, 64; Smith 1996, 41.

⁴⁶ Games: Versnel 1970, 73, 74, n. 3, 130, nn. 2–3. Funeral: Polyb. 6.53.7; Ov. *Fast.* 6.363 ff.; cf. Suet. *Aug.* 31.5 on the Forum Augustum (*statuas omnium triumphali effigie in utraque fori sui porticu dedicavit*).

CHAPTER 1

he had refused a triumph. Equally inappropriate would have been his appearance in the toga, since it would not have served to perpetuate the fiction that the return of the Parthian standards was, in some sense, a victory. The decision to be depicted in armor would thus have effected, in this sense, the visualization of his *recusatio*, not only of the triumph but of its attendant *ornatus*; for much the same reason an equestrian statue would not do, since it would have potentially alluded to the celebration of an *ovatio*. On his return in 19 BC, Augustus, we are told, no doubt with a keen eye to such matters, entered the city inconspicuously, by night.[47]

Thus, the cuirass provided a dramatic alternative. Augustus's appearance in a guise that did not fully and conspicuously declare his status reminds us that, in 19, as in 27 at the Pantheon, he no longer needed to be represented in a manner that acknowledged the actual grandeur of his position. Yet the choice of a military image is telling.

There is more to be said about the historical context of 19 BC that serves to explain this statue's appearance. A great deal of attention has been paid to the transformation of Augustus's status in the year that the Prima Porta statue was probably dedicated. For it was in this same year that, upon his return from the east, both the third attempt to define Augustus's constitutional position took place and the traditional access to the triumph was blocked.[48]

---

[47] Triumphs refused: see Girardet 1993, 212–14, on Augustus's refusals as an aspect of his "traditionalism" and a rejection of an association with those who had celebrated more than three triumphs—all were dictators. Fiction: cf. *RGDA* 29, where, immediately following his account of the recovery, *devictis hostibus*, of standards lost in Spain, Gaul, and Dalmatia, Augustus offers his claim that he "compelled" (*coegi*) the Parthian standards' return; cf. Dio 54.8.2. Return in 19 BC at night: *RGDA* 4.1 and Dio 54.10.3–4; Dio 54.8.3 mistakenly has Augustus enter the city on horseback (an *ovatio*?), so Rich 1990 *ad loc.*; further, Cassiod. *Chron.*, *sub anno* 576 (= 19 BC) has Augustus refuse the customary chariot. *Recusatio*: Wallace-Hadrill 1982, 36–37. *Ornamenta triumphalia*: Suet. *Tib.* 9.2; Dio 54.24.7; discussion in Abaecherli Boyce 1942; Gordon 1952; Eck 1999. According to Suet. *Aug.* 73, Augustus not only favored simple furnishings in his house, but often wore the *vestis domestica* unless custom dictated otherwise; see the comments of Alföldi 1970, 127–28.

[48] Ferrary 2001a, 2001b; Cotton and Yakobson 2002.

The striking correspondence between the last elaborations of Augustus's so-called "constitutional settlement," the curtailment of the triumph for Roman commanders who were not members of the imperial house, and the celebration of the return of the Parthian standards—to which the Prima Porta statue is so demonstrably related—is neither a matter of mere chronology nor simply fortuitous. All three of these historical events require comment.

We may begin with the "constitutional settlement." The sequence of events by which Augustus's new role was established is well known. In 27 BC, he "transferred the republic from [his] power to the dominion of the senate and people of Rome"; he was then granted his new name and multiple provinces for ten years, which were regularly to be renewed.[49] In 23, he surrendered the consulship; now he was a *privatus*, yet one who would wield official authority nevertheless: he was granted tribunician power, possibly annually and perpetually, as well as the right to speak first in the senate; he was awarded *imperium maius* against that of the (other) proconsuls, and—what is central to our discussion—he was relieved of the necessity of having that *imperium* renewed whenever he crossed the *pomerium*. Thus, after 23, although Augustus was a *privatus*—that is, he held no public magistracy—he not only controlled a huge army but held the legal right to enter not only Italy but the city of Rome with his *imperium* intact.[50]

It has been noted that these changes to Augustus's status seem to have resulted in a genuine loss of power, for while he held "greater *imperium*" with respect to other proconsuls in the provinces, his powers at Rome were

---

[49] Dio 53.13.1 and 16.2; the renewal as a reassertion of senatorial and popular sovereignty: Cotton and Yakobson 2002, 195.

[50] Settlement of 23 BC: Dio 53.32.5, with Brunt 1977, 96; Cotton and Yakobson 2002, 196–97 (on the grant "to allow Augustus' *imperium*, whenever and for as long as he possessed it, not to laspse—as it normally did—when he crossed the *pomerium*"); Syme 1939, 336–38, outlines the political aspects. Thus, henceforth, Augustus's *imperium* was valid in Rome and Italy (and even when in his provinces [Cotton and Yakobson 2002, 199]). Cf. Eder 1990, 110: after 23 BC, Augustus was "a *privatus*, without office, backed by a huge army . . . through his *imperium proconsulare* and his *tribunicia potestas*, however, he was so deeply integrated into the administration of the empire that the new *res publica* could not operate efficiently without him." Cf. further, Richardson 1991, 8; the situation is excellently summarized in Gruen 2005.

CHAPTER 1

manifestly not the equivalent of the consuls'.⁵¹ At this moment, however, Augustus's exercise of *imperium* and its various competences *in Rome* were of little practical consequence, since he left for the east early in the following year. In the ensuing period, the political and social situation deteriorated, and upon his return in 19 BC, things were rectified, in part, by the granting to Augustus of new powers. Among other privileges, he was now awarded that of *iurisdictio* at Rome, and the right to twelve lictors with *fasces* within the city, just like the consuls, between whom he would sit on public occasions. The sum of these developments, together with his existing powers, not only rendered Augustus once more the most powerful man in the state, but in 19 they allowed him to exercise both his *imperium* and his *auspicia* within the city *and* in his provinces—both *domi et militiae*. But Augustus already, since 23, had the right to return to the *urbs* with his *imperium* intact—that is, *imperium militiae*, military might, not civil jurisdiction. The new privileges of 19 were not a substitute for those of 23 but an addition, and above all, his new emblems of power (*fasces* and *sella*) were the manifest confirmation of his extraordinary status, which thus rendered the geographical and functional distinctions about *imperium* moot. The status of Imperator Caesar Augustus was now elevated, on a new legal foundation, and his right to "cross the *pomerium*" was one of its highly visible distinctions.⁵²

The second of the events of 19 BC that calls for comment is the restriction of access to the triumph. Now, given Augustus's new prerogative, one of the problems with the triumph was that it allowed, if only for a single day, a special grant of "military" *imperium* to be held within the *pomerium*.⁵³ This was purely celebratory, not a matter of legislated status; indeed, Valerius Maximus points out that "it was customary for a general about to celebrate a triumph

---

⁵¹ Jones 1951; Brunt and Moore 1989, 12; Girardet 1990b and 1993; Ferrary 2001a; Hurlet 2001, 171–73; Cotton and Yakobson 2002.

⁵² Deterioration of political situation: Girardet 1990b. Augustus's privileges: Dio 54.10.5; Syme 1979, 308; Hurlet 2001, 170–72 (signs of the civil powers of the consulate). While Augustus's statue may have originally held the *hasta* in her left hand, I am not persuaded by Parisi Presicce 2013, 126 (following Alföldi 1959), that one should regard this as the symbol of his tribunician power; in her treatment of the presumably related imagery on the coinage, Küter 2014, 251–52, is similarly skeptical.

⁵³ Livy 45.35.3–4 (Paullus in 167) and 26.21.1–13 (Marcellus in 211) give the sequence by which *imperium* was extended: tribunes bring a motion *ad populum* on the authority of the senate.

to invite the consuls to dinner and then to request them not to come, so that on the day of his triumph nobody of higher official rank be at the same dinner table."[54] But, in a world in which the ceremonial had long held great significance, even the appearance of power posed problems for a monarchy that refused to acknowledge itself. The triumph had to go.

The story of the triumph's appropriation by the imperial house after 19 BC hardly needs retelling.[55] Yet it should be stressed that one of the pillars on which the curtailment of such honors was erected had long been in place, yet lying dormant on account of the civil wars: the *lex Pompeia de provinciis*.[56] The reinstatement of some of this law's provisions provided the means for the triumph's demise.[57] For in 52, acting against corruption (and possibly against Caesar), Pompey had pressed for and obtained a law that decreed a five-year interval between consulship and proconsulship, which technically prevented the consuls from departing for their provinces before the end of their consular year as holders of a valid *imperium* and *auspicia*, as had long been Republican practice. We have already seen (at note 31) that Caesar had also endeavored

---

[54] Val. Max. 2.8.6.

[55] Cf. the accounts in Hickson 1991 and Itgenshorst 2004, esp. 449–52.

[56] Dio 40.56.1-3, with Gruen 1995, 457–58, who disputes the notion that the *lex Pompeia* was effected to thwart Caesar—perhaps not, but surely it did; see further Magdelain 1968, 55, who notes the consequence that *imperium militiae* would henceforth be held only by promagistrates, since the consuls would no longer depart during their year in office while they were still in possession of the auspices (there were only three exceptions between 51 and 44 BC); extensive discussion in Ferrary 2001a, 105–15; Hurlet 2001, 160–61, with reference to Cic. *Div.* 2.76 and *ND* 2.3.9, where Cicero complains of the promagistrates' lack of the auspices (see n. 59 below).

[57] In 27 or 19 BC? Dio 53.14.2 dates this to 27 BC; Suet. *Aug.* 36.1 does not specify a date; see the comments of Hurlet 2001, 200 and 173, for the context of 19 BC, although the argument (174) that this rendered the proconsuls incapable of the auspices is contradicted by the case of Cicero (see following note). Moreover, after 27 BC, there were only three triumphs: that of Sex. Appuleius in 27 BC, delayed (Schumacher 1985, 213) although earned in the year following his consulate of 29 BC; Atratinus, whose triumph followed his consulate by twelve years; and that of Balbus, who was, however, adlected to the consulship from his status as a *privatus* (Vell. 2.51.3). Cf. Hurlet 2001, 167 and n. 48, as well as 174 and n. 73, suggesting that his auspices may have been vitiated since he departed Rome while not yet officially a magistrate. The *lex Pompeia* was not simply reactivated (Ferrary 2001a, 112); Hickson 1991, 128, suggests that the reorganization of the provincial administration in 27 BC "was probably the most significant factor in the actual reduction of triumphs," with no mention of the *lex Pompeia*.

CHAPTER 1

to enforce a separation between consulship and promagistracy in order to deprive the consuls of access to troops. In 27, the renewal of these technicalities was complete, and the consulship was effectively transformed into a civic magistracy. And as a result, the proconsuls would leave for their provinces as *privati*.[58] Thus, unlike the magistrates, whose powers were acknowledged by favorable auspices and a *lex curiata* (an *ad hominem* piece of legislation passed by the curiate assembly that confirmed that its recipients held the right to their *imperium et auspicia*), promagistrates departed the city without such a law having been passed and only assumed those powers attendant on their assigned commands *in provincia*.[59] Before Pompey's triumph *sine magistratu* in 79, this was grounds for the refusal of a triumph (as it had been in the case

---

[58] Consulate as civic magistracy: Magdelain 1968, 51–52; Girardet 1990b; Hurlet 2001, 173. Former consulars summoned to serve: thus Cicero went to Cilicia in 51 BC (Linderski 1981); see Cic. *Fam.* 3.2.1. Proconsuls depart as *privati* (i.e., with a new grant of *imperium*): Versnel 1970, 187; Hurlet 2001, 173.

[59] Cf. Magdelain 1968, 51–52 (powers conferred by "une loi special et rend superflue l'intervention des curies"). This seems the only way to explain the apparent contradiction between a series of testimonia: (i) the refusal of a triumph to Scipio, a *privatus*, in 210 (see Versnel 1970, 169 and n. 5, with sources), although such grounds for refusal would end with Pompey; (ii) the seeming legitimacy of Cicero's claim to triumph in 50 BC (*Att.* 6.3.3.; Linderski 1981); (iii) the initial refusal of a triumph to C. Pomptinus on the grounds that *negant . . . latum de imperio*, although Cicero denies this (*Att.* 4.18.4, but cf. Staveley 1956, 89); (iv) Appius Claudius's (*cos.* 54) claim that a *lex curiata* was not a requirement for a proconsul to proceed to his province (Cic. *Fam.* 1.9.25, *QFr.* 3.2.3, with Nicholls 1967, 266–67, and Versnel 1970, 337); and (v) the perplexing comment of Cicero that "for many years our wars have been conducted by proconsuls and propraetors who do not have the right to take auspices" (*Div.* 2.76). Three things stand out. First, Cicero's complaint about the promagistrates' lack of the auspices must be related to the rise of *legati*, promagistrates who possessed neither independent auspices nor *imperium* (see the further discussion in chapter 2). Second, promagistrates, despite the lack of a curiate law, are known to have triumphed: Pompey in 79 BC; so too Pomptinus (*procos.* 63), who was appointed as a promagistrate while a *privatus* and who triumphed, at least according to Cicero, with an unusual *lex curiata* (*latum insulse*), despite objections, in 54 BC. And third, Appius is said by Cicero to have declared that he would not only forgo the lot for his province, but would go to Cilicia in 53 BC *sine lege suo sumptu* (*Att.* 4.18.4), a sham declaration of his independence that was undermined by his attempt to acquire the *lex* by bribery (*Att.* 4.17.2); he was acclaimed in 53 BC (see Combès 1966, 456) but did not triumph. Brennan 2000, I:18–20, outlines the attendant problems, although his conclusion that "the [curiate] law can have conferred only *auspicia militiae*" (19) is, as I have tried to suggest (cf. chapter 2), not the whole story. The *lex curiata* seems to have constituted a formal legal acknowledgment of powers already conferred by election (similarly, in part, Versnel 1970, 349–51).

of Scipio in 210). But by the end of the Republic such extraordinary commands had become all the more so. In fact, not one of the three men who triumphed after 27 was in violation of the spirit, if not the letter, of the revived Pompeian arrangements. Two of them—Sextus Appuleius and Sempronius Atratinus— were assigned to their provinces a number of years following their consulates, while Balbus was never a consular. All three assumed their stations in the provinces as *privati cum imperio*, almost certainly without a curiate law, and all were allowed to triumph.[60]

All these developments were overshadowed by the third event of 19 BC, the momentous return of the Parthian standards, an event commemorated on the coinage throughout the Roman world (figure I.9), in the forum by the much-discussed arch attested for 19, and, above all, by the statue from Prima Porta—all elements of the new visual language of power.[61]

The arch, despite its customary label, was *not* itself triumphal as a monumental form; that distinction belonged properly to both the chariot statue and the *Fasti* it bore.[62] Nor was the cuirass-type statue: its selection for the Prima Porta monument presupposes a deliberate rejection of triumphal imagery— an imagery that was in this instance abjured by Augustus and Agrippa and, from 19 BC on, effectively refused to others. This "*anti*-triumphal" theme must have taken precedence in the Prima Porta statue's design and conception, and

---

[60] Extraordinary commands: Ridley 1981. *Auspicia*: Vell. Pat. 2.115.3 attests the requirement of the *auspicia* for the triumph, and the bestowal of the *ornamenta triumphalia* to *legati* who did not possess them, such as was the case for L. Passienus Rufus and Cossus Cornelius Lentulus; see Eck 1984, 138–39, and Schumacher 1985, 215–16. Triumphs after 27 BC: Sextus Appuleius, *cos.* 29, triumphed in 26 BC; L. Sempronius Atratinus, *cos. suff.* 34, triumphed in 21 BC; and L. Cornelius P. f. Balbus (*RE* 70), who was *procos.* in Africa, triumphed in 21–20 BC, though he never held the consulate; Balbus was not the *consul suffectus* of 40 BC referred to by Vell. 2.51.3 (Groag in *RE* 4: 1270; *pace* Rich 1990, 203, and Hurlet 1997, 390, n. 108, and Hurlet 2001, 167, n. 48), nor the L. Cornelius ___f.___n. in 32 (Broughton at *MRR* 3:63); this was probably his great uncle (*RE* 69 [*patruo*]=Plin. *HN* 5.36); the Velleius passage refers to 48 BC, when the younger Balbus was an envoy of Caesar (see *MRR* 2:265); nor is it likely that Balbus was the L. Cornelius ___f___n. who was *cos. suf.* in 32 BC (Broughton in *MRR*, 3:63). Here I partly revise my earlier view of the role of the curiate law (in Koortbojian 2010).

[61] Prima Porta statue: Rose 2005 surveys the materials and bibliography. I am not persuaded by the down-dating to 17 BC argued by Simon 1991 and Hölscher in *Kaiser Augustus* 1988, 386–87. Visual language of power: Zanker 1988; Wallace-Hadrill 1990.

[62] Arch: Wallace-Hadrill 1990; Rich 1998. Chariot sculpture and *Fasti*: Hickson 1991, 134.

CHAPTER 1

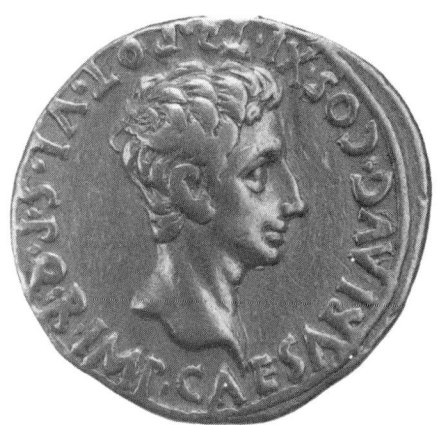 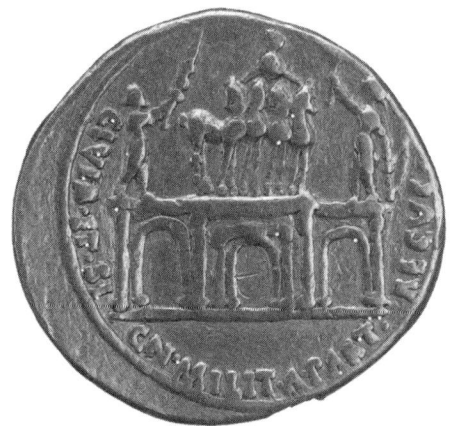

I.9 *Aureus* depicting the Parthian arch of Augustus, Rome. Spanish mint (Colonia Patricia?), ca. 18–17 BC. *RIC* I², no. 131 = *BMC* 427 = Giard I, no. 1228.

the choice of the cuirass-type—just as in the case of Caesar's *statua loricata*—allowed Augustus to appear as *imperator* rather than triumphator.[63] This theme was continuously asserted as Augustus not only declined additional triumphs but accepted in their stead ever greater *supplicationes* as a vehicle for celebration and continued to accrue acclamations for the victories of his field commanders earned under his auspices.[64] The interpretation of these celebrations as "pseudo" or "disguised" triumphs misses the point: just as Augustus no longer needed to hold an official magistracy to wield power, he no longer required the public approbation that signaled its effective employ. Florus had grasped the essence of Augustus's program: "He was so great that he despised whatever a triumph might bestow."[65]

Finally, careful attention to the significance of the statuary repertory demonstrates as well that there is no compelling reason for the ubiquitous yet tacit assumption that the cuirass-type of the Prima Porta statue was chosen *solely* so

---

[63] *Contra* Hickson 1991, 130–31: "it was only the triumphal procession and not the image of *triumphator* which Augustus sought to avoid" (131); cf., however, 132, on the "permanent personal possession" of the *praenomen imperatoris*. Cf. the tendentious view of Lange 2016, 278, n. 77.

[64] *Supplicationes*: Billows 1993. Acclamations: Barnes 1974 and Schumacher 1985.

[65] "Pseudo-triumphs": Torelli 1982, 54 (à propos of Augustus's *reditus* in 13 BC and the deposition of the laurel on the Capitol). "Disguised triumph": Settis in *Kaiser Augustus* 1988, 420 (à propos of the Ara Pacis). Florus 2.54 (*sed iam tantus erat Caesar, ut triumpo augeri contemneret*).

that its breastplate might bear its symbolic imagery. Indeed, if the presentation of the Parthian narrative had been the only significant element of the monument, it might have been shown to much greater advantage in relief on the statue's base, as such narratives were on other occasions, as on the so-called altar of Domitius Ahenobarbus or, in symbolic form, as on the base of the Bocchus monument.[66] The choice of a *statua loricata* must have had other motives as well.

❧

The foregoing discussion, it is to be hoped, has suggested one. Upon his return to Rome in 19 BC, Augustus's *imperium consulare* was that vested in him in 27 to be held in his assigned provinces; it was this power that after 23 he was no longer compelled to lay down when he crossed the *pomerium*, his surrender of the consulate notwithstanding.[67] There was no need for Augustus to seek senatorial approval and ratification from the *comitia tributa*, as there was in the case of the extension of *imperium* required for the celebration of a triumph; nor was there need of a reaffirmation of that power by means of another *lex curiata*; nor, one assumes, was there the corollary requirement of a renewal of his auspices whenever Augustus returned to Rome.[68] So, while the additional powers granted Augustus upon his return in 19 indeed elevated his *civil* status, they did not disguise the real basis of his position, his military *imperium*, which was, in turn, enhanced by the disempowerment of the consulate. After 19, events had ensured that Augustus had no rivals in military power and that, despite his status as a *privatus*, he had powers equal to those of the consuls. Thus, as the vehicle for the memorialization of the return of the Parthian standards, Augustus's *statua loricata* visibly declared him to be Imperator Caesar Augustus at Rome—not simply in his provinces, and more important,

---

[66] Domitius altar base: Kuttner 1993. Bocchus monument: Hölscher 1979; Hölscher in *Kaiser Augustus* 1988, 384–86, with bibliography; Kuttner 2013.

[67] The lack of the consulate, and thus technically of *imperium domi*, would cease to be an aspect of imperial rule with Caligula's continuous consulships.

[68] Roles of the senate and *comitia tributa* in the triumph: Richardson 1975, 58–62. Renewal of auspices: Varro *Ling.* 5.143 (*pomerium* marking the place where *auspicia urbana finiuntur*); Cic. *Div.* 1.33 (on Ti. Gracchus's violation of augural law, *quod inauspicato pomerium transgressus esset*), with Linderski 1986, 2204–5.

permanently. In contrast to the similar statue of Caesar, an image predicated on the traditionally Republican legal standing of the dictator, Augustus's statue set before the *populus Romanus* the image of his new, unprecedented legal status and, in so doing, rendered obsolete the old notion of a strict division between *domi* and *militiae*. In this way, the statue forcefully manifest the new reality of empire, a new meaing of *imperium*, and a new conception of rule. This is what it meant for Augustus to "cross the *pomerium*."[69]

Vitellius at the Bridge

Finally, and briefly: the argument for a ban on the appearance of a living, armed *imperator* within the *pomerium* takes as one of its most forceful pieces of evidence a famous passage in Tacitus, recounting Vitellius's arrival at Rome on 17 July in the year 69 BC:

> Vitellius, mounted on a distinguished horse, wearing the *paludamentum*, and girded by arms, had set out from the Milvian bridge, driving the senate and people before him; but he was dissuaded by his courtiers from entering Rome as if it were a captured city, and so he changed to a senator's toga, arranged his troops in good order, and made his entry on foot.[70]

This is held to be a version of the *mutatio vestis*, that exchange of military to civic attire (or the reverse) required to cross the *pomerium*.[71] Vitellius abandoned the *paludamentum* and *balteus*—for this is surely the significance of Tacitus's *accinctus*—and donned the *toga praetexta* of a magistrate. Nevertheless, his troops followed him, his thirty-four cohorts "distinguished by the names of their *gens* and their kinds of arms" and his centurions, "with gleaming arms and decorations." One imagines, following Tacitus's description, that this would have appeared much like a triumph—save for the obvious lack of the customary chariot and the other requisite *ornamenta*.[72]

---

[69] After 19 BC: Girardet 1990b. New conception of rule: Richardson 1991.
[70] Tac. *Hist.* 2.89; cf. Suet. *Vit.* 11.1.
[71] Alföldi 1970, 123–27; Kleiner 1983, 295–96; Wellesley 2000, 102.
[72] Cf. Suet. *Vit.* 10.2: "For when he had begun his march [to Rome, after the death of Galba], he rode through the midst of cities like one is conveyed in a triumph."

Although the new emperor's actions acknowledged that the toga was his proper attire in the city, it is clear that this aspect of decorum did not apply to his troops. The solution was clearly a compromise. Why did Vitellius change?

Vitellius was no ordinary general. He had been acclaimed by his troops on the German frontier in January, and his status as *imperator* had been recognized by the senate's acclamation on 19 April (celebrated by the Arval Brethren with offerings on 1 May, *ob diem imperii*), when he was no doubt also granted tribunician power (celebrated by the Arvals on 30 April, *ob comitia tribuniciae potestatis*).[73] So, at his *adventus*, Rome had already bestowed upon him all those powers that had come to signify the position we know today as that of the emperor.[74]

It would seem that these powers were conveyed by *senatus consulta* and then enacted by comitial legislation, for this is the force of the *lex de imperio Vespasiani*.[75] What survives of this complex statute attests that those powers eventually accumulated by Augustus and his successors were enacted on precedent and bestowed at once upon later emperors, a procedure that can be traced back to Tiberius.[76] Those who drafted this *lex* were mindful of how, as in the case of Vitellius, there might be a long interval between acclamation by the troops and the essential actions of both senate and people. Thus, its eighth clause makes explicit that the *acta*, *gesta*, *decreta*, and *imperata* effected during the interim were to be recognized as both lawful and binding, "just as if they had been undertaken according to the order of the people or plebs"—a fiction of the kind we shall examine in chapters 2 and 3.[77] Moreover, since the *lex*'s seventh clause appears to exempt the new emperor from any "obligation to observe those laws from which his predecessors had been freed," one is led

---

[73] Acclamation by troops: Tac. *Hist.* 1.56.2. Recognition by the senate: Tac. *Hist.* 1.56.2. Celebrations by the Arvals: Scheid 1998d, no. 40, lines 81–82, 84–85.

[74] Cf. Tac. *Hist.* 2.55: "The senate at once [upon receiving the news of Vitellius's acclamation] voted for Vitellius all the honors that had been devised during the long reigns of other emperors"; with Brunt 1977, 100–101, and Scheid 1992, 230.

[75] Brunt 1977, suggesting its correspondence to *senatus consulta*. Comitial legislation: Crawford, in *RS* I, p. 550. *Lex rogata*: Hurlet 1993, 265; Scheid 1992, 237 (the Princeps "exerce ses fonctions par la volonté du peuple romain"); further, Nicolet 1988.

[76] Dio 53.18.4 ("bestowed upon the emperors at one and the same time"); Brunt 1977, 98. Cf. the essays in Capogrossi Colognesi and Tassi Scandone 2009.

[77] Brunt 1977, 106, dating the clause's warrant to the time of Vitellius.

CHAPTER 1

to assume, when considering it in combination with the clause that follows, that something similar obtained upon Vitellius's acclamation in 69 BC. Thus, when he entered Rome, even before legislation granted the traditional powers and prerogatives of his new office, he might have been free to exercise them.

Among these powers and prerogatives was, as we have already seen, *imperium*, held and exercised both *domi et militiae*, and the consequent right to "cross the *pomerium*" without its diminution. What is more, Tacitus's detailed account makes no mention of Vitellius retaking the auspices upon his entry to the city; thus, his *auspicia* were also valid, both *domi et militiae*.[78] So, upon his arrival with his troops at Rome, despite the obviously military character of his claim to rule, the senators appealed to tradition, and tradition prevailed. The living image of the new ruler was to be that of the *civilis princeps*, and his *mutatio vestis* was not a matter of public or augural law but of established precedent, one enshrined in the custom that decreed that the centuriate assembly meet outside the *pomerium*.[79] In the truest imperial fashion, just as Augustus had claimed "to accept no office contrary to custom" and yet assumed unprecedented powers, so Vitellius bowed to the *mos maiorum* that bade him change his garb, yet asserted *another* imperial tradition, one that declared that his power to command was valid at home as well as abroad.[80] He too, like all emperors after Tiberius and all who would follow, held the right to "cross the *pomerium*."

---

[78] For the requirement, see Cic. *ND* 2.10–11, *Div.* 1.33, 2.75, with Mommsen 1887–1888, I:100–103 = 1889–1896, I:114–18; Linderski 1986, 2204.

[79] Cf. Versnel 1970, 353, on Gell. 15.27.5.

[80] Augustus's claim: *RGDA* 6.1.

2

Octavian's *Imperium Auspiciumque* in 43 BC and Their Late Republican Context

Aged nineteen years old I mustered an army at my personal decision and at my personal expense, and with it I liberated the state, which had been oppressed by a despotic faction. For this reason the senate passed honorific decrees admitting me to its body in the consulship of Gaius Pansa and Aulus Hirtius, at the same time giving me consular precedence in stating my opinion, and it gave me supreme command [*imperium*]. To prevent the state from suffering harm, it ordered me as *propraetor* to take precautions together with the consuls. In this same year, moreover, the people appointed me consul, after both consuls had fallen in war, and *triumvir* for settling the state.[1]

The historical background to the famous opening of Augustus's *Res Gestae* is well known; so too the first *princeps*'s penchant, amid his account, for omissions and obfuscations, as a host of other texts and modern commentators reveal.[2] Central to this passage is the young Octavian's first command (*imperium*). Its enactment is readily dated, as Cicero reports the meetings of

---

[1] *RGDA* 1.1; text and trans. from Cooley 2009; cf. Scheid 2007. The episode that forms the basis for what follows plays virtually no role in Alföldi 1976, despite its title.

[2] Surveyed recently by Vervaet 2010 and Rich 2010.

CHAPTER 2

the senate on 1 January 43 BC and the days that followed at which the appointment was made. In turn, the calendars fix his precocious assumption of power and its symbols, the *fasces*, to the 7th: *Imp. Caesar Augustu*[*s primum fasces sumpsit*] *Hirtio et Pansa* [*cos.*] (*Fasti Praenestini*); *VII Idus Ianuar. E*[*o die Caesar*] *primum fasces sumpsit* (*Feriale Cumanum*).[3]

Several issues that emerge here are fundamental to an understanding of Octavian's rise to power; a few have long attracted scrutiny, commentary, and differing opinions, and some are discussed (along with several related problems), in differing proportion, in what follows. Chief among these are, first, how was Octavian's status different from that of elected magistrates who held commands? Second, how was his independent *imperium* conferred upon him? And third, how was his independent right to the *auspicia publica*, which was requisite for the full and valid execution of that command, conveyed?

Magisterial Investiture

The grant of Octavian's powers did not follow the customary procedure for the conferral of *imperium* upon magistrates of the state, a process that is sporadically documented in the sources.[4] Long-standing practice required an election by the *populus* in the centuriate assembly. A sitting magistrate would take the auspices and, if the signs were favorable, have the people summoned to the *comitia*; after the vote, the presiding magistrate offered a prayer for the election's good fortune. All had to take place on a single day, or else the entire process would need to be repeated, *ab initio*.[5]

---

[3] Cic. *Phil.* 5.45; cf. 14.28; the first notice is in 3.5. The date: Stein 1930, cited in Linderski 1984, 79, n. 26 = 1995, 152, n. 26. *Fasces senatus dedit*: Cic. *Phil.* 11.20. Praeneste: *Inscr. Ital.* XIII.2,113 = *CIL* I, p. 230 = *EJ*, 44. Cumae: *Inscr. Ital.* XIII.2,392 = *CIL* XII.4333 = *ILS* 108 = *EJ*, 44. Precocious: as Corey Brennan has pointed out to me, *fasces sumere* does not seem to be a technical term, and in the *Fasti Cumanum* it mimics the similar recording of Octavian's donning of the *toga virilis* (18 or 19 October 48 BC) in what was conventional ritual language = *EJ*, 53. Spannagel 2009 provides enlightening discussion of Octavian's early career.

[4] Amalgamation of the sources and discussion in Mommsen 1887–1888, I:608–22 = 1889–1896, II:278–93; Linderski 1996, 179–80; Lintott 2003, esp. ch. 5; Benoist 2005; Van Haeperen 2007.

[5] Summons: Varro *Ling.* 6.91. Prayer: Lintott 2003, 45; Cic. *Mur.* 1; Livy 3.64.9–10, with Mommsen's reconstruction of the *rogationis carmen* (Mommsen 1887–1888, III:391, n. 1 = 1889–1896: VI, pt.1, 450, n. 1); cf. *Ad Herr.* 4.68; Dion. Hal. 7.59.2. Single day: Cic. *Phil.* 2.82; App. *BCiv.* 1.14.

Elections were usually held long before the end of the year, often months before the inauguration of those newly elected.[6] When that day came, a new magistrate would take the auspices at home, at dawn, and later he was accompanied by senators to the Capitol. It stands to reason that, before ascending the hill, he convened the *comitia curiata* (in the old Comitium before its demise, and afterwards at the rostra), where he carried the *lex* that acknowledged that his auspices were *recte* and that his appointment was *iustus*. This was the famous *lex curiata*, which Cicero explains as a "double vote" in the election of magistrates.[7] Then, on the Capitol, the vows of the previous year's consuls were resolved, sacrifices were performed, prayers were said, and vows were made for the well-being of the state; finally, an initial meeting of the senate was called, before which the new consuls would once again auspicate, and after which the allotment of the provinces would take place—if this had not already occurred.[8]

There were several other aspects of a senior magistrate's appointment, although their precise timing and sequence are debated (I shall return to this below). Within five days of entering office, magistrates took an oath to observe the laws.[9] And at the initial meeting of the senate, a date would be set for the celebration of the *Feriae Latinae*, before which the consuls' departure for their provinces is said to have been forbidden (although this is hardly borne out by our sources).[10] And lastly, in times of war—before the start of the consular

---

[6] Time between election and entry to office: Mommsen 1887–1888, I:583 and n. 1 = 1889–1896, II:247 and n. 3; Vaahtera 2001, 119, n. 105.

[7] *Recte* and *iustus*: see n. 31 below. "Double" vote: Cic. *Leg. Agr.* 2.26.

[8] *Auspicia*: Dion. Hal. 2.5.1. *Processus consularis*: Ovid *Fast.* I, 79–81. Auspices and sacrifice on the Capitol: Livy 21.63.14–15; cf. Varro *apud* Gell. 14.7.9 (*immolareque hostiam prius auspicarique debere*); Livy 22.9.7. Various *hostiae* attested: Ovid *Fast.* I, 83–84, *Pont.* 4.4.31; Livy 31.5.4–5 (201 BC), 36.1.2 (191 BC), and 42.28.7 and 42.30.8 (171 BC). *Voti Soluti*: Livy 41.14.7–15, with Scheid 1998b, 209–11; cf. Livy 33.44.2. Prayers: Livy 31.5.4 (201 BC), 36.1.2 (191 BC), and 42.30.8 (171 BC). *Vota*: Cic. *Verr.* 2.5.34.14 (*votaque pro imperio suo communique re publica*); Livy 21.63.7. *Vota pro salute rei publicae*: Cic. *Sull.* 34.7; Vell. 2.22.2.8; cf. Ovid *Pont.* 4.4.30 and Livy 42.28.9. Auspication before senate meeting: Varro *Ling.* 6.91. Allotment and its timing: discussion and sources in Stewart 1998, ch. 1; Rosenstein 1995.

[9] *Iurare in leges*: Livy 31.50.6–8, with Drogula 2015, 33; cf. Millar 1989, 145; Plin. *Paneg.* 64, with Mommsen 1887–1888, I:619–20 = 1889–1896, II:291.

[10] Meeting of the senate: Ovid *Pont.* 4.4.35–36. *Feriae Latinae*: discussion and sources in Smith 2012 and Marco Simon 2011. Celebrated at various times: in winter (Cic. *Div.* I.18 [*cum tumulos*

year was aligned with the calendar on 1 January in 153—a magistrate would often quickly depart for his *provincia*, where he would serve, after making his vows on the Capitol. In times of peace, the departure from the *urbs* would customarily wait until the end of the year, a practice legitimated in 81 by Sulla.[11]

Privatus cum imperio

But there is little evidence that all—or, indeed, any—of these rituals transpired in those instances when *imperium* was granted to *privati*, particularly after the passage of the *Lex Pompeia* of 52 BC, when *all* promagistrates were to be appointed, *de iure*, as private citizens (*privati cum imperio, sine magistratu*).[12] Such was Octavian's status at the time of his initial command of 43, as Cicero states explicitly:

> *Demus igitur imperium Caesari, sine quo res militaris administrari, teneri exercitus, bellum geri non potest; sit pro praetore eo iure, quo qui optimo.*
>
> [Let us therefore give Caesar the command, without which no military affairs can be administered, no army held together, no war waged; let him be propraetor with the fullest power of a regular appointment.][13]

Albano in monte nivalis]); in late March 199 BC (Livy 32.1–9); on the third day before the Nones of May and repeated (due to a *vitium*) on the third day before the Ides of August in 176 BC (41.16.1); 12 April in 168 BC (44.19.4); 1 June in 171 BC (42.35.3); in January 48 BC within eleven days of Caesar entering office (Caes. *BCiv.* 3.2).

[11] Regularization of the consular year: 15 March in 222 BC? (Livy 31.5.1–2, with Mommsen 1887–1888, I:599 and n. 6 = 1889–1896, II:267 and n. 2; cf. Livy 21.63.1–2); 1 January in 153 BC (Livy *Per.* 47, with Michels 1967, 98–100). Rapid departures for war: e.g., Flamininus in March 217 BC (Livy 21.63.8 and 22.1.5–7) and Aemilius Paullus in April 168 BC (44.19.4). Sullan reorganization: Balsdon 1939 and Brennan 2000, II:388–91 (both detailing the late Republican exceptions).

[12] *Privati*: Béranger 1973. *Lex Pompeia*: Dio 40.30.1, 46.2.1–2 and 56.1; this may be said despite the suspension of the *lex* given the outbreak of civil war. Discussion in Marshall 1972, 890 ("this *lex* only functioned properly in 51/50"—the demands of civil war intervened). The *Lex Iulia* of 49 BC appears to have abrogated some of its provisions (Girardet 1987); cf. Ferrary 2001b, 105–7; Hurlet 2006, 34, both with bibliography.

[13] Cic. *Phil.* 5.45. *Optimo iure*: Botsford 1909, 186–88; cf. Dio 46.35.4 ("the distinction and authority of praetor").

Cicero was addressing the senate, and Octavian's command was conferred by a *senatus consultum*. His was an *imperium extraordinarium*, as the orator would later report, issued to a *privatus* on account of the emergency presented by Anthony's siege of Mutina. And in spite of his youth, it was accompanied by the simultaneous decree of other honors, recounted by Cicero and confirmed (as we have seen) by the *Res Gestae*: notably Octavian's adlection to the senate (despite his not having yet entered upon the *cursus*) and the bestowal of the privilege of speaking before the *patres*.[14]

In January, Octavian was encamped at Spoleto. Cicero makes no mention of those essential, traditional, and (seemingly) constitutional aspects of magisterial appointment that formed the basis of the conferral of power, no acknowledgment of a vote by the people, nor of a *lex curiata de imperio*, which would have required the youth's presence. Here we see one of the differences between the magistrates and those *privati cum imperio* who were appointed as promagistrates: "The former [were] installed in Rome after an *auspicatio* and in a special ceremony, whereas the latter had to do without such an official installation."[15]

Was Octavian's *imperium* granted by the senate alone, as Cicero's speech might be held to imply?[16] It is well known that Livy similarly fails to consistently mention the full procedure for appointments, despite the fact that he acknowledges extraordinary powers to have customarily been conveyed *populi iussu* or *ex auctoritate patrum*, and that the sources suggest that special commands may have *usually* required the authority of both.[17] But not always: in 210 BC, Scipio was elected, in a surprise vote by the centuries in the campus;

---

[14] Extraordinary command for a *privatus*: Cic. *Phil*. 11.20; other honors: *Phil*. 5.46. The purpose of the *senatus consultum* was parsed by Cicero at *Phil*. 3.5 (*ut rem publicam . . . defendere*). Discussions of *imperia extraordinaria* in Jameson 1970 and Gruen 1995, 534–43.

[15] Quotation: Versnel 1970, 344. Van Haeperen 2012, 91 (and repeated in Van Haeperen 2017, 396), speaks, strangely and surely mistakenly, of Octavian's inability, since he was not at Rome, "y prendre . . . auspices d'entrée en charge ni donc y bénéficier d'une *lex curiata*"—but since he was not a magistrate, neither act would have applied.

[16] Magdelain 1968, 25, n. 2, and 53.

[17] Extraordinary powers: Livy 26.2.1. Livy's omissions: Ferrary 2003; cf. Feldherr 1998. Conferral of special commands: Brennan 2000, II:646, on Livy 26.2.1. Cf. Badian 1996, 187–89, for similar omission of details in Livy's accounts of the tribunate; Scheid 1998c, 214, on Livy's penchant for "passant sur les actes de routine."

CHAPTER 2

evidence for the procedure for *prorogatio* is similarly spotty.[18] And for the late Republic, the example of Cicero's own appointment, in 51, as proconsul for Cilicia, is telling: the post was "decreed by the senate and fixed by popular law."[19] Nevertheless, it is equally clear that by the later first century the senate had long since accrued the power and the right to act alone in the not unrelated matter of prorogations of *imperium*. Thus, given that Cicero's account of Octavian's appointment marked a moment of political crisis, the orator should most probably be taken at his word that this was a *senatorial* act.[20]

Proconsuls and propraetors were not appointed to a magistracy—their commands (*militiae*) and their competencies were *extra ordinem*.[21] This was true even when the *imperium* of a consul or praetor was extended by means of prorogation, and it was surely all the more so in the case of the appointment of an inexperienced youth like Octavian. Magistrates were elected in the *comitia centuriata*, but (as we have noted) that election was also confirmed by a law in the *comitia curiata*; promagistrates were appointed by *senatus consulta*—and no *lex curiata* would be carried for a privatus, not even for an ex-consul such as Cicero. About this, Cicero had been unequivocal: "[It] is unheard of and absolutely without precedent that a magistracy should be assigned [*detur*] by a *lex curiata* to a man who has not previously received it in some comitia."[22] There were precedents for such appointments *sine magis-*

---

[18] Scipio: Livy 26.18.6–10. *Prorogatio*: Livy 8.23.12, 8.26.7 (in 326 BC) and 10.22.9 (in 295 BC); cf. Livy 9.42.2 and 10.16.1.

[19] Cic. *Fam.* 15.9.2 (*senatus consulto et lege*), 15.14.5 (*hanc provinciam quam et senatus et populus annuam esse voluit*); cf. *Fam.* 2.7.4 (defending the senate's decree and the laws of the land); *Att.* 7.7.4 (*nec enim senatus decrevit, nec populus iussit me imperium in Sicilia habere*) and 6.6.3. Discussion: Fanizza 2014, 66 and nn. 51–52, who believes the law in question to be the *lex curiata* (unpersuasive). Cicero's correspondence and the technicalities involved: Marshall 1972.

[20] Senate's powers: Ferrary 2003; Brennan 2000, I:73–75 (on Livy 8.23.10–12) and 188–89 (citing Polyb. 6.15.6 on the senatorial prerogative). Crisis: cf. Vervaet 2009, 412, n. 27, on the similarity of Pompey's assignment in 78: "unlikely that the authorities in Rome bothered to pass a *lex curiata* . . . and the senate again resorted to this procedure [in 43 BC] when it sanctioned the young Octavianus' command"—yet why should one think that a *lex curiata* was called for? Cf. Vervaet's comments cited in n. 22 below.

[21] Brennan 2000, I:102–3, gives the rare exceptions.

[22] Cicero's appointment in 51 BC: cf. chapter 1, n. 58. "[It] is unheard of": Cic. *Leg. Agr.* 2.26–28 (*iam hoc inauditum et plane novum, uti curiata lege magistratus detur, qui nullis comitiis ante sit datus*), with Vervaet 2014, 308–11, 311: "What Cicero here objects to is that the curiate law would be passed on behalf of individuals who had not first been properly elected by all the tribes. . . . It was technically impossible to pass a *lex curiata de imperio* on behalf of a citizen who

tratu. Spain saw many: Publius Cornelius Scipio, later Africanus, was sent as a promagistrate, a *privatus cum imperio*, in 210 BC; Lucius Cornelius Lentulus and Lucius Manlius Acidinus in 206; and Titus Quinctius Flamininus in 205. The procedure, although much curtailed by the rise in the number of praetorships, continued—perhaps most notoriously with Pompeius's extraordinary commands from 82 onwards, sporadically until his consulship in 70, and then after. Octavian's case was one among many. In moments of crisis, such as when Octavian was appointed to his command *propraetore* in 43, senatorial decree must have sufficed; similarly, the emergency explains why the consuls Hirtius and Pansa departed for Mutina, in the dead of winter, without attending the *Feriae Latinae*.[23]

Lex curiata

A *lex curiata* was clearly not a requirement for an extraordinary command, nor even (as we shall see) for an elected magistrate. Yet this law looms large in most discussions of *imperium auspiciumque*: what was its purpose?

The curiate law was a customary aspect of magisterial investiture. On the one hand, it has been variously thought that it bestowed imperium, *imperium militiae*, or the auspices; none of these views can be sustained, however, in the face of the ancient testimonia, despite their lacunose state and, at times, confusing if not contradictory reports. On the other hand, the curiate law has been held to have confirmed or ratified any or all of these—interpretations that have more to recommend them. But what was confirmed, and by whom?[24]

---

had not first been properly invested with a lawful magistracy"; *contra* Linderski 1996, 166, à propos of Caes. *BCiv* 1.6.5–7 and Cic. *Fam.* 3.2.1, who suggests no such distinction between the grant of imperium to magistrates and *privati*: "*privati* [consulars who were appointed promagistrates] ... could not receive the imperium simply by a decree of the senate, it had to be bestowed upon them by a legislative act: first, it would appear, by a law in the centuriate or tribal assembly to be followed by the lex curiata de imperio"; similarly Fanizza 2014, 67 (referring, unpersuasively, to Cicero's posting to Cilicia). Cf. Toher 2004, 183, who points out that no *lex curiata* was passed for Octavian until his election to the consulship—neither one for his adoption (citing Dio 45.5.3–4 and Florus 2.15.2–3) nor, implicitly, one for his first command.

[23] Scipio: Livy 28.38.1 (*ductu auspicioque*). Lentulus and Acidinus: Livy 28.38.1 (*propraetoribus*). Flamininus: Livy 29.13.6. The progressively increased number of praetorships: Lintott 2003, 107 and n. 59 (concisely), and Brennan 2000 (in detail); discussion in Jashemski 1950, with comprehensive lists in the appendices. Pompeius: Vervaet 2006 and 2009. Hirtius and Pansa: Dio 46.33.4.

[24] Survey and criticisms in Vervaet 2014, 300–351; cf. Stasse 2005.

CHAPTER 2

Much depends on the sequence of inaugural rituals, and the significance of that sequence. Recently, Van Haeperen has proposed a very suggestive interpretation: by means of the *lex curiata*,

> un *magistratus iustus* serait donc un magistrate élu par le peuple, confirmé par les dieux lors de la prise d'auspices initiale, et, sur cette double base, revêtu d'une loi curiate: un magistrate "irréprochable aux yeux des hommes et des dieux."
>
> . . . une loi curiate resterait necessaire afin de conférer le *magistratus iustus*, après que la personne choisie eut obtenu l'assentiment des dieux.
>
> Un magistrate ne pouvait être considéré comme pleinement *iustus*, par le vote de la loi curiate, que s'il avait été élu selon les règles et obtenu l'assentiment de Jupiter lors de sa prise d'auspices initiale.[25]

The *lex curiata*, as it followed the newly elected magistrate's initial *auspicatio*, was the legal confirmation—the stamp of approval—that the auspication was positive, that the magisterial appointment could be regarded as *optimo lege et iure*, and that the sanction of Jupiter that came with the magistrate's initial enactment of the rite was officially acknowledged.[26] One imagines that the magistrate asked of the god whether his election had been *fas*, and Jupiter had, by means of the birds, conveyed his assent; the *lex curiata* thus ratified the quality of a magistrate's auspices with respect to both law and custom and declared him a *magistratus iustus*. We recognize here how the Romans' elected office-holders were approved by both gods and men.[27]

If Van Haeperen's interpretation is correct, the *lex curiata* offered not merely a "surplus of legitimacy," but an additional acknowledgment of a mag-

---

[25] Van Haeperen 2012, 86, 90, and Van Haeperen 2015, 226, respectively; cf. Humm 2011 and 2015 (accepting Van Haeperen's view).

[26] *Contra* Magdelain 1968, 29, for the reverse sequence.

[27] On the formula *fas est*, see Catalano 1960, 310; Versnel 1970, 335; Linderski 1986, 2195, 2291; Hickson 1993, 53–54; Fiori 2014a, 81. *Optimo lege et iure*: a conventional formula signaling the objective sense of the law, conceived "globally and autonomously," and applied to its full extent; see Mantovani 2008; Broggini 1966. Cf. Vervaet 2014, 314 (quality of auspices); 321 (*lex* not only for military auspices).

istrate's standing: *iustus*, but in what sense?²⁸ At issue is the *ius publicum*, and, unsurprisingly, there are augural connotations. Cicero implies that three augurs were customarily present at the passing of the *lex curiata*, and Dionysius refers to the role of *ornithoskopoi*.²⁹ These two ancient authorities suggest different yet not mutually exclusive aspects of the comitia's task and how it was carried out. The latter reveals that it was the *pullarii*—that is, neither the *augures* themselves nor the newly elected magistrate—who carried out the observation of the birds, while the former suggests that augurs were present at the passing of the *lex* to ensure that the signs revealed in the initial auspication, and their reporting, were in accordance with augural law. Therefore, *iustus* should be understood in this context not merely as a political expression signaling full accordance with legal statutes, but equally as a fundamentally religious term portending the augural propriety of both those statutes and their employ.³⁰ Cicero speaks on numerous occasions of the *ius augurum*, and of the requirements of the priesthood's fulfillment of its responsibilities, both *recte*, that is, without religious fault, and *iusta*, in accordance with the *ius* established by religious tradition, the two terms serving, at times, synonymously.³¹ Thus, the language of our sources reiterates the approval of both men and gods: magistrates entered office *optimo lege et iure* as a recognition

---

²⁸ Surplus of legitimacy: Stasse 2005, 384; Van Haeperen 2012, 82, 84; cf. Vervaet 2015, 216 and n. 38.

²⁹ Cic. *Att.* 4.17.2. *Ornithoskopoi*: Dion. Hal. 2.6.2–3, with Vaahtera 2001, 119–22; Van Haeperen 2012, 76, with bibliography; Linderski 1986, 2191, n. 164 (not "the *augures publici*, but . . . low-class *apparitores*, no doubt the *pullarii*, who were paid by the state"); cf. *ILS* 1886, 1907; *contra* Vervaet 2014, 319, n. 54 ("ranking citizens from prominent Roman colonies and *municipia* across Italy").

³⁰ Cf. the augurs' role in the lot: Rosenstein 1995; Stewart 1998.

³¹ *Ius augurum*: Cic. *Senect.* 12 (*iuris auguri*), *Dom.* 39 (*iure augurum*); cf. *Lex Coloniae Genetivae*, 66 (*de auspiciis quaeque ad eas res pertinebunt augurum iuris dictio iudicatio esto* [concerning auspices and whatever things shall pertain to those matters, jurisdiction and right of judgment are to belong to the augurs]: *RS* I: no. 25, 3–4, and trans., p. 423). *Iustus=recte*: cf. Gracchus's outburst reported at Cic. *Nat. D.* 2.11 ("am I not *iustus*? I put the names to the vote as consul, as augur, and with the auspices taken"), and *Leg.* 2.21 (*quaeque augur iniusta . . . defixerit*). Commentary in Behrends 1970, esp. 18–21; cf. Linderski 1986, 2185, 2204–5; Linderski 1996, 182–83; Humm 2011, 115; and Humm 2015, 232; *contra* Vervaet 2015, 216–17, n. 38, who, while perhaps correctly insisting on the relevance of *iustus* in the formula *iustum imperium et auspicium* solely to *imperium* (note, however, that the grammar of such a formula is ambiguous; cf. Gildersleeve and Lodge 1895, § 290), nonetheless does not do justice to the term's wider purchase and religious dimension that are attested by our sources.

of their acceptance by the former and as an acknowledgement of the assent of the latter.

And what of the promagistrates? Despite their lack of a *lex curiata*, the conventionalization of appointments *pro consule* and *pro praetore* established an equality among the positions of command—for the character of *imperium* and *auspicia* was the same for all who possessed them, independently, at the same rank, whether that of a consul or praetor.[32] All such commanders served as representatives of the *SPQR*, despite differences in their assigned competencies and the spheres in which these were to be carried out, but they were representatives who differed fundamentally in kind: in the manner of their legal standing and of their religious sanction. As we have seen, the procedure for establishing these essential qualities of magisterial appointment was manifold and fixed by tradition. By contrast, Octavian's command, like that of all those who were appointed *sine magistratu* with an independent *imperium*, would acquire its religious sanction differently.[33]

Octavian's *Auspicia*

Octavian's possession of his own auspices is vouchsafed by the sources, yet the basis of his *ius auspicandi*, and the manner of its assumption, is seldom the subject of detailed analysis. On the seventh of January, the new commander not only received the *fasces* but took the auspices, as we learn from the evidence provided by the Narbo Altar's inscription (AD 12):

VII Idus Ianuar. Qua die primum imperium orbis terrarum auspicatus est.

[On the seventh day before the Ides of January, on which day, for the first time, (Octavian's) command over the whole world was (validated by) auspication.][34]

---

[32] Livy 8.32.3: *praetores iisdem auspiciis quibus consules creati.*
[33] Cf. Magdelain 1968, 25: "L'existence d'un statut legal, établi isolément [as in the case of the *senatus consultum* for Octavian] . . . rend inutile une loi curiate."
[34] *CIL* XII.4333 = *ILS* 112 = Sherk 1988, no. 7c.

The religious character of this notice is complemented by an anecdote related by Pliny the Elder:

Divo Augusto Spoleti sacrificanti primo potestatis suae die sex victimarum iocinera replicata intrinsecus ab ima fibra reperta sunt, responsumque duplicaturum intra annum imperium.

[When Divus Augustus was sacrificing at Spoleto on the first day he was in power the livers of six victims were found with the bottom of their tissue folded back inward, and this was interpreted to mean that he would double his power within a year.][35]

This (or Pliny's source) was later quoted, in part, by Suetonius:

Et immolanti omnium victimarum iocinera replicata intrinsecus ab ima fibra *vict paruerunt, nemine peritorum aliter coniectante quam laeta per haec et magna portendi.*

[While he was sacrificing, the livers of all the sacrificial victims appeared to be folded back on themselves from the bottom lobe; none of the experts interpreted this as other than portending great success.][36]

In this instance, repetition enhances credibility, and there can be little doubt that, when the news of the senate's actions reached Octavian's encampment at Spoleto, he comported himself in accordance with tradition and sought the gods' validation for the command that had been bestowed. Collectively, these sources specify *sacrificium* and *extispicium* and imply *auspicia*; how, and on what basis, were the rituals performed? Three broad questions present themselves, and these are treated here in an ascending order of significance and in increasing detail.

---

[35] Plin. *HN* 11.190.
[36] Suet. *Aug.* 95; cf. Wardle's commentary (2014). The anecdote is echoed in Dio 46.35.4 and Obsequens 69.

CHAPTER 2

What did sacrifice, and subsequent haruspicy, have to do with Octavian's assumption of *imperium*? It was customary that the new consuls would offer prayers and sacrifices on the day of their inauguration, beseeching the gods that things be *bene ac feliciter* for the state, particularly in times of war. *Extispicia* followed, and *haruspices responderunt*, as omens were sought, as if to confirm the efficacy of sacrifice and prayer. The rites were central to the successful deployment of *imperium*.[37]

The *haruspices* are reported to have played a significant religious role in Roman politics from the middle Republic onward. They customarily accompanied commanders in the field; as Cicero says, *qui nihil in bello sine extis agunt*. These individuals were merely technically adept *apparitores* rather than members of the illustrious *LX*, who were most likely an imperial development.[38] Examples of their role and function are well attested: in 215 BC, Fabius enlisted the *haruspices* in order to respond to prodigies; in 176, and again in 171, Livy reports that the consuls sacrificed on the day of their entry into office and informs us that haruspicy followed. By the late Republic, even colonial magistrates (*duoviri* and *aediles*) were attended by haruspices, if the stipulations of the *Lex Coloniae Genetivae* are to be considered customary.[39] And the sources report that the most famous commanders are all known to have had personal *haruspices*: Sulla, his Postumius; Verres, Volusius; and Caesar, most famously, Spurinna. Why shouldn't the young Octavian—who is known to have done so on other occasions—have employed one at Spoleto?[40]

---

[37] E.g., Livy 36.1.2–3, 42.30.8. Scheid 2015, 255, notes the conventional employment of the "deux actes divinatoires."

[38] *Haruspices*: overviews in Rawson 1978; Guittard 2002–2003; sources collected in Wissowa 1912, 543–49; Haack 2003 treats the famous *LX* of the imperial period. As *apparitores*: Wissowa 1912, 548, citing Cic. *Verr.* 2.2.10.27 and 2.3.60.137. Quotation: Cic. *Div.* 1.95, who explicitly contrasts the role of *extispicia militiae* with the *auspicia domi*; Scheid 2015, 259, describes the role of *haruspices* as "une function romaine permanente."

[39] 215 BC: Livy 23.36.10 (*haud facile litari haruspices respondebant*); 176 BC: Livy 41.14.7–41.15.1ff; 171 BC: Livy 42.30.8 (*haruspices responderunt*). *Lex Coloniae Genetivae*: *RS* I: no. 25, lxii, 12–40.

[40] Postumius: Cic. *Div.* 1.72; Aug. *Civ.D.* 2.24; cf. Obsequens 56b. Volusius: Cic. *Verr.* 2.3.11.28 and 54; cf. Cic. *Verr.* 2.2.10.27 and 33. Spurinna: Cic. *Div.* 1.119, with the commentary of Rawson 1978 and Weinstock 1971—despite Julius's well-known ambivalence (Suet. *Iul.* 81; Val.

OCTAVIAN'S *IMPERIUM AUSPICIUMQUE*

How was Octavian's right to the *auspicia publica*—for this is what is attested by the calendar entries—conferred and/or confirmed? The Narbo inscription makes clear that these were not *auspicia privata*. Octavian, a *privatus*, could only auspicate on behalf of the *SPQR* if the *senatus consultum* that appointed him *propraetore* and granted him his assignment conveyed, along with *imperium*, the *auspicia*. His independent command, *extra ordinem*, was a competence to be exercised solely with respect to the goals, geographical theater, and temporal extent of his allocated task, all of which constituted his *provincia*; this was, perforce, *imperium auspiciumque militiae*.[41] The same would appear to have been true for all promagistrates appointed as *privati* with an *independent* command, and several examples from the very end of the third century are unambiguously attested, as we have already seen; perhaps the most famous example is that of Pompeius's command in 78 BC against Lepidus.[42] Thus, the appointment of 43 as a command with independent *imperium auspiciumque* was hardly unusual in Republican military history.[43]

Max. 8.11.2r); similarly Pompeius, if Cic. *Div.* 2.53 is to be believed. Even Constantine would consult them: *Pan. Lat.* 12(9), 2, 4, with Barnes 1981, 52–53; cf. Wheeler 2008. Octavian and the *haruspices*: Plin. *NH* 11.195 (before Actium). Attitudes toward portents and omens: Suet. *Aug.* 90–92; cf. Suet. *Aug.* 96.2 on the multiple sacrifices and reading of the *exta* at Perugia (commentary in Wardle 2014 *ad loc.*).

[41] Extraordinary command's distinct purpose: Ferrary 2001b, 110–11. *Imperium* bringing with it the right to the *auspicia*: Bleicken 2016, 90; cf. Vervaet 2014, 20–21: "There is every indication that the possession of independent *imperium* . . . and that the *auspicium publicum* . . . was one of the foremost *iura* embedded in the *ius imperii*."

[42] Third-century examples: given at n. 23 above, to which add M. Valerius Laevinus in 201 BC (Livy 31.3.2–3: *cum imperio . . . propaetor missus*) and Cn. Cornelius Blasio and L. Stertinus in 199 BC (Livy 31.50.11: *pro consulibus imperium esse in Hispanae iussit*). Full list in Jashemski 1950, ch. 1, and appendices, although dates are given here according to *MRR*. Pompeius in 78 BC with independent *imperium pro praetore*: Plut. *Pomp.* 16.2 (*hegemon*) and 17.4 (*proconsule?*); analysis in Boak 1918, cited and followed by Jashemski 1950, 89, Jameson 1970, and Vervaet 2009, 408, with the full bibliography.

[43] *Contra* Giovannini 1983, 33–37, 41 (nonmagistrates have no auspices). Vervaet 2014, 346, regards this, excessively, as a special situation: those who held their *imperium extra ordinem* either did so "by virtue of a curiate law . . . or alternatively by means of a special provision. This special clause may well have been part of the constitutive statute (or, most exceptionally, a *senatus consultum*) that invested them with the independent *imperium*." As has been suggested here, a *lex curiata*

CHAPTER 2

Cicero had famously condemned the decline of *religio*, and in particular those proconsuls and propaetors who did not have the auspices (*qui auspicia non habent*) and who conducted wars without any auspices at all (*nullis auspiciis administrantur*). Were these the *duces* who "only begin to wage war when they have laid down (*posuerunt*) their auspices"?[44] The distinction between Cicero's use of *auspicia habere* and *auspicia ponere* has, unfortunately, also caused confusion. These two formulae need to be understood in opposition—that is, the former signifies that one possesses the capacity to take the public auspices, and the latter the act of relinquishing that capacity in accordance with religious regulations: *ponere* cannot in this passage be construed as anything other than the counterpart to *habere*.[45]

To whom was Cicero referring? The object of his scorn was *negligentia nobilitatis*, and his comment constituted a condemnation of recent practice.[46] But magistrates had traditionally gone to their provinces at the end of their term of office, and while they would have laid down (*posuerunt*) their *auspicia urbana* upon departure from the *urbs*, they would then have assumed, as promagistrates, the auspices anew, together with their *imperium*, which was granted them as an aspect of their *provincia*. So, which promagistrates had no *auspicia*? These must have been the *legati*, many of whom had begun to be more and more frequently appointed at proconsular or propraetorian rank, with a delegated *imperium* and no auspices.[47] Many were former magistrates, or even promagistrates who had previously been in possession of their own auspices. They were the *duces* who waged war despite the fact that they had laid down their auspices when their office had expired; their new role was an aspect of civil war's effect on Rome's military institutions and *mos maiorum*. This was the focus of Cicero's sarcasm—and perhaps implicit here is an attack on a prac-

---

was unlikely, and it is hard to see the procedure as having been special, since it obtained in every instance when a *privatus* was appointed to a command or a proconsul had his assignment prorogued.

[44] Cic. *Nat. D.* 2.9; *Div.* 2.76.

[45] *Contra* Tarpin 2003, 287–88 and n. 49; cf., more persuasively, Dalla Rosa 2011, 250–52, and Dalla Rosa 2014, 86–91.

[46] Giovannini 1983, 78.

[47] *Legati*: Varro *Ling.* 5.87, with Benoist 2012. Similar conclusion in Vervaet 2014, 348–49. By contrast, Giovannini 1983, 43–44, 77–79, and Rich 1996, 102–3, regard all promagistrates as lacking auspices—wrongly, as the case of Octavian shows.

tice that, by the date of the *De Divinatione* and the *De Natura Deorum*, was commonplace: Metellus Scipio and Caesar employed such *legati*, but the practice had been given prominence by its widespread use by Pompeius. The context of Cicero's condemnation was the state of politics as well as that of religion.[48]

In the case of Octavian's command, what is striking is that he was not appointed as a *legatus*, and that the example of Pompeius's campaign against the pirates in 67 BC, and in Spain after 55, was *not* employed by the senate in their attempt to aid the consuls Hirtius and Pansa. Unlike those appointed by Pompeius to military commands as *legati pro praetore* with a delegated *imperium*, Octavian's status was that of an independent commander, with full *imperium auspiciumque*, at praetorian rank, a fact seemingly confirmed by the *supplicationes* voted him together with the consuls.[49] As the passages in the *De Divinatione* and the *De Natura Deorum* make plain, given his views, Cicero could hardly have proposed any other sort of appointment.[50]

❧

How was it that Octavian might first take the auspices beyond the *pomerium*, in the military sphere (*militiae*)? "Le cas d'Octavien prenant ses auspices de depart à Spolète, en recourant d'ailleurs probablement à une fiction juridique, se situe dans un context bien trop exceptionnel pour être érigé en règle générale"; so Berthelet.[51] Such a judgment assumes that there actually was such a thing as "departure auspices," that a juridical fiction allowed for them to be acquired

---

[48] Some examples of recent *legati* who were former magistrates include: (of Caesar) Calenus in 48 BC (*pr.* 59) and Gabinius in 48 BC (*pr.* 61, *cos.* 58); (of Metellus Scipio) Varus in 46 BC (*pr.* 53?) and Longus in 46 BC (*pr.* 58); (of Pompeius): Afranius in 46 BC (*cos.* 60), Petreius in 46 BC (*pr.* 64?), and Ampius Balbus in 46 BC (*pr.* 58); further examples in Girardet 1987, 319–24 (cited by Ferrary 2001b, 108, n. 31). That *legati* were awarded triumphs (so, apparently, Q. Fabius Maximus and Q. Pedius in 45 BC, for which see Vervaet 2014, 81–82 and notes)—without independent *imperium* and/or auspices—added fuel to the fire: for the practice, see Lange 2016, 72 and nn. 12–13.

[49] Cic. *Phil.* 14.11.

[50] Augustus's reorganization of the provincial commands in 27 BC returned to the Pompeian model: according to Dio (53.13.1–8), those assigned to Augustus's provinces, his *legati pro praetore*, were military men with only a delegated *imperium*; see the commentary of Rich 1990, *ad loc.* Pompeius's *legati* in 67 BC: App. *Mith.* 94; Plut. *Pomp.* 25.2–3; Dio 36.23.4, 37.1.2, with Jameson 1970.

[51] Berthelet 2015, 166.

CHAPTER 2

outside of Rome, and that the scenario at Spoleto in January of 43 BC was highly unusual. All three assumptions require scrutiny and shall be treated in reverse order.

Octavian's undertaking of his extraordinary command must be seen in the context of those attested for regular magistrates. By custom, one entered a magistracy—the conventional formula appears to have been *magistratum inire*—at Rome; while men were often elected *in absentia*, they were, as best we can tell, then summoned to the *urbs* for the various rituals that accompanied the taking of office.[52] All of those rituals—election in the *comitia centuriata*, the passing of the *lex* in the *comitia curiata*, and the vows, sacrifices, and meeting of the senate on the Capitoline—all took place in *loci inaugurati*.

The importance of the *urbs* for the magistrates' proper inauguration and subsequent conduct of their commands is exemplified by those occasions when a *vitium* was perceived to have brought their auspices into doubt, thus necessitating a commander's return for his auspices' retaking, the *repetitio auspiciorum*.[53] During the Italian campaigns, this posed no great logistical problem. Thus, in 325 BC, L. Papirius Cursor returned from Samnium; so too, in 302, a dictator (M. Valerius Maximus Corvus?) from the territory of the Marsi in central Italy; in 216, M. Iuniuis Pera from Casilinum; and in 215, Q. Fabius Maximus from Cales—all *auspiciorum repetendorum causa*, returning to Rome as required.[54]

But, at times, the ritual acts of political life were required when magistrates were far from the city, and with the constant warfare that led to the growth of empire, this necessitated greater flexibility. The precedent had long been set, even within Italy: for example, in 460 BC, augurs were sent to Lake Regil-

---

[52] Magistrates *creati in absentia*: Livy 24.43.5; 24.9.9. Magistrates elected and then summoned to Rome: Livy 24.43.9.

[53] This clashes with the view of Mommsen (1887–1888, III:629 = 1889–1896, VI:2, 251) when he commented on Varro, *Ling.* 5.33, that the Romans took the auspices in all the Latin towns in the same way as at Rome. It is not clear whether the rites of the *Feriae Latinae*, held in the sacred precinct on the Mons Albanus, were celebrated similarly, *in loco inaugurato*, if not also *auspicato*, for the augural status of the Mons Albanus is not reported in the sources; cf. Marco Simon 2011, 125 (following Grandazzi 2008).

[54] Livy 8.32.4, 10.3.3–8, 23.19.3–5, 23.36.9–10; discussion in Linderski 1993, 62; Berthelet 2015, 125. The case of Papirius is corroborated by the Arezzo elogium (*ILS* 53 = *CIL* VI.1318).

lus, "commanded to present themselves . . . there to inaugurate a place where the auspices could be taken and matters brought before the people [*locumque inaugurari ubi auspicato cum populo agi posset*]." Or, in 357,

> *Ab altero consule . . . legem novo exemplo ad Sutrium in castris tributim de vicensima eorum qui manumitterentur tulit. Patres, quia ea lege haud parvum vectigal inopi aerario additum esset, auctores fuerunt; ceterum tribuni plebis, non tam lege quam exemplo moti, ne quis postea populum sevocaret, capite sanxerunt.*

> [the . . . consul (Gnaeus Manlius) . . . got a law passed in his camp before Sutrium—the men voting by tribes—which levied a tax of one-twentieth on manumissions. The Fathers sanctioned this law, since it brought in no small revenue to the empty treasury; but the tribunes of the plebs, troubled less by the law than by the precedent established, had it made a capital offence for anyone thereafter to summon the people (to the *comitia* away from Rome)].[55]

Cum populo agere was the technical term for the passing of laws, and the *comitia* in which this occurred were inaugurated places (*templa*)—thus, the *locus inauguratus* at Lake Regillus—and this is implicit in the calling of the *comitia tributa* at Sutrium. In the early Republic, there seems to have been no other regulation about where they might be held—for why else should we hear that in 357 BC the tribunes felt the need to legislate a prohibition of such meetings *in externo solo*, so as to protect their veto, which was valid only within a mile of the *pomerium*?[56]

In a famous passage, Servius (Danielis) reports that a remedy had eventually been devised to resolve such issues that attended Rome's expansion. For it is explained that commanders had the capacity to auspicate outside the *pomerium* in the case of distant conflicts:

---

[55] Livy 3.20.6 and 7.16.7, respectively; commentary on the latter in Botsford 1909, 202, 297, and Oakley *ad loc.*

[56] *Cum populo agere*: Väähtera 1993; Linderski 1993, 59: "to pass the laws and to elect the magistrates, is possible only *auspicato*" (citing Livy 3.20.6).

CHAPTER 2

Sed hoc [revertere ad captanda rursus auspicia] servatum a ducibus Romanis, donec ab his in Italia pugnatum est, propter vicinitatem; postquam vero imperium longius prolatum est, ne dux ab exercitu diutius abesset, si Romam ad renovanda auspicia de longinquo revertisset, constitutum ut unus locus de captivo agro Romanus fieret in ea provincia, in qua bellabatur, ad quem, si renovari opus esset auspicia, dux rediret.

[This (return to the *urbs* for the retaking of the auspices), however, was preserved by the leaders of the Romans, while fighting in Italy, on account of proximity (to the *urbs*); but once the empire was greatly extended, lest the commander be absent from the army for a long time if he had to return to Rome for the *renovatio auspicii*,[57] a specific place in the captured territory would be made (as it were) Roman within that *provincia* in which he was fighting, of which, if the auspices needed to be renewed, the commander might avail himself.][58]

Not all who suspected that their auspices were flawed availed themselves of such a solution, including, most famously, C. Flaminius. It is not at all clear if this was a matter of a *vitium* or of the general's sheer arrogance, since the tradition is clearly hostile, and the accounts of Livy and Cicero diverge sharply and significantly.

First, Cicero. He implies that Flaminius was indeed a magistrate and was held to have auspicated, by means of the *tripudium*, yet to have refused to acknowledge the validity of the signs; the disaster at Lake Trasimene ensued.[59] For Cicero, Flaminius serves as one example among many of what comes to pass when the rites of religion are neglected.

---

[57] As Catalano 1960, 81, pointed out (followed by Berthelet 2015, 166, n. 102), Servius here confuses *renovatio auspiciorum* and *repetitio auspiciorum*.

[58] Servius *Aen.* 2.178; Mommsen 1887–1888, I:100 = 1889–1896: I:115; *contra* Magdelain 1968, 52–53. See also Vervaet 2014, 88, n. 59; Berthelet 2015, 166, with bibliography; noted by Scheid 2012a, 118–19; extensive discussion in Bianchi 1997, 92–121.

[59] Cic. *Div.* 1.77; cf. 2.21, 67, and 71; Cic. *Nat. D.* 2.8 (*Flaminius religione neglecta*); cf. Plut. *Fab.* 2.3–3.1; Livy 22.9.7 (*plus negligentia caerimoniarum auspiciorumque quam temeritate atque inscitia*).

By contrast, Livy offers a much more complex account. Elected to his second consulship for 217 BC, Flaminius left Rome for Gaul in secret, apparently *non inauguratus*—thus, as a *privatus*. Livy reports that several days later he entered on his magistracy (*magistratum iniit*) at Ariminum and duly sacrificed.[60] Should one assume this to mean that Flaminius attempted—unsuccessfully—to auspicate as well as sacrifice, *ex urbe*?[61] Livy makes plain that this was a doomed enterprise; according to the senators,

> *Magistratus id* [viz., *auspicium*] *a domo, publicis privatisque penatibus, Latinis feriis actis, sacrificio in monte perfecto, votis rite in Capitolio nuncupatis secum ferre; nec privatum auspicia sequi, nec sine auspiciis profectum in externo ea solo nova atque integra concipere posse.*
>
> [Magistrates . . . carried this (*auspicia*) with them when they set out from home—from their own and the nation's hearth—after celebrating the Latin Festival, sacrificing on the Alban Mount and duly offering up their vows on the Capitol; but a private citizen could neither take the auspices with him nor, if he had left Rome without them (i.e., as a non-inaugurated magistrate), receive them new and complete on foreign soil.][62]

Three important questions follow from Livy's account. First, in what sense was Flaminius a magistrate? Despite his election to his office, he had failed to perform before his departure *all* of the requisite rituals that would have made him a magistrate with *iustum imperium et auspicia*: the first auspication at home, the carrying of a *lex curiata*, the celebration of the *Feriae Latinae*, and the *nuncupatio votorum* on the Capitol before his departure. He was thus effectively rendered a *privatus*. Livy perhaps exaggerates, yet pointedly; technically, Flaminius was no magistrate:

---

[60] Livy 21.63.5–12 (*consulem inauspicato factum*), with Weisseborn and Müller 1887–1912, *ad loc.* (*vitio creatus*). Cf. Val. Max. 1.6.6 (*Flaminius inauspicato consul creatus*); Badian 1996, 199–200 and n. 17 (elected *auspicato* but there was a *vitium*).

[61] See Scheid 2015, 253: "J'aurais tendance à supposer qu'il aura en fait pris les auspices et formulé les voeux pour la nouvelle campagne dans le prétoire de son camp près de Cortone, ce qui respectait la forme, mais était contraire à la coutoume." Cf. Livy 26.2.2–3 on 211 BC.

[62] Livy 22.1.6–7.

CHAPTER 2

Revocandum universi retrahendumque censuerunt et cogendum omnibus prius praesentem in deos hominesque fungi officiis, quam ad exercitum et in provinciam iret.

[With one accord (the senators) voted to recall him and drag him back and compel him to discharge in person all his obligations to gods and men, before he went to his army and his *provincia*.][63]

Second, why couldn't Flaminius (or anyone else), as a *privatus*, take the auspices with him to the military sphere? For Livy, this is clear: Flaminius couldn't bring them with him because, although he was elected, he was not duly installed, and his auspices had not been confirmed by a *lex curiata*—those rituals that would have made him a *magistratus iustus*. Thus he didn't have the *ius auspicii* that such investiture would have bestowed on him. Since he hadn't taken the auspices and they hadn't been acknowledged by the *lex curiata*, he could not "take them with him," as any *iustus magistratus* would have done, when he departed for his province while still in office. Technically, Flaminius had never *had* the auspices to begin with.

Third, why couldn't Flaminius successfully receive the auspices, "new and whole," on foreign soil? And why could he not avail himself of the juridical fiction referred to by Servius that allowed for the *repetitio auspiciorum* far from Rome? Here we find the fundamental difference between our two accounts. According to Cicero, Flaminius, as consul, held the *ius auspiciorum*, but his fatal error was his refusal at Ariminum to abide by the results of the *tripudium*'s revelation of a *vitium*; there was no need to return to the *urbs* for the *repetitio auspiciorum*, since, in Cicero's account, the problem was not a flaw in his capacity to take the auspices, but his unwillingness to abide by them. For Livy, however, Flaminius's magistracy itself was *iniustus*, because *inauspicato*, as it had been in 223 BC. His auspices could not be "repeated" since they had not been bestowed to begin with.[64]

---

[63] Livy 21.63.11–12.
[64] Cf. Weisseborn and Müller 1887–1912, *ad* Livy 22.1.6 ("Kein iustum imperium, kurz ist nicht Konsul"). *Contra* Linderski 1993, 69, n. 31, who assumes that the *vitium* concerned Flaminius's failure to perform the "departure auspices," which he regards as not concerned with "the

OCTAVIAN'S *IMPERIUM AUSPICIUMQUE*

And fourth, why not "new and whole"? Since a promagistrate—notably Octavian in 43 BC—could assume his auspices away from Rome, this question still stands. And why does Livy say, in general, that a *magistrate* who left Rome without the auspices, thus *iniustus*, would be unable to assume them *ex urbe*? At issue is a distinction between the magistrates and the promagistrates. The latter were assigned their *provincia* with the requisite competencies for the fulfillment of their tasks (*imperium auspiciumque* that were valid *militiae*), and they assumed these capacities upon leaving the *urbs*. By contrast, duly elected magistrates required installation in office, at Rome, *auspicato*—that is, a new magistrate required the curiate ritual that confirmed his auspices were *nova et integra*.[65] This was a rite that could not be fulfilled without a meeting of the thirty lictors who made up the curiate assembly, which met, by custom, within the *pomerium*—and thus could never be convened *in externo solo*.[66]

The Status of Commands

The history and diversity of magisterial and promagisterial appointments during the Republic set Octavian's *imperium* and his auspices in their broad context. Five differing scenarios with a correspondingly distinct status are reported by our sources and may be briefly articulated.

(1) A *magistratus iustus* was one properly installed—by a vote of the people, the taking of the auspices, and the passage of a *lex curiata*. Before the end of his term of office, a magistrate would customarily proceed to a provincial command, assigned usually by sortition, where he would serve after his magisterial year, *pro magistratu*. He would

---

whole office of the magistrate, but solely his particular field of action: the sphere *militiae*." This appeal to "the auspices of departure" is in accord with neither Livy's account nor the rest of our evidence (discussed below).

[65] The formula *nova et integra* appears to be neither simply pleonastic nor a technical term for the auspices; cf. the usage at Cic. *Verr.* 2.1.51.133, and *Balb.* 17; Florus 1.33.7; Plaut. *Cas.* 626.

[66] The *comitia curiata* met within the *pomerium*: Livy 5.52.15–16. Whether or not this was a requirement and was what prevented the Thessalonican "elections" of 49 BC is hardly certain (cf. the discussion in Vervaet 2014, 336–37). The new magistrate, who quite probably carried his own *lex*, would need to present himself before the *comitia*; so too Fanizza 2014, 62.

CHAPTER 2

go to his *provincia decreta* with *iustum imperium auspiciumque* and maintain those powers, in accordance with his assignment by senatorial decree. And thus it was in this sense that they "took their auspices with them" (as Livy puts it).

(2) The commands of such ex-magistrates, serving *pro magistratu*, were often extended by the senate (*prorogatio*). Others—*privati*—might be appointed by the senate to a command as promagistrates, either with a vote of the people (for example, Cicero in 51 BC) or without such a vote (for example, Octavian in 43), and without a *lex curiata*; thus, they were appointed merely by decree of the senate. Their assignment would carry with it the *imperium* and auspices requisite for their task—both of which were held solely *militiae*.

(3) As we have seen, it might come to pass that a magistrate was elected and assigned his *provincia*, yet if the auspices were not taken, there could be no *lex curiata*—such appears to have been the case of Flaminius. He was thus *inauspicatus* and could not be properly *inauguratus* and therefore a *magistratus inustus*.

(4) Lastly, an elected magistrate, one *creatus* in the *comitia centuriata*, with a *provincia* decreed by the senate, might assume office, and thus the right to the auspices, without the passage of a *lex curiata*. This was the fate of Appius Claudius, who was elected consul for 54 BC together with L. Domitius Ahenobarbus. Political controversies raged during their year: the elections were delayed, a reality compounded by the prosecution of Gabinius, and in September the revelation of a bribery scandal—with all of the candidates charged—saw to their postponement yet again; by December the elections and other fundamental arrangements had still not taken place.[67] Accord-

---

[67] Cic. *Att.* 4.15 (27 July), 4.16 (1 July), 4.17 (1 October) and 4.18 (end of October); *QFr.* 3.1.15 (September) and 3.1.24 (September); *Fam.* 1.9 (December). Tribunician obstruction: Cic. *QFr.* 3.2.2–3 (11 October 54) (*consules comitia habere cupiunt; rei nolunt, et maxime Memmius*); *QFr.* 3.3.2 (21 October 54) (*comitiorum cottidie singuli dies tolluntur obnuntiationibus*); thus Rosenstein 1995, 52 ("tribunician obstruction of passage of a *lex curiata* prevented the consuls from casting lots for their provinces"), following Shackleton-Bailey 1980, *ad loc.*; cf. Vervaet 2015; similarly Fanizza 2014, 60; cf. Magdelain 1968, 21 ("ce n'est pas l'absence de loi curiate des consuls, mais le jeu de l'*obnuntiatio*").

ing to Cicero, Appius had served his consulship despite the fact that he had not carried a *lex curiata*; while he had been granted a province by the decree of the senate in accordance with his election, the sortition of provinces had not occurred. According to Cicero, in a famous passage:

Appius in sermonibus antea dictitabat, postea dixit etiam in senatu palam, sese, si licitum esset legem curiatam ferre, sortitutum esse cum college provinciam; si curiata lex non esset, se paraturum cum college tibique successurum, legemque curiatam consulil ferri opus esse, necesse non esse; se, quoniam ex senatus consulto provinciam haberet, lege Cornelia imperium habiturum quoad in urbem introisset.

[Appius was in the habit of saying in private, and later said publicly in the senate, that, if passage was given to a curiate law, he would draw lots for a province with his colleague; but if there was no curiate law, he would come to an arrangement with his colleague and supersede you (Lentulus). A curiate law, he contended, was something a consul should have, but did not absolutely need. Since he had a province by decree of the senate, he would hold military authority under the lex Cornelia until he reentered the city boundary.][68]

All of this clearly had little effect on his carrying out of the responsibilities of his office at Rome, since, as Cicero suggests, the consuls were nevertheless able to convene the senate—an act that required the taking of the auspices. While Cicero does little to clarify the matter, his comments (*rem ad senatum detulerunt; consules comitia habere cupiunt*) suggest that this occurred and one could not possibly comprehend his silence about the consequences if it had not. That a consul's carrying out of his responsibilities and conducting of the state's business *auspicato* did not require a curiate law may be inferred, since Appius had surely taken the auspices upon assuming his consulship, even if no curiate

---

[68] Cic. *Fam.* 1.9.25. Cf. Cic. *QFr.* 3.2.3 (*Appius sine lege curiata confirmat se Lentulo nostro successurum*); Cic. *Att.* 4.18.4 (*Appius sine lege suo sumptu in Ciliciam cogitat*).

CHAPTER 2

law followed.⁶⁹ Cicero's correspondence suggests that Appius was consul, but technically not a *magistratus optimo lege et iure*. And as if in acknowledgment of this state of affairs, Appius himself had said that he would take up his *provincia decreta* at his own expense (*suo sumptu*) without the authority of the senate's *ornatio provinciae*.⁷⁰ Finally, when did Appius depart for his province? For this had a bearing on his status, regardless of the question of his *lex curiata*. If he had not left Rome by the end of the year, his magistracy would have expired. Thus, he would have departed as a promagistrate—a *privatus cum imperio*—with the requisite *imperium auspiciumque* that formed part of his senatorial assignment, but no longer with those powers associated with his office.⁷¹

"Auspices of Departure"

There is still the question of the "auspices of departure" taken prefatory to the assumption of command. Did such a thing exist? Here we encounter an example of how powerful interpretations are sustained in the face of the attestations of our sources.

Many scholars have long claimed that departure auspices were a necessary ritual, parallel to the auspices taken upon one's entrance into a magistracy. These were among the things that Flaminius is said to have famously neglected.⁷² But it seems relatively clear that all magistrates would have been expected to take the auspices before their departure, as they would before any significant action, whether in the *urbs* or in the field: thus Cicero's *nihil publice sine auspiciis nec domi nec militiae*.⁷³ Yet, following the influential views

---

⁶⁹ Cf. Vervaet 2015, 222, n. 55, who believes that the taking of the auspices required the *lex*—for reasons that escape me; the idea seems to derive from Magdelain 1968, 26.

⁷⁰ Cf. Vervaet 2015, 222, n. 56 ("Ap. Claudius eventually departed Rome without a curiate law *de imperio*"); and further, Vervaet 2014, 333–36, for the implication that "without a *lex curiata de imperio* for the consuls there could be no *s.c. de provinciis ordinandis*." There is an obvious parallel with one who triumphed *suo sumptu*, in defiance of the senate's long-standing prerogative for the bestowal of the honor.

⁷¹ Magdelain 1968, 54, outlines the technicalities.

⁷² Investiture and departure auspices as distinct: representative views include Magdelain 1968; Linderski 1993, 63; Humm 2011, 80; Berthelet 2015, 119–20; Magdelain 2015; see further below.

⁷³ Cic. *Div.* 1.3; cf. 1.95 (*nihil in bello sine extis agunt, nihil sine auspiciis* [*domi?*]); *Nat. D.* 2.9 (*in his bella quibus rei publicae salus continetur, nullis auspiciis administrantur*); examples in

of Mommsen and Magdelain, the "auspices of departure" have attained a distinctive status as a specific Roman institution—despite the virtual absence of any such report in the sources.[74] Indeed, all of the reputed attestations (with one famous exception, to be discussed below), speak only of the *vota nuncupatio* on the Capitol, which have been consistently confused with the auspices.[75] Rüpke recognized the dilemma posed by the sources regarding such auspices and noted the prevalent confusion of *vota* and *auspicia*: "It is probable that auspices were usually taken before leaving the city, but the sources do not allow us to give them a special meaning." In fact, two of the most famous cases adduced, Flaminius and Marcellus, are negative *exempla*—noting not their performance of such a rite but its disregard; perhaps this is telling. It suggests that we deal here with *mos* rather than a legally established practice.[76]

The sole and exceptional testimony to the taking of auspices before departure would appear to be a fragment from a work on the consulate written by L. Cincius, an antiquarian of the Augustan era; the passage is preserved in Festus:

Praetor ad portam nunc salutatur is qui in provinciam pro praetore aut pro consule exit: cuius rei morem ait fuisse Cincius in libro de consulum potestate talem: Albanos rerum potitos usque ad Tullum regem: Alba

---

Livy 34.14.1 and discussion (and other examples) in Vervaet 2014, 315; Livy 5.52.15 treats those matters that require the auspices within the *pomerium*.

[74] Mommsen 1887–1888, I:63–4 and 99 = 1889–1896, I:72–73, 113–14; Magdelain 1968, 36–42; Magdelain 2015, 43.

[75] *Vota*: Livy 21.63.9; 22.1.6; 41.10.5; 42.49.1; 45.39.11; Cic. *Verr.* 2.5.34; Festus 15L concerns another rite, despite attempts (e.g., Humm 2011, 79) to associate it with departures. *Vota* confused with *auspicia*: Dalla Rosa 248, n. 20, and 249, n. 26, on Livy 2.1.5–7; Vervaet 2014, 83 ("auspices of departure taken on the Capitol") and 320 (less clear that the auspices were taken on the Capitol, although implied re: Livy 22.1.5–7); Berthelet 2015, 123 (on Verres and Flaminius); Humm 2011, 79 (departure auspices on the Capitol in Auguraculum); 80 (Flaminius fails to take them in 217 BC); Sánchez 2014, 34–35, for the same confusion re: Livy 21.63.5–9; 39 ("correspond très probablement à la prise des auspices de depart"); Lange 2016, 28, on Verres's vows ("auspices") on the Capitoline before departure.

[76] Rüpke 1990, 45–46 ("Es ist wahrscheinlich, dass üblicherweise vor dem Auszug Auspizien genommen wurden, aber ihnen eine besondere Bedeutung zuzumessen, erlauben die Quellen nicht"). Similarly, Fiori 2014a, 90 and n. 130 (there were only vows). *Mos*, not *lex*: similarly Van Haeperen 2007, 33.

CHAPTER 2

deinde diruta usque ad P. Decium Murem consulem populos Latinos ad caput <aquae> Ferentinae, quod est sub monte Albano, consulere solitos, et imperium communi consilio administrare: itaque quo anno Romanos imp<erato>r<e>s ad exercitum mittere oporteret iussu nominis Latini, conplures nostros in Capitolio a sole oriente auspicis operam dare solitos. Ubi aves addixissent, militem illum, qui a communi Latio missus esset, illum quem aves addixerant, praetorem salutare solitum, qui eam provinciam optineret praetoris nomine.

<aquae> = cf. Livy 1.51.9, with discussion in Sánchez 2014, 14–15. *imprs* = *imperatorem*: Coli 1951, 163, following Huschke; so too Ziolkowski 2011 and Drogula 2015, 29; the emendation is unnecessary and unconvincing; rightly rejected by Sánchez and earlier by Momigliano 1969, 416. *conplures* = *consules*: Coli 1951, 163; so too Oakley 1997, I:340. *illum quem aves addixerant*: excised by Ziolkowski as an interpolation.

[The praetor is now saluted at the gate, he who went to his *provincia* in the place of a praetor or a consul. About the origin of this custom, Cincius, in his book on the consul's powers, says that the Albans ruled (the League) up to the reign of Tullus; then, once Alba was destroyed, up to the time of the consul Decius Mus, the Latin people had the custom to gather at the Ferentina spring, which is below the Mons Albanus, and to decide about the command by general agreement. Thus, in any year when it behooved the Romans to send commanders to the army by order of the Latin League, many of our (past leaders?) were accustomed to take the auspices at the sun's rising on the Capitol. As soon as the birds assented, the soldier who had been sent by the whole of Latium was accustomed to salute as praetor the one whom the birds approved, who obtained that *provincia* by being named praetor.][77]

---

[77] Festus 276–77L. Discussions and various translations in Oakley 1997, I:340, Berthelet 2015, Stewart 1998, Drogula 2015; most thorough treatments in Fiori 2014a, Ziolkowski 2011, and (exhaustively) Sánchez 2014, to all of which the following is inevitably indebted.

A difficult text: possibly corrupt, interpolated, and lacunose, as scholars have not failed to suggest; the last of these possibilities is the most troublesome. So Schwegler concluded, as Ziolkowski points out, noting that "the sudden switch from the movements of the political center of the Latin League to the modalities of choosing a Roman commander for the allied army, marked by *itaque*, quite unwarranted in the present text, clearly indicates a substantial lacuna."[78] Perhaps. But some of its information may be corroborated, and certain questions it raises may be answered—with one major exception, as we shall see.

According to Cincius, a praetor was one who had been assigned a *provincia*—for in the period to which he refers (from the age of Tullus to the consulate of Decius), all Roman magistrates would seem to have been known as praetors.[79] These men obtained (*obtinere*) their provincial assignments by the lot (*sortitio*), by agreement among the magistrates themselves (*comparatio*), or, especially in times of crisis, by *senatus consultum*. Any magistrate who had been assigned a *provincia* was the object of an auspication (for sortition was an augural act), and one should assume that observation of the auspices reported here—*operam dare auspicia*—was intended to seek the gods' approbation for the task.[80]

The auspices were taken at sunrise (*a sole oriente*),[81] and Cincius's report of the performance of the rite *in Capitolio* immediately calls to mind the taking of the auspices on the day of the magistrates' inauguration, when this was done on the Capitol in anticipation of a meeting there of the senate. Yet Cincius's *quo anno*, coupled with the use of the past tense, suggests an iterative, occasional effect, implying that the need for Roman commanders by the Latin League was not constant, but nevertheless occurred repeatedly: this must refer to all those who were installed *in the past* as the league's commanders, in any year that such an event came to pass, and suggests that the auspication was

---

[78] Schwegler 1868–1872, II:344, n. 2, cited by Ziolkowski 2011, 470, with further bibliography.
[79] Livy 7.3.5, with Lintott 2003, 104 and Brennan 2000, I:20–23.
[80] Stewart 1998, chaps. 1 (*sortes*) and 4 (*comparatio*); similarly Sánchez 2014, 26. As an augural act: Fiori 2014a, 92–93.
[81] Cf. Enn. *Ann.* 92 V = 87 Sk (*simul aureus exoritur sol*), with Linderski 2007b, 3–5; Livy 8.23.15 (*consul oriens de nocte*) with Linderski 1986, 2173, n. 94; Gell. 3.2.10, Censor. 23.4, Livy 10.40.2, and Festus 474L—all cited by Mommsen 1887–1888, I:101, n. 3, and 102, n. 1 = 1889–1896, I:116, nn. 2–3.

performed to ratify their assignment.[82] Finally, to what did the birds assent? This cannot be the gods' selection of the commander, since that is not how *provinciae* were assigned; Cincius must refer to the approbation of the gods for the one chosen by the customary procedures for the task of leading the league.[83] Cincius reports an ongoing practice, and the *conplures nostri* should be understood here as all those *magistrati praeteriti* to whom the task had been allotted.[84]

Magistrates are generally believed to have left for their *provincia* after making their vows on the Capitol. Despite the silence of our sources, they surely took the auspices before departing as well—but doing so was hardly exceptional, and the fact that Livy never mentions this might well be held to suggest that it was so commonplace as to be unworthy of mention. We *never* hear directly of a query put to the gods as to whether it was *fas* for a commander to depart—indeed, this is not what Cincius relates.[85] Given the evidence we do have, it would seem that there was no "special" auspical rite for departure at all—and that these auspices were no different from those taken before *any* action.

There appears to have been one fundamental distinction between magistrates and *privati cum imperio*, one somewhat disguised by our ancient authorities and often misconstrued by our moderns. That is, consuls and praetors had *imperium* and *auspicia*, both *domi* and *militiae*, because of their investiture and entry in their magistracy, which granted them an urban com-

---

[82] Momigliano 1969, 416. I am not persuaded as to the relevance of Sanchez's proposed comparanda (2014, 15–20). Equally unpersuasive is the argument of Drogula 2015, 31, that the archaic practice was to select commanders "through auspication."

[83] That Cincius describes some sort of auspical competition between magistrates, on the model of Romulus and Remus, seems hardly convincing; he cannot have referred here to the choice of one commander among several candidates: cf. Sánchez 2014, n. 73ff; 39; Ziolkowski 2011, 468–69, on the idea of a competition among the magistrates: "sheer absurdity."

[84] *Complures nostri*: Caesar *BGall.* 1.52.5 used the term in a broad, general sense, yet here contextualization is essential. Coli 1951, 163, emended to *consules*, although this has not met with assent; Schwegler 1868–1872, II:344 and 345, n. 2 (cited by Ziolkowski 2011, n. 19) proposed *augures*—although without further comment or substantiation; similarly Sánchez 2014, 31, following Momigliano 1969 (comparing Dion Hal 2.4). But the action attributed to these figures is not one that the augurs performed: magistrates possessed the *spectio*, while the augurs held the right to *nuntiationes* (for the most part *negative* signs appearing unasked—the *auspicia oblativa*); cf. Ziolkowski 2011—neither magistrates nor augurs.

[85] *Fas est*: n. 27 above. On Livy's omissions, cf. n. 17 above.

petency as well as their assignment of command (*provincia*); they possessed the *ius auspicandi* in each sphere in conformity with the demands of their public office.[86] Thus, if they took the auspices when departing from the Capitol, these would be *auspicia urbana*. By contrast, nonmagistrates (*privati*) could only take the auspices *after* they had departed, as they entered on their *provincia* (taking this in *both* its qualitative and territorial senses), since their assignment endowed them solely with the right to the auspices *militiae*, as a fundamental aspect of their command.[87] Despite the often ingenious arguments of numerous scholars for the institutional importance of such "auspices of departure," *privati*—like Octavian in 43 BC—could *only* take the auspices beyond the *pomerium*.[88]

Monumentum imperium auspiciumque?

Octavian's grant of an independent command in January of 43 BC had its sequel in the distinctions bestowed in the wake of what was declared—largely on the basis of arguments made by Cicero—to be his initial achievement. When word reached Rome in mid-April reporting the routing of Antony's forces, the lifting of the Mutina siege, and the soldiers' acclamation of their leaders, the success of Octavian's appointment was honored, despite his less than significant role at Forum Gallorum.[89] Cicero proclaimed him as *imperator* in the senate and championed the proposal of *supplicationes* in honor of the consuls and the *propraetor* that had been made by the young commander's father-in-law, Servilius, extending them to an unprecedented fifty days.[90]

In addition, at some point over the next months, a gilded monument, decreed for Octavian in January, was set up at the rostra, which would permanently acknowledge not only his *imperium* but also his new status and, above all, his youth. Velleius reports that "the senate honored him with an equestrian statue, which is still standing at the rostra and testifies to his years

---

[86] Richardson 1975, 59–60; Rich 2014, 210, with bibliography.
[87] *Contra* Rüpke 1990, 46–47.
[88] Recognized and elaborated (paradoxically!) by Magdelain 1968, 52–55, who for so long was the champion of the concept of "auspices of departure."
[89] Letter of Servius Sulpicius Galba to Cicero: Cic. *Fam.* 10.30 (15 April 43 BC).
[90] Cic. *Phil.* 14.11, 29, 37; cf. Dio 46.38.1; Ovid *F.* 4.673–76. Broad discussion in Bellen 1985.

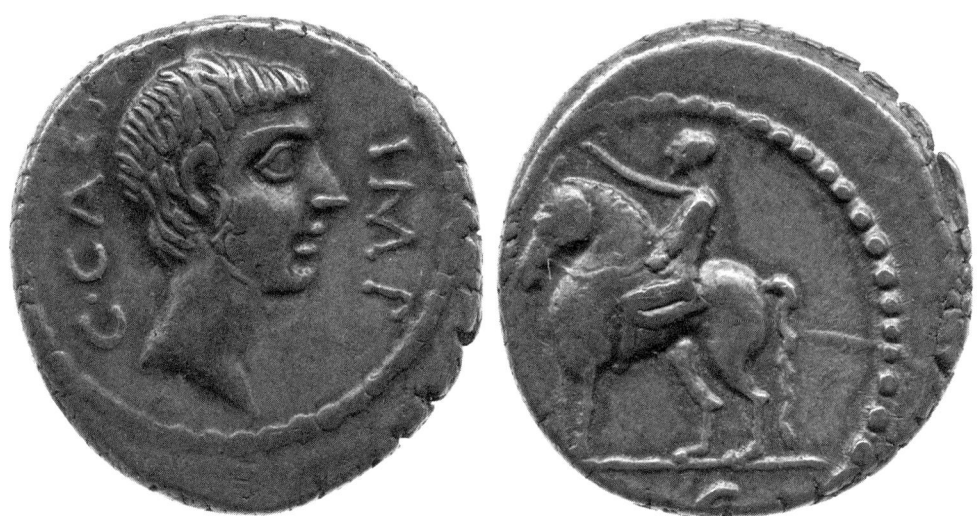

II.1 Octavian [C. CAESAR. IMP], *denarius*. Italy, site of mint unknown, 43 BC. *RRC* 490/1.

by its inscription," and the famous opening of Augustus's *Res Gestae*, "*annos undeviginti natus . . .* ," may well have echoed the statue's *titulus* and its exorbitant claim.[91] An image of the statue appeared almost immediately on the coinage issued by Octavian himself (figure II.1): its legend, C. CAESAR. IMP, confirms that it dates after the Mutina acclamation of 16 April, yet before 19 August, when Octavian would be elected to the consulship; the S.C. on the reverse acknowledged the senate's decree of the statue.[92]

Whenever the statue was erected, and whatever its final appearance,[93] it took its place alongside what were surely its models—those erected in honor of Sulla (in 80 BC?) and Pompeius (at some unknown point in the following

---

[91] Vell. 2.61.3: *Eum senatus honoratum equestri statua, quae hodieque in rostris posita aetatem eius scriptura indicat*. *RGDA* 1, recalling the statue: Mannsperger 1982, 336.

[92] *RRC* 490/1; discussions in Mannsperger 1982; Bergemann 1990, cat. L25; Sehlmeyer 1999, 249–51. Wallace-Hadrill 1986, 75, noted the innovation of Octavian's appearance on both obverse and reverse. Dating of the coin implies its place of minting: discussion and bibliography in Woytek 2003, 472–73, suggesting Bononia; cf. Wallmann 1977, 32, who suggests that this was minted at Rome after Octavian's arrival during the summer.

[93] Much debated, as there are two other variants of the type whose legends date them in successive periods of 43 BC: COS PONT AUG (after 19 August) and III VIR R P C (after 27 November); cogent summary and bibliography in Sehlmeyer 1999, 249–51.

decades), removed after Pharsalus in 48, and replaced on Julius's order in 44—as well as two others more recently decreed for Lucius Antonius (perhaps in 44 when he was *tribunus plebis*), and for Marcus Aemilius Lepidus (in January 43).[94]

Attitudes toward such an extravagant honor as a gilded equestrian statue were changing rapidly, as were those held concerning their honorees—all fueled by the complexity of political realities at the onset of civil war. In early February of 43 BC, Cicero, when proposing a statue commemorating Servius Sulpicius, denigrated Sulla's equestrian monument when referring, by contrast, to Sulpicius's "wonderful liking for the moderation of our ancestors and censured the indulgence of the present age." Sulpicius would have a *statuam pedestrem aeneam in rostris*; it was still standing in the mid-second century AD.[95] Alternatively, already in the preceding January, Lucius Antonius had been ridiculed by Cicero, who mocked the honors to which his statue's inscription alluded; under the circumstances, just how much longer his statue remained standing can only be surmised. But the fate of Lepidus's monument is telling: it had been proposed in January of 43 BC, the senate's decree would be acknowledged in April, and yet by July the statue had been set up and already torn down. Seldom were Roman honors so short-lived—but the changing patterns of alliance with the outbreak of civil war had dramatic effects.[96]

Octavian's statue is the only one of the three equestrian monuments set up in 44/43 BC that survived the civil wars. Its gesture, like that of Sulla's statue a generation before, signaled an address, and both men's raised arms were surely to be understood as if directed to their assembled troops, although at the rostra they would seemingly address their fellow citizens in Rome.[97] But at the dawn of civil war, Octavian's statue and its gesture would no doubt serve (or so we might imagine his partisans to have thought) as a summons to his cause. At such a moment of crisis, it may well have given visual form to

---

[94] Entries for each in *LTUR* II, s.v. *eques*, give the sources (all by E. Papi); Lahusen 1983, 14–18, collects all the statues known to have been erected *in* or *pro rostra*; cf. Sehlmeyer 1999, 63–66, 231–34, 245–51.

[95] Cic. *Phil.* 9.16; cf. 13. Second-century attestation: Sextus Pomponius in *Dig.* 1.2.2.43.

[96] Lepidus's statue proposed January 43 BC: Cic. *Phil.* 5.40–41. Decree acknowledged 11 April BC: Cic. *Phil.* 13.8–9. Statue set up and already torn down by July: Cic. *ad Brut.* 1.15.9; cf. 1.12.1.

[97] See chapter 4 on Constantine in the forum.

CHAPTER 2

Cicero's unsuccessful plea in the senate that January to signal the state of the *res publica* by the cessation of normal affairs:

> ... *tumultum esse decrevi; iustitium edici, saga sumi dixi placere, quo omnes acrius graviusque incumberent ad ulciscendas rei publicae iniurias, si omnia gravissimi belli insignia suscepta a senatu viderent.*

> [... the senate should decree a *tumultus* ... a closing of the courts ... that the military cloak (the *sagum*) be assumed, so that all men, if they saw all the symbols of a very serious war adopted by the senate, might with greater zeal address themselves to the avenging of the injuries of the state.][98]

The changing of attire (*sagum sumere*) had long served to symbolize the mood of the Roman populus.[99] Was this signaled by Octavian's costume on his statue? Was it intended to signal a call to arms, and—by the end of 43 BC—to symbolize the specifically military aspect of the new *triumvir*'s assigned task, *rei publicae constituendae*? Despite the summary engraving of nearly all of the surviving dies for the coins of 43 representing Octavian's equestrian monument,[100] his depicted attire is ambiguous: he is clearly shown without the toga, which would have evoked his citizen's role (as on the coin depicting Sulla's statue or that of Philippus); unencumbered by a cloak wrapped about the hips (as was the equestrian image on the *Caes Divi f* coin); or similarly, lacking that garment fluttering behind him while at a gallop (as on coins of Fonteius Capito and Licinius Nerva).[101] What was apposite—and perhaps appropriate? Given his acclamation as *imperator*, one might imagine that Octavian here appeared—as others had before him, and as the emperors

---

[98] Cic. *Phil.* 6.2; cf. Dio 46.29.5.
[99] *Mutatio vestis*: Alföldi 1934, 5–9 = 1970, 123–27; Galinier 2012; cf. chapter 1.
[100] The website *Coinage of the Roman Republic Online* (http://numismatics.org/crro/) lists six examples of 490/1 and four of 490/3; cf., however, the commentary of Sehlmeyer 1999, 251, n. 258 ("oft zu grob gearbeitetet sind").
[101] Discussion of costumes employed for equestrian statues and on the coins: Bergemann 1990, 4–6; Koortbojian 2008, 81. The cited examples: Sulla (*RRC* 381); Philippus (*RRC* 425); *Caes Divi f* (*RIC* I², no. 262); Fonteius Capito (*RRC* 429); Licinius Nerva (*RRC* 454).

would after—in the eminently recognizable costume of his military status: *loricatus*.¹⁰² The symbolism was surely intentional—and all the more so given the bellicose reality of the march on Rome that immediately followed its appearance.

Octavian marched on Rome in August to demand the consulship, and his troops encamped beyond the Quirinal. The next day he crossed the *pomerium* and entered the city: in doing so, the fact that—legally—he had lost his *imperium* mattered little, as Octavian's show of force clearly sufficed to override any scruple about *Staatsrecht*. Not only Caesar had set the precedent, but Antonius too—so Cicero:

Etenim in contione dixerat se custodem fore urbis seque usque ad Kalendas Maias ad urbem exercitum habiturum. . . . Et quidem se introiturum in urbem dixit exiturumque, cum vellet.

[For he (Antonius) had declared in a harangue that he would be the city's guardian, and would keep his army by the city till the Kalends of May (44 BC). . . . And he said indeed that he would enter and go out of the city when he chose.]

Quid vero? Quod in contione dicere ausus est se, cum magistrate abisset, ad urbem futurum cum exercitu, introiturum quotienscumque vellet?

[But what of the fact that he (Antonius) dared to say at a public meeting that, when he had laid down his office, he would be present close to the city with an army, and would enter it as often as he pleased?]¹⁰³

Already at the age of nineteen, the extraordinary character of Octavian's powers was manifest, above and beyond the law, which, over the following decades, would adapt to him rather than he to it. Within months, the *Lex Titia* would empower the *triumvirs* with consular power, both *domi et militiae*, and

---

¹⁰² Cuirassed commanders on the coinage: *RRC* 291, 454, and possibly 293. Cuirassed statues of the emperors: Stemmer 1978. Octavian *loricatus*: most similarly on *RRC* 518/2?

¹⁰³ Cic. *Phil.* 3.27; *Phil.* 5.21, with commentary in Sumi 2015, 138–41.

CHAPTER 2

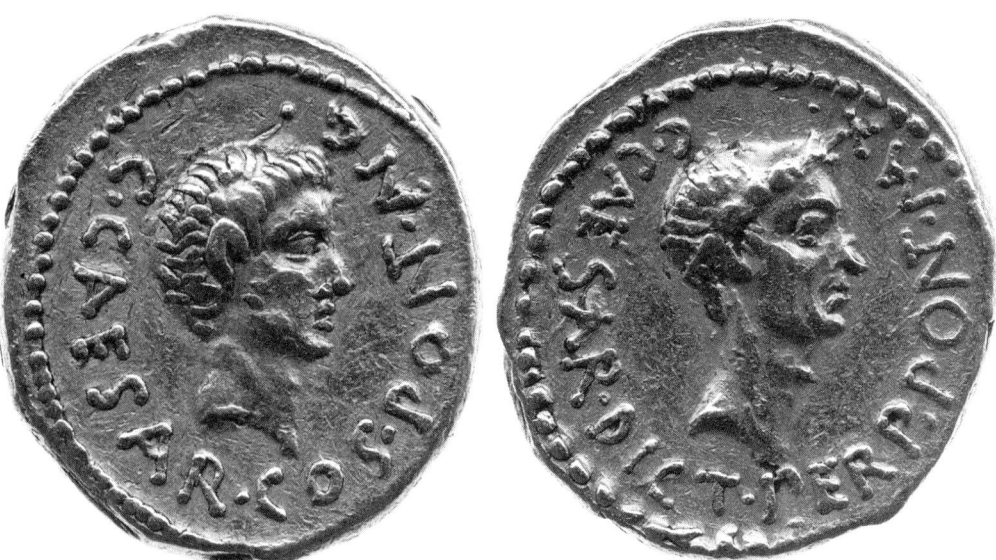

II.2 Octavian [C. CAESAR. COS. PONT. AUG.], *aureus*. Italy, site of mint unknown, 43 BC. *RRC* 490/2.

Octavian, granted Italy and the West as his *provincia* by the arrangements at Brundisium, would continue to move freely in and out of Rome, rendering the long-standing pomerial ideology of the Republic a thing of the past.[104]

He withdrew from the *urbs* before the elections, and on the nineteenth of August Octavian was awarded the consulship; this too, along with his entry into the pontifical and augural colleges, was acknowledged soon by new gold coins, on whose reverse (figure II.2) there now appeared the laureate head of Caesar, as an announcement that the youth had also seized the mantle of the caesarian party.[105]

By the onset of winter, after November of 43, the second of the equestrian statue coin-types was issued after the formation of the triumvirate (figure II.3).[106] On this coin, Octavian would now hold aloft the *lituus*—the symbol

---

[104] *Lex Titia*: App. *BCiv.*, 4.2–3, 4.6–7; Dio 46.55–56; Livy *Per.* 120. Pomerial ideology overturned in the Augustan era: see Girardet 1990b for the subsequent decade, and Ferrary 2001a and 2001b for what followed.

[105] *RRC* 490/2.

[106] *RRC* 497/1.

OCTAVIAN'S *IMPERIUM AUSPICIUMQUE*

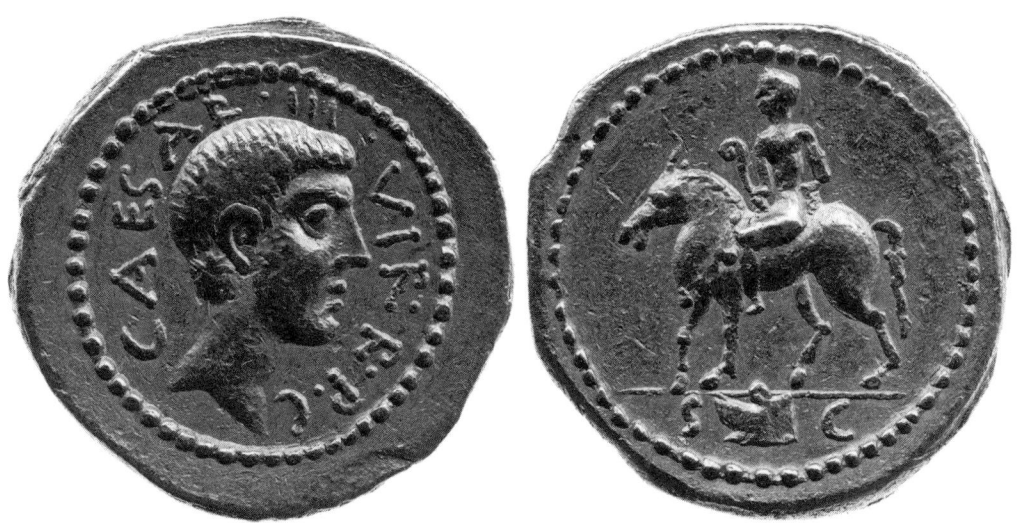

II.3 Octavian [CAESAR *IIIvir* R.P.C.], *aureus*. Italy, site of mint unknown, 43–42 BC. *RRC* 497/1.

of his membership in the augural college (which had been announced by the legend on the earlier coin's second state, *RRC* 490/2). This was perhaps in answer to Antonius's declaration, on the first of his coins issued as *triumvir*, of his membership in the same priesthood.[107] But it was also a reminder, at least implicitly, that now, as a magistrate, Octavian held the auspices—now *domi* as well as *militiae*. Here on the coins, if not on the statue itself, one finds, by the following year, confirmation of Octavian's *imperium auspiciumque*; he would be the possessor of both for more than fifty-six years.[108]

---

[107] Wallmann 1977, 33; cf. the portrayal of Antonius's and Octavian's numismatic rivalry in Newman 1990.

[108] Calculating the duration: Spannagel 2009. Lifelong *imperium*: Jones 1951 remains fundamental; Girardet 1995. Magisterial treatment in Ferrary 2001b. *Auspicia*: Hurlet 2001.

3

Roman Sacrifice and the *Ritus Militaris*

Sacrifice was only one of many attested Roman rituals, but it is arguably the one whose *imagery* was most ubiquitous throughout the Roman world.[1] This imagery is known in virtually all of the artistic media—at every possible scale, from the minuscule to the monumental, in many varied contexts, both public and private—and its use extended from the center of the *urbs* to every corner of Rome's *imperium*. Most if not all of the familiar examples that survive are of imperial date; had we a greater repertory of extant mid-Republican monuments than the coinage, we would no doubt have a clearer sense of how honors had traditionally been afforded to the gods and a better impression of the shape of the tradition in which our surviving monuments must be set. We might also know just how early an imagery was established for a distinctly Roman *ritus*, and when what appear to be its constitutive elements were codified in practice.

The Costumes of Sacrifice

The Romans did indeed have a *ritus*, as the highly conventional form of these monuments and the literary sources attest. The full panoply of the ritual might

---

[1] Huet 1992 remains essential and has been updated by a sequence of studies—among them, Huet 2005, 2008a, 2008b, and 2012—and a monograph is promised; in the interim: Huet et al. 2004, with extensive bibliography.

include offerings of incense and wine, the accompaniment of musicians, and the presence of those technicians, the *cultores* and the *ministri*, who performed the actual immolation of the animal victims. All of this would have been followed by the offering to the gods and the customary banquet that ensued. The monuments reveal the consistency of the practice, even when they emphasize one or another of these aspects, whether a mere libation, a libation accompanied by the use of incense, the offering of foodstuffs, or the slaying of the animal victims.[2] The entire sequence of actions and events established a hierarchy between men and gods, and the varied repertoire, from the most abbreviated to the most fulsome, marked the intensity, if not the significance, of an appeal to the divine—for the purpose of such behavior, it hardly needs saying, was to propitiate the gods: to ask their favor or to give thanks for favors received. Sacrifice was both a contract with the gods and the form in which that contract was communicated with them.[3]

In all aspects of such ritual, the Romans customarily performed the central act of the *ritus* with veiled head.[4] This was the *ritus Romanus* (figure III.1), the normative manner for sacrifice, and its role in Roman life extended throughout imperial times. It was not the *only* way the Romans sacrificed; they also practiced other modes, most famously, the *ritus Graecus*, that special form employed for the celebration of a particular set of gods—notably Hercules, Saturn, Apollo, and Ceres—not all of whom were in fact Greek: the form of the rite did not correspond to the ethnic associations of the gods who were its object. This Greek manner of observance was conducted *capite aperto*, and often with one's head wreathed with laurel.[5] It is most readily seen on the monuments that represent that thoroughly Roman institution, the *Ludi Saeculares*, at which various gods were honored *Graeco ritu*. The guise in which this *ritus* was enacted is seen, for example, on an ornate marble tripod base of Augustan date (figure III.2), where one of the *XVviri* makes an offering,

---

[2] Ritual sequence: Prescendi 2007; Scheid 2012b, 86–87; the entries related to sacrifice in Huet et al. 2004, 183–235.

[3] Rüpke 1990, 145.

[4] *Caput Velare*: Freier 1963; Livy 10.7.10 (*cum capite velato victimam caedet*); cf. Cic. *Nat. D.* 2.10; Livy 8.9.5 (Decius's *devotio*); Plut. *Quaest. Rom.* 10; Verg. *Aen.* 3.403–7; Dion. Hal. 12.16.2–4.

[5] Scheid 1995 and 1996. Earliest attestation in Cato *Orat.* 77 (Malcovati)=Prisc. *GL* 2.377 (Keil) (*Graeco ritu fiebantur Saturnalia*).

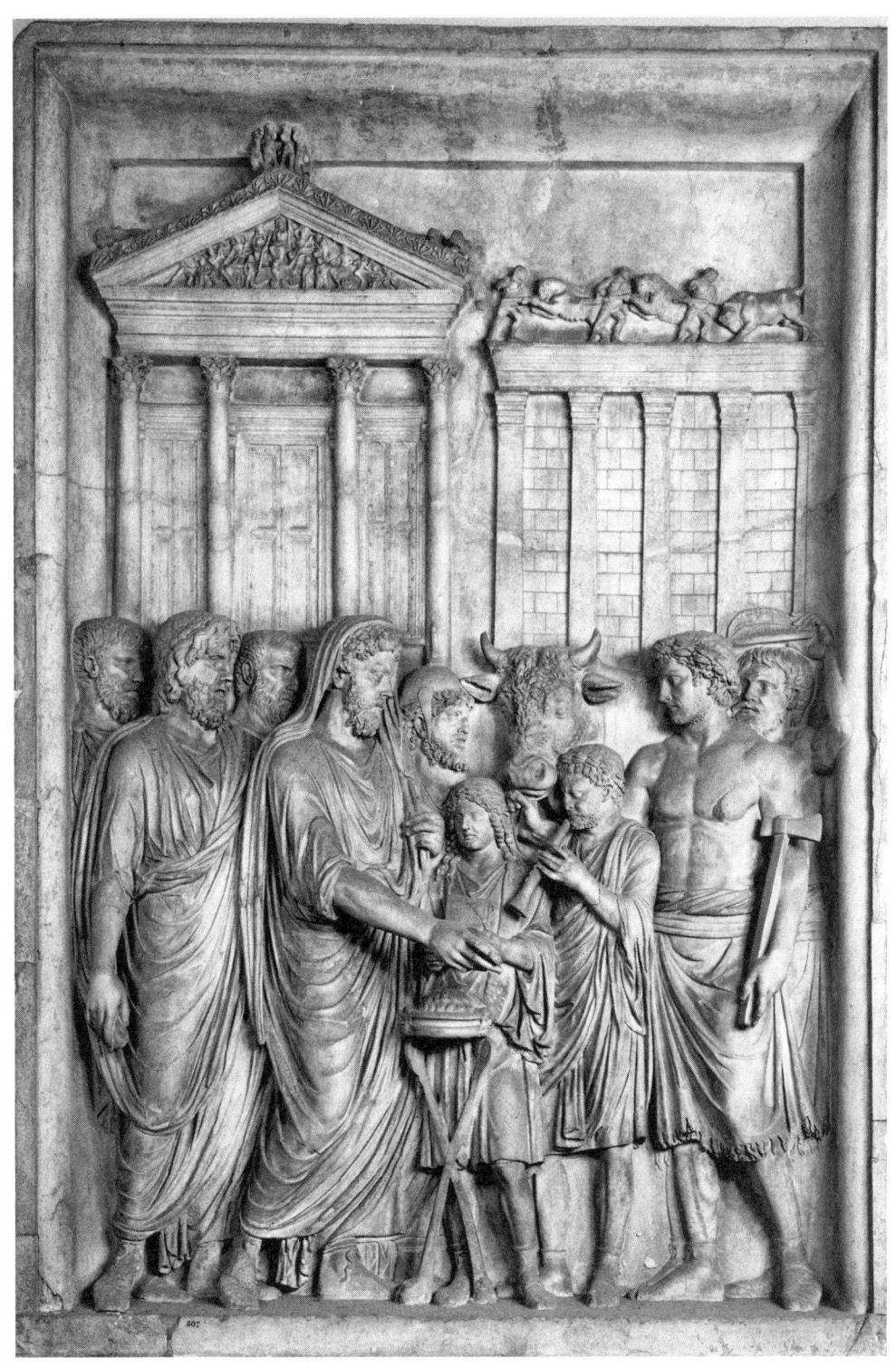

III.1 Sacrifice of M. Aurelius. Ca. AD 180. Marble. Rome, Musei Capitolini.

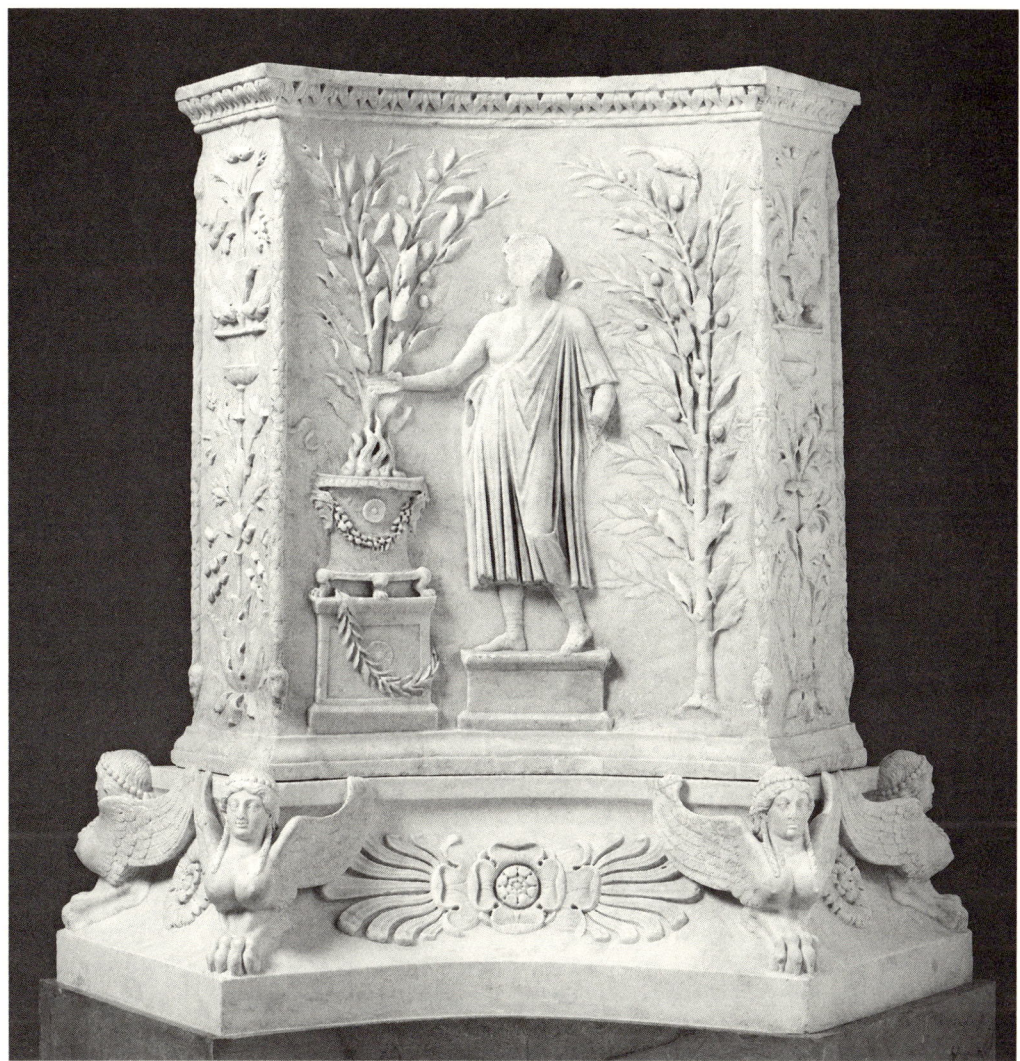

III.2 Tripod base with *XVvir*. Augustan. Marble. Paris, Louvre.

no doubt in reference to the games of 17 BC, and on Domitian's bronze coinage (figure III.3), where the emperor sacrifices *capite aperto* to the Moirai at the *ludi* of AD 88.[6]

There were other modalities of cult practice, although of these we have only the slightest hints in the sources: we hear of the *cinctus Gabinus*, the *Albanus*

---

[6] *Ludi Saeculares*: texts in Schnegg-Köhler 2002 and Pighi 1965; numismatic evidence in Scheid 1998a and Grunow Sobocinski 2006.

CHAPTER 3

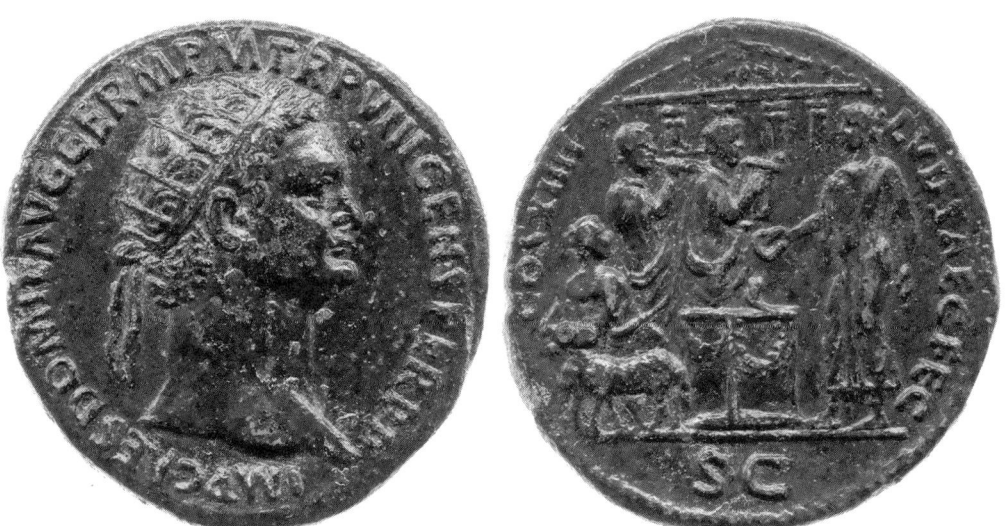

III.3 Domitian, *dupondius*, AD 88. *RIC* II, Rome, no. 381 = *BMC* II, no. 430 = Giard III, no. 464.

ritus, and of the *mos Etruscus*. The last of these, with its implicit relationship to haruspicy, is probably recorded on an unusual relief of Trajanic date (see figure III.14). The first is thought to be depicted on the Paris Census relief (figure III.9), but the appearance of the Alban rite is, unfortunately, lost to us.[7]

In other circumstances, there were yet other forms—most strikingly, those specifically associated with the military sphere, on land and at sea, which are invoked repeatedly in our sources.[8] Yet certain distinctive aspects of military sacrifice are attested solely by the monuments and despite their compelling evidence, their character and function have never been recognized. It is these that are the focus of what follows.[9]

---

[7] *Cinctus Gabinus*: Cressendi 1950; Dubourdieu 1986 and 1988. It has been suggested that the *cinctus Gabinus* appears on the Paris Census relief: Huet 2012, 49 and n. 11; Maschek 2018, 39. *Albanus ritus*: Livy 1.7.3. *More Etrusco*: Glinister 2009.

[8] Generally, Rist 1920. At sea: Baudy 1998, 215–21; Perea Yebenes 1997.

[9] Kleiner 1983 remains the sole specific treatment of the imagery of military sacrifice, although the article fails to take its full measure; other discussions shall be cited below. Cf. Huet 2012, 60 ("Une règle ou une coutume, qui nous est pas parvenue, devait probablement exister"). There is no acknowledgment of this distinctive form of religious ritual amid the extensive treatments of Stoll 2001 and Schmidt Heidenreich 2013. Recently Scheid 2017 has acknowledged the emperor's appearance in the ritual scenes of Trajan's column "als Kaiser, als Imperiumsträger."

RITUS MILITARIS

Trajan's column provides the best evidence. There, the emperor appears in numerous scenes of the Dacian campaigns, far from Rome, in three different forms of attire: in the cuirass and *paludamentum*, the customary uniform of a Roman commander in the field; in traveling garb, the *tunica* worn with the *paludamentum*, or at times the *sagum*, at times the *paenula*; and, on three occasions, the toga, while performing the *suovetaurilia*. All of these pose problems of interpretation that require explanation.[10]

First, the "travel costume."[11] On three occasions, Trajan sacrifices en route to the front. Scene 86 (figure III.4) depicts the arrival of Trajan and his entourage in a port along a river. He wears a tunic and what appears to be the commander's *paludamentum*, and he is shown sacrificing upon arrival—at the river port, outside the center of the city, as the wall at the upper right suggests. Trajan performs the rite, strikingly, with his head uncovered, *capite aperto*. Behind, a young *camillus* offers the *acerra* with the incense, and at the right, alongside the altar, a bovine lies, already dead, presented to the emperor by the *victimarius*. Is this scene the initial offering, known as the *praefatio*? If so, it is conjoined to the full ritual, with the *praefatio* taking place while the *immolatio* has already occurred, which would have been followed by the sacrifice proper of the meat and then banqueting, for the large gathering of men, women, and children—citizens of this northern town—is surely meant to imply that they will, in turn, feast as a result of the emperor's largesse. Similarly, in scene 91 (figure III.5), Trajan appears before an arched entrance to a building in *tunica* and *paludamentum*, and again he pours a libation with his head uncovered, while a young attendant offers the incense box to the accompaniment of a flute-player, and this time four bovines are led to the altar. Once again we find a crowd of civilians—men, women, and children—who gather, no doubt, to witness the event and to take part in the feasting that will ensue. And in scene 99 (figure III.6), at the famous bridge over the Danube built by Apollodorus at the site of the city of Dobreta, the emperor again sacrifices *capite aperto*. He is clad in traveling garb, although in this instance his cloak is not pinned

---

[10] The bibliography is immense; see, *inter alia*, Lehmann-Hartleben 1926; Gauer 1977; Lepper and Frere 1988; Settis 1988; Coarelli 2000; Stefan and Chew 2015; Mitthof and Schörner 2017.

[11] *Reisekostüm*: The account of Lehmann-Hartleben 1926 has been followed (explicitly or implicitly) by nearly all subsequent scholars.

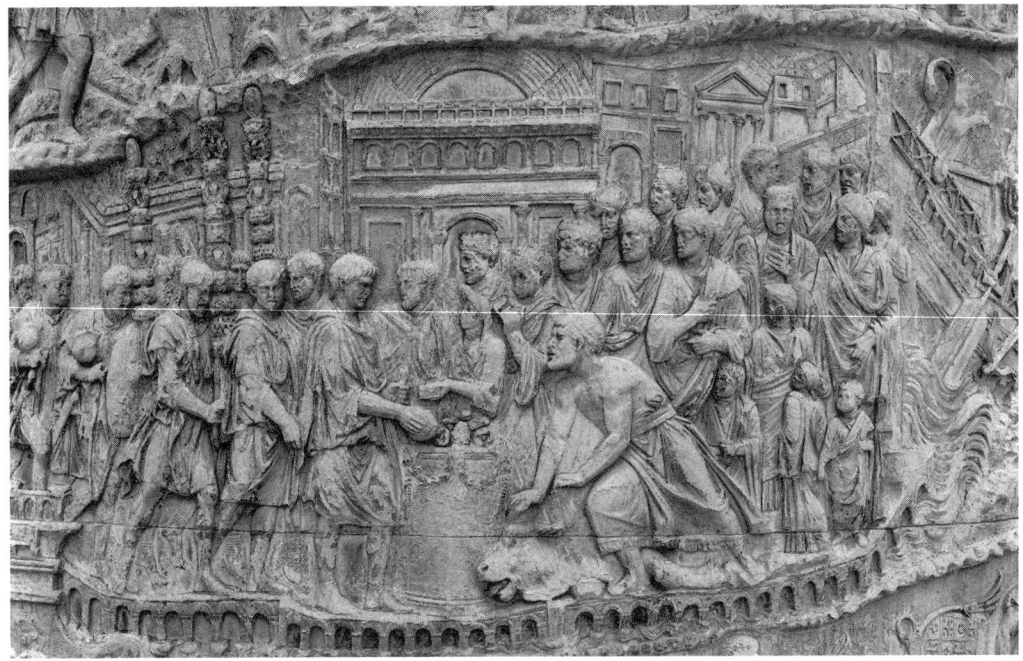

III.4 Column of Trajan, detail: scene 86, sacrifice. Rome.

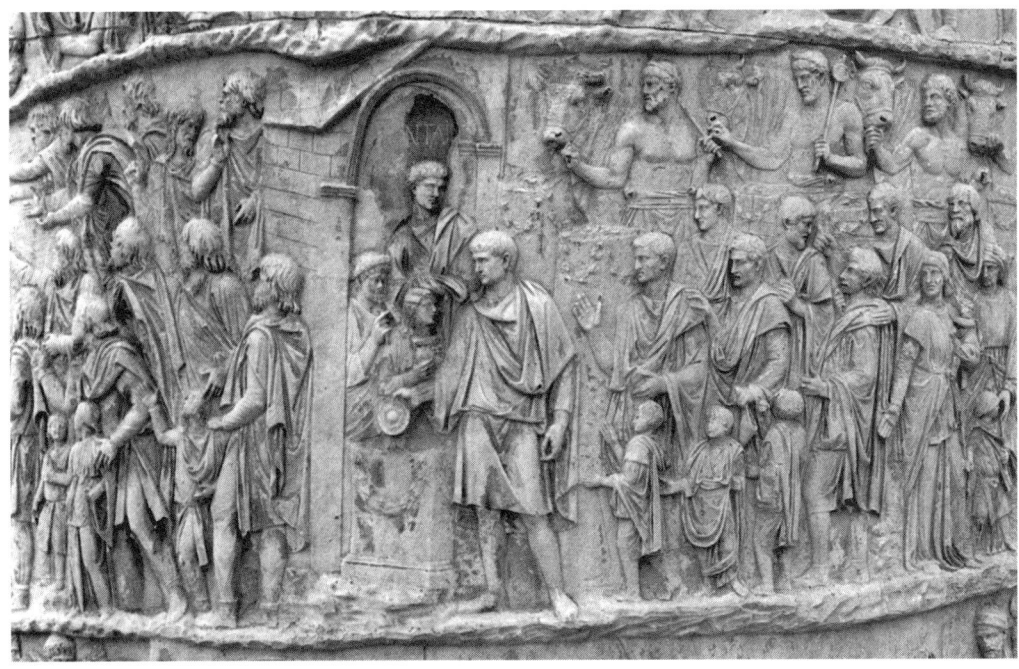

III.5 Column of Trajan, detail: scene 91, sacrifice. Rome.

RITUS MILITARIS

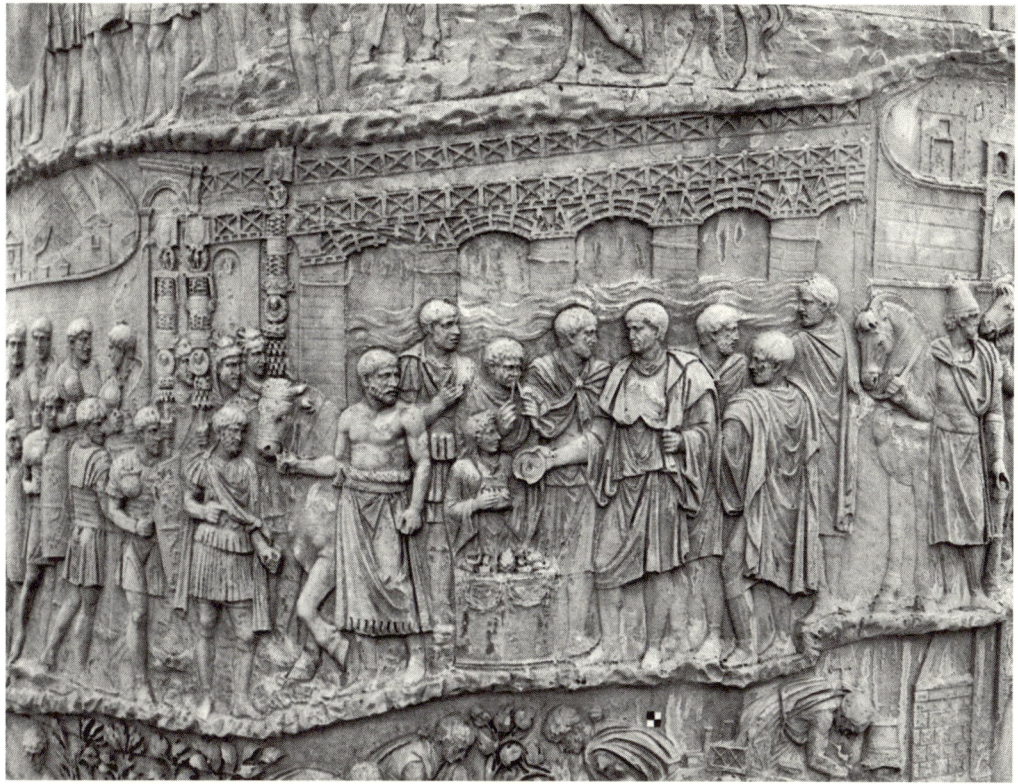

III.6 Column of Trajan, detail: scene 99, sacrifice. Rome.

at the shoulder; he once again pours a libation; and a *camillus* and a musician accompany the rite. Here the altar holds numerous offerings, probably foodstuffs, and the *victimarius* leads a bovine for slaughter.[12]

---

[12] Offerings: Winkler 1991; Scheid 2017. *Paludamentum*: an antiquarian problem obtrudes—the length of the depicted cloaks is not always the same. The *paludamentum*, when worn over the cuirass, apparently hung to the knees (scenes 6, 9, 11, 14, 18, 27, 40 *et alia*) and was customarily pinned on the shoulder with a *fibula*. What has been termed the "traveling cloak," worn over a tunic, was sometimes of equal length (e.g., scenes 33 and 46); at times it is pinned on the shoulder (scenes 84, 86, 90–91, and 100), and sometimes not (as in scene 98, where the garment of one of his lieutenants is pinned, while others show their cloaks clasped on their chests). Victims: Ryberg 1955, 121–22, assumes the single victim was a steer (*bos mas*) for Jupiter; cf. Scheid 2017. Settis 1988, 167, assumes that this scene suggests an imminent *extispicium*. Distinction between the types of *hostiae*: this is not possible, although it is again likely that one was a *bos mas* for Jupiter, the others *tauri* for male divinities (such as, e.g., Mars, Hercules, or the *Genius* of the emperor)—thus Ryberg 1955, 121–22. Scheid 2017, 148, suggests that the

CHAPTER 3

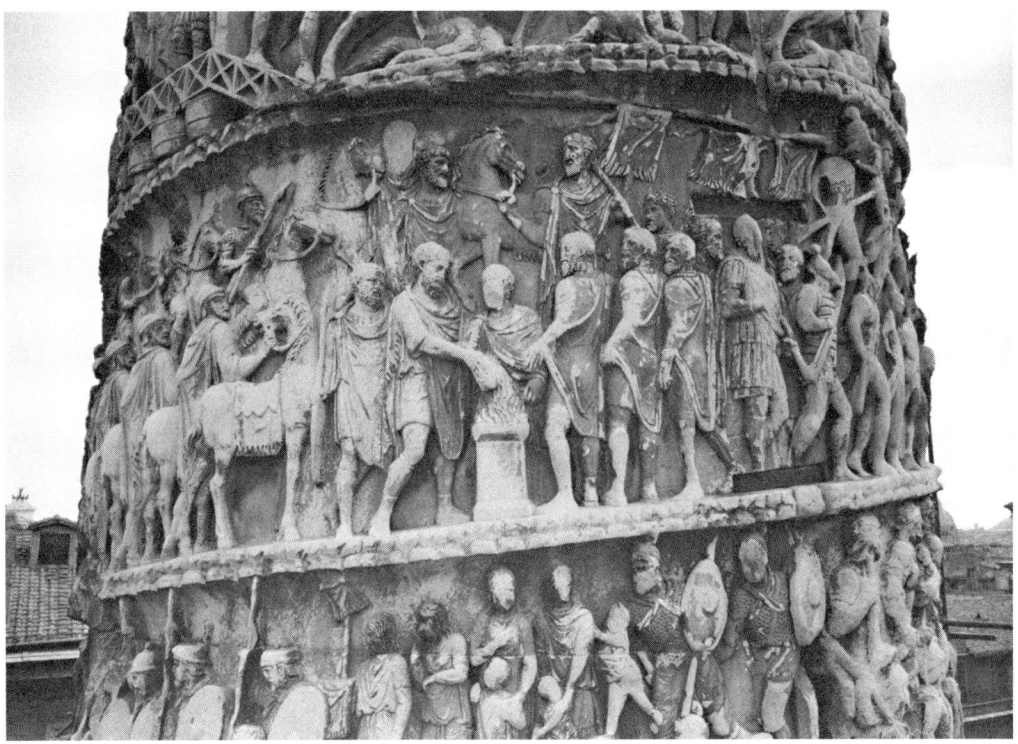

III.7 Column of Marcus Aurelius, detail: scene 75, sacrifice. Rome.

The same imagery is found again on the Antonine column. In scene 75 (figure III.7), Marcus, in traveling garb—*tunica* and *paludamentum*—makes his libation over a blazing altar, once again, *capite aperto*.[13] The presence of his entourage and their horses again suggest an arrival, although precisely where is not at all clear. Here the scene shows the sacrificial rite in its most abbreviated form, with no accompanying ministrants or musician, no offering save for wine; I shall return, in due course, to this sort of pictorial "condensation."[14]

Although these appearances of the emperor in tunic and cloak may be understood as a display of the proper "traveling attire" of the Roman military, this hardly suffices to explain the appropriateness of this costume and the

---

four bovines appearing in ritual scenes on the Marcus column were offered to the Capitoline triad and *Salus Publica*.

[13] Scheid 2000; Griebel 2013; the *ritus* is not addressed in Beckmann 2011.
[14] Griebel 2013, 113 ("auf die kaiserliche *libatio* reduziert"; "eine stark verkürzt Ikonographie").

bared head for the sacrificial rites. It has not gone unobserved that an appeal to a *Reisekostüm* clarifies little:

> Given the strong reference to traditional sacrifice in these scenes, it is all the more surprising that in the three instances where the emperor performs the sacrifice himself, attired unconventionally and unrealistically in the *tunica* and *sagum*—that is, in travel garb—he should be regarded simply as being en route, an interpretation that is in no way satisfactory.... In any case, the fact that in all of the *lustratio* offerings his mantel is shown pulled over his head, and in the case of the other offerings is not, should be considered in any attempt to explain and make these scenes comprehensible.[15]

Two things may be asserted with some confidence. First, it is clear that the *Reisekostüm* was conventional for travel on campaign, and forms one aspect of the proper attire in the military sphere—despite the fact that there is little agreement about the identity of the cloak. Whatever its specific name, it was among those costumes for the military sphere that were all generally referred to by the term *paludatus* according to Festus and Veranius.[16] In most representations it is pinned with a *fibula* on the shoulder and would thus appear, given its correspondence to the cloak worn by the emperor *loricatus*, to be the *paludamentum*.[17] But Trajan also appears in a shorter cloak that closes, often pinned, at the front (scene 34, at the dock by the warships); is this the *paenula*? Whatever its name, it was often worn by the lictors in military settings—although the texts

---

[15] Gross 1940, 44: "Bei der starken Anlehnung an altüberlieferte Opferszenen an diesen Stellen ist es um so verwunderlicher, daß der Kaiser die drei Male, wo er sonst selbst opfert, unkonventionell und wahrheitswidrig in Tunika und Sagum bzw. Im Reisegewand sole betont werden, daß der Kaiser eben unterwegs sei, befriedigt keineswegs, doch vermag ich keine bessere zu geben; jedenfalls muß der Umstand, daß bei allen Lustrationsopfern der Mantel über dem Hinterkopf gezogen dargestellt wird, bei allen anderen Opfern nicht, bei jedem Erklärungsversuch berücksichtigt und verständlich gemacht warden."

[16] Festus 298L (*Paludati in libris auguralibus significat, ut ait Veranius, armati, ornati. Omnia enim miltaria ornamenta paludata dici*); cf. 439L (for the Salii, *paludatas cum apicibus*). The broad sense of *paludatus* was recognized by Kuttner 1995.

[17] Gross 1940, 45, thinks that this is the *sagum* ("militarischen Zivilkleid"), a self-contradictory formulation that destroys any sense of what appears to have been a deliberate distinction.

merely inform us that in military situations the lictors were *paludati*.[18] This cloak is discerned on the Cancelleria reliefs (especially B); the so-called Nollekens relief; the Pozzuoli arch fragment in Berlin; and the Anacapri *adventus*. But if this is indeed the *paenula*, why should the emperor wear it? Gross considered it the proper costume for sea travel, although scenes on Trajan's column suggest that this was not always the case.[19] And according to the Scriptores Historiae Augustae, while this garment was used by the tribune of the plebs, it was never worn by the emperor.[20] Despite the details with which the emperor's costume are rendered, given the lack of consistency of the depicted costumes themselves, it seems impossible to definitively associate the images with the names recorded by our sources, and even more difficult to determine with certainty whether, in every instance, these details have a precise significance. All one can say with confidence is that a proper description of the emperor's appearance on campaign was *paludatus*.

Second, the detailed account of the sacrificial scenes on both the columns, and their correspondence to real practice, surely extended to this conventional military costume in which the ritual is performed. Thus, in all of these scenes we have examined, given their unambiguous topographical context and the official status of their imagery on monuments of the state, the emperor's costume during the sacrificial rite while on campaign—above all, his bared head—must be understood as the appropriate comportment for honoring the gods in the military sphere. This is confirmed by the fact that in other representations of military imagery, Roman soldiers or commanders are similarly depicted, at times explicitly in battle armor, sacrificing with their heads uncovered. This form of *ritus* is attested on a wide array of monuments: the *fides exercitus* coins of Trajan; on a *Feldherr-sarkophage* now in Mantua; on a rather crude funerary relief now in the Vatican's Galleria Lapidaria; on one of the wall paintings

---

[18] Lictors *paludati*: Varro *Ling.* 7.37; Livy 31.14, 41.10, 45.39.11. Sette 2000, 35, suggests that the lictors wore the *paenula* and cites their appearance on the Cancelleria reliefs; this would also appear to be the case with the Hermitage bust of a lictor, recently discussed by Pollini 2017, 114, n. 74 (and his fig. 13), whose front-clasped cloak is most likely the *paenula*—*paludatus* only in the broad sense (as Kuttner 1995).

[19] Gross 1940, 45; cf. scenes 35 and 79 on Trajan's column, where, in scenes of ship travel, the emperor's cloak is pinned on the shoulder.

[20] S.H.A., *Hadr.* 3.5–6.

from Dura Europos; and on another state monument—the Arch of Galerius at Thessalonica.²¹ In all of *these* scenes, as on the columns, a Roman soldier—or, explicitly, the emperor—sacrifices in a costume appropriate to the ritual's performance in the military sphere, whether expressly cuirassed or simply in tunic and cloak. This signals not merely that the setting of such events is that of a campaign, but that, just as on the great columns at Rome, such military scenes are carried out in a fashion that is at odds with the customary form of Roman ritual. Since all of these soldiers bare their heads as they sacrifice to the gods above, these are obviously not scenes enacted according to the *ritus Romanus*.²²

One must conclude that all of these images represent yet another normative mode of honoring the gods, one effected solely in the military sphere—one that might be termed the *ritus militaris*. This modality of sacrifice has nothing to do with which gods are the focus of cult. For here what is at issue is the sphere of the Romans' actions rather than the particular Roman gods that govern them. That is, while the *ritus Romanus* must be understood as the manner in which cult was performed in the domain of Roman *civic* acts, the *ritus militaris*, as the designation suggests, was the fashion appropriate to those of the *military* realm. In all of the imagery we have examined, we comprehend the representation of a basic distinction between the character of social and political functions, civic and military, and an acknowledgment of these two opposed domains by means of the *form* of sacrifice that was appropriate to each; this imagery was *both* realistic and ideological. Justification for such a

---

²¹ The Dura painting poses two problems: (1) Does Terentius sacrifice before three Roman emperors or three Palmyrene gods? Kaizer 2006 and Dirven 2007 survey scholarly argument and bibliography, to which add Kantorowicz 1961, 378, and fig. 25, for the scene of a sacrifice, *capite aperto*, to Jarhibol, who wears Roman military costume, as do the three "gods" before whom Terentius makes his offering. (2) Does Terentius sacrifice *capite aperto* by custom as a Roman commander or according to the rite for Palmyrene gods? The Palmyrene monuments show that both forms of the rites were employed, and the difference between them is never questioned; for a survey of the monuments, see Drijvers 1976, with bibliography.

²² The only acknowledgment known to me of the idea that sacrifice *capite aperto* held military significance is a merely implicit suggestion made by Perea Yebenes 1997, 53: describing the rites depicted on Trajan's column, he notes that "en los varios sacrificios intermedios [i.e., after departure for campaign], como principio o fin de escalas de viaje marítimo, se hacían ritos más sencillos, libaciones o libación + sacrificio, y en estos casos invariablemente un animal único, y siempre es un toro. Sólo en los *suovetaurilia* el pontífice máximo, en este caso el Emperador, aparece *capite velato*."

CHAPTER 3

distinction was enshrined in Roman culture by the separation of *res domi* and *res militiae*, a distinction much attested by our sources and much discussed by scholars—and thus one that hardly requires elaboration.[23]

Ritual, Fiction, Ideology

Yet one of the most celebrated examples of "military" sacrifice, that found on one of the two famous silver cups from Boscoreale (figure III.8 a-b), would appear to pose a problem for the interpretation sketched here. On this cup Tiberius is depicted sacrificing in armor and wearing the *paludamentum*, and thus this scene seems to contradict the correspondence that the columns have revealed between the costume adopted for the rite and the locale of its enactment. That is, while Trajan and Marcus sacrifice in armor or in the military *Reisekostüm* on the frontier of the northern provinces, here Tiberius appears explicitly in military guise, and yet he sacrifices within the *pomerium*, at the heart of the city of Rome, before the Temple of Jupiter on the Capitoline—a setting where one might have expected him to appear in the civilian toga and to act according to protocols of the *ritus Romanus*.

There have been many attempts to resolve this fundamental difficulty posed by the cup's imagery. Four distinct interpretations have been offered to explain the Boscoreale cup's strange depiction of the emperor sacrificing in armor on the Capitol.

(1) This is a representation of the traditional announcement of vows, the *nuncupatio votorum*, offered by Tiberius on the Capitol in 12 BC before his departure to Pannonia.[24]
(2) It is the sacrifice on the Capitol that culminated one of Tiberius's triumphs—either that of 8/7 BC, over the Sugambi, or that of AD 12, after his Pannonian victory.[25]

---

[23] Rüpke 1990 provides a full account and bibliography. Cf. the discussion in chapter 1.
[24] Héron de Villefosse 1899.
[25] Strong 1907, and revived, in part, by Vervaet 2014, 86, n. 57, who seems not to have recognized the force of the arguments in Kuttner 1995 nor to have grasped the significance of the "sacrifice in armor."

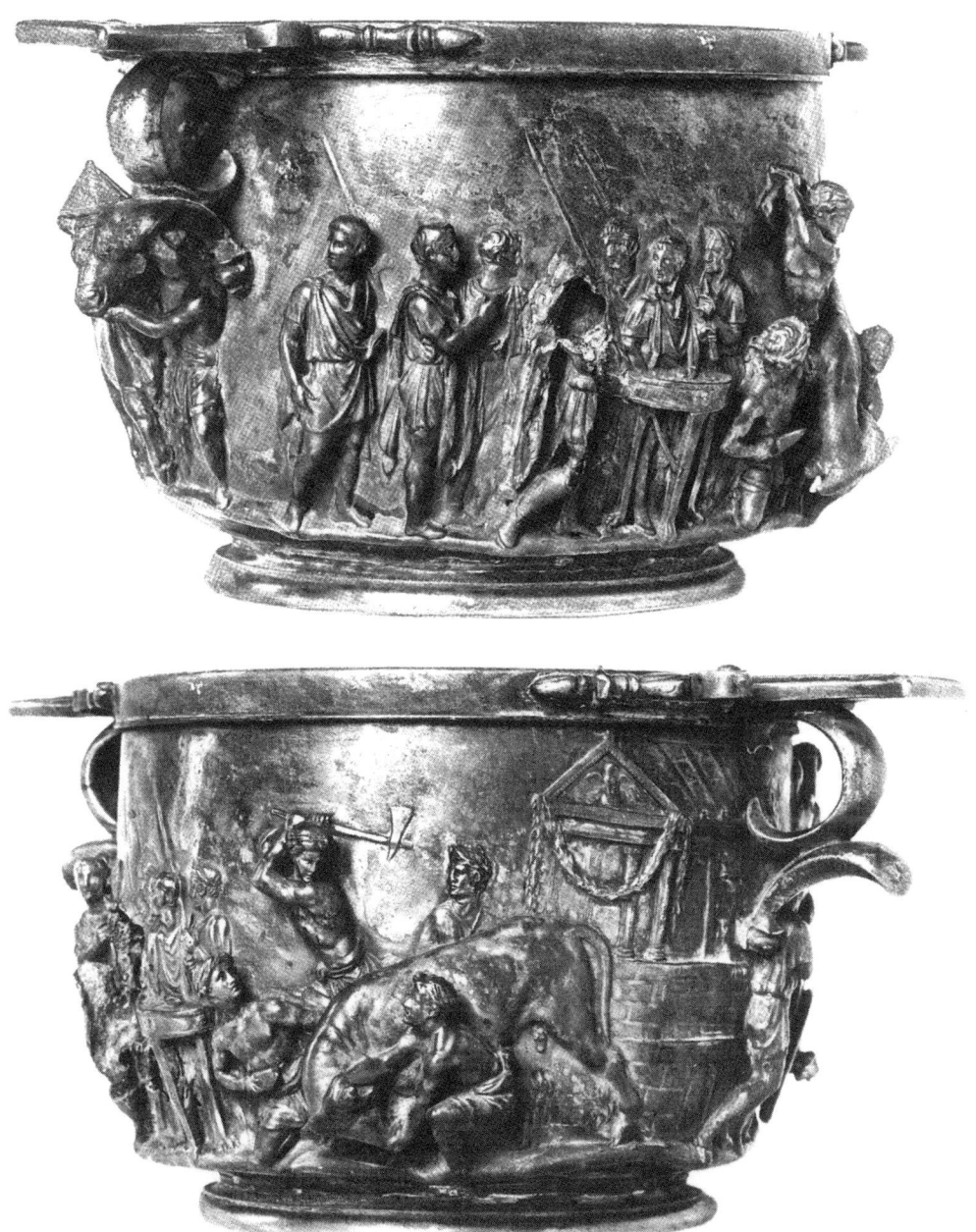

III.8a/b Tiberius sacrificing before the Capitoline temple. Boscoreale cup. Ca. 9–7 BC. Silver. Paris, Louvre.

CHAPTER 3

(3) Since the triumphator is in armor, the scene cannot occur on the Capitol in Rome, and should depict either the triumph on the Mons Albanus or an event at the foot of the Capitol—whatever it represents, it takes place outside the *pomerium*.[26]
(4) The scene is not truly historical, but an aspect of Rome's mythic "history"—and the problem of the setting can be ignored because this is a representation of Aeneas, not Tiberius.[27]

The interpretation of the scene as the departure rite, the *nuncupatio votorum*, known to have taken place on the Capitol, is surely correct—and has been gradually refined over the last fifty years: Tiberius sacrifices on the Capitol to Jupiter, in armor, before his departure on campaign.[28] The *nuncupatio votorum* sought the gods' approval for taking the field for battle—and the campaign, we might say, actually began with the vow. This was communicated by the accompanying sacrifice, whose ritual allowed men to commune with the divine—and this is what is *actually* shown, since one readily recognizes the difficulty of depicting the vow itself in a recognizable form.[29]

This interpretation is confirmed by a series of sarcophagi that depict the very same scene, in the same setting—a sacrifice in armor before the Capitoline temple, signaling the conclusion of the *nuncupatio votorum*.[30] And the consistent presentation of these commanders sacrificing *capite aperto* suggests that this was how Tiberius once seems to have comported himself on the Boscoreale cup, before it was so severely damaged. The *nuncupatio* was a military act: not only did one perform the ceremony in armor, but one did so according to the appropriate protocols and sacrificed *capite aperto*; this too is the *ritus militaris*.

But why is this form of the rite enacted at the heart of Rome? This is a matter of topography, of politics, and of religion. One must conclude that what

---

[26] Mons Albanus: Polacco 1955. Foot of the Capitol: Pollini 1978.
[27] Kleiner 1983.
[28] Kähler 1958–1960, Koeppel 1969, Hölscher 1980, and Kuttner 1995.
[29] Similarly, Hickson Hahn 2007.
[30] Reinsberg 2006 presents the monuments and their bibliography fully, yet offers no convincing explanation of our problem.

is at stake in these various representations of sacrifice is not the actual place of their occurrence, but the function they served there and their religious efficacy: what mattered was the kind of action for which the approbation of the gods was sought.[31] Thus, on the Boscoreale cup, a clash of certain well-known Roman institutions that distinguished *domi* from *militiae* produces what amounts to a legal and religious *fiction*: for the *nuncupatio*, a Roman commander performed a quintessentially Roman ritual *as if he were not at Rome, but in the field*—and in the manner and costume appropriate to such a setting.

In this sense, the cup's imagery is not unlike a certain aspect of Roman legal practice, one often employed for political purpose—the not-uncommon expediency by means of which the jurists acted in situations "as if" they were true: a state of affairs might be construed, falsely, as fact; assumptions might then be derived—and in turn legal consequences, at odds with an actual situation, deduced—that served when legislative precedent was lacking in order to convey a benefit, impose an obligation, or exact a penalty.[32] Numerous examples survive in the writings of the jurists, where such fictions were frequently employed in order to treat noncitizens as if they were: the *fictio legis Corneliae* confirmed testamentary enactments as if the beneficiaries, who had died in enemy lands, were citizens; similarly, according to Gaius, aliens might be treated as citizens so that judgments might equally be rendered for or against them; and Julian and Ulpian would concur that "it is accepted at civil law that whenever the fulfillment of a condition is prevented by one who has an interest in its nonfulfillment, the condition is to be treated as though it had been satisfied."[33]

Such fictions might operate more broadly as well. For example, the military character of the proconsuls and propraetors—those field commanders who were appointed as *privati* to lead Rome's troops on campaigns far from the *urbs*—performed in this capacity exactly *as if* they were duly elected magistrates.[34] Similarly, in the imperial age, the Roman army—by then largely comprising

---

[31] Cf. Catalano 1960, 198, on "sfera di atti."
[32] Succinct account in Long 1875; details in Thomas 1995 and Richardson 1995; cf. also Ando 2011a and, more extensively, Ando 2011b.
[33] *Fictio legis Corneliae*: *Dig.* 35.2.1. Gaius: *Inst.* 4.37. Julian: *Dig.* 35.1.24. Ulpian: *Dig.* 50.17.161.
[34] Richardson 1995.

CHAPTER 3

newly made citizens from the provinces as well as mercenaries of many ethnic origins—was still the *exercitus populi Romani*: that is, it might still be claimed that the army was that of *Rome's* people.[35] More pertinently, the effacement of topographical distinctions, similar to what appears in the case of the Boscoreale cup, is found repeatedly in the legal sources—as when Gaius resolves the problem of the inability, *in provincia*, to consecrate a site publicly or to perform those private acts that render a place *religiosus*: the legal remedy was that "even if [provincial ground] is not *religiosus*, it is treated as though it were. Similarly, whatever in the provinces is not consecrated on authority of the Roman people is properly not sacred, but it is nevertheless treated as if it were."[36]

But the most apt comparison for the *nuncupatio* on the Boscoreale cup is found in the practices of the Fetial priesthood and the adaptation of their reputedly ancient rite for the declaration of war—the casting of a spear into enemy territory from its border—to the exigencies of a growing empire.[37] Two decades before the making of the Boscoreale cup, Octavian is reported to have revived the priesthood and, in 32 BC, to have performed the rite *at Rome* before embarking for the Battle at Actium:

> [The senators] put on their military cloaks [*chlamydas*] as if he [Antonius] were close at hand, and went to the temple of Bellona, where they performed, through Caesar as *fetialis*, all the rites preliminary to war in the customary fashion.[38]

The spear was apparently thrown at a small column; the historicity of this custom is vouchsafed by Ovid and Festus, and its purpose explained by Dio when the rite was enacted by Marcus Aurelius two hundred years later: the emperor would depart "after hurling the bloody spear, that was kept in the temple of Bellona, into what was supposed to be the enemy's territory."[39]

---

[35] Herz 2002, esp. 81 and 95. Cf. Hölscher 2006, 36–38, on some of the ways in which such fictions were perpetrated on the *populus* at Rome.

[36] Gaius, *Inst.* 2.5–7. The broad legal context is treated in Ando 2011b.

[37] Kuttner 1995, 125, recognizes a parallel between Fetial ritual and the *nuncupatio*, but does not fully grasp its nature.

[38] Dio 50.33.4–5.

[39] Ovid *F.* 6.205–8; Festus 30L; Dio 72.33.3.

And the topographical "fiction" would be explicitly described, its aetiology provided, and the role of the column explained, by a commentary that survives in Servius (Danielis):

> When in the time of Pyrrhus the Romans were about to wage war against an overseas enemy and did not find a place in which to carry out this ceremony of declaring war by the fetials, they saw to it that one of Pyrrhus's soldiers should be captured, whom they made to buy a plot in the Circus Flaminius, so that they could fulfill the rule for declaring war as though in hostile land. Later a column was dedicated at that place in front of the temple of Bellona.[40]

Given the not-uncommon role of such fictions as an accepted aspect of Roman legal institutions, a parallel interpretation of the Boscoreale cup's unusual imagery seems inescapable: the *nuncupatio votorum* was an act of the military sphere, enacted at the heart of Rome, "as if" it was conducted on the subsequent campaign in the field. This was because it was the *sphere of human action* that determined what was sought from the gods, and this fixed the proper *ritus* for the practice of cult. That sphere was ideological, not geographical, just as was the distinction the Romans made between *domi* and *militiae*.[41] Although we have seen numerous examples from the columns in which the location of the scenes in the provinces determined the relevant domain of activity, what the Boscoreale cup demonstrates is that the *locus* of an act and the legal and religious sphere to which it belongs need not actually correspond.

Other images representing *another* institution and its rite confirm this interpretation. A famous relief from the Campus Martius (figure III.9) depicts the *lustratio*, long believed to be that performed at the closing of the census—the

---

[40] Serv. Dan. *Ad Aen.* 9.52. The fullest discussion and bibliography is in Rich 2011 (who is skeptical about the historicity of Servius's account), from which I take the translation. The same idea is found at Serv. Dan. *Ad Aen.* 2.187: cf. the commentaries in Wissowa 1912, 152; Bianchi 1997; Rüpke 1990, 52; Scheid 2012a, 119.

[41] Giovannini 1983; see also the discussion in chapter 1 and, recently, Berthelet 2015, 186–94, with bibliography.

CHAPTER 3

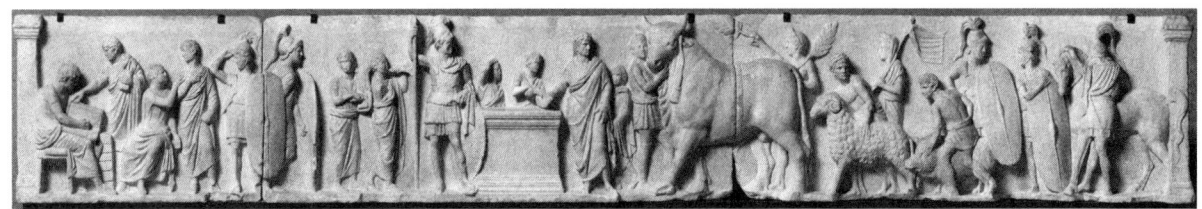

III.9 Census/*lustratio* relief, "Altar of Domitius Ahenobarbus." Late Republican. Marble. Paris, Louvre.

act presumed to be unfolding at the work's left end.[42] This occurred, according to tradition, at five-year intervals and determined the assignment of rights and duties to the citizenry; its concluding rite was carried out in the Campus Martius, where the major sacrifice of the *suovetaurilia*—the sacrifice to Mars of a sow, a ram, and a bull—was enacted and then followed, as the sources relate, by procession *into* the city.[43] Yet recently this consensus view of the relief's imagery has been effectively challenged, as it has been shown that on the basis of various attributes it is unlikely that one or both of the censors actually appears.[44] For the togate figure sacrificing at the center does not wear the senatorial shoes commensurate with the censor's status, and the presumed censor seated at the left, despite his senatorial footwear, sits not on the curule chair of such a magistrate but on a simple stool. Instead, it has been suggested, this scene should be that of another institution at which the *lustratio* was performed, also by convention in the Campus Martius: the *coloniae deductio*, the ceremony that marked the foundation of new colonies.[45] This institution, performed by a three-member board (*IIIviri*), did not always comprise sitting magistrates or men of consular rank,[46] and thus the two figures long presumed to have been censors, together with the third significant figure on the Paris frieze, carrying the *vexillum* (and apparently attired in the *cinctus Gabinus*),

---

[42] See Schmid 2007/2008 and Lohmann 2009, both with an extensive bibliography.

[43] Census in Campus, *suovetaurilia*, and *lustratio*: Livy 1.44.1–2., 4.22.7, 40.45.8; Varro *Rust.* 2.1.10, 3.2.4–5; Dion. Hal. 4.22. Procession to the Capitoline: Livy 45.46.15. Discussion and bibliography in Gargola 1995, 78–82.

[44] Maschek 2018.

[45] *Coloniae deductio*: Varro *Ling.* 5.143, with Versnel 1975; Ogilvie 1961; Eckstein 1979; Bispham 2006. New interpretation: Coles 2017; Maschek 2018.

[46] Coles 2017.

may well belong to the *deductio*.⁴⁷ For the founding of new colonies was preceded by a sacrificial ritual that would also appear to have been performed *capite velato*, according to the *ritus Romanus*, outside of the *pomerium*, in the presence of troops, at an altar of Mars. So, whether a representation of the census or the *deductio*, the sacrificial *habitus* displayed on the Paris relief declares it a civic rite performed beyond the boundary of the city, and demonstrates how the religious character of the *ritus* employed might not correspond to the specifically geographical sphere in which it was exercised.

What appears to be an analogous scene is represented on the columns (figures III.10 and III.11), where both Trajan and Marcus, similarly *togatus* and *capite velato*, officiate at the *suovetaurilia*. These images have long been recognized as depictions of yet another *lustratio* ritual central to the military's encampment, the *lustratio exercitus*. On both columns, the act is performed according to the *ritus Romanus*, despite its actual geographical setting in the provinces. Here, too, the emperor's comportment signals that his action, always prefatory to battle, belongs to the *civic* sphere, and that the *lustratio*—wherever it was performed—was conceived as a civic act, despite the fact that it was an offering to Mars; that is, it defined its participants' rights and obligations to their community—military, political, and fiscal—and established that community's unity along with the privileges to be held within it.⁴⁸

But the sequence and setting of the *suovetaurilia* implied on the Paris *lustratio* relief—whether a depiction of the census or the *deductio*—have been reversed on Trajan's column. The civic rite now *follows* the procession and takes place within the wall of the camp—just the opposite of how the rite was performed at Rome, where it was traditionally conducted outside the *pomerium* and followed by a procession (census: into the city; *deductio*: to the new foundation). As this civic ritual was adapted for military employment in the provinces, its elements underwent a reversal.⁴⁹

---

⁴⁷ Maschek 2018, citing Cic. *Phil.* 2.102; cf. Varro *Ling.* 6.93, and the materials cited in n. 7 above.

⁴⁸ The idea that the *lustratio* represented a purification was effectively refuted by Versnel 1975, and reaffirmed recently by Scheid 2016. Related types of *lustratio*: Cic. *Div.* 1.102.

⁴⁹ Censor with the *vexillum* leading the *exercitus centuariatus* from the campus into the city: Varro *Ling.* 6.93; Livy 45.46.15. *Vexillum* carried to the *coloniae*: Cic. *Leg. Agr.* 2.86; *Phil.* 2.102. Despite the unambiguous evidence of the columns, Dio 47.38.4 and Plut. *Brut.* 39 describe as un-

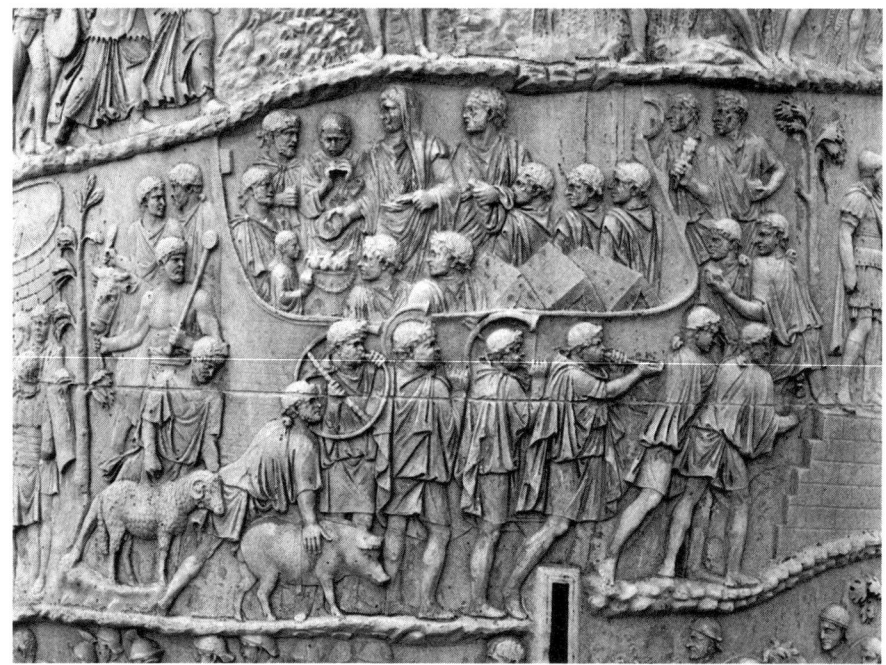
III.10 Column of Trajan, detail: scene 103. Rome.

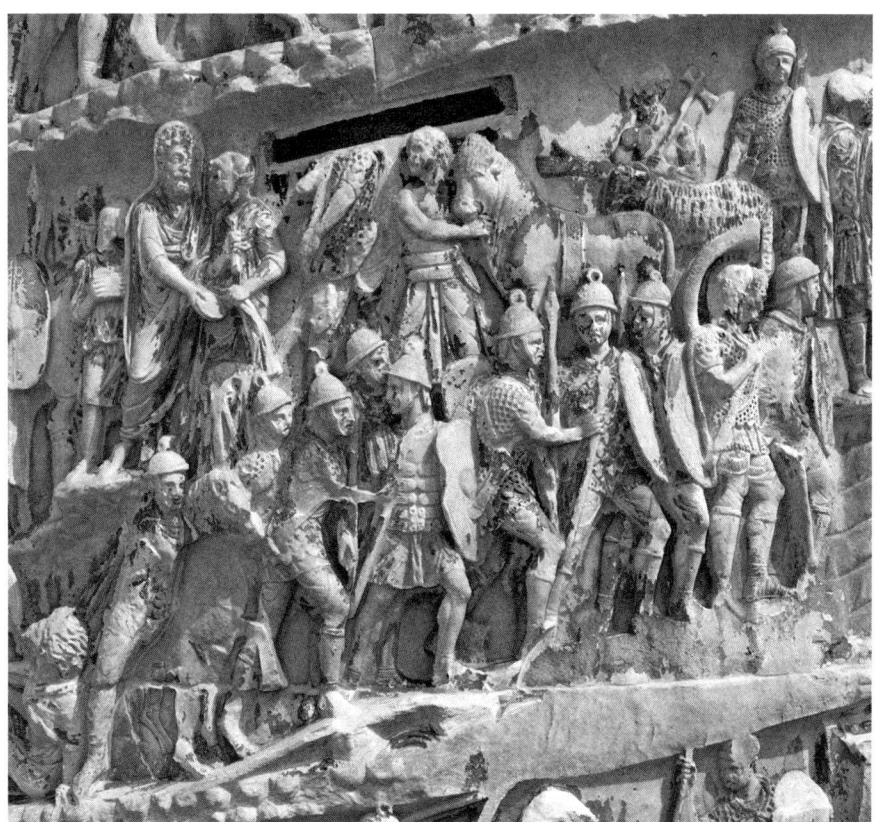
III.11 Column of M. Aurelius, detail: scene 30. Rome.

This can be explained. The institution of the *lustratio exercitus*, like the related role that the *lustratio* played in the census and in the founding of colonies, was designed, or merely evolved, as an echo of the mythic founding of Rome itself.⁵⁰ Indeed, all forms of the *lustratio* were civic acts performed, outside of Rome or in the provinces, in the service of Roman dominion and its civic existence. The census charted and ordered the growth of the city, and both *coloniae* and *castra* were conceived as expansions of Rome herself: for the notion of *novae urbes* held within it that of the original *urbs* itself; that of the *castrum* was little different.⁵¹ Thus, the two great historiated columns demonstrate that the temporary home of the legions was to be understood as an extension of the city of Rome: in the traditional language of Roman ideology, the *castrum* was—paradoxically—*domi*, not *militiae*.⁵²

Although all of these *lustrationes* were civic acts, despite the site of their enactment, there was an essential difference between the events to which each of them applied. In the case of the census, the rite signaled the reentry into the city; for the *coloniae*, it marked a departure for the subsequent foundation of a new city; and in the case of the *castrum*, the rite was an aspect of preparation for departure from an *altera patria* for battle.⁵³ In all three instances, one glimpses how these institutions describe a pattern of relationships between the civic sphere and what lay outside its boundary. And in this they point out the opposition of the *lustratio* to the *nuncupatio*: in the latter, a military act takes place in the city, while in the former, a fundamentally civic act takes place on campaign. In this sense one recognizes that these were reciprocal fictions.

The following charts—which set the relationships out schematically—reveal the essential correlations to the *ritus* employed. If we regard these as

---

usual the carrying out of the sacrifice within the camp—not "in the open field, as the custom is" (Plutarch); cf. Gargola 1995, 79 ("one atypical case").

⁵⁰ See the materials cited in n. 45 above.

⁵¹ *Coloniae*: Gell. *NA* 16.13.9 (*quasi effigies parvae simulacraque*); cf. Torelli 2014 and Sewell 2014. *Castra*: Livy 44.39.4 (as *altera patria*); Cic. *Phil.* 5.27 (*urbis propugnaculum*). *Castrum* as civic space: Scheid 2017, 146.

⁵² Cf. Livy 7.12.9 and 7.21.9 on the properly *civic* appointments of Gaius Sulpicius (358 BC) and Gaius Julius (351 BC) as dictators, while *in castris* (commentary in Oakley *ad* 7.12.9, noting the institutionalized fiction).

⁵³ *Altera patria*: Livy 44.39.4. Departure for battle: sources assembled by Versnel 1979, 112, n. 47.

CHAPTER 3

being based on the traditional view of Roman geographical ideology, with the *pomerium* serving as the fundamental division between the civic and military realms, one sees something like this:

WITHIN THE *POMERIUM*	BEYOND THE *POMERIUM* OR *IN PROVINCIA*
Boscoreale cup: sacrifice (*capite aperto*)	Trajan's column: sacrifice (*capite aperto*)
	Trajan's column: *lustratio* (*capite velato*)
	Paris relief: *lustratio* (*capite velato*)

From this perspective, the different forms of the *ritus* suggest no coherent explanation; there appears to be no logic to the performance of the ritual *capite velato* or *capite aperto*. But if we consider these matters as a reflection of a purely ideological distinction between *kinds of actions*, not only does their reciprocal nature emerge clearly, but the relevance of their actual geography (and of the pomerial ideology) evaporates:

CIVIL ACTION (*CAPITE VELATO*)	MILITARY ACTION (*CAPITE APERTO*)
Paris relief: *lustratio* in Campus Martius	Boscoreale cup: sacrifice on Capitolium
Trajan's column: *lustratio in castra*	Trajan's column: sacrifice *in provincia*

What such an analysis reveals is that for the institution of the *lustratio exercitus*, the military camp was understood, according to tradition, as what might be called *altera pars Romae*; similarly, for the enactment of the *nuncupatio*, the Capitoline was, also by tradition, conceived as what might equally be termed *altera pars militiae*. The monuments we have been examining represent for us two exceptional situations in which radical transformations of custom—of the sacrificial *ritus*—had become institutionalized. While the realism of their represented scenes of ritual signaled official legal and religious realities, their "symbolism"—their fictions—evoked other, ideological claims. Here we find yet another proof that, despite the long-standing tradition of scholarship that regards *domi* and *militiae* as mutually defining conceptions, these were neither primarily nor fundamentally a matter of the realities of geography. The ideology that divorced *res civiles* from *res militares* depended on the establishment of legal and religious "fictions" that the Romans were so often willing to employ. And from this point of view, the truly *Roman* counterpart to the *ritus Romanus* was not the *ritus Graecus*, which acknowledged the gods with Greek practice, but the *ritus militaris*, which admitted a distinction between how, where, and why cult was offered to the Romans' own divinities.

Nuncupatio et extispicium

Several other monuments that are at times associated with the *nuncupatio votorum* and specifically with the departure of commanders have a place in this discussion. Given the evidence presented here, *none* of these can properly be so interpreted.

A (probably) late Republican relief now in the Vatican (figure III.12) depicts an armed figure sacrificing before a statue of what appears to be the god Mars. Yet there is nothing here that speaks of imminent departure, an interpretation perhaps undermined by the second statue that once stood at the relief's now-lost right side—and thus there is no good reason to think that this represents the formal announcement of vows as an aspect of a commander's leave-taking. So too the protagonist's plumed helmet distinguishes him from the portrait repertory of military commanders and strongly suggests that the subject matter of the relief (and its protagonist's identity) is mythological.[54]

---

[54] Vatican relief: bibliography and discussion in chapter 1, n. 15 above. In Koortbojian 2010, 250, n. 16 (there as a *nuncupatio*), I had failed to grasp the real nature of the image, for if this relief depicts the *nuncupatio*, its proper recipient of cult should have been Jupiter. Mythological subject: Kaschnitz von Weinberg 1937; Simon in Helbig[4] 1963, I: no. 1122; Felletti Maj 1977; Kleiner 1983; Kuttner 1995; Holliday 2002.

CHAPTER 3

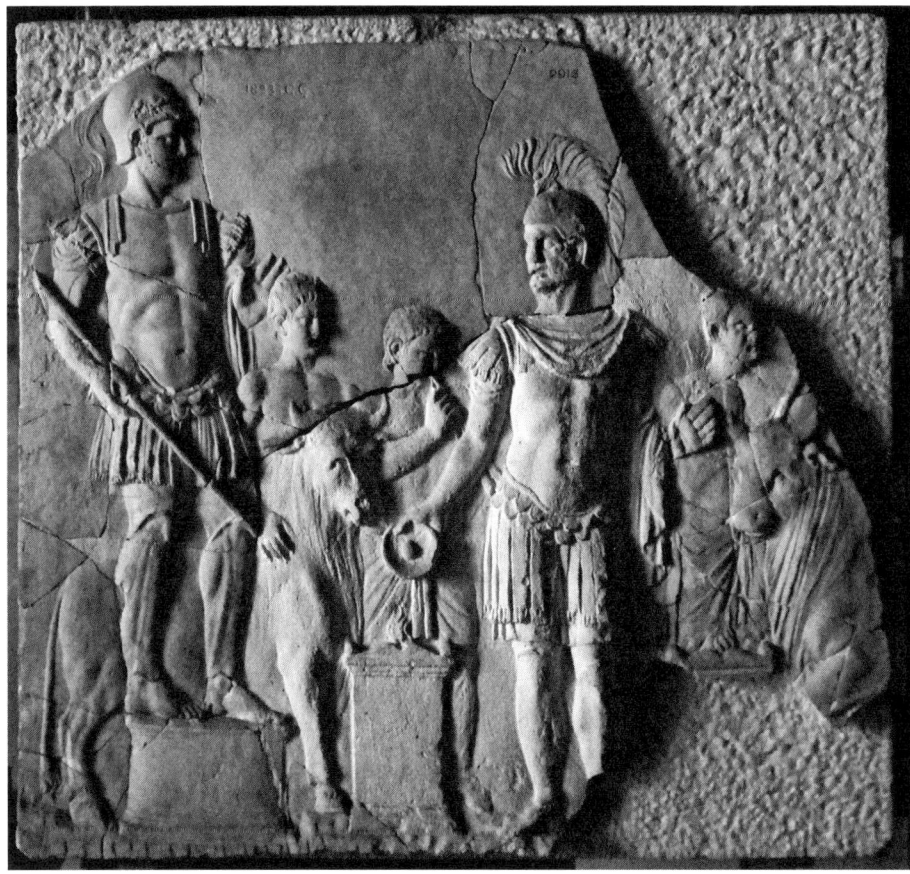

III.12 Sacrifice relief. Late Republican. Marble. Musei Vaticani.

A second monument, the so-called Altar of the Vicus Sandaliarius (figure III.13), displays a combination of civic acts, in an unspecified setting, although this is surely to be understood as taking place at Rome.[55] The taking of the auspices and the implication of sacrifice that the relief depicts are both, given the dated inscription, rightly associated with the departure of Gaius (standing at the left) for the eastern campaign in 2 BC. Yet his toga argues against this being a representation of the *nuncupatio*, which, as the Boscoreale cup shows and the reports of Livy confirm (see below), was a set of vows made in military dress, immediately before departure. Rather, the Vicus Sandaliarius altar amalgamates, indeed celebrates, other attested *civic* religious rituals

---

[55] What follows corrects part of my own interpretation in Koortbojian 2013, 73–77, where the bibliography is cited; see, recently, Marcattili 2015 (unpersuasive).

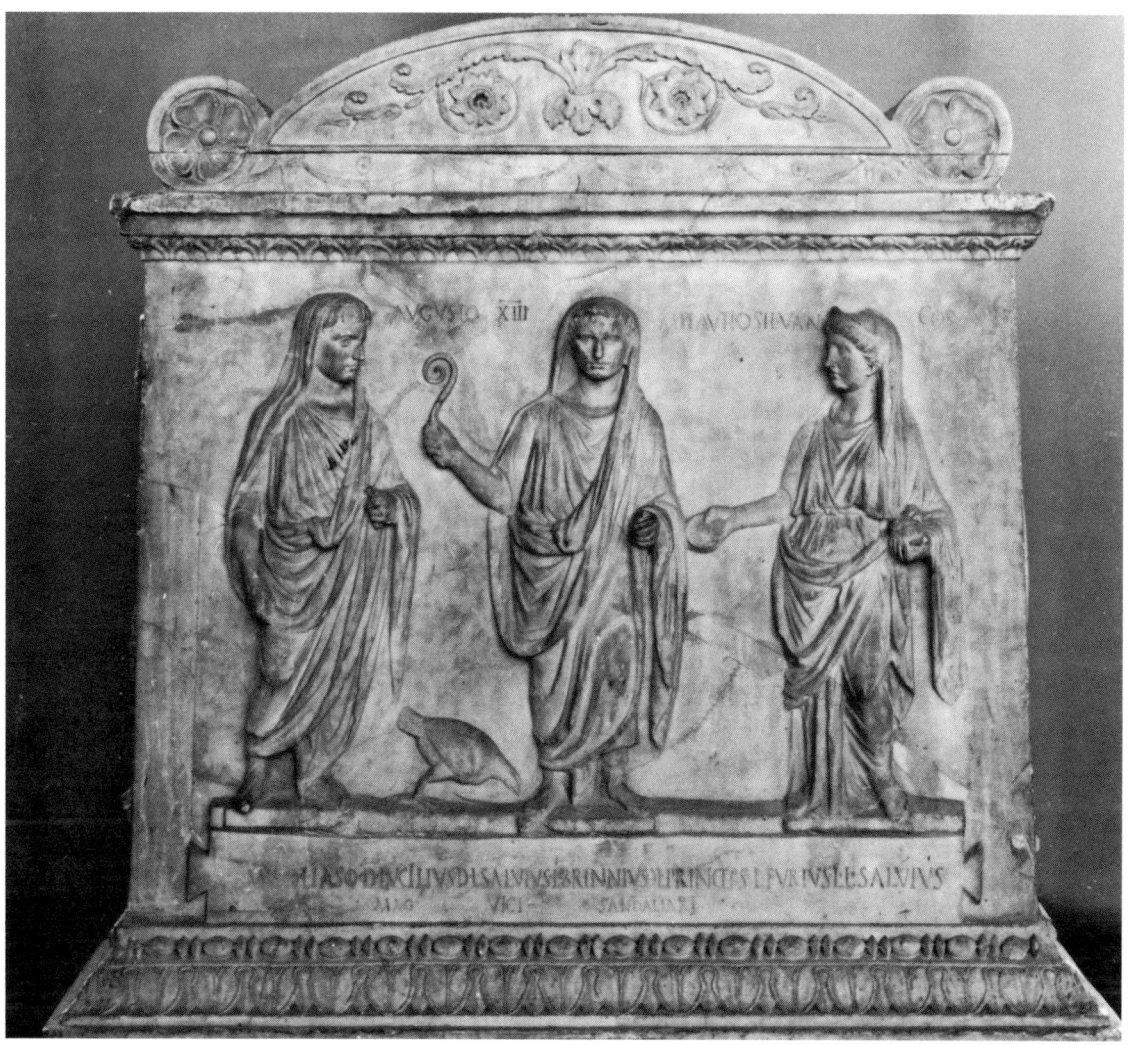

III.13 Altar from the Vicus Sandaliarius. 2 BC. Marble. Florence, Uffizi.

that were associated with the Romans' preparations for war. (I return to these civic rituals below.)

A third example, a relief depicting an *extispicium* (figure III.14), formerly in the Borghese collection and now in the Louvre, has also been long associated with the *nuncupatio votorum*—here too an association without solid foundation.[56] The scene, set before the Capitoline temple, depicts an assembly of

---

[56] Louvre relief: Ryberg 1955, 128–30; Tortorella 1985 and 1988; Grunow Sobocinski and Thill 2018; all with bibliography. Interpretation as a *nuncupatio*: this was the (unpublished) opinion of

CHAPTER 3

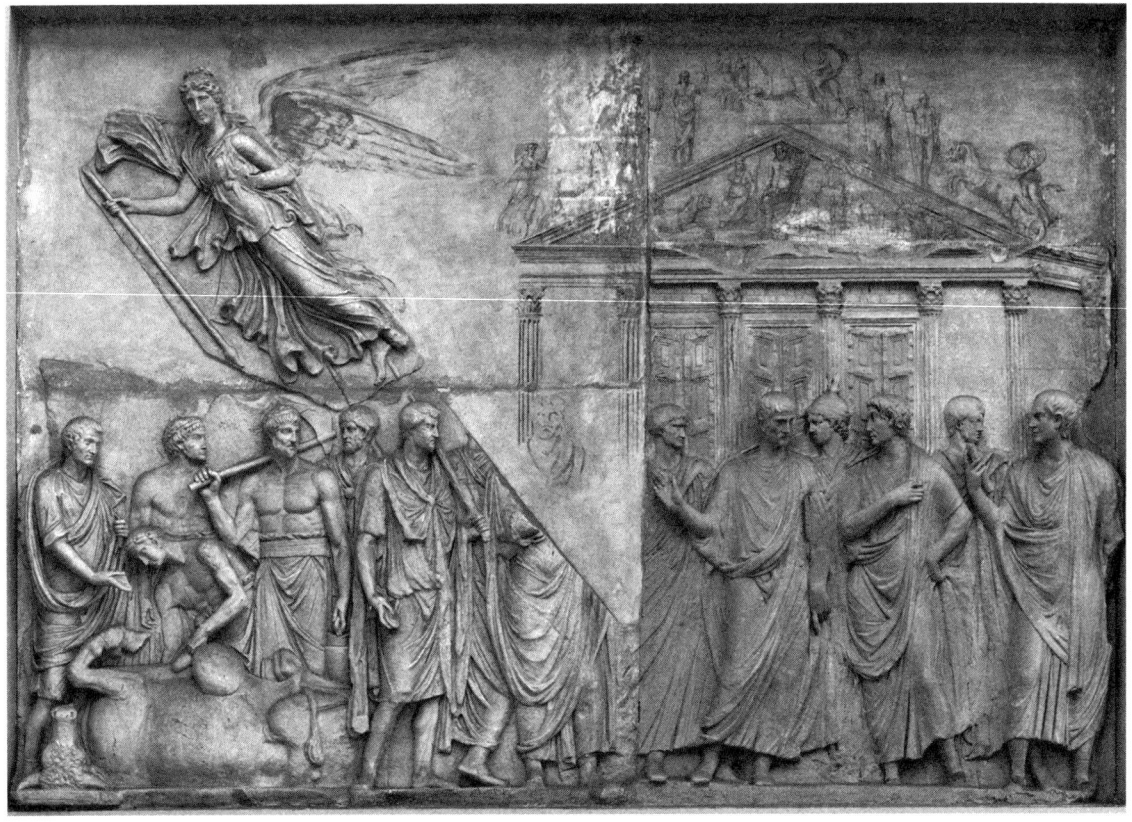

III.14 *Extispicium* relief. Early second century AD. Marble. Paris, Louvre.

togate men in discussion and, at the left, a scene of extispicy presided over by a *haruspex*. The presence of Victoria flying above has been presumed to suggest that this represents a scene of prophecy following upon sacrifice, in this instance, divination, *more etrusco*, by means of the sacrificial beast's entrails. Yet the costumes of the protagonists do not signal an imminent departure, nor do they suggest a military context.[57] For on our surviving state monuments

---

H. Stuart Jones cited by Wace 1907, 240; followed by Ryberg 1955 and Tortorella 1988, as well as Oppermann 1985, 72–78; Haack 2003, 109; Torelli 2011, 141.

[57] It is the prominence of Victoria, flying above, and the axes affixed to the *fasces* that have been held to augur for an impending military campaign: however, Victoria often marks the *adventus* (see next note), and the axes appear, at times, contrary to custom (and, apparently, *Staatsrecht*: cf. Koeppel 1969, 144, n. 41 ["die Künstler sich nicht streng an das Staatsrecht hielten"]), in other

of first- and second-century date, Victoria's presence might signify *either* an *adventus* or a *profectio*[58]; here, however, she signals *neither*, since this scene too represents another ritual amid the preparations—not the departure—for war. For there is abundant evidence that, while sacrifice was performed as an aspect of the *nuncupatio*, the *extispicium* was customarily enacted in the context of a civic ritual as a means of prophesizing at the start of the year, when war lay on the Romans' horizon. Livy's account of the start of the year 171 BC (at that point, in March) sets forth the concatenation of many of the relevant events:

> The consuls, *ex senatus consulto*, offer sacrifices of *hostiae maiores* at all the temples where the *lectisternia* were held; assured their prayers were approved by the gods, they reported to the senate that the rites had been performed; the haruspices, having performed their rite [*extispicium*?], gave their report to the senate; the *patres* instructed the consuls to present their resolution to the popular assembly (*centuriata*), which they passed; the senate decreed that the lots should be drawn by the new consuls for their *provinciae*; legions were enrolled, troops were allotted, and the commands were arranged.[59]

Livy goes on, at great length, detailing the many preparations, and their impediment by controversy, for the imminent war with Perseus—preparations that lasted, according to Livy, for months prior to the newly installed commanders' departure:

> In order that the magistrates might set out sooner for their provinces, the Latin Festival was held on the first of June; and after this ceremony

---

scenes of an arguably civic character—notably, on the frieze known as Cancelleria B; further examples from the private sphere in Schäfer 1989.

[58] *Profectio* and *adventus*: Koeppel 1969. The larger debate revolves, principally, around the interpretation of the Cancelleria reliefs; summary of the positions in Keller 1967 and, subsequently, Petruccioli 2014; Maggi 1993 demonstrates the amalgamation of the iconographies on the late imperial coinage.

[59] This drastically abridges and paraphrases Livy 42.30.8–42.31.9. New Year of 171 BC in March: sources and discussion in Michels 1967, 97. Later evidence for New Year's vows in the dossier of the Arvals: Scheid 1990, 289–383.

CHAPTER 3

had been completed the praetor Gaius Lucretius, having sent ahead everything needed for the fleet, set out for Brundisium.[60]

At roughly the same time (*per hos forte dies*), Livy reports that the consul who had drawn the province of Macedonia, Publius Licinius, also prepared—at last—to depart: "after announcing his vows on the Capitol, [Licinius] set out from the city in military dress" (*votis in Capitolio nuncupatis paludatis ab urbe profectus est*). The *extispicium* that presaged his victory was, at this point, already long past.

So one realizes that the imagery of both the Vicus Sandaliarius altar and the Louvre relief relate events that belong, within the conventional chronology of the Romans' arrangements and planning for war, at the start of the lengthy buildup to the departure for battle—not only the time-consuming preparations of the troops but the many rituals that marked the often months-long wait for the campaigning season during the height of summer. Many of these rituals were of a civic nature, performed by the magistrates in their elected capacity—as both of these monuments show; the *nuncupatio votorum*, by contrast, was not among them: it belonged to the military sphere.

Three Problems

Three other things also call for comment. First, our sources say next to nothing, explicitly, about sacrifice in the field; at best, details are implied. For example, amid his account of the campaign against the Gauls led by Gnaeus Manlius (*cos.* 189), Livy tells of how Manlius

> encamped that day at the base [of the mountains]; the following day, having offered sacrifice and obtained favorable omens from the first victims, he divided the army into three columns and began the advance against the enemy.[61]

The mention of the *castrum*, the multiple victims, and the subsequent departure of the troops suggest that the sacrifice was the *suovetaurilia* offered at

---

[60] Livy 42.35.3.
[61] Livy 38.20.6–7: *eo die sub ipsis radicibus posuit castra; postero, sacrificio facto, cum primis hostiis litasset, trifariam exercitum divisum ducere ad hostem pergit.*

the *lustratio exercitus*, despite Livy's paucity of detail. More often, however, we hear that a sacrifice occurred—and nothing of *how* it was conducted, or by what rite. Nowhere is the sacrificial *ritus* and its differing forms acknowledged.[62]

Second, the mode of offering *capite aperto* was not a consequence of appearing in military garb, since nothing precluded someone wearing the cuirass and *paludamentum* or the *tunica* and *sagum* from covering his head during sacrifice. Nonetheless, this appears to be attested only twice on the surviving monuments: on a relief from Aesernia (figure. III.15), a *suovetaurilia* is conducted by Attalus Nonius, slave of Marcus, wearing the *tunica* and with his head covered by the *ricinium*; and on a dedicatory altar from Eining (figure III.16), the military prefect T. Flavius Felix makes an offering to the Severan house, the Capitoline triad, and the *Genius Cohortis*, wearing the tunic and mantle (the *sagum*?), *capite velato*.[63] Such images demonstrate that, in the military sphere, should it be appropriate, the means to cover the head was ready-to-hand.[64]

And third, there is one literary attestation that seems to suggest that such a costume—military garb, with head covered—might have once appeared in statuary form. Livy reports that a statue was set up at Praeneste in the year 215 BC for one Marcus Anicius:

> There formerly stood in the forum of Praeneste a statue of the man, wearing a cuirass and draped in a toga, with his head covered, together with three images [*signa*: of gods?]. It had an inscription on a bronze plaque, stating that Marcus Anicius had paid his vow on behalf of the soldiers who were in the garrison at Casilinum. The same inscription was placed beneath three images of gods set up in the Temple of Fortune.[65]

---

[62] Cf., e.g., Livy 44.37.13; Val. Max. 1.6.4 and 9.7 *mil. Rom.* 2.

[63] Aesernia relief: Scheid 1994 and Huet 2012, 53–54, with a full bibliography; Eining altar: Huet 2008a, 59, and cat. 8 (tunique et manteaux, *capite velato*); Kempkes and Sarge 2009, 106; Schmidt Heidenreich 2013, 128–29, and cat. C246.

[64] Note that on the so-called Nollekens relief the emperor appears *capite velato* over the laurel crown: Pollini 2017, 119.

[65] Livy 23.19.18: *statua eius* [= M. Anicius] *indicio fuit, Praeneste in foro statuta, loricata, amicta toga, velato capite, et tria signa cum titulo lamnae aeneae inscripto, M. Anicium pro mili-*

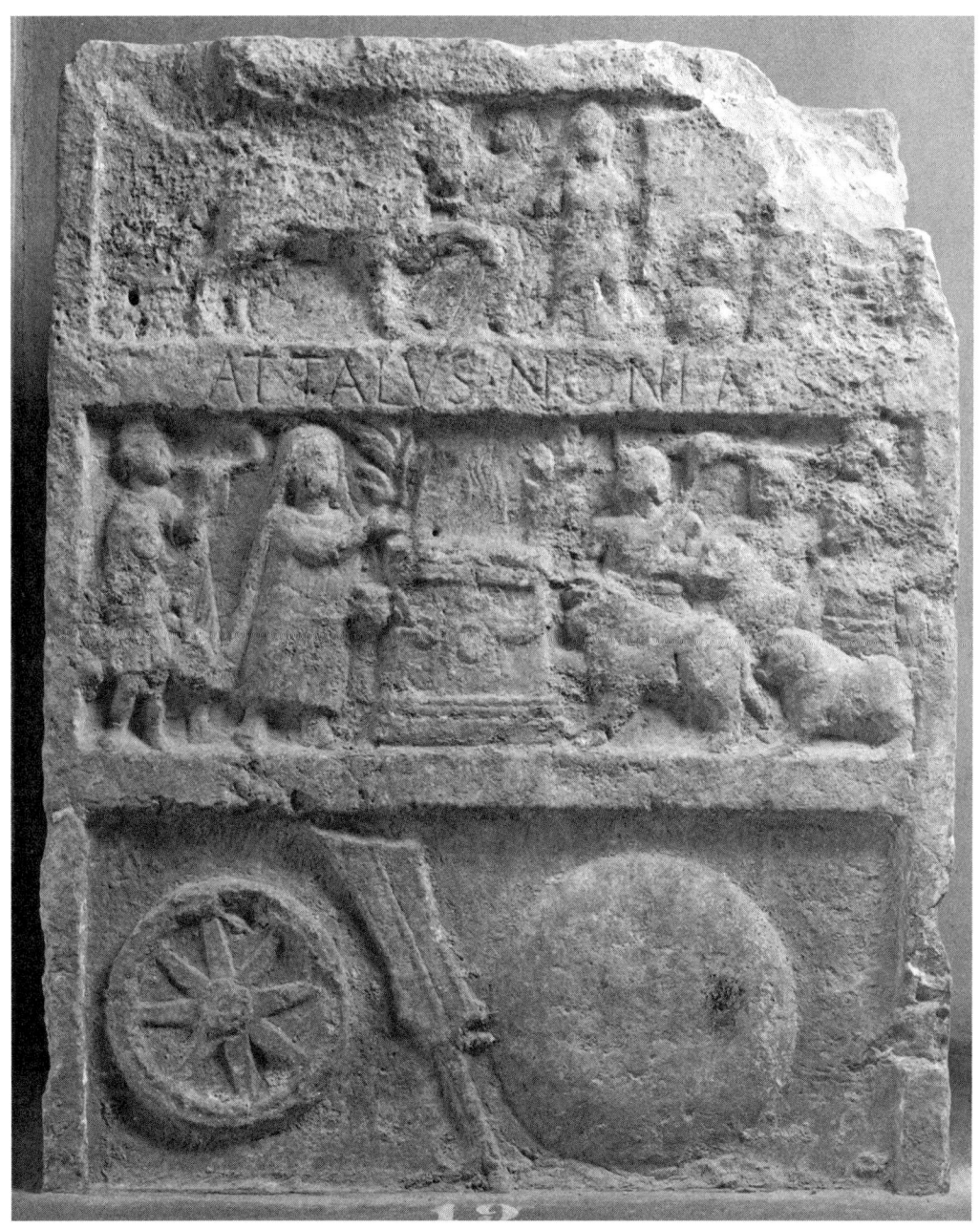

III.15 Relief of Attalus Nonius. Augustan. Marble. Aesernia, Museo Civico.

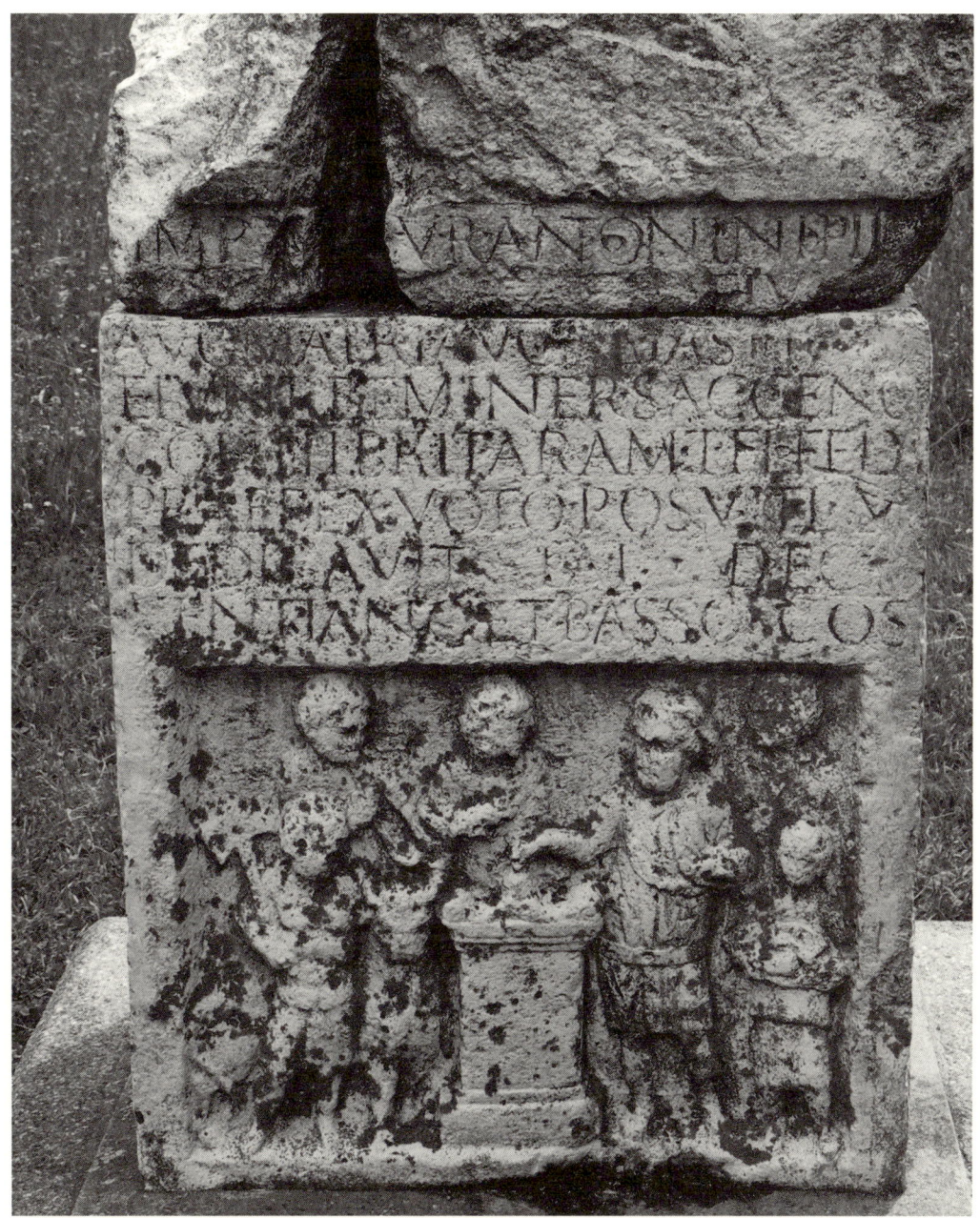

III.16 Altar of T. Flavius Felix. AD 211. Marble. Eining.

CHAPTER 3

The description of Anicius's statue is most puzzling and was surely garbled by Livy's source, yet it is far from clear in what manner. There are several ways to construe this passage.

(1) Was this a *single* statue, as Livy's text states? If this was indeed a single statue (*statua . . . fuit*), it would appear to be a *hapax* amid our monumental record, for one did not wear the cuirass while draped in the toga. And if Livy's tripartite description of a single statue's appearance was accurate, was *amicta toga* intended in this instance, despite its misnomer, to signal the conventional draping about the waist of the *paludamentum*,[66] which in this instance was pulled up to cover the head? Not only would this be wholly unconventional as a costume, but on account of Anicius's veiled head it would *not* be an example of the ritual comportment by which such a cuirassed figure would presumably have distinguished himself—the *ritus militarus*.

(2) Or are we confronted by an even more distorted passage that has mistakenly amalgamated *three* different statues—one *paludatus*, one *togatus*, and one *capite velato*? Three portraits of Anicius, in these three guises, would have referred to his three different social roles (soldier, citizen, and religious officiant).[67] These cannot have been the *tria signa* in the Temple, which are surely those that marked the fulfillment of the *votum* and are distinguished from the traditionally honorific *statua*.

(3) But were there two? One in the cuirass and another in the toga *capite velato*? Livy's text, as it stands, with his use of the singular form

---

tibus qui Casilini in praesidio fuerint votum solvisse. Idem titulus tribus signis in aede Fortunae positis fuit subiectus. Et tria signa has been queried by editors, at times bracketed (Madvig), and at times deleted (Ulrich, Moore), although this is both unnecessary and illogical: the *statua* cannot have been the votive(s) referred to by the inscription. This example was pointed out to me by Tonio Hölscher, and I have profited greatly from reading his unpublished essay "Eine mehrfache Statuenehrung aus der Zeit der mittleren Republik?" Sehlmeyer 1999, 122–23, gives the earlier bibliography, although he fails to detect the problem addressed here; so too, Galinier 2012, 202–3; cf. Cressendi 1950, 451, who noted the unusual character of the example.

[66] One would have expected some form of *cinctus*.
[67] Koortbojian 2008.

(*statua . . . fuit*), would seem to preclude this, despite the fact that the costumes described suggest it, with their unmistakable reference to military *virtus* and religious *pietas*.⁶⁸

Which of these possibilities is convincing? Each poses problems. Three statues would be without comparanda at this early date in the Roman west; two would have been equally so, although such paired statues might well have been intended to honor Anicius for both his *pietas* and his *virtus*—the two commonly associated virtues so central to mid-Republican ideology signaled, on the one hand, by his military costume and, on the other, by the customary form for sacrifice, *capite velato*.⁶⁹ Two statues were, nevertheless, most likely. For a simultaneous claim to both *pietas* and *virtus* posed a distinct problem for the statuary repertory, and such a double valence may well have caused confusion. The only conventional means to effectively signal both *virtus* and *pietas* would have been inapposite, given the report of Anicius's honors: the image of him sacrificing as a *triumphator* did, on the Capitol, in the *toga triumphalis*. Indeed, the tradition of honorific statues had addressed itself, by and large, to one virtue at a time.⁷⁰ But as we have seen on monuments large and small, the double invocation of *pietas* and *virtus* was also visibly manifest by the depiction of the *ritus militaris*.

Comprehending the Rites and Their Forms

The *ritus militaris* must be understood as an aspect of Rome's institutionalization of its military realities. In our attempts to provide convincing accounts of this—as of all aspects of social, cultural, and political history—we are forced to ask: How tightly were the Romans bound to such institutions? How monolithic a role did the *forms* of such rituals play in Roman life? And how might we measure the communicative force and cogency of the images we have been examining? The evidence of the monuments is, from this point of view,

---

⁶⁸ So Hölscher, "Eine mehrfache Statuenehrung."
⁶⁹ Hölscher, "Eine mehrfache Statuenehrung"; for the paired virtues, cf. Simon 1985; Köves-Zulauf 2000 discusses the sources.
⁷⁰ Zanker 1979, 360.

CHAPTER 3

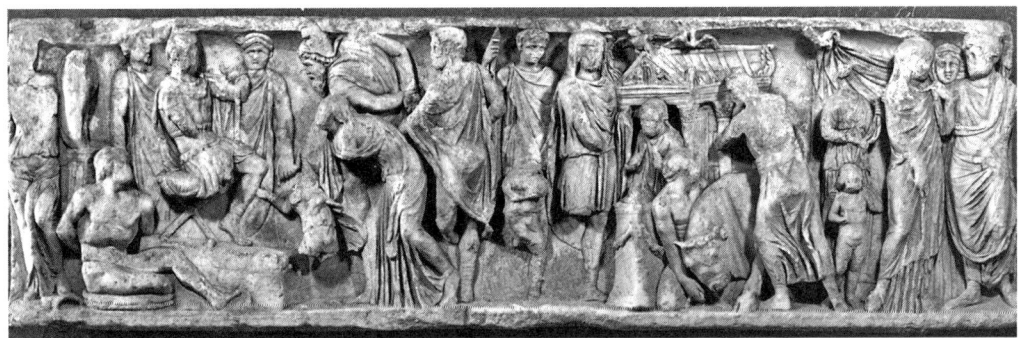

III.17 General's sarcophagus. Ca. AD 160–170. Marble. Villa Medici, Poggio a Caiano.

perplexing, for there are clear exceptions to the typology that has been traced in the preceding pages—several of which require scrutiny.

On the so-called *Feldherr-sarkophage*, despite the serial nature of their imagery, the distinction we have been tracing *seems*, at times, to have been ignored, as we see on the sarcophagus from Poggio a Caiano (figure III.17). Here a commander, *tunicatus et paludatus*, performs the *nuncupatio*—as the presence of the Temple of Jupiter Optimus Maximus suggests—yet here he sacrifices *capite velato*. The same conundrum is posed by the Eining altar (figure III.16), where Flavius sacrifices seemingly in his military capacity as *praefectus cohortis III Britannorum*, once again, *capite velato*. In the face of such imagery, we are forced to ponder, on the one hand, whether the traditional rites and their conventional forms were actually comprehended—or, at the very least, whether they were always considered binding for the efficacy of the rite—or, on the other hand, whether the precise details of ritual practice have given way on such monuments to the most conventional image of religious action.

By contrast, on the Bridgeness relief (figure III.18) from Scotland, an Antonine panel commemorating the completion of a section of Hadrian's Wall, the *lustratio* of the camp in the far reaches of Britain is performed.[71] On the right end panel, a group of soldiers from the Second Legion Augusta, identifiable by their inscribed *vexillum* held aloft, gather around an altar. The *suovetaurilia* is enacted by their togate commander, accompanied by a musician and an oddly posed figure who can only be intended to represent one of the *ministri*

---

[71] Phillips 1972–1974 points out that the architectural features are part of the slab's overall design and are not intended as a representation of the action's setting; Keppie and Arnold 1984.

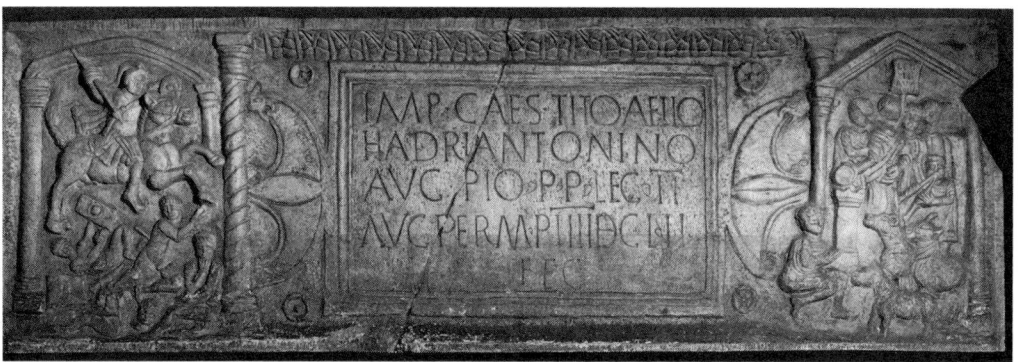

III.18 Inscribed panel from Hadrian's Wall, from Bridgeness. Antonine. Marble. Edinburgh, National Museum of Scotland.

of the rite. Strangely, in this instance, the commander appears to perform this civil act, *togatus, capite aperto*: was his bared head a misplaced reference to the commander's military status, or simply an unconventional depiction of the *suovetaurilia*, one that failed to recognize the ritual's proper form and its protocols?[72]

Again, we might consider the example of several other sarcophagi that adapted and elaborated the "generals"-type—and which display even more peculiarities. For the conventional scene of the *nuncupatio votorum* was, at times, decontextualized—as one sees on the famous Rinuccini and Balbinus sarcophagi. On the former (figure III.19), the Capitoline temple has vanished, and there is no longer anything, save for an awareness of the typology, to suggest that this sacrifice is to be associated with the *nuncupatio* and the commander's departure; this is now a symbol of *pietas*.[73] By contrast, on the so-called Balbinus casket (figure III.20), the *parapetasma* stretched across the background, the conventional symbol for an interior setting, suggests a similar divorce from the tradition. In both scenes we recognize that their imagery is no longer tied to the rite from which it so clearly derives. And on the Balbinus sarcophagus, the temporality of the *nuncupatio* has been dramatically transformed—as we see Balbinus crowned by Victoria, signaling that the scene takes place, not before his campaign (= *nuncupatio*), but *after* his victory (= thanks offering).

---

[72] Heller 2016, 369 ("probably also *capite velato*") is surely mistaken, but signals conventional expectation.

[73] Rodenwaldt 1935.

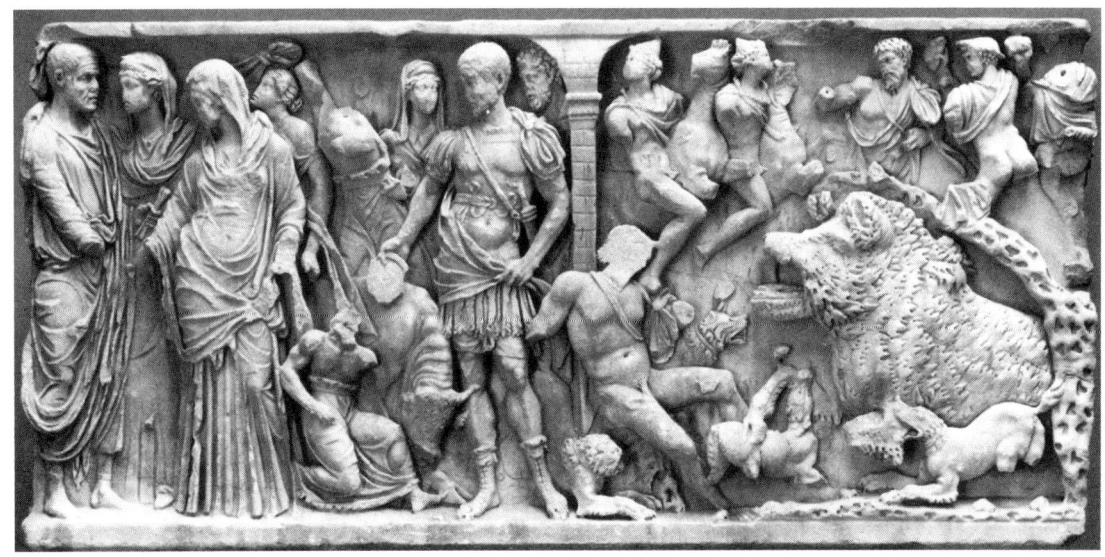

III.19 Rinuccini sarcophagus. Ca. AD 200–210. Marble. Berlin, Staatliche Museen.

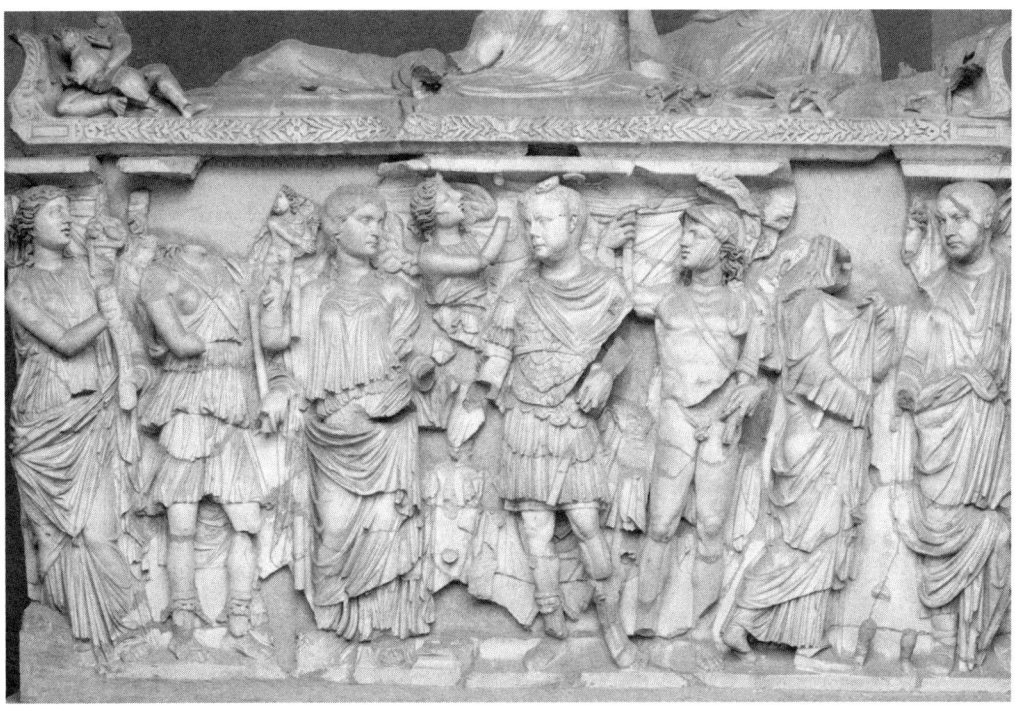

III.20 Balbinus sarcophagus. Ca. AD 238–240. Marble. Rome, Museo di Pretestato.

From these few examples, one recognizes that, on both private and public monuments, from both the late Republic and the high Empire, what has long been understood by scholars as the appropriate *ritus* for a major Roman divinity might well have been performed unconventionally (and not infrequently) by the depicted protagonist. These instances may well have been exceptional—but we have no way of knowing *how* exceptional. Or to put this another way: what has been claimed here is that a distinction between civil and military imagery was normative; but how normal? Our evidence does not provide us with an effective answer.

Lines of Inquiry

Yet other questions may be pursued. Why did such exceptions come into being? Why do such departures from what appears to have been a longstanding convention occur? These questions, prompted by this imagery, call for attention, and it is with these that we shall conclude. For simply explaining these instances as *mistakes* seems less than compelling—indeed, perhaps this would be no explanation at all. Four lines of inquiry suggest themselves, and perhaps all played a role in the history of the sacrificial *ritus* that we have been examining. A brief sketch of these approaches to the problem posed by these monuments seems in order.

First, are our attempts to systematically study institutions more than the making of modern myths? Are the aetiologies to which we grant historical status no more than hypotheses? This possibility is exemplified quite vividly by the current trend in scholarship that seeks to rebut those long-familiar claims for an overarching coherence of Rome's characteristic legal and social traditions—such as that represented, perhaps above all, by Mommsen's vision of *Staatsrecht*. Two of the examples that have been examined here might be seen to exemplify the problem. The Bridgeness *suovetaurilia* relief seems to combine the proper costume for the rite (*togatus*) with the wrong *habitus* (*capite aperto*): should this be construed as some form of ad hoc compromise between a depiction of the status of the practitioner (military) and the proper mode of the *ritus* (civil), or as merely a sign of ignorance or indifference? Was the statue of M. Anicius described by Livy an example of the same phenomenon? Or, to take the example of scene 30 of the Marcus column, with its *suovetaurilia* of merely

CHAPTER 3

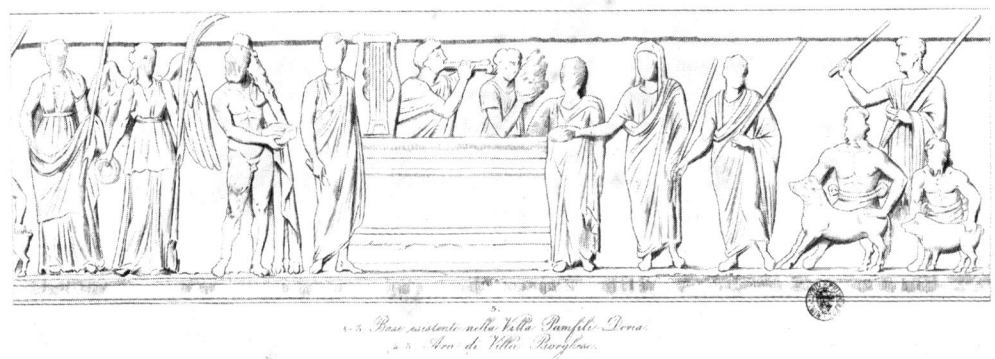

III.21 Hercules altar. Late Republican. Drawing (after *Mon. d. Inst.* VI/VII). Rome, Galleria Borghese.

two *hostiae*, we might ask whether most Romans were actually aware of which animal victims were the proper offerings to the different gods, and on which occasions. That is, we should inquire whether or not the Romans shared *our* concern with what has come to be considered an antiquarian approach to the past's institutions. To put this more pointedly, we need to ponder whether the attested sacrificial practices—such as those so carefully outlined by Cato[74]— should serve as the example for the behavior of *all* Romans, at all times.

Second, it is clear that in some instances, the *ritus* varied in the offering of cult to one and the same divinity: was the distinctiveness of each form and its context even noticed? The most striking example is provided by the cult of Hercules. A small late Republican altar (figure III.21), now in the Galleria Borghese, depicts a multi-figured scene of sacrifice, apparently dedicated to Hercules as well as other gods—clearly Victoria, and possibly Iuventas (who was known to be *Herculis uxor*), although the last identification is much debated.[75] Whoever these figures are, there can be little doubt that, given his proximity to the group surrounding the altar, the offering depicted is made, at least in part, if not primarily, to Hercules *Invictus*. Yet cult was most famously offered to this god at the Ara Maxima, *rito Graeco*, with bared

---

[74] Cato *Agr.*, with Scheid 2005, 129–60.
[75] Ritter 1995, 57–60, with bibliography. Reifferscheid's claim (1863) that the figure holding the cithara to the immediate left of the altar represents Apollo, and thus should be considered a member of the divine group, was rejected by Goethert 1931: despite his large scale, this figure cannot be Apollo, who never appears in Roman art as a *togatus*.

head—not *capite velato*, as here. The setting, its protagonists, and its *ritus* all demonstrate that this is not a representation of the famous altar in the Forum Boarium, and that this is most certainly meant to suggest another of the Hercules shrines at Rome, which were numerous. Did the Romans recognize a difference in custom and practice? Similarly perplexing—perhaps more so—is the roundel from a lost Hadrianic state monument, now on the Arch of Constantine (figure III.22), depicting sacrifice to the same god. Hercules is enthroned above the emperor, who sacrifices *capite velato* in the familiar tunic and cloak. Again, the most renowned Roman cultic context—that offered at the Ara Maxima—demanded a bared head for the *ritus Graecus*. What these two monuments—the small altar and the Hadrianic roundel—reveal is that the fame accorded the Ara Maxima rite in our sources was in all likelihood exceptional, and that the practice of cult, and its representation on the monuments, knew a variety of forms—just as did the god himself: *Invictus, Bullatus, Cubans, Custos, Fundianus, Musarum, Olivarius, Pompeianus*, etc.[76]

A third approach would focus on what could be called "artistic shorthands," a practice that might well be conceived as a consequence of a repetitive image-repertory and its serial production. That is, the monumental series to which many of the examples we have examined belong suggest that some display not so much an uninformed rendering of the rites they depict, but an approximation of their conventional form—whether deliberately or unconsciously produced. A form of pictorial *condensation* might, in some cases, have governed (and may well explain) the reduced number of participants, or the conflation of traditional elements of ritual. So, the Poggio a Caiano sarcophagus (figure III.17), from this point of view, might be considered an example of the repetition of the much more common *habitus* for sacrifice—the *ritus Romanus*. Or, on the Marcus column (figure III.11), the isolated *suovetaurilia*, which appears without its proper setting within the *castrum* that declares it to represent the *lustratio*, might be similarly understood as a reduction of the full ritual to its most recognizable element. The coins of Septimius Severus, issued in celebration of the *Ludi Saeculares* of AD 204 (figure III.23), pose the same problem. In contrast to the precedent of the Flavian issues marking the ceremonies for the year 88 by the Greek rite (figure III.3), those of Septimius

---

[76] All of these, and others, are noted by entries in *LTUR* III (1996).

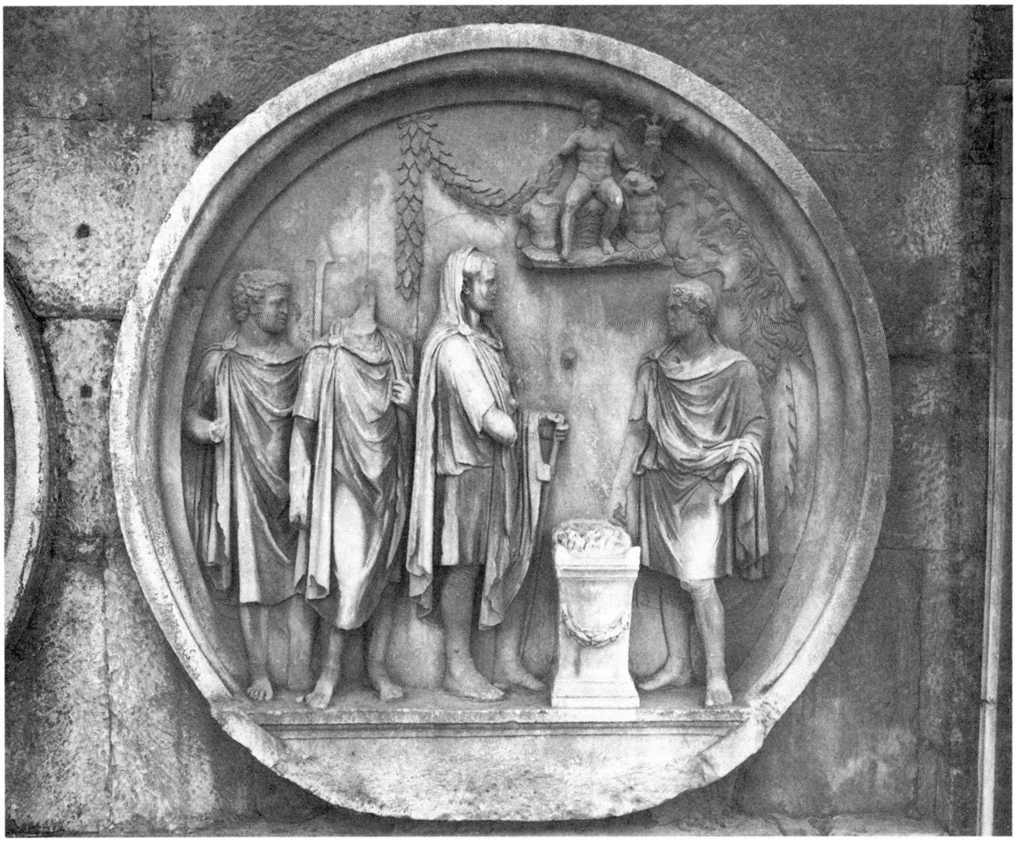

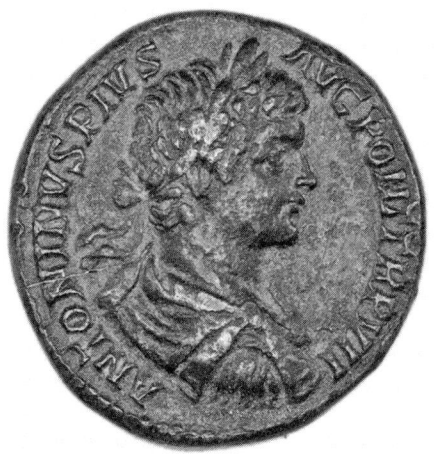

III.22 Sacrifice to Hercules. Hadrianic. Marble roundel on the Arch of Constantine, Rome.

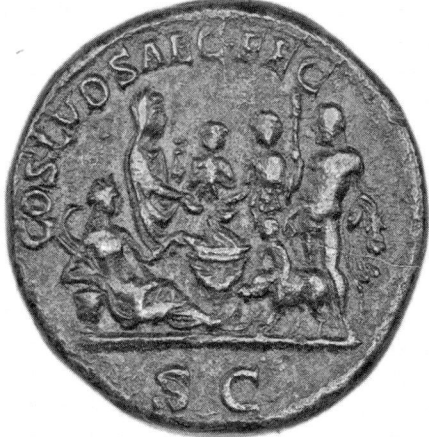

III.23 Septimius Severus, *sestertius* for *Ludi Saeculares*, AD 204. *RIC* IV.1, Rome, no. 761.

depict the sacrifices to the *Moirai* and to Terra Mater by the togate emperor, making his offering *capite velato*.⁷⁷

Lastly, to adopt a fourth point of view, we might ask: do institutions have their own "life-cycles"? Social and religious rituals had been carefully codified during the late Republic by scholarly treatises—the ancient sources report so many of these—yet this phenomenon has left comparably little trace in texts of imperial date. Did the very regularity of custom and ritual inure practitioners to their full meanings?⁷⁸ A suggestive example is provided by a contrast. On another of the Hadrianic roundels from the Arch of Constantine (figure III.24), this time the sacrifice to Diana on the hunt, the emperor pours his libation, now with his head properly veiled for the *ritus Romanus*. Yet some two hundred years later, at Piazza Armerina (figure III.25), on the Small Hunt mosaic, we encounter the same iconography, and another sacrifice to Diana in the forest. On the mosaic, the *dominus*, similarly clad in tunic and cloak, makes the same libation at the rustic altar below the goddess of the hunt's statue—but now, *capite aperto*, despite the fact that the ritual is neither Greek *nor* military. Had the proper form of the religious practice seen its day?

Much has been written about the third-century abandonment of mythological themes and their allegorical significances (particularly in the funerary realm) and the turn toward more rational modes of expression and their corresponding imagery—what in German has been called *Entmythologisierung*.⁷⁹ Even a cursory reading of Macrobius might well suggest that a parallel abandonment of traditional ritual practice and its meanings had occurred—what one might deem an *Entritualisierung*. For there is no doubt that the antiquarian researches of the early fifth century demonstrate an attempt to reconstruct

---

⁷⁷ Cf. Scheid 1998a, 31: "La representation des princes sacrifiant tête voilée renvoie à l'acte sacrificial lui-même plutôt qu'au rite grec: il s'agit du mode sacrificial le plus courant"; cf. Rowan 2012, 59–60. Given its lack of specificity about the recipient of the offering, the Augustan aureus from Spain—on whose reverse Augustus (?) appears *capite velato* at an altar, flanked by a *praeco*, above the legend LUDI SAECUL(ares)—does not pose the same problem (BMC I, no. 431, and pl. 10.4 = *RIC* I², no. 138, and pl. 3 = Simon 1993, 85, no. 40, and Taf. 3, Abb. 2).

⁷⁸ Cf., recently, Ando 2011b, 55, on rituals "slipping from intelligibility" in the second century AD.

⁷⁹ Survey of attitudes in Koortbojian 1995, 138–41; cogent discussion by Zanker in Zanker and Ewald 2012, 254–60; cf. Koortbojian 2015.

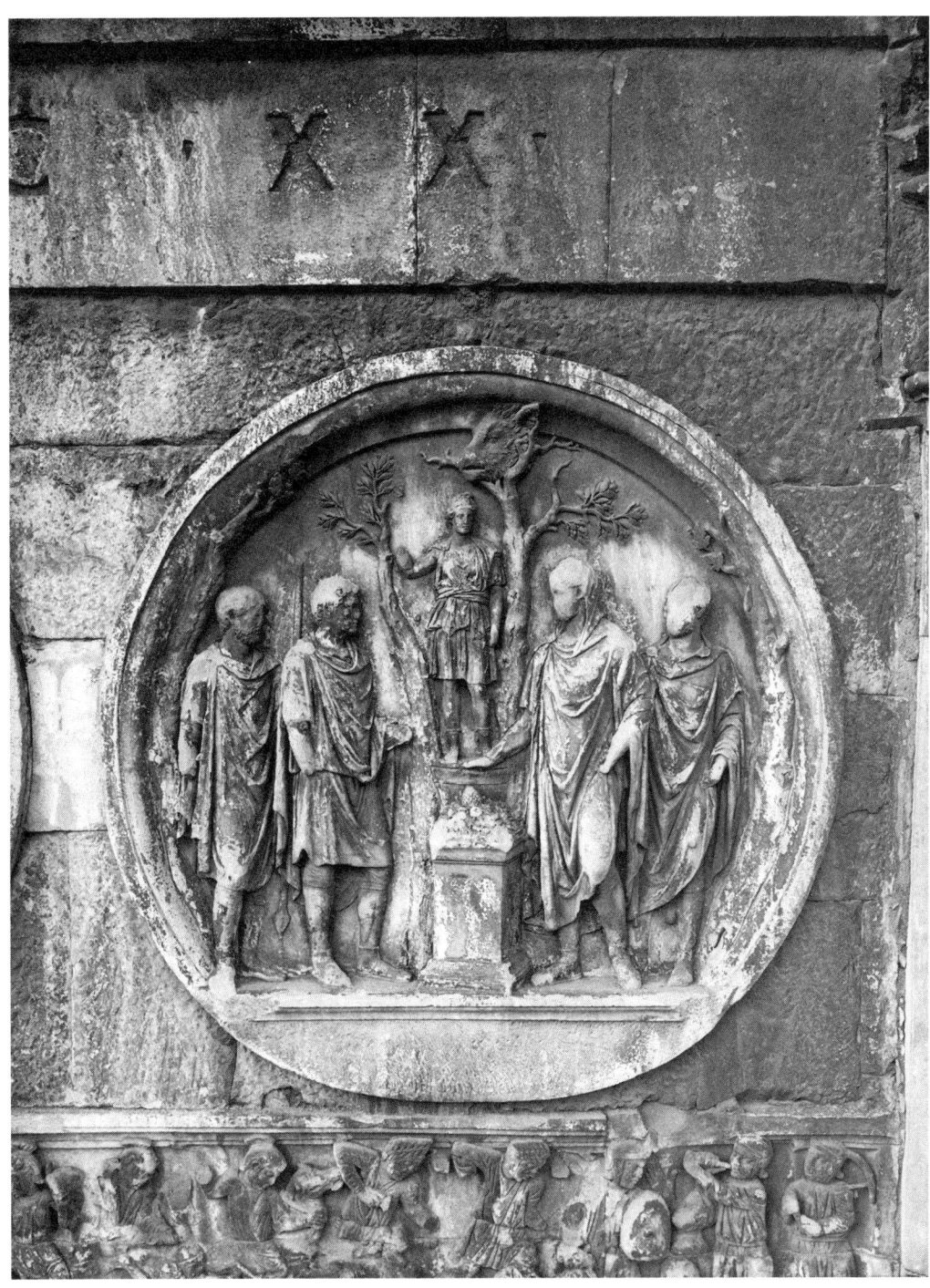
III.24 Sacrifice to Diana. Hadrianic. Marble roundel on the Arch of Constantine, Rome.

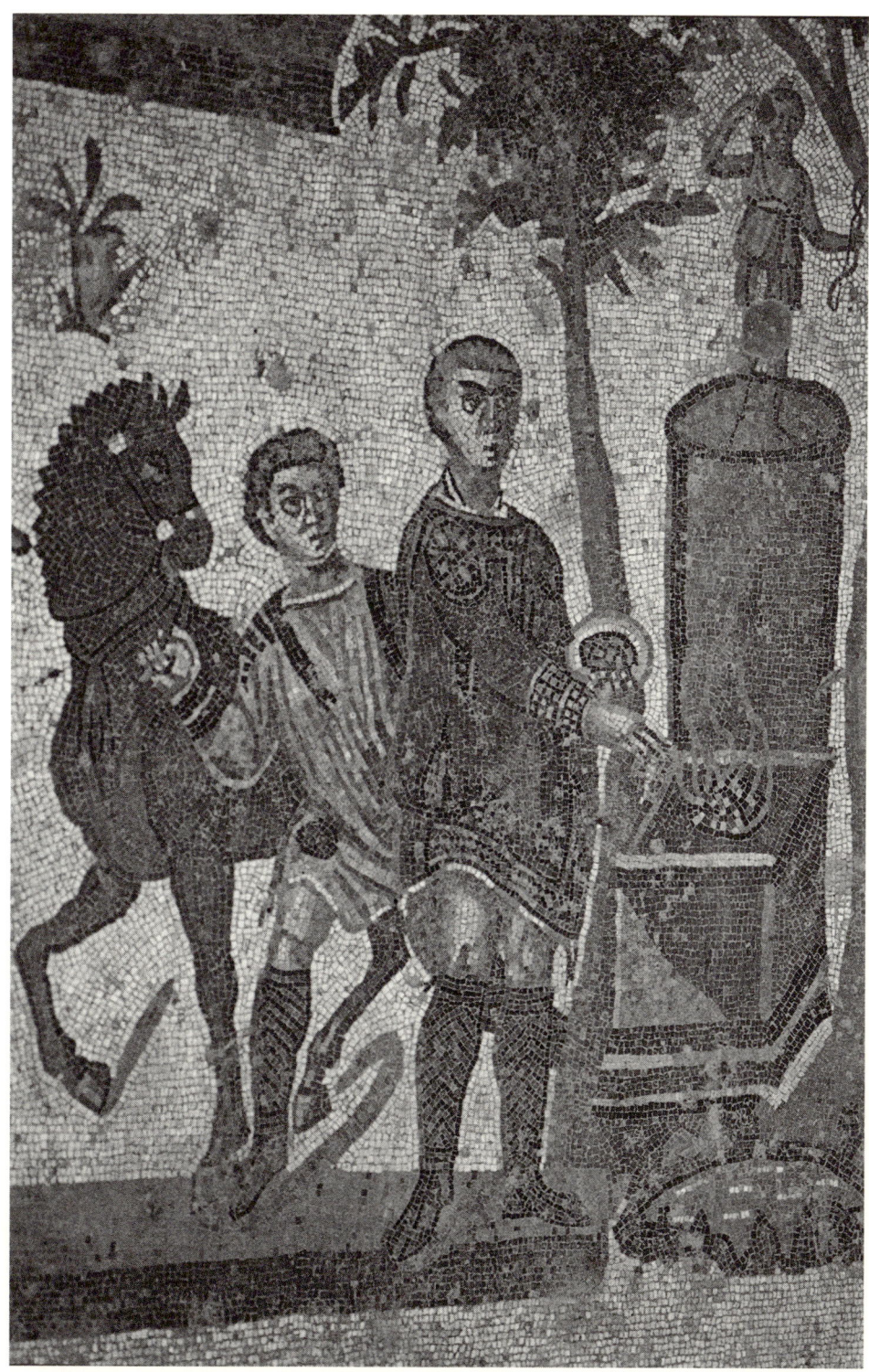
III.25 Detail: Small Hunt mosaic, Piazza Armerina.

"lost" institutions and rituals. The normative value of even such essential social acts as sacrifice became routinized with repeated use, and the commonplace fact of their ubiquity may well have led to a diminution—indeed, the extinction—of the profound relation to reality that such scenes, and the practices they depicted, were intended to record. It is demonstrable that, for Macrobius and his circle, what had once been practices seemingly vital to social and religious life had long since become a mystery. And it is, perhaps, this sort of social "forgetting" that explains the peculiar history displayed for us on the monuments of so central a practice as the sacrificial *ritus*.

4

Constantine's Arch and His Military Image at Rome

The many questions that surround the Arch of Constantine in Rome (figure IV.1) have long been debated.[1] What follows will have little to say about the notorious crux, *instinctu divinitatis*,[2] the problem of the emperor's Christianity,[3] the question of the emperor's relation to *Sol Invictus*,[4] or the programmatic use of its *spolia* reliefs.[5] Rather, the emphasis will be threefold. First, this chapter will focus on the roles of the *SPQR* and the emperor in the arch's design. Although the commission of the arch was surely an act of the senate—notwithstanding the fact that by the early fourth century AD the formula was traditional and regularly invoked despite political realities—what possible role did Constantine, or his conception of his role in the *urbs*, play in the arch's imagery? For it is hardly conceivable that the senate's vision of Constantine's rule was incompatible with his own. Second, what follows will examine the meaning of the claim *triumphis insignem*—that is, that an arch, still customarily associated with triumph by the fourth century, was in this instance bestowed for a new purpose with a unique rationale, in a particular historical context, despite a lack of any persuasive evidence that an official triumph was actually

---

[1] Basic discussion and bibliography in Capodiferro in *LTUR* I:86–91 (1993); succinct overview in Liverani 2005.
[2] Hall 1998; Lenski 2008.
[3] Surveys by H. Drake, M. Edwards, and A. D. Lee in Lenski 2006b.
[4] Lenski 2012a; Bardill 2012, chaps. 5 and 6.
[5] Faust 2011; Liverani 2011; Prückner 2008; Elsner 2006; Liverani 2004.

CHAPTER 4

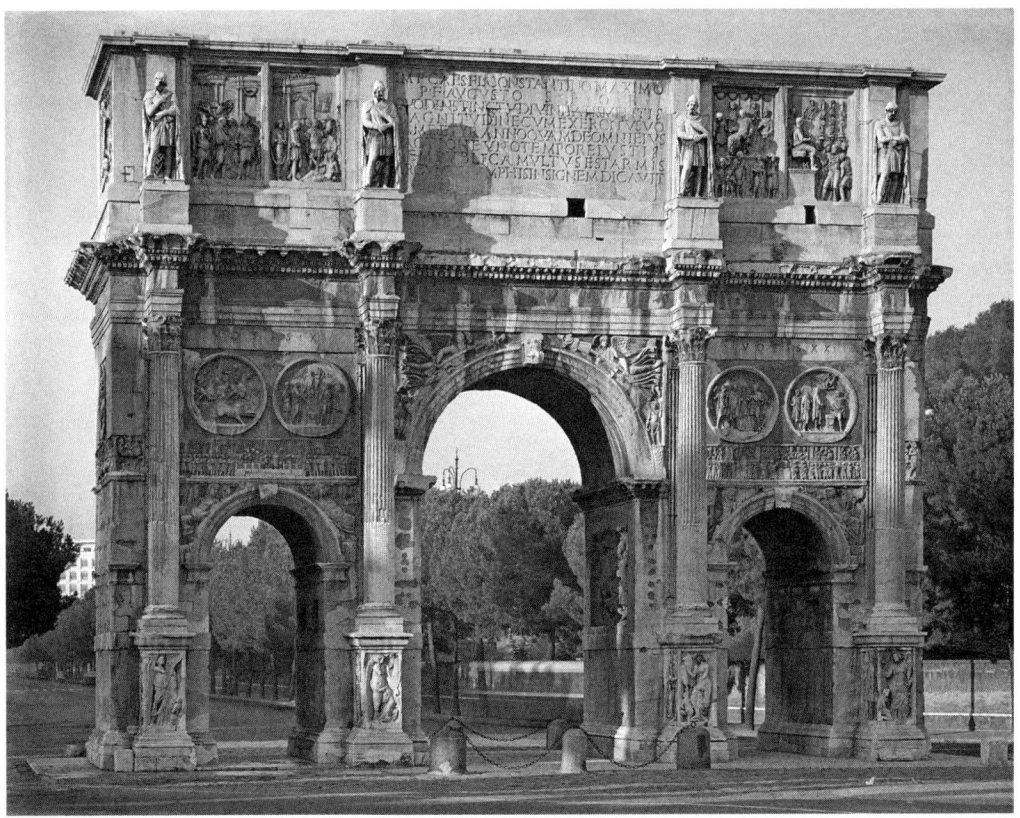

IV.1 Arch of Constantine, AD 315. Rome. North face.

celebrated. And finally, this chapter will elucidate the arch's evocation of the emperor's role, both at home and abroad, as both *civilis princeps* and *imperator exercitus*. For the Constantinian frieze's representations of the latter role, *at Rome* (figure IV.2; cf. IV.15), was central to the senate's message—beyond that proclaimed by the arch's monumental inscription—as it conveyed an unusually martial image set before the citizenry.[6] Before his entry on 29 October 312, following his victory at the Milvian Bridge, Constantine had never set foot in Rome and would do so only twice thereafter.[7] Yet an important aspect of the arch's message, as we shall see, was that he would not hesitate, once again, to "cross the *pomerium*"—in arms—should his authority to rule be threatened.

---

[6] Cf., similarly, Giuliani 2000, 271–72.
[7] *Contra* Van Dam 2018.

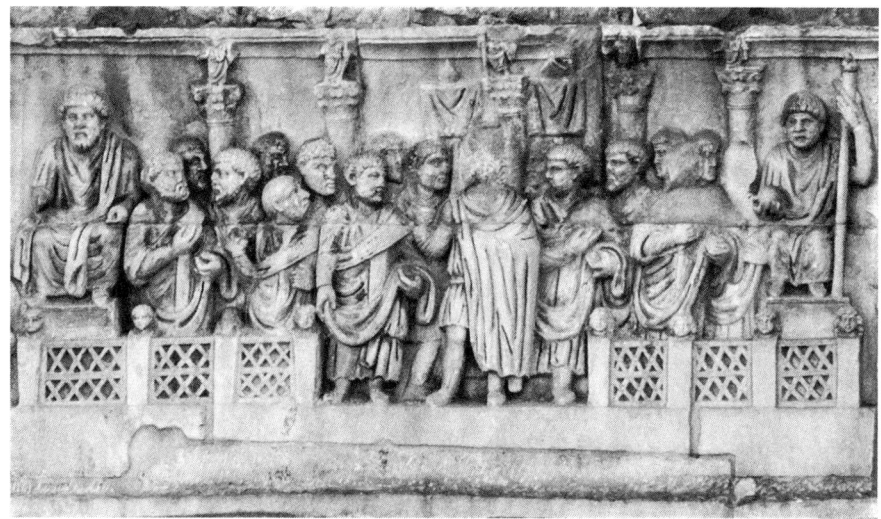

IV.2 Detail: Arch of Constantine, Rome. *Adlocutio* scene.

The Choice of a Monument and Its Design

Whose, and what, intentions are to be gleaned from the arch's monumental inscription and its sculpted imagery? Its prominent text is specific—*SPQR* . . . *dicavit*—and despite the fact that some still regard the emperor himself as the agent of its design and its message, the view that this was a senatorial monument has become, by and large, the *communis opinio*.[8] But, if true, in what sense did the senate exercise its prerogative? What latitude did the senators have? And to what extent should we regard its patronage as having been effected freely, and to what extent in consultation with—or indeed, in anxiety about—the views of Constantine himself?[9] A fair assessment of the significance

---

[8] Giuliani 2000, 273–74, presents a summary and emphasizes Constantine's probable role in certain decisions (284); Popkin 2016, 68 and n. 89, cites those who regard Constantine as responsible and those who see senatorial patronage (69, n. 90). Representative is Prückner 2008, 59 ("Wir können daher vom Bogen so sprechen, als habe ihn Konstantin selber entworfen") and 60 ("Was wollte er Rom und der Welt mit ihnen sagen?"); cf. Lenski 2008, 218–19, on the roles of emperor and senate, and Wilson Jones 2000, 72 ("The Senate may have built the arch, but it did as the emperor bid"); cf. Prusac 2012, 127 *et passim*, for Constantine's "direct involvement."

[9] The case for the senate's role is best made by Lenski 2012a; symptomatic are the comments of Elsner 2000, 171, with n. 28, and 2006, 256 ("obvious . . . that the Senate would not have built . . . an arch that he positively disapproved of"), yet hardly probative.

CHAPTER 4

of the emperor's image, and his *military* image in particular, depends on an appraisal of his own role in that representation.

But first, why an arch? Only two established monumental types of sufficient grandeur availed themselves—*columna* and *arcus*. If the reuse of building materials that is now evident on Constantine's monument should suggest shortages of raw material of marble newly imported, the mammoth undertaking of a new column would seemingly preclude its choice. The monumental arch had other advantages. By the dawn of the fourth century, it was a long-established form, and one whose fundamental architectural character was well known across the Empire; it was among those typical structures that are understood to have been commissioned at Rome by emperors who had not set foot within the *pomerium*.[10]

Constantine's arch had a familiar model for both its architectural form and its dimensions, and its reworking of the Severan example in the forum was fundamentally conservative as a matter of architectural practice, a practice with precedent.[11] The old argument, recently revived, that the arch was merely the remaking of a similar earlier structure remains unpersuasive; it appears much more likely that the architectural fabric, oddly pieced, was assembled from the *spolia* of earlier monuments and other materials ready to hand—a not uncommon practice; even the use of *spolia* for the arch's decoration was hardly an innovation, as the remnants of the Arcus Novus and the Arco di Portogallo attest.[12] Nevertheless, as has long been recognized, Constantine's arch survives as a most singular monument, although one whose contemporary message remains to be fully unraveled.

Despite its adherence to a long-established typology, it is hard to imagine the senate's initiative without some measure of acquiescence by the emperor, for certain aspects of the arch's form and decoration might well have

---

[10] Humphries 2003 and 2015 for the bridge of Gratian and the arch of Gratian, Valentinian and Theodosius by the Pons Aelius, as well as the porticus nearby.

[11] Reuse: Pensabene 2006. Relation to Severan arch: Wilson Jones 2000 gives comparative dimensions and analysis; cf. De Maria 1988, 203–11. The unpublished Maxentian inscription discovered by A. La Regina atop the arch would suggest as much: see Marlowe 2010, 204, n. 20. Precedent: Trajan's Benevento arch based on Titus's: Wilson Jones 2000, 66–67, and bibliography in n. 72.

[12] Old argument: Frothingham 1912; its revival: Melucco Vaccaro 2001 and Conforto 2001. Earlier use of *spolia* on arches: Laubscher 1976; Mayer 2002, 197–99.

required it.[13] Three have been the subject of query. First, the reuse of *spolia*: whether or not the political significance influentially suggested by L'Orange was intended, should one imagine that the senate proceeded with its notable employ of secondhand architectural components and preexisting sculpture—in contrast to newly carved reliefs—without authorization of some kind?[14] Second, the possible absence of the apparently traditional *quadriga* atop the arch: would the emperor have countenanced such a conventional monument in his honor that dispensed with what was perhaps its most prominent sculptural element?[15] And third, the *explicit* reference to civil war in the inscription: is this conceivable, given the long-standing Roman tradition that forbade triumphal honors in such circumstances and forced earlier monuments—notably Augustus's Naulochos and Actium monuments—to dissemble their commemorative function?[16]

An assumption of a dialogue between senate and emperor concerning the broader political motivation for Constantine's arch and its imagery has become a commonplace of interpretations. Yet the central issue is arrogating their relative roles and demonstrating if and how they are documented by our sources, rather than merely imagined by our hypotheses.[17] Moreover, as a historical problem, such a possible dialogue was fundamentally dependent on the manner and frequency of communication in the later Roman world between Rome and the new centers of empire. In those instances in which correspondence can be dated, transmission times could vary—due to distance, weather, mode of transport, or

---

[13] *Contra* Salzman 2016, 21–22, who attempts, without sufficient or persuasive arguments, to limit Constantine's role ("not personally engaged with its planning and execution").

[14] L'Orange and von Gerkan 193; cf. Pensabene 2006, 140. Similarly, architectural *spolia* were employed at Old Saint Peter's (Brenk 1987). These may well have included monuments damaged by the fires of AD 283 and 307 reported in the Calendar of 354 (Machado 2006, 161).

[15] Giuliani 2000, 284; cf. Magi 1956–1957, who argued for such a statue. Note that neither the depiction of the arch of Septimius nor that of Tiberius shown on the Constantinian frieze includes its presumed attic statuary.

[16] Civil war triumph: Lange 2012, 43 ("improbable . . . without the approval of Constantine"), and 2016 sketch the tradition; discussion in Mayer 2006, 142–43, 149, Wienand 2015b, and Popkin 2016, 69–70 and notes. The "rule" against a triumph in civil war: Val. Max. 2.8, with Lundgreen 2014 and Havener 2014.

[17] Cooperation: Bravi 2012, 458 ("Probabilmente questi uomini *religiosissimi* [Volusianus, Rufinus, et al.] furono i principale ideatori del programma figurative dell'Arco"). Post-Constantinian relations between emperor and senate: Humphries 2003.

CHAPTER 4

a sense of bureaucratic urgency; letters from any of the capitals could take weeks or months or, in the rare case, years, to reach their destination.[18]

Thus, different sorts of arguments avail themselves concerning the emperor's involvement, not only for a major monument like an arch but for other architectural and artistic enterprises—some of which may be briefly surveyed.

In the case of public building, several well-known fourth-century examples of the emperor's role are both relevant and revealing. First, Eusebius, quoting Constantine's letter of AD 326 to Macarius on the building of the Church at the Holy Sepulchre, suggests the limits of the emperor's interests:

> It is thus for your own Good Sense to make such order and provision of what is needed that not only a basilica superior to those in all other places, but the other arrangements also, may be such that all the excellences of every city are surpassed by this foundation. As to the building and decoration of the walls, be advised that our friend Dracillianus, who exercises his office among the *praefecti illustrissimi*, and he who is governor of the province, have been entrusted by us with its care. For my Religious Care has ordered that craftsmen and labourers and everything they may learn from your Good Sense to be needed for the building work should forthwith be supplied by their provision. As to the columns or marble, you should after a survey yourself write promptly to us about what you may consider to be of most value and use, so that whatever quantity and kind of materials we may learn from your letter to be needful may be competently supplied from all sources. It is right that the world's most miraculous place should be worthily embellished. As to the vault of the basilica, whether you decide that it be coffered or in another style of construction I would wish to learn from you. If it were to be coffered, it might also be decorated with gold. In short, in order that your Holiness may make known with all speed to the aforementioned magistrates how many labourers and craftsmen and what other expenditures are required,

---

[18] Jones 1986, I:401–3; Corcoran 2000, 157–58, and Eck 1996, with examples, discussion, and bibliography; cf., more broadly, Millar 1992, 213–27; Moatti 2007.

take care to refer immediately also to me not only the matters of the marble and pillars, but also the lacunary panels, should you judge that best.[19]

Nearly sixty years later, Symmachus, in his capacity as *praefectus urbi*, wrote to the Emperor Valentinian II (AD 384) concerning the scandalous failure of a new bridge over the Tiber before it was completed, and he also noted the excessive costs for the construction of a new, unnamed basilica—projects begun under Valentinian's predecessor, Gratian. Both debacles were due to a feud between the two senators in charge: Cyriades, *vir clarissimus, comes et mechanicae professor*, who had been succeeded in the responsibility by Auxentius, also *vir clarissimus*. From Symmachus's two surviving letters devoted to the two affairs it is clear that the emperor was primarily concerned that an investigation should be conducted into the question of faulty engineering, but that there should also be an accounting of the funds spent on both projects and where to lay the blame for failure and mismanagement. Two years later, at the beginning of 387, the matters were still not settled, as Symmachus's letter to Flavius Eusignius, the praetorian prefect, reveals.[20]

Successive emperors continued to engage with the problems surrounding the basilica. In AD 386, Theodosius, writing to Sallust, then *praefectus urbi*, on behalf of Valentinian II and Arcadius, remarks that the prefect had "made known to our Serenity's ears by carefulness of suitable language the entire site and aspect of the place, for it has been proper that we, better informed, order what must be ordered." And beyond the expected scrupulousness over expenditures, a major question concerned the reorientation of the new basilica, built on the site of a small and east-facing (probably hall-style) church established a generation earlier under Constantine, and its relationship to the Via Ostiense and the river. An old roadway that ran behind the Constantinian church and along the river was restored, and a new road was to be built that would lead

---

[19] *VC* 3.31.2–32.2, trans. Cameron and Hall 2010; noted by Johnson 2006, 293–94; trenchant interpretation in Liverani 2003a, 205–6; broader context and other testimonia in Lenski 2016, ch. 9, esp. 181 and no. 8.

[20] Symmachus *Rel.* 25 and 26 (AD 384); *Ep.* IV, 70 (AD 387). Basilica: identified as S. Paolo fuori le mura by Chastagnol 1966, followed by the commentary of Marcone 1987, and as the Basilica Piniana by Liverani 2003b.

worshipers directly to the worksite. And the emperor notes that the ground should be level,

> lest any unevenness may obscure the splendor of the more enlarged edifice, so that in every facade there is the finest beauty, which the design shows ought to be observed immediately in the front [elevation] of great buildings.[21]

The surviving documents for all three of these examples demonstrate that the initiative for these building projects, and most of the details concerning their planning, construction, and elaboration, came, not from the emperors, but from local officials who sought the rulers' consent and, above all, their financial support.[22] In each instance, the emperor's basic concern was threefold: that he should be apprised of the costs that would be paid from his private purse; that these new structures be testaments to his patronage; and that they should be bigger and more beautiful than other buildings of their type—a vision made plain in the same letter to Sallust:

> To us [sc. Valentinian, Theodosius, and Arcadius], upon consideration of the veneration already sacred from long ago, desiring to adorn [*ornare*] the Basilica of Paul the Apostle for the sake of sanctity of religion, to enlarge (its plan) [*amplificare*] so as to serve a greater number of the faithful, (and) to raise it (i.e., the building) to a greater height [*attollere*] on account of a zeal for devotion.[23]

---

[21] *CSEL* 35 = Günther 1895, I:46–47, no. 3; translated from Coleman-Norton 1966, II, no. 211 (adapted); discussion in Chastagnol 1960, 349–53. For the Constantinian-era structure, the *iter vetus*, and the change in orientation for the *Basilica Nova*, I follow Liverani 1989; see further Liverani 2003a, 207–8, and Brandenburg 2005–2006. Theodosian basilica: Brandenburg 2005, 114–30.

[22] Cf. Lenski 2016, 193 ("projects whose original conception is reported to have come from someone other than the emperor himself"); similarly, Liverani 2003a.

[23] As cited in n. 21 above. I follow Liverani 2003a, 208, who suggests that *attollere* should signify the physical height of the structure; cf. Brandenburg 2005–2006, 250, n. 50. If the Constantinian basilica had been a simple hall church, small in scale (so Brandenburg 2005, 103), it would be understandable that the nave of the new five-aisled basilica—larger than old Saint Peter's—would have stood dramatically taller; this would seem to be the significance of the emperor's comment

By and large, one sees a pattern, one owed, in large measure, to the conservative nature of artistic and architectural production: in most instances, new monuments conformed to type—this was surely the case with bridges and basilicae—and thus little consultation on the specifics of *form* was relevant. What was required was discussion (as we have seen) of scale, the nature of materials, and a desire that, by these means, the result would be a *decor* that would be regarded as *summus*.[24]

The same pattern held for the commission of honorific statuary, which was also, at times, a gift to the emperor from the senate, at times a gift from the emperor to the senators. For example, in AD 384 Symmachus wrote to Theodosius and Arcadius concerning a proposed statue for Theodosius's father:

> Because any return, compared with your benefactions, can be only slender, this noble order of senators has discovered a pleasant way of making a return to prove its gratitude. It has solemnly honored with equestrian statues, and has thus enrolled among ancient names, the author of your [Theodosius's] family and line who was formerly general in Africa and in Britain.[25]

The *prisca nomina* were those to be read on the *tituli* of all such statues, publicly displayed as civic honors. Equestrian monuments were perhaps the most exalted of the customary forms: as they were thoroughly conventional, Symmachus had no need to provide a description nor any reason to announce their site, as such statues were usually set up in *celeberrimi loci*.

There are testimonia to similar instances of such joint accountability for a variety of monumental types. In the Constantinian period, statues were set up by the senate that proudly displayed their imperial letters of sanction.[26] Other sculptural forms might also be the subject of imperial consultation by correspondence. So Ambrose, in a letter to Theodosius, had informed the

---

siquidem in omni moenium facie decor summus est, quem servari oportere prima statim fronte magnarum aedificationum demonstrat intentio.

[24] Cf. in general the comments of Zanker 2010.
[25] Symmachus *Rel.* 9.4, trans. Barrow 1973.
[26] Weisweiler 2012a and 2012b; Chenault 2012.

emperor after the death of Valentinian II (AD 392) of his discovery of "a beautiful porphyry sarcophagus" (*labrum*) that would be *aptissimum* for the purpose of holding the late ruler's remains, "since Maximianus, the colleague of Diocletian, was so buried."[27] And it is the imperial portrait that most assuredly exemplifies the emperors' collaboration, despite the paucity of contemporary documentation. For the initial rendering of an emperor's features was surely made from life and designed—if only initially—in the subject's presence. Such renditions established the types that were to be reproduced, and our late antique sources suggest that *imagines* were circulated as part of a ceremony that acknowledged the right to rule; Lactantius reports that Constantine's "laureled" portrait was sent to Galerius, and according to Zosimus it was exhibited in Rome in 306. These images were replicated, for better or for worse, depending on the skill of the sculptor and, at times, the nature of his material and the character of his medium.[28] And lastly, there is the coinage. It is long believed that, throughout Rome's history, not only was numismatic imagery centrally controlled, but it reflected a deliberate set of choices sanctioned by the emperor's authority. Yet with the multiplication of mints—at court centers at great distances from one another—it is not at all clear that detailed models were widely circulated; instead, it may have been the case that "local artists had to content themselves with slight indications of the characteristics of the emperor to be depicted, such as 'young,' 'clean-shaven,' 'aquiline nose.'" Indeed, it has been suggested that coins marked with the letters S M (*Sacra Moneta*) were an affirmation of imperial presence and "of the emperor personally employing the services of the mint thus named."[29] The effectiveness of an image's political

---

[27] McLynn 1994, 337–38; Mayer 2002, 195.

[28] Lact. *De Mort. Pers.* 25; Zosimus 2.9.2. The lineaments of the imperial portrait system hardly need rehearsing; summaries in Pfanner 1989, Smith 1997, esp. 176–79, and Fejfer 2008, 404–29. Late antique sources on the circulation of *imagines*: Lact. *De mort. Pers.* 25, Constantine Porphyrogenius's *De Caeremoniis* (tenth-century), P. Cairo Cat. II, n. 67183, with Bruun 1976a. By analogy, the eighteenth and nineteenth centuries provide extensive evidence for the production of portraits "from life," despite a sculptor's relatively limited access to his subject (sometimes none at all), especially in the case of those of the highest rank: Baker 2014, 183–93.

[29] Quotation: Bruun 1976a, 129; cf. Bruun 1976b, 10, for "slightly adjusted portraits of Licinius, i.e., there is no genuine Constantinian portrait that could have been employed as a model at that mint [Thessalonike] at that time"; similarly, Giudetti 2013, 185. Absence of widely dissemi-

message, as both the coinage and the sculpted portraits reveal, was not wholly dependent on the fidelity of a likeness taken from life.

❧

What do the sources tell us about an emperor's interest in the monuments—those set up in his name? It is a spare report, to be sure, but nonetheless a coherent one. Several things stand out.

First, it is clear from even these few texts that the emperor desired his representation to respond effectively to his political concerns, whether these were expressed by monuments initiated by his subjects or by himself. There is a vivid sense that a ruler wished that such acts of *publica magnificentia et munificentia* should reflect well on him and should redound to his credit. Put simply, it was no doubt every ruler's desire that works associated with the imperial name and paid for from the imperial purse should be bigger, finer, more elaborate, and built of the most obviously costly materials—that they should be, in every sense, impressive. And as we have seen, it was no small matter that the emperor felt assured that he got his money's worth.

Second, concerning the senate's initiatives at Rome, it is also clear that that body continued to play a role and to exert its authority. But this was an authority that Constantine appears to have regarded as one newly reinstated: he claimed to have restored not only the senate but the people and the city itself to its "original liberty and nobility," and this is reflected in the rededication of so many of Maxentius's architectural undertakings in the name of the new emperor.[30]

Lastly, it is evident that the same latitude—to propose major projects to the emperor and to dedicate independent efforts in his name—was extended to cities and their magistrates across the Empire. This was the complex reality of political honors throughout the fourth century, and it applied to the production of the emperor's image just as it did to those monuments that embroidered

---

nated detailed models for the coin portaits: cf. figures IV.17–21, 23–25. *Sacra Moneta*: Sutherland in *RIC* VI, 43 and 90–92, followed by Bruun 1976b, 17.

[30] "Original liberty and nobility": Rufinus *HE* 9.9.11; cf. *Pan. Lat.* XII (9), 20. Maxentian buildings: Cullhead 1994, 49–60.

CHAPTER 4

and enhanced it. Thus, the emperor's representation, in all its senses, must be measured—and the degree to which that can be described compellingly as a self-representation must be assessed—in much the same fashion; Constantine's military image was no different, as we shall see.

Arcum triumphis insignem dicavit

Did Constantine triumph in AD 312? Was his Roman arch its memorial? Debate continues. Yet the circumstance of his Roman *introitus* or *ingressus* (to employ the least prejudicial terms), together with several aspects of the arch's imagery, suggest that, despite the reference to *triumphi* in the inscription, the traditional rite, in both its political ceremonies and its religious rituals, was unlikely to have been celebrated.[31] For instance, as has long been noted, since Constantine entered the city the day following his victory, there was no time for the elaborate preparations that were customary for the celebration of a triumph, and given the political situation of the preceding year, there is no reason to believe that Constantine's march on Rome signaled that such a celebration was imminent. This was, after all, civil war, and just as the advances of Caesar and Octavian had been the cause of great alarm in the capital at the close of the Republic, and similarly that of Septimius in 193, so too, that of Constantine. The victor of 312 may well have been greeted with enthusiasm by the *populus Romanus*, but our evidence suggests that it was hardly the hope of many in the senate. Public celebration was surely impromptu.[32]

The depiction on the arch of Constantine's entry (figure IV.3) shows him, contrary to Roman triumphal tradition, sitting in a *carucca* rather than stand-

---

[31] Summaries of the debate, its bibliography, and the various interpretations of the relationship between *triumphus* and *adventus* in Fraschetti 1999, Curran 2000, Giuliani 2000, Lange 2012, and Wienand 2015b (although his claim [177] that Constantine's entry was "indisputably regarded by contemporaries as a genuine triumph" seems overconfident). Historical context: Lenski 2006a. Triumphal tradition and its imperial transformations: Liverani 2017.

[32] No time for preparations for the *pompa*: Giuliani 2000, 278, following Kuhoff 1991, 165; Stephenson 2009, 147; Lange 2012, 42. This assumption is reinforced by the rumors that immediately circulated about whether or not Maxentius was dead: *Pan. Lat.* 12 (9), 17, 3, and Zosimus 2.17. Prior marches on Rome: Birley 1988, 155–57, with reference to sources; Curran 2000, 70, followed by Bodnaruk 2015, 152.

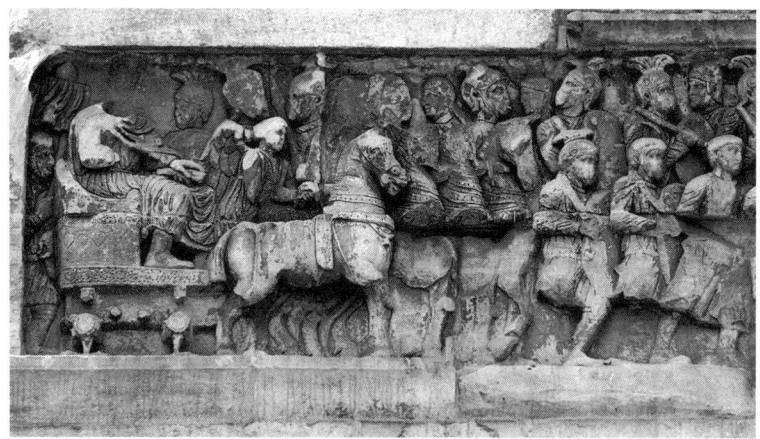

IV.3 Detail: Arch of Constantine, Rome. *Adventus* scene.

ing in a *quadriga*, at the end of a parade that displays none of those customary features of the long-established ritual, and most troublingly, it celebrates, explicitly, a victory over Roman troops.³³ Many have declared the scene an *adventus*³⁴; however, this does little to resolve what is perhaps the most fundamental question about the represented event. Whether *triumphus* or *adventus*, what is *not* shown is that aspect common to both rituals, and most significant for the triumph—sacrifice. For not only was it an essential feature of the triumph that the emperor ascended the Capitoline and made his offering in the Temple of Jupiter Optimus Maximus, but this was so of his arrival anywhere—as is made abundantly clear, for example, on the Column of Trajan (see figures III.4, 5, and 6). Even the arrivals of the proconsuls and provincial governors were celebrated with offerings, as both our sources and other state monuments attest. Despite the presence on the arch's attic of a reused

---

³³ Triumphal ritual's traditional aspects: discussion and critique in Beard 2007. *Carucca*: Lenski 2012a, 183–84; more thoroughly in Goddard 2011, although since the early third century the *adventus* was most commonly shown as taking place on horseback (Klose 2015, 103–4). No triumphs for civil war: see n. 16 above.

³⁴ *Adventus*: Calendar of AD 354 (*Fasti Furii Filocali*) = *Inscr. Ital.* XIII.2, 257, and 527 for 29 October (*adventus divi*); discussion in Lehnen 1997, 183–87; Curran 2000, 71; Humphries 2009; Faust 2011; Lenski 2012a; Popkin 2016. Conflation of triumph and *adventus*: cf. Wienand 2015b, 175, citing Rüpke 1990, 235 ("der Kaiser...der jeden Auftritt zum Triumph Machen kann"); Haake 2016, 273–74 ("triumphalen adventus"), following Lehnen 1997.

Aurelian scene of that emperor's *lustratio* while far from Rome on campaign (as the soldiers in uniform make plain), the absence of any reference to Constantine's Capitoline sacrifice on the contemporary frieze, or elsewhere on the arch, is striking.[35]

The arch's imagery, in these various respects, hardly conforms to that of a traditional triumph; the monument's inscription is equally unconventional, in both its language and its message:

IMP. CAES. FL. CONSTANTINO MAXIMO / P. F. AUGUSTO S.P.Q.R. / QUOD INSTINCTU DIVINITATIS MENTIS / MAGNITUDINE CUM EXERCITU SUO / TAM DE TYRANNO QUAM DE OMNI EIUS / FACTIONE UNO TEMPORE IUSTIS / REMPUBLICAM ULTUS EST ARMIS / ARCUM TRIUMPHIS INSIGNEM DICAVIT.

[To the emperor Caesar Flavius Constantinus the greatest, dutiful and blessed, Augustus, the Senate and the People of Rome, because, by the inspiration of divinity and by the greatness of his mind, with his army he avenged the state with righteous arms against both the tyrant and all of his faction at one and the same time, *arcum triumphis insignem dicavit*.][36]

This was a masterful display of political rhetoric, most unusual among the surviving *comparanda* from Roman arches. The customary formalistic litany

---

[35] Absence of sacrifice: Straub 1955; Fraschetti 1999, 9–75, on "l'abbandono del Campidoglio"; cf. MacCormack 1981; Humphries 2009, 31; contrast the role of the Capitoline ideology in Maximian's triumph at Trier in *Pan. Lat.* X (2), 6, 4–5 (with commentary of Ando 2017, 406–7). Hekster 1999, 739 (citing Künzl 1988, 62), suggests, unpersuasively, that, as there was no official triumph, there was no need to sacrifice; indeed, sacrifice was an aspect of *adventus*: e.g., Suet. *Galba* 8.2 and an inscription from Aphrodisias concerning the entry of Q. Vibius Egnatius Sulpicius Priscus (= Reynolds 1982, no. 48), with discussion and bibliography in Bérenger 2009. Sacrifice occurred anywhere across the empire when officials made their appearance (see Lehnen 1997, 181–83), and is amply attested on the Column of Trajan in scenes 80, 84, 86, and 91. Aurelian *lustratio* panel: Ryberg 1976, 37–43; cf. the discussion in chapter 3: the damaged and restored relief most probably would have originally depicted Marcus *capite aperto* as he performed the rite. It has been suggested that the selection of elements of the Trajanic frieze and from among the Aurelian panels deliberately avoided those scenes—the Sacrifice on the Capitol and the Triumph (now Museo Conservatori)—that made direct reference to the Capitoline cult of Jupiter; see Ruysschaert 1963 and Fraschetti 1999, 27.

[36] *CIL* VI.1139 = *ILS* 694, trans. partly based on Lee 2016, 80.

of imperial titles is noticeably brief, leaving space for a substantial rationale for the monument, including the senate's acknowledgment of the divine and its testimony to Constantine's worthiness (*mentis magnitudine*), as well as praise for the army. The claim for vengeance against a faction was surely to have recalled the language of Augustus's *Res Gestae*, whose monumental display, one assumes, was still standing before the Mausoleum in the Campus Martius. But here, strikingly, this constituted a deliberate and unprecedented justification for civil war (*iustis armis*), as well as a claim that such a victory deserved its memorialization in this grand architectural form.[37]

But if Constantine did not celebrate a traditional triumph—one voted by the senate and conforming to time-honored ritual—why build him an arch? And to what does the inscription's *arcum triumphis insignem dicavit* refer? The phrase has posed distinct translation difficulties, which reveal an obvious discomfort with the formulation; this is perhaps all the more acute given the perceived ambiguity of *instinctu divinitatis*, and the question of whether or not either of these phrases should be taken literally.[38]

Several things require comment. First, the inscription literally states "triumphs"—despite the fact that Constantine had never previously celebrated one, as the plural form declares; nor, as we have seen, do the arch reliefs unambiguously depict one. A decade later—in AD 326—after the defeat of Licinius left Constantine sole ruler, a medallion (figure IV.4) would proclaim INNUMERI TRIUMFI AUG N. Although such exaggeration heralding the new state of affairs might be regarded as merited, *triumphator* does not appear as an aspect of Constantinian titulature until the 330s. Thus, in the inscription, it is hard to see how *triumphi* can have been intended to mean anything more than "triumphal."[39]

---

[37] Rhetoric: Kuhoff 1991, 165 ("ein Meisterwerk politischer Formulierungskunst"); comparanda for previous Italian arches in De Maria 1988. Reference to *Res Gestae*: bibliography in Popkin 2016, 65–66; cf. at 67 ("deserving celebration in monumental form"); similarly Van Dam 2007, 48–49 ("a miniature *Res gestae* for Constantine").

[38] Metaphorical language: Raeck 1998; Fraschetti 1999, 52–58; Giuliani 2000, 282; Prückner 2008, 63 ("ganz allgemein, 'triumphal'"); cf. Tortorella 2013, 639 ("è tutta all'insegna dell'ambiguità").

[39] Plural *triumphi*: cf. Giuliani 2000, 281. Holloway 2004, 20, argues, unpersuasively, for the plural form as exaggeration suggesting "total victory." INNUMERI TRIUMFI: *RIC* VII, Trier, nr. 469; Mittag 2017, 434; Wienand 2012, 483–505 ("ewiger Triumphator"); Haake 2017, 385; Humphries 2008. *Triumphator* as an aspect of Constantinan titulature: Grünewald 1990, 147–50; cf. the list in Wienand 2015b, 177n.

CHAPTER 4

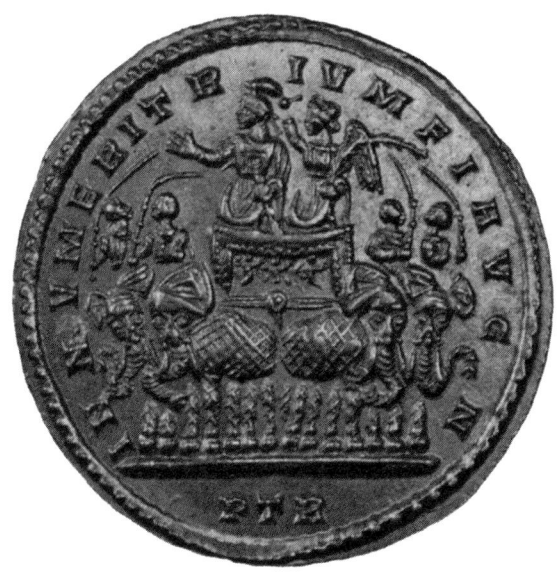

IV.4 Constantinian gold medallion, AD 326. *RIC* VII, Trier, no. 469.

Second, the crucial line *arcum triumphis insignem* has seemed to pose problems. At times, this has been rendered as if *insignem* were a substantive in apposition to *arcum* (that is, as if the inscription read *insigne*, giving the neuter accusative), and thus the phrase has been rendered as something like "an arch, the mark for triumphs," or "als Zeichen für seine triumphe."[40] Yet in the inscription, *insignem* can only be an adjective modifying *arcum*, suggesting something along the lines of "an arch, famous for its triumphs."[41] Moreover, several of the adjectival translations suggest a reference to the arch's sculpted reliefs (for *insigne* was indeed used in this fashion), and these suggest that those *triumphi* were actually a reference to the reliefs on the arch's narrative frieze, as in "decorated with his victories," "decorated with triumphal images," or in some instances implicitly understanding those "triumphs" to have been Constantine's, as in "resplendent with his triumphs" or "distinguished by [repre-

---

[40] Hall 1998; Prückner 2008. For usage as a noun, cf. Plin. *HN* 7.19 (*diadema regium insigne*); Cic. *Pis.* 73 (*pacis est insigne et otii toga*); ILS 5570 = CIL VIII.210 (*arcum quoque cum insignibus*).
[41] Frothingham 1912. Marlowe 2004, 211–13.

sentations of] his victories."⁴² But the best example of such a reference to an arch's representations—Suetonius's *ianos arcusque cum quadrigis et insignibus triumphorum*—actually employs the noun, and in that instance the pairing with *quadrigis* makes it doubly clear that a substantive is intended, that a monument's decoration is being evoked, and, by implication, that an arch so embellished was the award for the celebration of a real triumph.⁴³

The central question is whether, when proclaiming *arcum triumphis insignem*, the senate was acknowledging that the traditional role of the monumental type it had erected was employed in the customary celebratory fashion, declaring that Constantine's *introitus* in 312 was indeed, literally and "officially," a triumph; or calling attention to the arch's decoration and proclaiming that its reliefs' depictions of the emperor's victories were, figuratively speaking, "triumphal." This is hardly clear. But in this aspect, as in others, the imposing precedent of Septimius's great arch in the forum may well have been decisive, since its inscription (the text of which is given below) was distinguished by the use of the adjectival form employed in the ablative: *insignibus virtutibus* ("by means of his signal virtues").⁴⁴ What matters, as we shall see, is how one should construe the message.

Third, the inscription reads *arcum*, not *hunc arcum*; why should one imagine that the monument refers, so conspicuously, to itself? It has been claimed that such usage was unprecedented, but this is hardly the case.⁴⁵ Indeed, when translating there is no grammatical reason to assume the definite as opposed to the indefinite article (as Latin employs neither), and thus it is equally reasonable to translate "an arch." The generalizing sense of the plural *triumphi*, together

---

⁴² The examples, in sequence, are drawn from, Curran 2000, Marlowe 2004, Barnes 2014, and both Lee 2016 and Lenski 2008.

⁴³ Suet. *Dom.* 13.2. Marlowe 2004, 212–13, following Raeck 1998, 346–47, adds the (now lost) text reported to have been displayed at Rome on an arch of Arcadius, Honorius, and Theodosius II (*CIL* VI.1196 = *ILS* 798): *arcum cum simulacris eorum tropeisq*(ue) *decora*[tum]; despite her recognition of "the adjectival construction *insignem triumphis*" on Constantine's arch, *simulacris* is here a noun.

⁴⁴ Cf. the adjectival use at Livy 5.41.2-3 (*virtutis insignibus*); 10.46.2-3 (*insigni . . . triumpho* ["by means of a distinguished triumph"]). Septimius's inscription: see below.

⁴⁵ Among those cited in the Heidelberg Epigraphical Datenbank: *AE* 1985, 879: Timgad, 170–71; possibly *AE* 1948, 2 = *CIL* VIII.22670: Leptis, 110; *CIL* VIII.24 = *CIL* VIII.10999: Tripoli, 163; *CIL* XIII.11810: Mainz, 231–60; *AE* 2002, 796: Medinaceli, 83–96.

CHAPTER 4

with the text's syntax, would perhaps seem to call for this broader significance: "an arch" was erected "because, by the inspiration of divinity and by the greatness of his mind, with his army he avenged the state with righteous arms against both the tyrant and all of his faction at one and the same time"—*not* as the conventional commemoration of an "official" Constantinian triumph.[46]

Finally, it was often the case with publicly dedicated monuments that their text included no verb—for it was understood that major public works, such as the arches of Septimius or Titus, as gifts of the *SPQR*, would have been made or granted in their dedicatees' honor. Therefore, as celebratory and honorific monuments offered to living men, it would seem unlikely that they would have been, from a religious point of view, dedicated (that is, to the gods) and thus would not have employed the technical term *dedicavit*. The Constantinian arch's inscription, specifying *dicavit*, should perhaps be translated as "devoted," as this verb choice might be seen to acknowledge the secular character of the honor, in the fashion of numerous other monuments vowed privately by elite Romans to their illustrious patrons and at times explicitly offered "most devotedly" (*dicavitissimus*).[47] In sum, *arcum triumphis insignem dicavit* should be understood as reporting that the senate had "devoted [to Constantine] an arch, [a monument] renowned for triumphs"—with the very clear inference that they had done so despite the fact that they had not officially awarded him one.

❧

One way to understand the paradoxes that mark the arch inscription's most debated elements—*instinctu divinitatis*, *mentis magnitudine*, and, as here, *arcum triumphis insignem dicavit*—is to see them as the product of yet another

---

[46] Not *hunc arcum*: similarly questioned by Liverani 2014, 12, n. 10. Unprecedented reference, *at Rome*, to the monument itself: Raeck 1998; followed by Giuliani 2000, 281; both too sweeping (cf. the materials cited in the previous note). Cf. Blonce 2014 more broadly on arches and their statuary and ornament.

[47] No verb: none on other Roman arches whose inscriptions are preserved, whether archaeologically or epigraphically; evidence collected in De Maria 1988. Technical, public sense of *dedicare*: discussion in Koortbojian 2013, 168 and n. 32, with bibliography. *Dicavitissimus*: definition in *TLL*; more than fifty examples in the Heidelberg Epigraphical Datenbank from across the Roman world.

set of Roman institutional "fictions."[48] On the one hand, one recognizes that, despite the inscription's implied reference to Maxentius and his Roman faction, the arch did not (indeed, could not) commemorate a civil war. This is made clear, albeit subtly, by the contrasting sense of the paired inscriptions on the arch's two facades that acknowledged both the *vota soluta* upon Constantine's *decennalia* and those *nuncupata* that looked forward to another decade of rule (VOTIS X VOTIS XX / SIC X SIC XX).[49] The first of these brief texts effectively undermines the allusion of the attic inscription, since the message of the passageway perpetrated the fiction that what was commemorated was *not* a civil war, "[for] if Constantine had reigned for ten years from 306 (= VOTA X), then Maxentius had not reigned at all."[50] In addition, the senate honored the new ruler with an *arcum triumphis insignem* despite the fact that, as best we know, a triumph was neither voted by that body nor celebrated with the conventional ritual. This second "fiction" was hardly an innovation, since the same might be said of the vow of Augustus's Parthian arch as well as Septimius's monument in the forum—for both serve as reminders that the *arcus* was not, in origin, or indeed in most instances, truly triumphal.[51] Despite the peculiarities of the arch's representations in both text and image, there can be little doubt about its display of Constantine's military image—for *that* was not a fiction.

Precedents

At some point, probably shortly after AD 312, the mints at Rome, Ostia, Ticinum, and Trier issued gold and bronze coins for Constantine (figure IV.5), all marked with the reverse legend SPQR OPTIMO PRINCIPI coupled with the image of military standards—in explicit imitation of Trajan's issues (figure IV.6).[52]

---

[48] See the discussion in chapter 3.

[49] *CIL* VI.1139 = 31245 = *ILS* 694, 4 and 5, with Buttrey 1983.

[50] Quotation: Harries 2012, 118; similarly, Humphries 2008, 95; 2009, 32; and 2015, 157 (Maxentius's rule "erased . . . from public memory").

[51] Did Septimius triumph? Discussion of sources and historiography in Popkin 2016, 170–73. *Arcus* as a Roman architectural form: Plin. *HN* 34.27, with Wallace-Hadrill 1990.

[52] Constantine: *RIC* VI, nos. 345–52 (Rome mint); cf. pp. 160, 348; cf. Chenault 2012, 122, who points out that this would have celebrated the two-hundredth anniversary of the dedication

CHAPTER 4

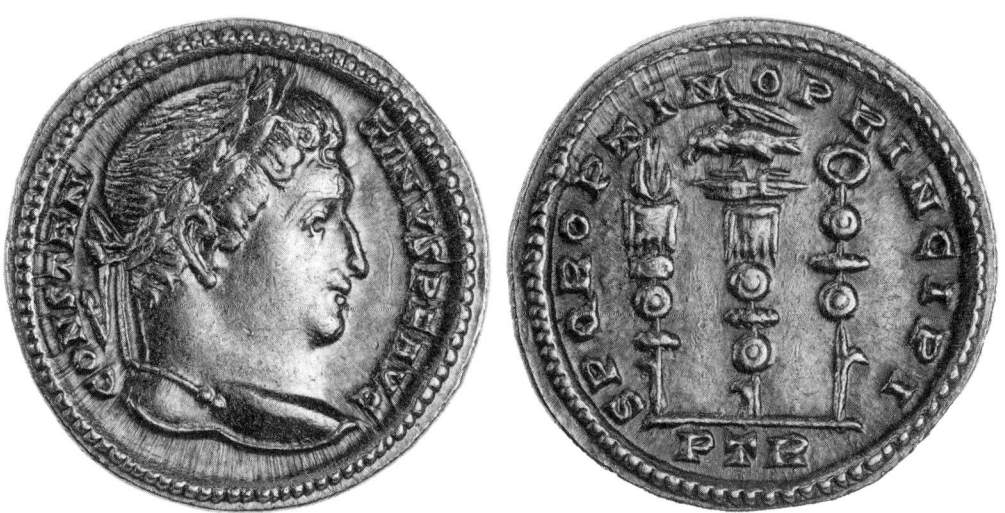

IV.5 Constantinian *aureus*, ca. AD 310–313. *RIC* VI, Trier, no. 815.

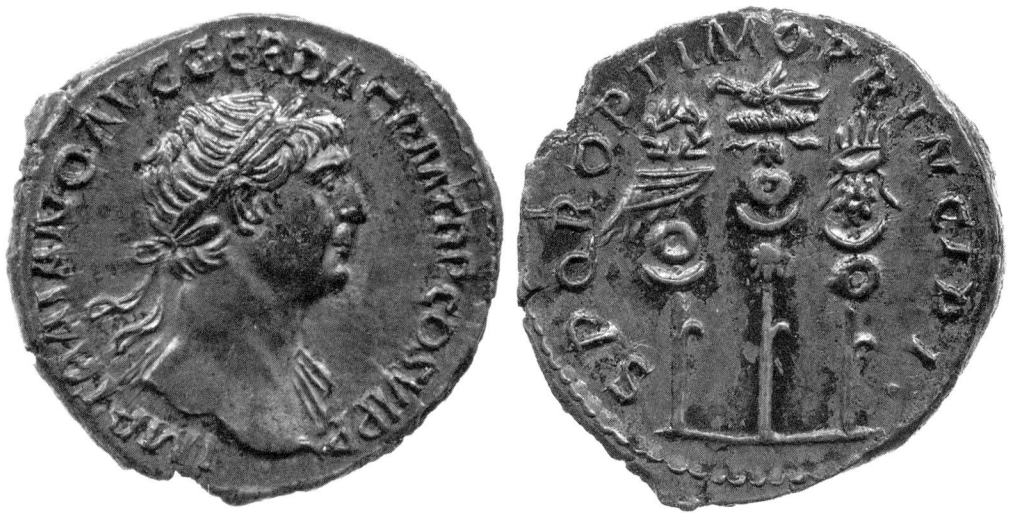

IV.6 Trajanic *denarius*, ca. AD 113–114. *RIC* II, Rome, no. 294

Mutual devotion between the emperor and his troops is self-evident in both instances, and the type advertises the profound role of military might in the reign of each emperor. These Constantinian coins are perhaps the sole

---

of Trajan's forum (112) and his column (113); discussion in Bleckmann 2014, 204–5; Wienand 2012, 215–16. Trajan: *RIC* II, nos. 294–95 (ca. AD 112–17).

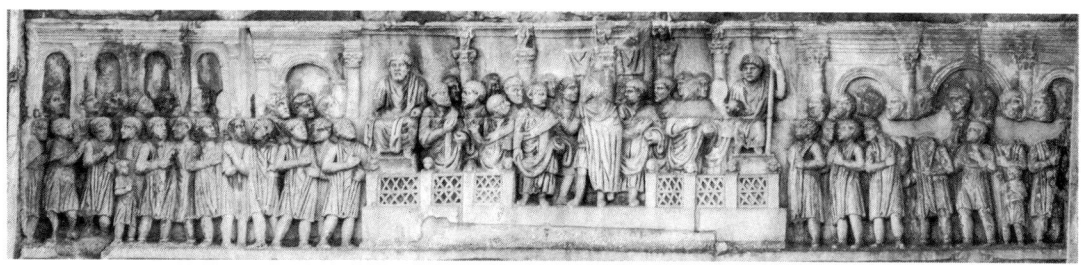

IV.7 Detail: Arch of Constantine, Rome. *Adlocutio* scene.

piece of independent evidence—other than the depiction of the statues of Hadrian and Marcus Aurelius on the rostra in his Roman arch's *adlocutio* scene (figure IV.7)—that might be enlisted in support of L'Orange's famous political interpretation of the arch's *spolia*, derived from monuments of Trajan, Hadrian, and Marcus Aurelius, as a recognizable mode of visual comparison between Constantine and his illustrious, "good" predecessors, and thus as a pictorial form of Constantinian panegyric.[53]

Yet the precedent of Septimius in the Constantinian era is equally palpable, if not more so—and not only in the architectural form of the Severan arch that provided the model for Constantine's. At least one other aspect of Severan tradition played a role, albeit one not often noted. The monumental inscription on Septimius's arch in the Forum Romanum reads:

IMP. CAES. LUCIO. SEPTIMIO. M. FIL. SEVERO. PIO. PERTINACI. AUG
    PATRI. PATRIAE. PARTHICO. ARABICO. ET
PARTHICO. ADIABENICO. PONTIFIC. MAXIMO. TRIBUNIC. POTEST. XI.
    IMP. XI. COS. III. PROCOS. ET
IMP. CAES. M. AURELIO. L. FIL. ANTONINO. AUG. PIO. FELICI. TRI-
    BUNIC. POTEST. VI. COS. PROCOS. <<P. P.

---

[53] L'Orange and von Gerkan 1939; trenchant discussion in Kinney 2012; Liverani 2004, 395, minimizes the association with the "good emperors," for according to the literary sources, as opposed to emulating these glorious predecessors, Constantine is reputed to have ridiculed them: Trajan was "wall ivy" (due to his penchant for seeing his name inscribed); Augustus, "an instrument of fortune"; Hadrian, "a studio painter"; Marcus, "a buffoon"; and Severus... (the fragmentary text stops here). The sources that relate these disparaging remarks are much cited: Bleckmann 1991, 343; De Caprariis 2003, 484; Liverani 2004, 394–96; Van Dam 2011, 128, n. 37; Chenault 2012, 122 and n. 120.

CHAPTER 4

OPTIMIS. FORTISSIMISQUE. PRINCIPIBUS>> [[*P. SEPTIMIO. GETAE. NOB. CAESARI*]]
OB REM PUBLICAM. RESTITUTAM. IMPERIUMQUE POPULI ROMANI. PROPAGATUM
INSIGNIBUS. VIRTUTIBUS. EORUM. DOMI. FORISQUE. S.P.Q.R.[54]

It is this inscription's final claim, offering the justification of the arch, that concerns us: "in recognition of the restoration of the state and the extension of the empire of the Roman people by means of their signal virtues, at home and abroad."

Here *insignis* appears in its adjectival form, modifying *virtutes*, as it does on the Constantinian arch. And here too the senators of the Severan era employed another Trajanic formula, a variation of a long-standing Roman conceit, whose language had appeared on the bases of three statues of Trajan once standing in that emperor's forum, where this language had been employed to assert both the breadth of military dominion and effective liberality of civil leadership at Rome: *optime de republica merito domo forisque*.[55] This is but a variant on the hallowed Roman topos of rule, *domi militiaeque*, a slogan that epitomized both spheres of an emperor's responsibilities. It had long been the benchmark of magisterial competence throughout the Republic.[56] Septimius's claims, and the tradition they evoked, served to anchor him to the political, geographical, and religious conceptions of Rome's imperial heritage. Although the grand sculpted panels of his arch had proclaimed his exploits in the field (*militiae*), as had the scenes that covered Trajan's column—on neither of which does one find any representation of the city of Rome—it was the assertion of

---

[54] *CIL* VI.1033 = *ILS* 425. See Brilliant 1967; Lusnia 2014, 75–84.

[55] Trajanic statue bases: all three reported at *CIL* VI.959 = *ILS* 292 (*duae valde mutilae, una paene integra*: Dessau, *ad loc.*); see Brilliant 1967, 94, n. 35. Fourth-century usage of *domi forisque*: cf. *AE* 1948, 6 a and b = *IRT* 562, 563 = *LSA* 2185 and 2186: ca. AD 355–361, statue base for Flavius Arcontius Nilus, governor at Lepcis Magna; *CIL* VI.1741 = *LSA* 1443: statue base from Rome for Memmius Vitrasius Orfitus, *PVR* 357–60, where the formula possibly means "at home and in public" (so Machado for *LSA*); *AE* 1953, 85, for a text from Bulla Regia honoring a victory of Constantius II (ca. 360?).

[56] Rüpke 1990, exhaustively. Early usage of *domi forisque*: discussion in chapter 1, n. 1. Later usage: S.H.A., *Pesc. Nig.* 6.10.3, *Maximinus and Balbinus*, 6.1.3, *Div. Claud.* 2.6.2, *Tacitus*, 16.6.2; similarly *domi bellique*: Sall. *Jug.* 41.7.

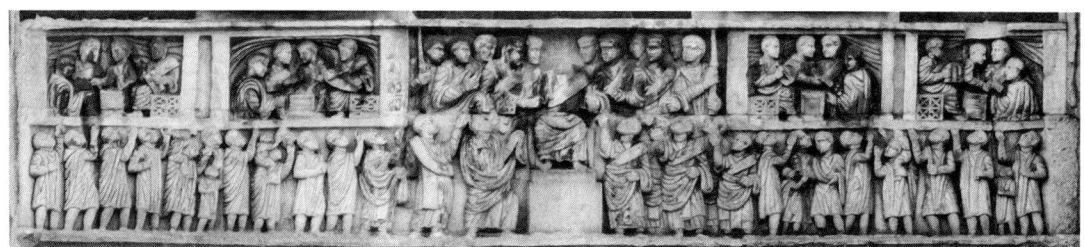

IV.8 Detail: Arch of Constantine, Rome. *Liberalitas* scene.

accomplishments *domi* that both emperors, renowned for their foreign campaigns, were concerned to proclaim. And although Trajan's famous institution of the *alimenta* had established the basis for his Italian endeavors on behalf of the populus, Septimius had effected no comparable domestic program. His architectural patronage in the capital before the erection of the forum arch had been considerable, yet in AD 203 the claim for the exercise of his *virtutes* at Rome was probably to be understood, in great part, as a proleptic hope for the future, one marked especially by the new *saeculum* that was about to be celebrated. And in this respect, it also provides a precedent for the assuredly optimistic assertion by the senators of the Constantinian age that the virtues of Maxentius's successor would offer to Rome's elite as well as its citizenry a brighter future, *domi forisque*.[57]

Although by the early fourth century the ideology of *domi militiaeque* was, to a large extent, out of step with contemporary realities and the role of the *urbs* within the expanse of empire, this old distinction between the civic and military spheres was granted dramatic visual form by the two Constantinian friezes on the arch's northern face. In the *liberalitas* scene (figure IV.8), the new emperor was depicted distributing largesse in a setting that may well have been intended to represent the Basilica Nova, and thus performing in his role as the new *civilis princeps*. The imagery of this institution of such personal imperial beneficence was now on permanent display and served to advertise the Romans' expectations for their new ruler. In this sense, the

---

[57] Trajan's *alimenta*: discussion and sources in Bennett 2001, 81–84. Septimius, largely absent from Rome for the previous decade, returned in AD 203 and celebrated the *Ludi Saeculares* the following year; overview in Birley 1988, 155–69. Proleptic claims: see the epigraphical dossier on *vota suscepta* assembled in Chastagnol 1988.

CHAPTER 4

liberalitas scene finds its parallel with the allegories depicted on Trajan's Benevento arch, the statue group in the Forum Romanum portrayed on the so-called *Anaglypha*, as well as on his coinage—all of which proclaimed Trajan's initiative, on behalf of the plebs, ensuring that children (especially male children) would have the sustenance required to nurture able-bodied citizens of the *populus Romanus* in the future. In the case of Constantine, the *congiaria* played a similar and important role, since such highly positive imagery had its counterpart in the negative tradition of sarcasm about the emperor's profligate liberality. Nonetheless, both the Trajanic and Constantinian images belonged to public monuments that not only heaped praise on these emperors but also, in declaring the hopes of their two eras' senatorial patrons for the continued *munificentia* of their reigns, served as yet another proleptic claim by the elite for the maintenance of what *they* surely regarded as the status quo.[58]

Imagines militiae Romae

The advertisement of Constantine's military role had more profound implications.[59] On his arch he appeared *loricatus* at the siege of Verona, and perhaps originally he was similarly garbed in the damaged scene of the Milvian Bridge. But the subsequent panel recounted how he entered the city of Rome with his armed troops, "in full regalia" (figure IV.3), escorted by the goddess of Victory, not as a triumphator clad in the *toga picta* in his *quadriga*, but as the new—and sole—*imperator*, riding in his *carruca* and wearing the customary traveling garb (*Reisekostüm*), *tunica* under the *paludamentum*. Indeed, only Constantine's bejeweled shoes suggest the scene's ceremonial character (although the emperor's destroyed head may well have been shown wearing

---

[58] *Civilis princeps*: Wallace-Hadrill 1982. Trajan's imagery of *liberalitas*: surveyed in Hannestad 1988, 174–86 and 193–94; the *arcus panis aurei* of the *Mirabilia* would seem to be yet another such monument—if only we knew to which emperor it should be attributed (and thus the interpretations of Torelli in *LTUR* I:98–99 and Tortorella 2013 are less than convincing). Constantine's "profligate" liberality: Zosimus 2.38; cf. Jul. *Caes.* 335B, Aur. Vict. 40.15, *Epit. de Caes.* 41.16; opposite view in Eus. *VC* 4.1.

[59] The panegyrical and numismatic evidence across Constantine's full reign is treated exhaustively in Wienand 2012. Cf. Cameron 2013, 106 (Constantine's "twin" elements of power—military success and political legitimation); similarly, Campbell 2005, 129.

CONSTANTINE'S MILITARY IMAGE

the jeweled helmet described in the sources, depicted on the Ticinum medallion, and exemplified by the helmet found at Berkasovo).[60]

In the *adlocutio* panel (figure IV.7; cf. figure IV.2), Constantine was shown addressing the *populus Romanus* in the forum, still clothed, the following day, in his *tunica et paludamentum*. Thus, he unabashedly appeared before the senators in military garb, as if he were their commander. The imagery transposes to the city of Rome a formula familiar from the Column of Trajan, which depicted that emperor's reception in the cities of the provinces. The contrast of civil and military costumes was well known from numerous monuments.[61] Their juxtaposition could not have been greater with the representation of the enthroned statues of Marcus and Antoninus flanking the group on the rostra, as well as with the standing Tetrarchs on their "Five-Column Monument" depicted behind—all *togati*—whose costumes made visible the claim not only for their political inheritance of the magisterial dignity of the Roman state and the *gens togata* but also, in the case of the Tetrarchs, for their *concordia*.[62] By

---

[60] "In full regalia": Lenski 2012a, 183. Costume: L'Orange and Gerkan 1939, 74–75; Zanker 2012, 92; Giuliani 2000, 276. *Toga picta* of the triumphator (and, in the fourth century, the consul): Aus. *Grat. Act.* 11 (*palmatae vestis* [cited by Wienand 2012, 484, n. 6]). *Tunica et paludamentum*: the description of Constantine's costume varies; he wears the long military cloak (known in Latin as the *paludamentum* or in Greek as the *chlamys*: for the basically interchangeable terms, see Hallett 2005, 132–37, and appendix D); this was worn over a tunic and draped across his knees (cf. the similar arrangement in the cosmic image of the seated *augusti* on the south pier of the Galeriuis arch [B, II, 21]; so too, Laubscher 1975, 70), but Constantine does not wear trousers (*braccae*, as L'Orange and Gerkan 1939, 74–75, states and, mistakenly, is too often followed [e.g., Koeppel 1990, 52, Zanker 2012, Lenski 2012a, 183, and Gehn 2012, 101]); the only unambiguous example of Roman military officers wearing *braccae* known to me is in the wall paintings from Dura Europos; for the custom of the *paludamentum* over the *tunica*, not the *lorica*, as the imperial costume at Rome by the high empire, see the comments of Laffranchi 1921, quoted by Alföldi 1970, 125, and cf. further below. Jeweled helmet: *Pan. Lat.* IV (10), 29, 5 (cf. VII [6], 6, 2). Ticinum medallion: Bleckmann 2014. Berkasovo helmet: Schmauder 2007. Cf. the fully bejeweled appearance of Constantine II at Amm. Marc. 16.10.6.

[61] Commander in the forum: similarly, Giuliani 2000, 273. Emperor's attire in the provinces: Trajan's column, scenes 25, 34, 56, 58, 60, 62–63, 65–66, 72–74; Marcus column, scenes 4, 9, 31–32, 41, 44, 49, 75, 80, 87. On the Septimius arch in the forum, the contrast of the *Reisekostüm* and battle garb (armed, in *paludamentum* and *lorica*) can be gleaned from the southwestern panel IV (visible in Brilliant 1967, pl. 87; cf. Bartoli's engraving, pl. 86a); finally, note the emperor on the attic panels of the Constantinian arch's *adventus* scene, with fringed *paludamentum* over the *tunica*.

[62] Cf. Bravi 2012, 456 ("sotto la tutela delle immagini dei Tetrarchi"); similarly Kähler 1964; Wrede 1981; Marlowe 2016; nevertheless, at times, a subtle hierarchy is observable (Hekster 1999, 720–21). Whether or not this is the eastern as opposed to the western rostra (Liverani 2007) would

contrast, Constantine's singularity, seeming to ignore his co-ruler Licinius, declared him to be sole ruler ("Maximus"); his youthful and clean-shaven appearance distinguished him from his older predecessors and announced a new age; and above all, his soldier's dress acknowledged his status as *imperator* and his military success ratified the foundation of his claim to rule.[63]

The presence of military men at Rome had grown steadily with the advent of empire, as troops were increasingly present from Augustus onward, if not within the city, then immediately outside its walls. And their representation on official public monuments had become equally familiar, reinforcing the reality, by the later first century AD, of the army's progressively more significant role in Rome's rule. Yet certain traditional formalities had apparently long prevailed—among them, the *mutatio vestis* that acknowledged the divorce of the spheres *domi* and *militiae*. Although there are few attested instances, Vitellius famously observed it; Septimius had not; Constantine, as the arch's reliefs show, deliberately and pointedly had ignored it, following his precedent; and later Constantius II would do so as well.[64]

---

matter little, although I have serious doubts about the hypothesis. Toga: cf. Cic. *Pis.* 73: *pacis est insigne et otii toga.*

[63] Cf. the postitive characterization of the "Five-Column Monument" by L'Orange and Gerkan 1939, followed by Mayer 2002, 176–78, and Zanker 2012, 95. For the long tradition of statuary on the rostra that forms the context of Constantine's appearance, see Bruggisser 2002. *Maximus*: see Lact. *De Mort. Pers.* 44, 11 (*primi nominis titulum*), with Grünewald 1990, 87, who dates the appearance of the epithet to AD 313 (although not consistently); cf. Wienand 2015b, 181 and n. 60. Clean-shaven: Smith 1997, 196–97 and n. 157 ("energetic militarism is represented . . . in the cropped hair and stubbled beard of camp life"). Claim to rule: similarly, Giuliani 2000, 286 ("Es ist ihre [i.e., the *SPQR*'s] Anerkennung, die aus dem Sieger, der immer noch in militärischer Tracht in ihrer Mitte steht, den legitimen princeps macht"); cf. the "theology of victory" in Fears 1981 and, for late antiquity, McCormick 1990. Military success: for Constantine's accomplishments before his march on Rome, see Barnes 2014, 71; downplayed pointedly by Wienand 2015b, 186.

[64] Soldiers and their representations in the *urbs*: Coulston 2000 and 2007, Busch 2007 and 2011, both with bibliography. According to Zosimus 2.34, Constantine removed troops from the frontier and stationed them in the cities (yet see the commentary of Ridley 1982, *ad loc.*, and materials cited there). *Mutatio vestis*: Mommsen 1887–1888, I:430–31 = 1889–1896 II:70; Alföldi 1970, 121–27; Giuliani 2000, 272–73. Vitellius: Tac. *Hist.* 2.89, Suet. *Vit.* 11.1. Septimius, by contrast, was said to have been armed: Herodian 2.14.1, yet cf. Dio 75.1.3–5. Cf. the similar conclusions of Gehn 2012, 101 ("radikal gewandeltes Verhältnis des Kaisers zum Senat") and note the bizarre refusal of Elagabulus at Herodian 5.5–6. See chapter 1.

CONSTANTINE'S MILITARY IMAGE

So, by the fourth century, the traditional distinctions between *domi militiaeque* survived as a hallowed aspect of Roman ideology—but no longer as a political reality. At the same time, the pairing of images of *liberalitas* and *adlocutio* emerged as contrasting symbols of the traditional imperial obligations to the historic, if no longer actual, center of power, both financial and military. A generation after the age of Constantine, on the Calendar of AD 354, the personification of Roma would appear (figure IV.9) with the symbolism of both aspects: a *putto* enacting the *sparsio*, and the figure of Victory on the Globe. And these symbols would be repeated in the images for the consuls for that year: Gallus, standing, with the *victoriola* (figure IV.10), and Constantinus II enthroned, dispensing the *sparsio* (figure IV.11).[65] This pairing of such conventional symbolic imagery for civic munificence and military prowess, much like that figured on the Arch of Constantine, acknowledged imperial duties and no doubt reflected senatorial attitudes during this period toward the absent sole ruler's responsibilities in the *urbs*.

In all of this the predominantly military imagery of the Tetrarchs had set the stage for their successor. The well-known statuary groups in Venice and the Vatican display the four, nearly indistinguishable military figures, whose mutual embraces signaled their reciprocal legitimacy, *paludatus* (or *chlamydatus*) and *loricatus*. The Venice group (figure IV.12) is further characterized by the "hand on sword" motif, reinforcing the imagery of armed readiness, while each figure in the Vatican foursome stands with the globe in hand, signaling universal concord, ensured by the parceling out of individual domains and sustained by martial dominance.[66] Yet the costume of other statues of

---

[65] Salzman 1990, 27, 34–35. For Constantius II's image and the *congiaria*, cf. Wienand 2012, 81.

[66] Tetrarch statues: bibliography and discussion in *LSA*, nos. 4, 439, and *LSA*, nos. 840, 841 (M. Bergmann). *Paludatus/chlamydatus et loricatus*: so too statuary examples in the Vatican and Turin and a lost one of Diocletian (*LSA*, nos. 1006, 1008, 1005). The tendency to discriminate between the long, draped late-imperial military cloaks—the *chlamys* and the *paludamentum*—especially because the latter was often shown bunched on the shoulder (what Oehler once called the *Schulterbauschtypus*), is a misunderstanding of their fundamental similarity as garments (although the fourth-century *chlamys* was arguably distinguished by its generally greater length); cf. the extended discussion in Gehn 2012, 22, who regards the *chlamys* that appears on most fourth-century statues as a fundamentally ceremonial garment (*Dienstgewand* and *habitus militaris*). "Hand on sword" motif: an apparently old topos—recall the response of Caesar's centurion to the intransigent senate, brandishing his weapon ("this will"), at Plut. *Caes.* 29.5 and *Pomp.* 58.2; Bergmann in *LSA*,

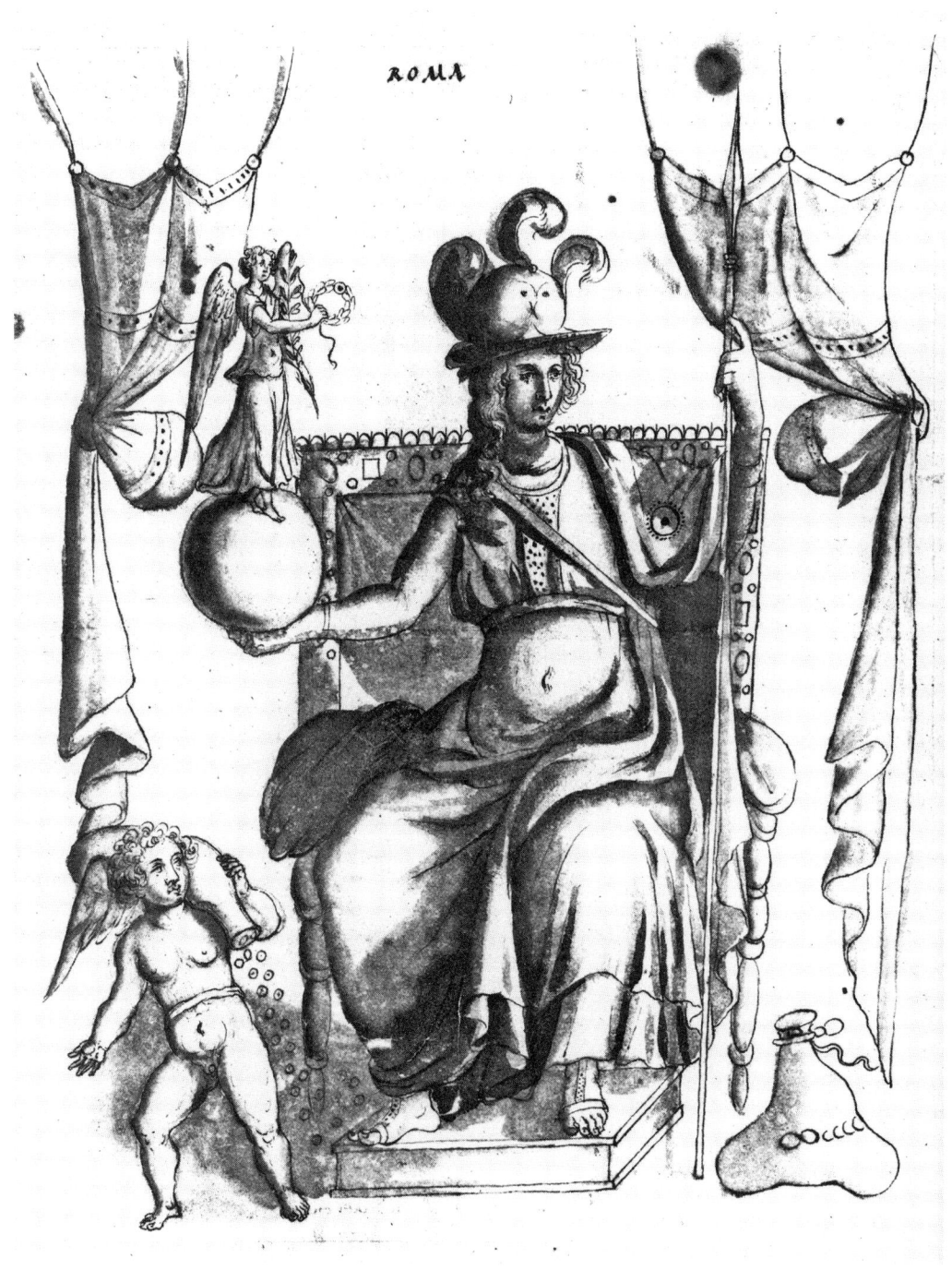

IV.9 Calendar of AD 354: Roma. Biblioteca Apostolica Vaticana, MS Barb. Lat. 2154, pt. B, fol. 2r.

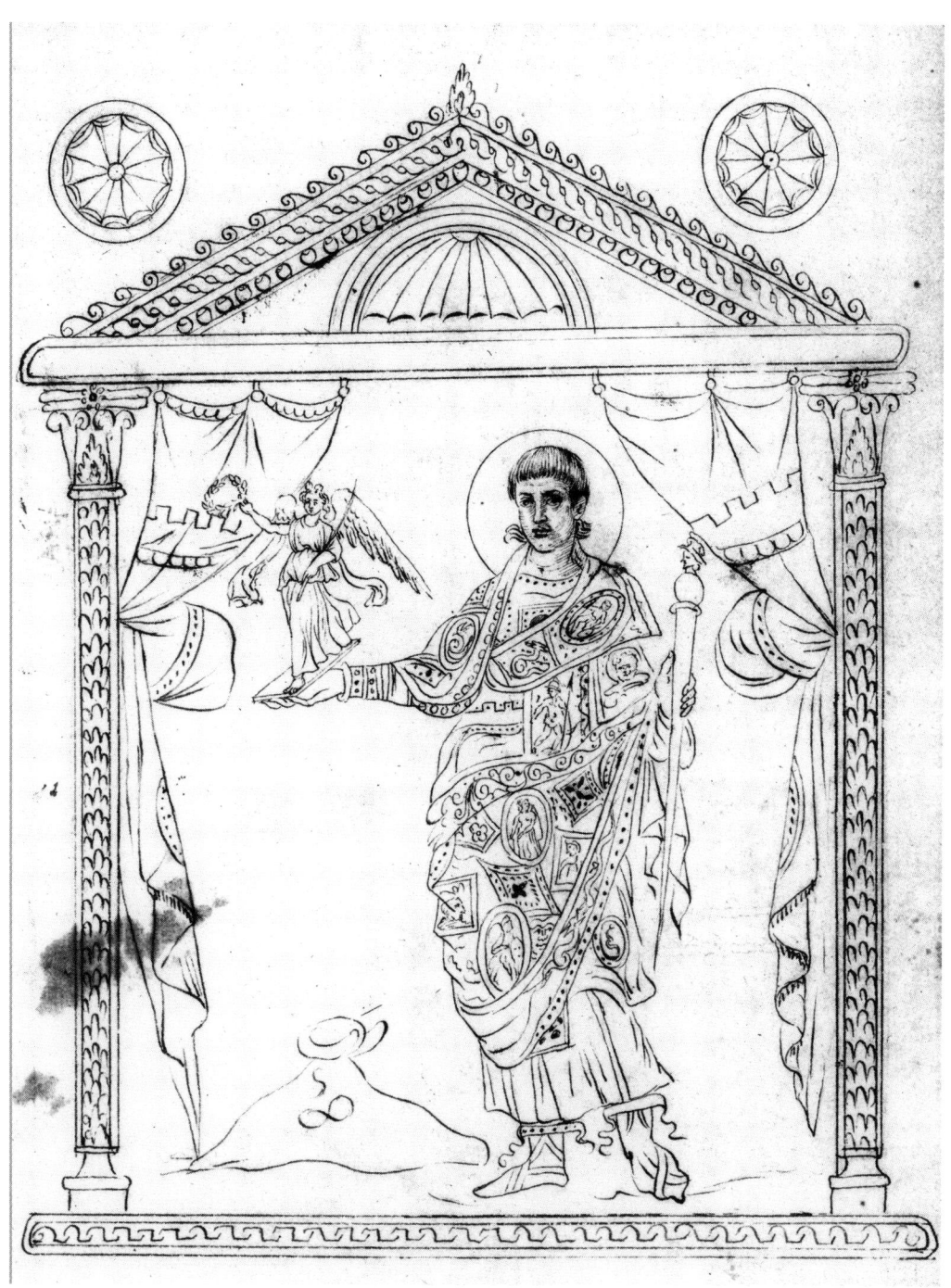

IV.10 Calendar of AD 354: Gallus. Biblioteca Apostolica Vaticana, MS Barb. Lat. 2154, pt. B, fol. 13r.

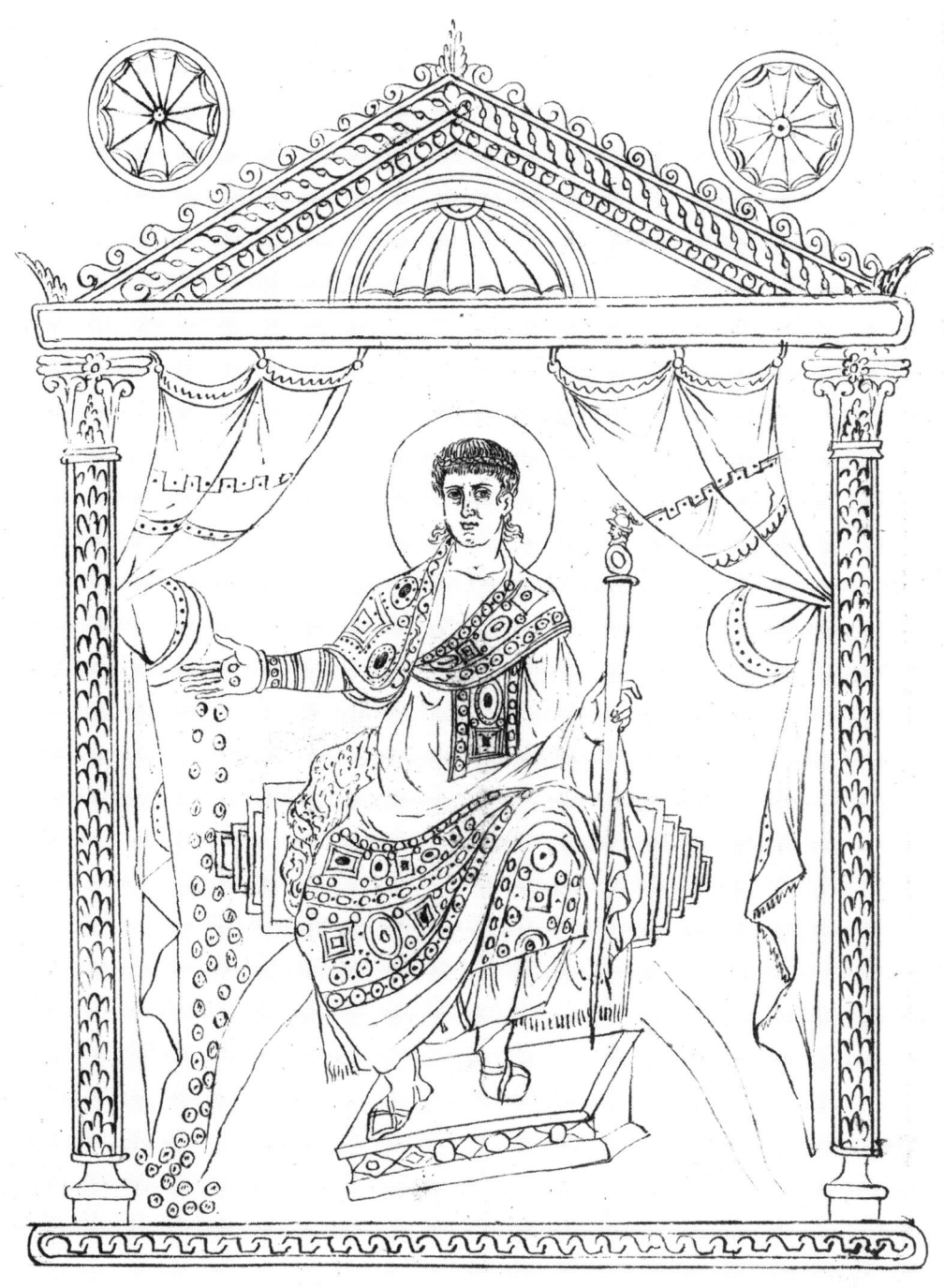

IV.11 Calendar of AD 354: Constantinus II. Biblioteca Apostolica Vaticana, MS Barb. Lat. 2154, pt. B, fol. 14r.

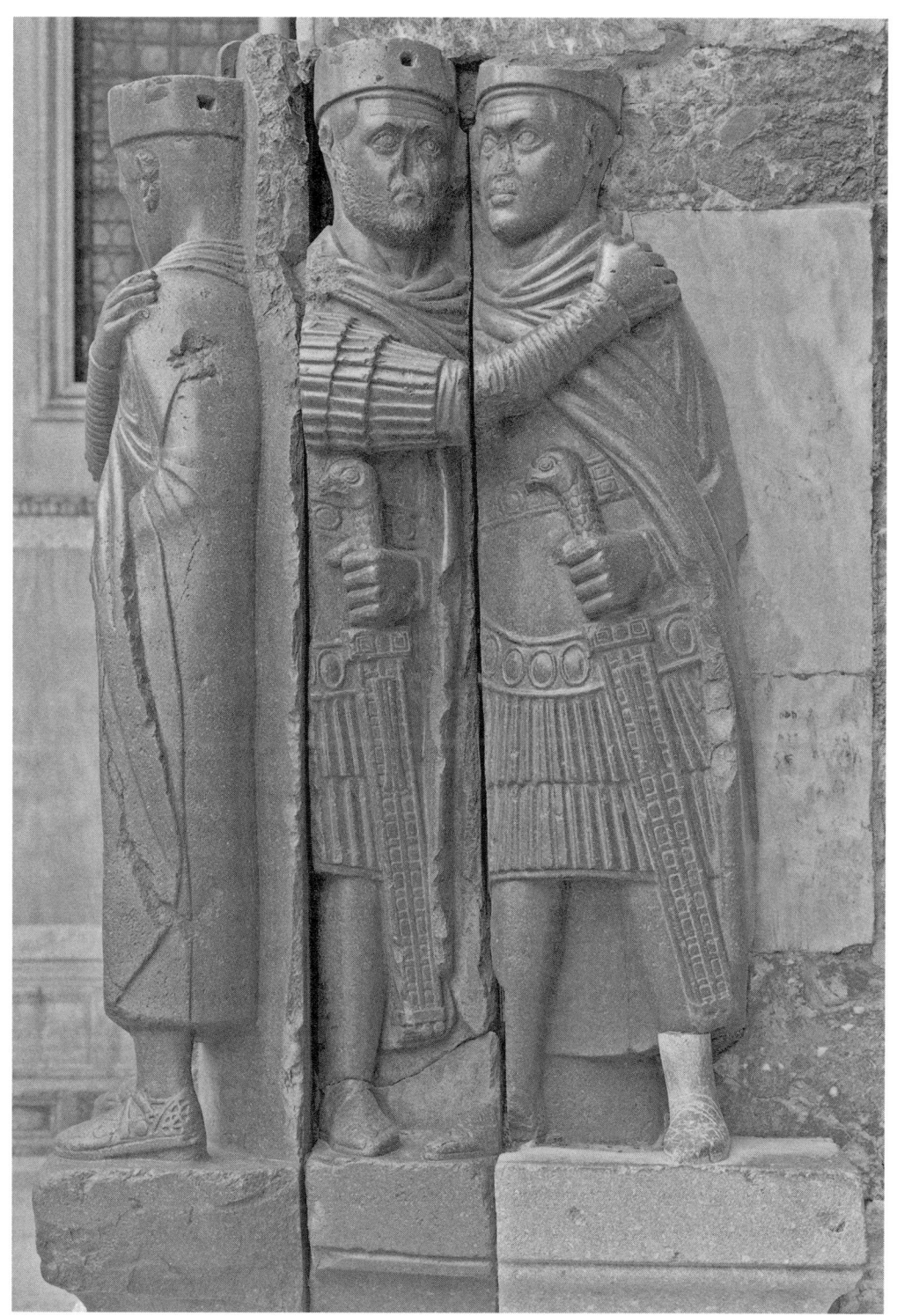

IV.12 The Four Tetrarchs. Ca. AD 300. Porphyry. Venice, San Marco.

CHAPTER 4

the period projected a somewhat different imagery. For example, a porphyry bust in Cairo displays the military cloak over the tunic, as do the under-life-size, headless porphyry statues in Berlin (figure IV.13), Vienna, and Ravenna and in fragments in London and Paris.[67] This was not battle attire, but the *Reisekostüm*; it connotes the emperor's military role, nonetheless, and suggests his engagement across the full extent of his dominion. It is thus that Constantine appears on the rostra in the *adlocutio* relief on his Roman arch (figures IV.2 and IV.7), where the costume is augmented visibly by his sword, protruding from under his cloak.[68] Whether or not this was how Constantine actually appeared in the forum on 29 October 312, one suspects that the senate's decision to have him depicted in this fashion was to be understood as an acknowledgment that, despite Constantine's *sedes imperatoriae* remaining in Trier—and then Sirmium, Serdica, and perhaps Thessalonica—he was ready to return to Rome rapidly, should reason arise.[69]

This message would be reinforced by the appearance of the equally aggressive imagery of those several *statuae loricatae* of Constantine that survive from the city of Rome—statues that would have contrasted dramatically with the togate images of Maxentius.[70] Those now on the Capitoline balustrade (figure IV.14) and at the Lateran are thought by many to have come from the imperial baths on the Quirinal. Both over-life-sized statues show the emperor *loricatus*, armed, with the *paludamentum* draped in different manners, and wearing the *corona civica*, signaling, in time-honored fashion, that he was to

---

no. 1010, "in calm preparedness" (followed by Bodnaruk 2015, 146), and Bergmann 2018, with similar examples; *contra* Bartocini 1932. Nearly indistinguishable Tetrarchs: the presence and/or absence of beards on the Tetrarch groups is convincingly dismissed as a conventionalized iconography by Bergmann in *LSA* (*loc. cit.*); *contra* Parisi Presicce 2012, who nonetheless remarks (109) the quartet's gesture of "reciprocal legitimacy." For the Tetrarchs as "adoptive brothers," see Kolb 1987, 44–47; cited and discussed by Shaw 1997, 339–40.

[67] Discussion in *LSA*, nos. 1007, 1009, 1010, 1011 (M. Bergmann), 1185 (M. Bergmann and U. Gehn); Bergmann 2018.

[68] *Reisekostüm* and sword: so L'Orange and Gerkan 1939, 86 ("das gewöhnliche Amst- und Militärkostüm"); Koeppel 1990, 58; Zanker 2012, 95 ("*Reisekleidung*").

[69] The emperor's *celeritas*: Lolli 1999, Lehnen 1997, 109–12, and Wienand 2012, 382 and 489 ("Reisegeschwindigkeit und Schlaflosigkeit"), all with the relevant texts from the *Pan. Lat.*; cf. similarly, Campbell 2005, 129. Constantine's *sedes*: Barnes 1982, 68–69.

[70] Hekster 1999, 734–35, following Evers 1992; yet cf. Constantine's known togate statues cited in n. 74 below.

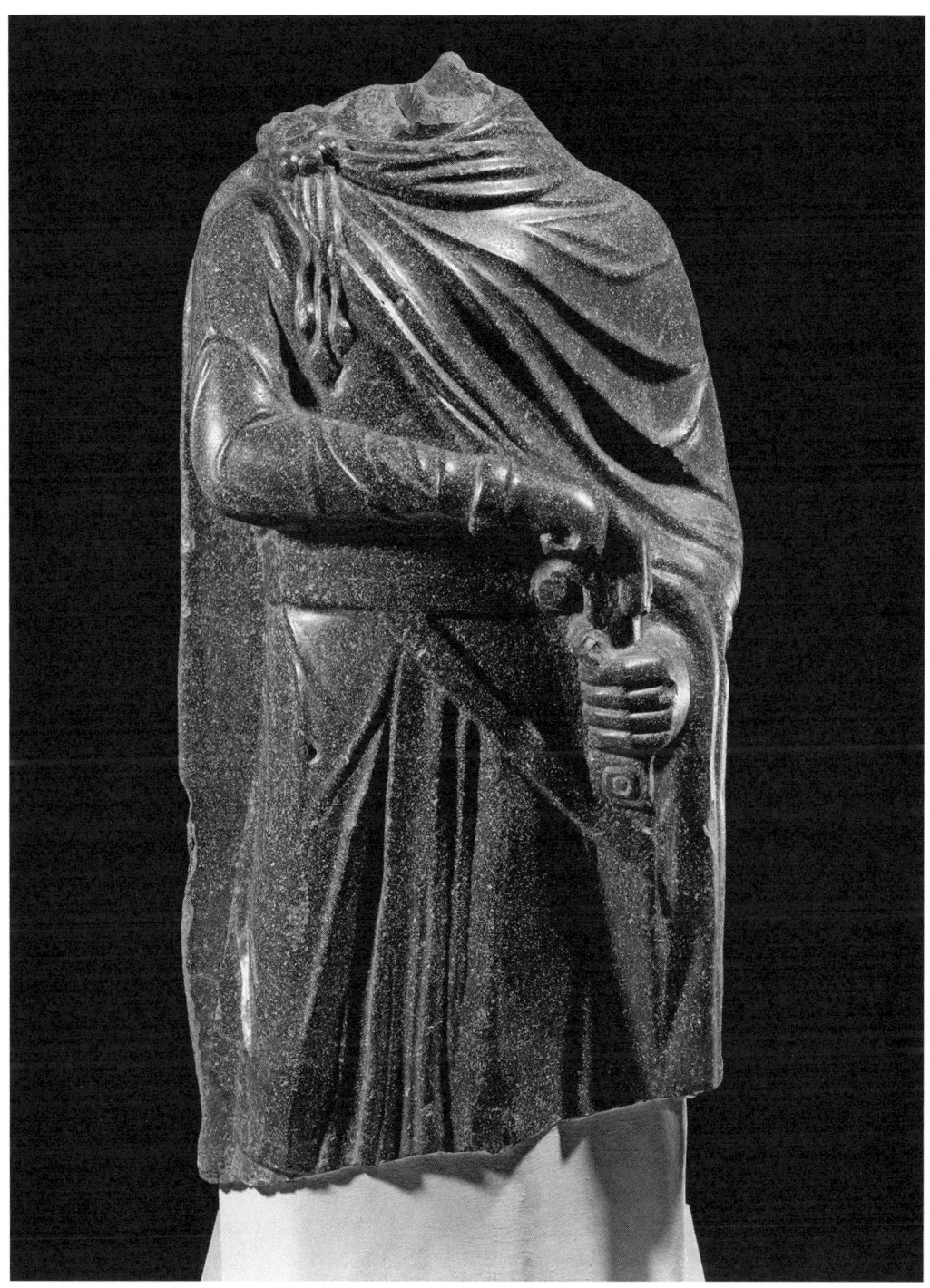

IV.13 Tetrarch. Fourth century AD. Porphyry. Berlin, Staatliche Museen.

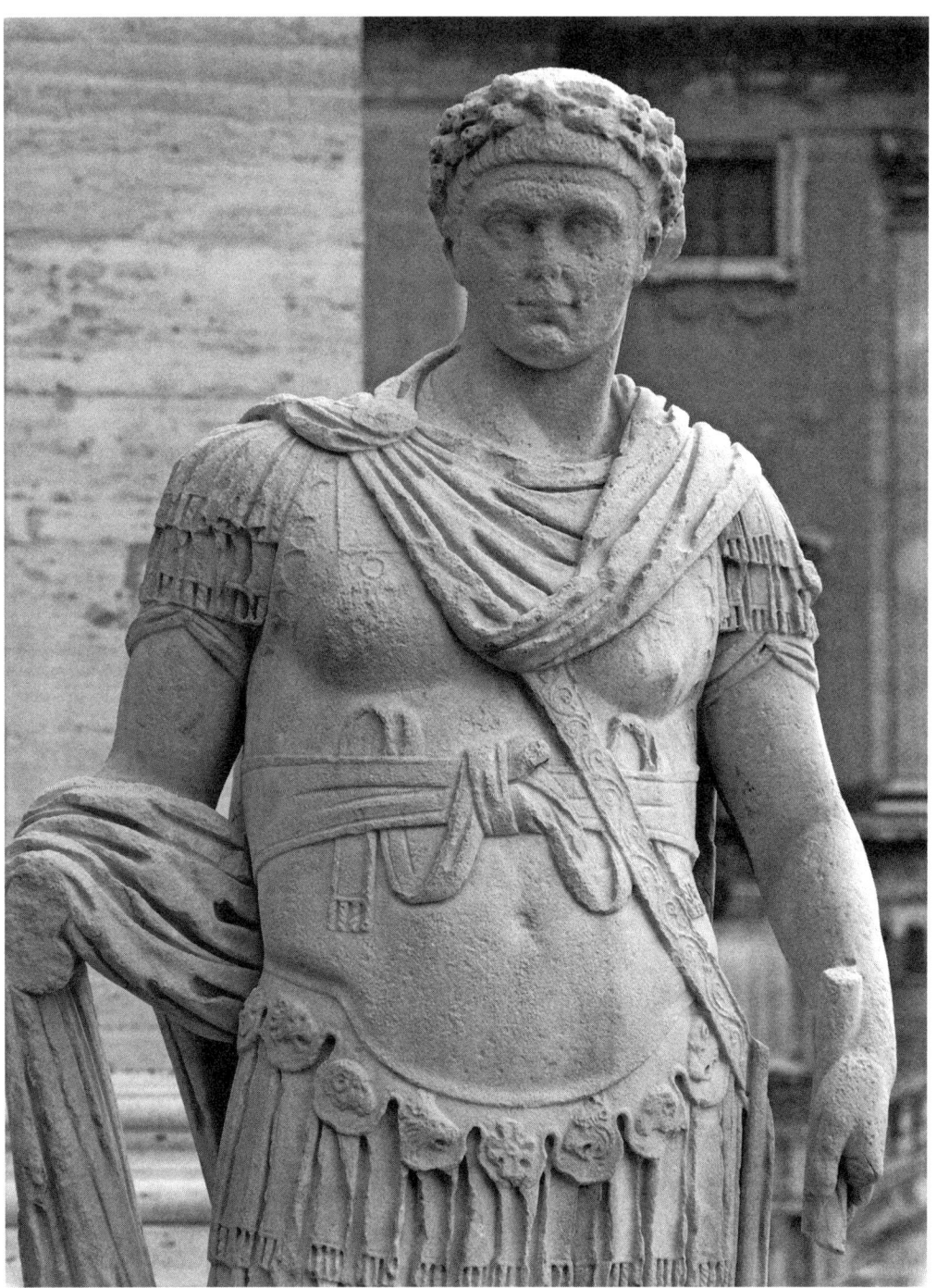

IV.14 Constantine *loricatus*. Early fourth century AD. Marble. Rome, Capitoline.

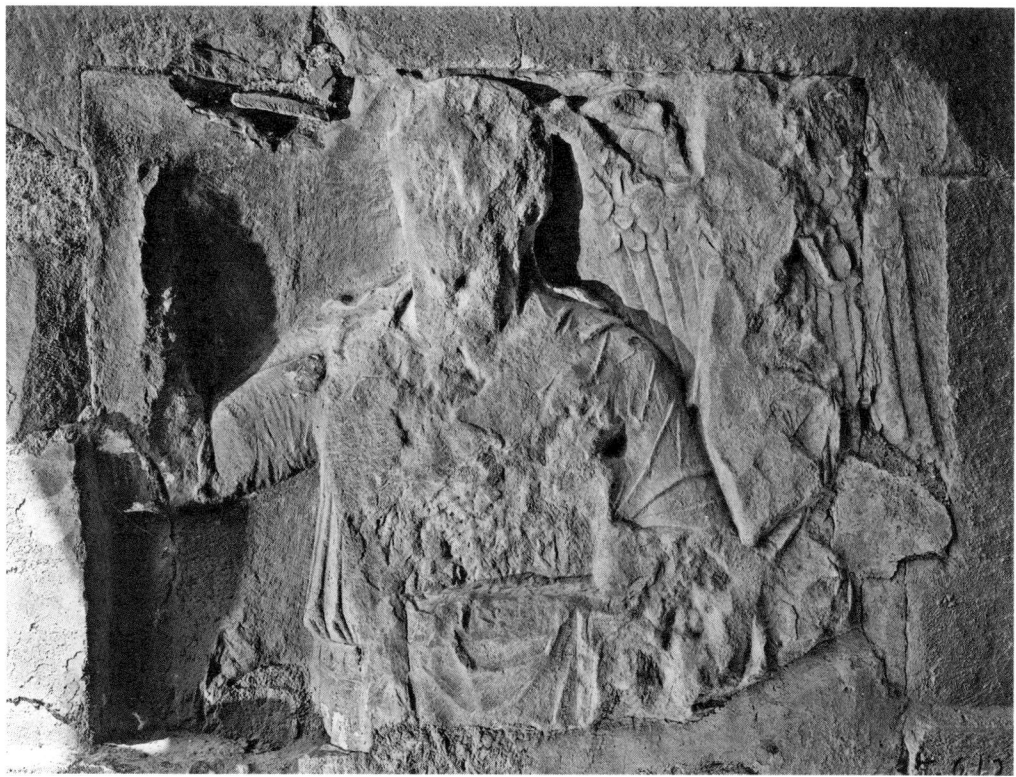

IV.15 Arch of Constantine, passageway relief. Marble. Rome.

be recognized as the savior of the citizens.[71] The military character of this imagery was echoed not only on the Roman arch in the bust-length portrait of Constantine in the central passageway (figure IV.15),[72] but quite possibly on the lost statue to which the head recently discovered in the Forum of Trajan originally belonged (figure IV.16).[73] This monumental presence of the armed ruler, emphatically a man, ready to act among men, contrasts dramatically with the ideology of a *deus praesens*: this was not a mythologizing vision but the representation of a pragmatic political reality. All of these statues—and

---

[71] Discussion and bibliography in Parisi Presicce 2005 and 2012. Differences in style and scale suggest that, if these (and possibly another) all came from a single dynastic group, it would have been one that was produced by accretion over a period of time. Sizes: Lateran, 3.22 m.; Capitoline, 2.75 m.; and another thought to represent Constantine II, 2.82 m.

[72] Lenski 2012a, 174–77.

[73] La Rocca and Zanker 2007, 146: "è supponibile che si tratti di un 'Einsatzkopf' un tempo pretinente a un'immagine loricate."

CHAPTER 4

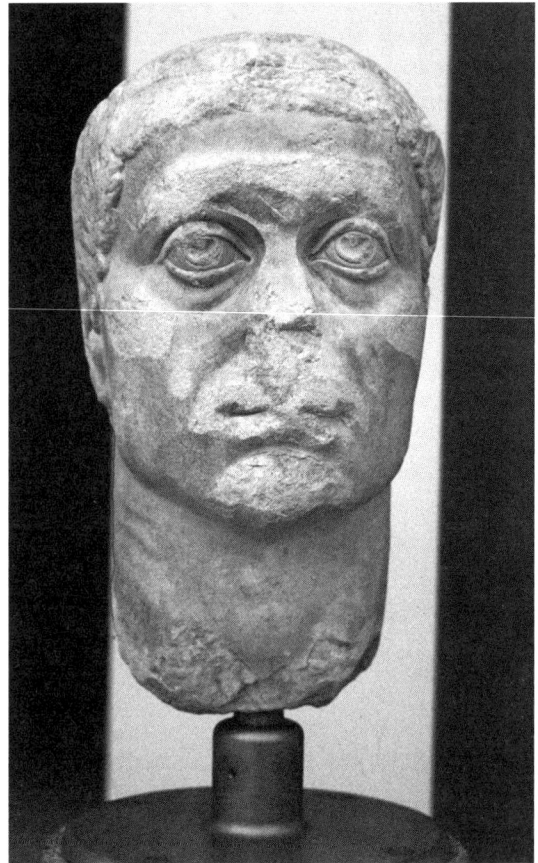

IV.16 Colossal Constantine portrait from Forum of Trajan. Early fourth century AD. Marble. Rome.

no doubt there were others as well—reiterated to the *populus* of the capital a consistent imagery of the emperor's martial character. While Tetrarchan in origin, and despite the radically youthful, clean-shaven portrait of Constantine that they bore, this imagery would be a continuing symbol of his authority to rule.[74]

---

[74] *Deus praesens*: MacCormack 1981, 22–32. Image of political reality: cf. La Rocca and Zanker 2007, 154 ("segni, simbolici e concreti"). Other statues: Aur. Vict. *Caes.* 40; for a togate statue of Constantine at Rome, a *statua civili (habitu)*: *CIL* VI.36953 = Grünewald 1990, no. 259, with Van Dam 2007, 48, n. 16, noting *CTh* 14.101 (AD 382), which would proscribe within the *urbs* the wearing of "the awe-inspiring military cloak." On the portrait-type, see Smith 1997 and La Rocca and Zanker 2007, all of whom, while focused on the portrait-type, undervalue the continuing

CONSTANTINE'S MILITARY IMAGE

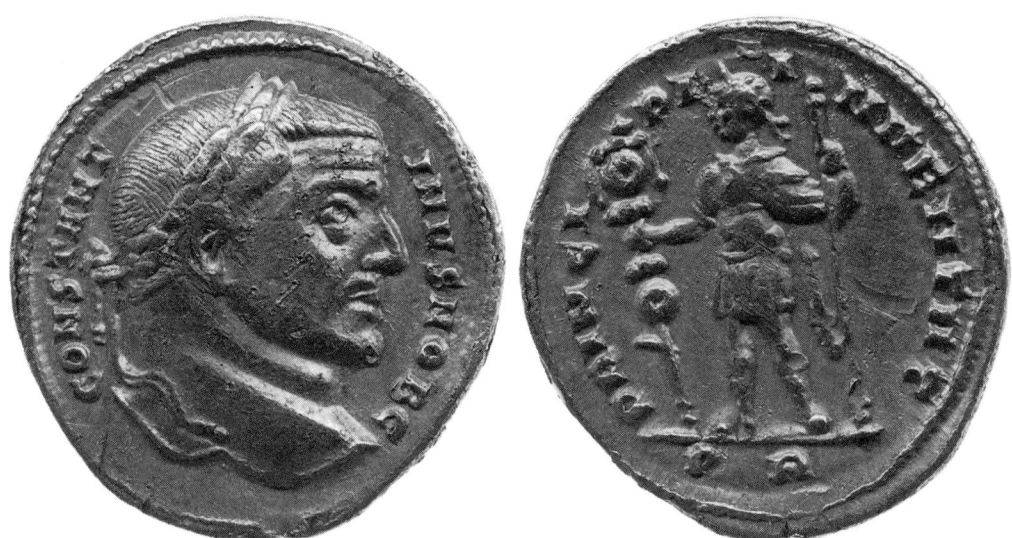

IV.17 Constantinian *aureus*, AD 307. *RIC* VI, Rome, no. 151: *principi iuventutis*.

Such an interpretation of the cuirassed statues' significance is confirmed by the militaristic appearance of Constantine on the coinage, which was accentuated by the youthful ruler's early representation with the heavy-set portrait-types, the cropped hair, and the short beards (figure IV.17) that were common to the Tetrarchs. But as soon as AD 306–307 the mint masters were rejecting this allusion that had marked some of Constantine's early issues, and they began to distinguish the newest member of the tetrarchic college by his youthful face—at times clean-shaven (figure IV.18), at times slightly hirsute (figure IV.19).

Yet the preponderance of reverse types—and above all, their legends—acknowledged the continuity of the Tetrarchic military ideology: *virtus militum*, *liberator orbis*, *perpetuitas augusti*, *ubique victores*, and *optimo principi* (figures IV.20, IV.21, IV.22, IV.23, and IV.5). The vast majority of coin obverse portraits produced at the Rome mint, especially from late AD 312 to 317, show Constantine in the cuirass and pair this with overtly militaristic reverse types and legends—and this is generally reflected in the production at all of the other western mints (figures IV.21, IV.23, IV.24, and IV.25). The militaristic imagery

---

military character on the coins and of the cuirassed statues. Praise formulae given in Kuhoff 1991, 169, with references to Grünewald 1990; already, albeit briefly, Alföldi 1948, 64.

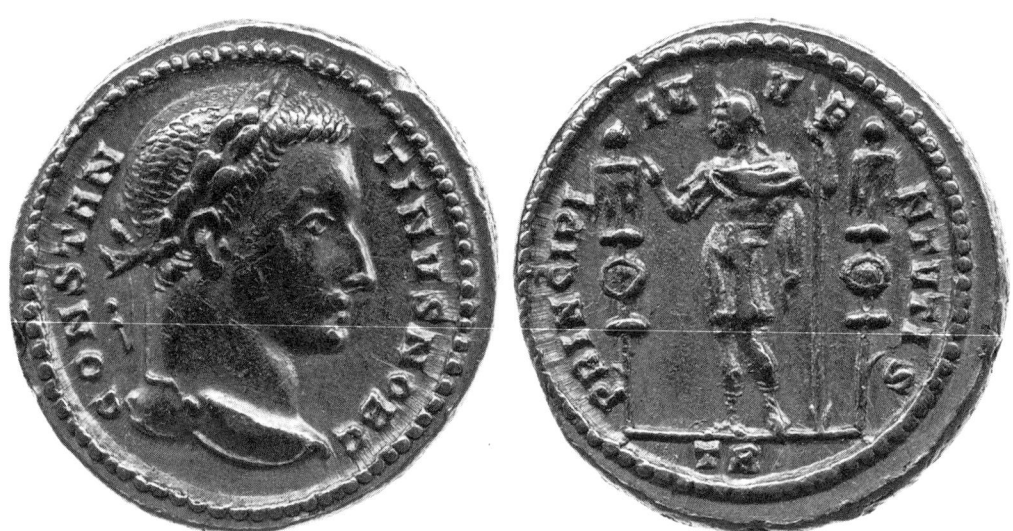

IV.18 Constantinian *aureus*, AD 306–307. *RIC* VI, Trier, no. 627: *principi iuventutis*.

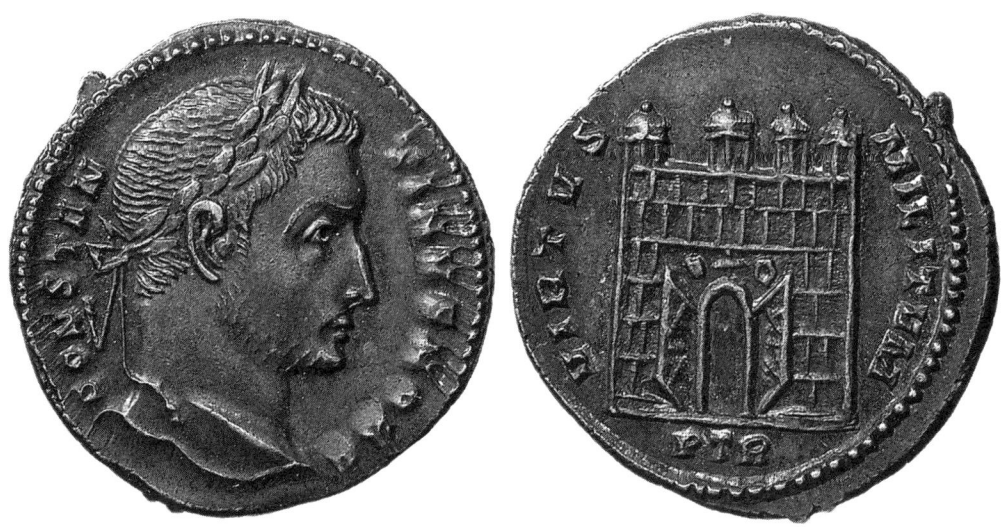

IV.19 Constantinian *argenteus*, AD 306–307. *RIC* VI, Trier, no. 636: *virtus militum*.

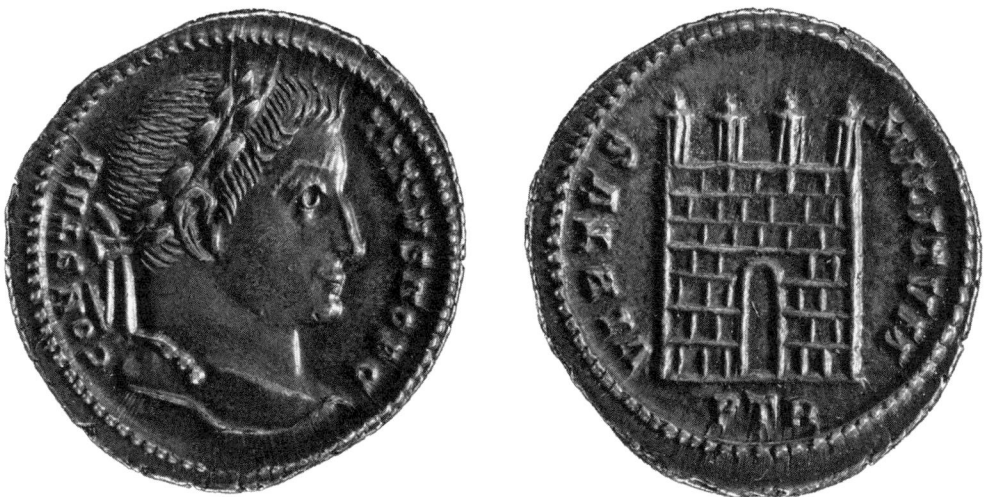

IV.20 Constantinian *argenteus*, AD 306. *RIC* VI, Trier, no. 638: *virtus militum*.

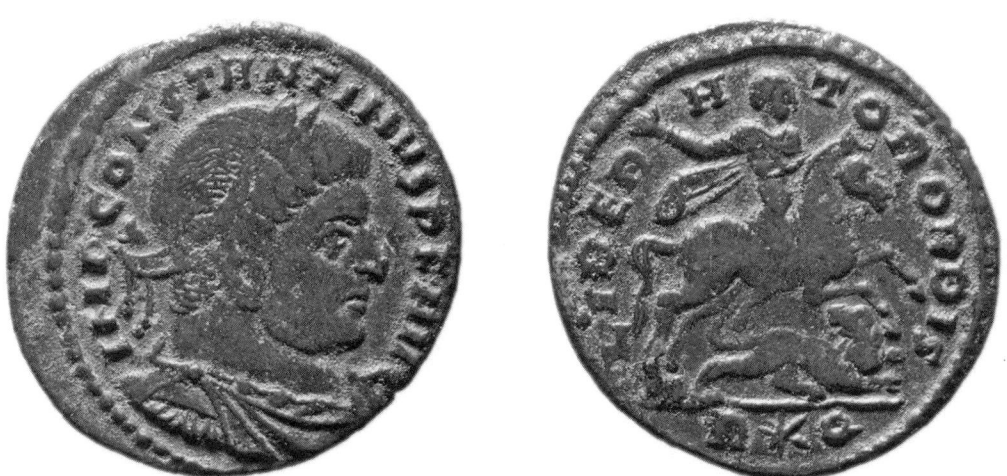

IV.21 Constantinian *nummus*, ca. AD 312. BM inv. no. B2142 (Rome) = Kent 1957, 454: *liberator orbis*.

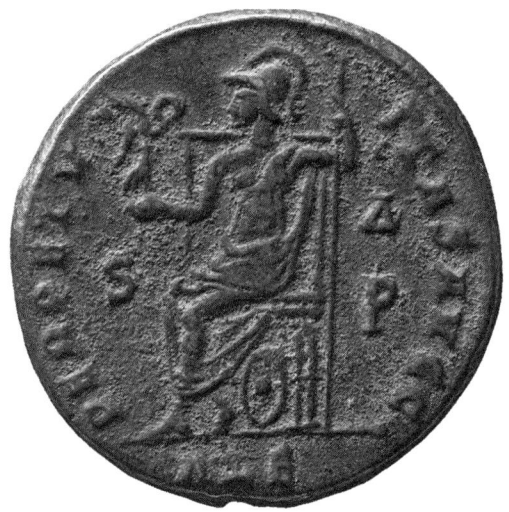

IV.22 Constantinian *follis*, AD 306–307. *RIC* VI, Alexandria, no. 63: *perpetuitas augg*.

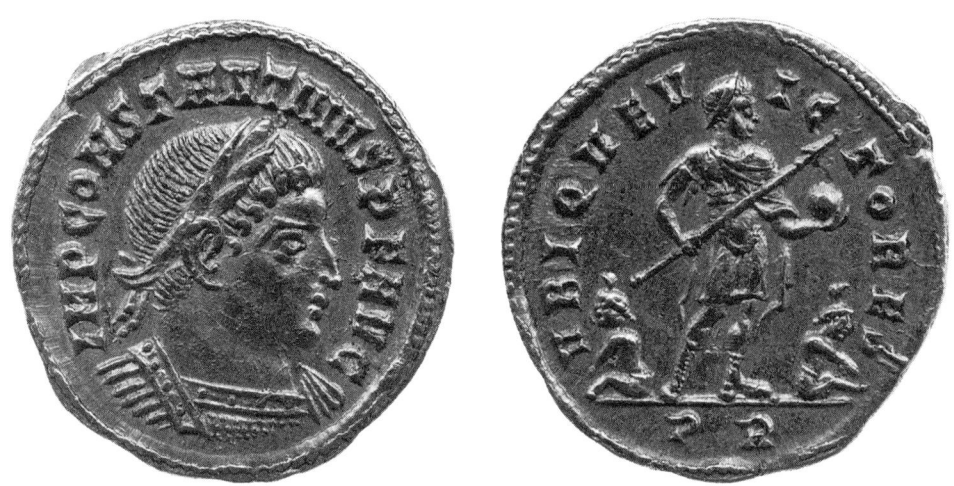

IV.23 Constantinian *aureus*, AD 312–313. *RIC* VI, Rome, no. 284 (add.): *ubique victores*.

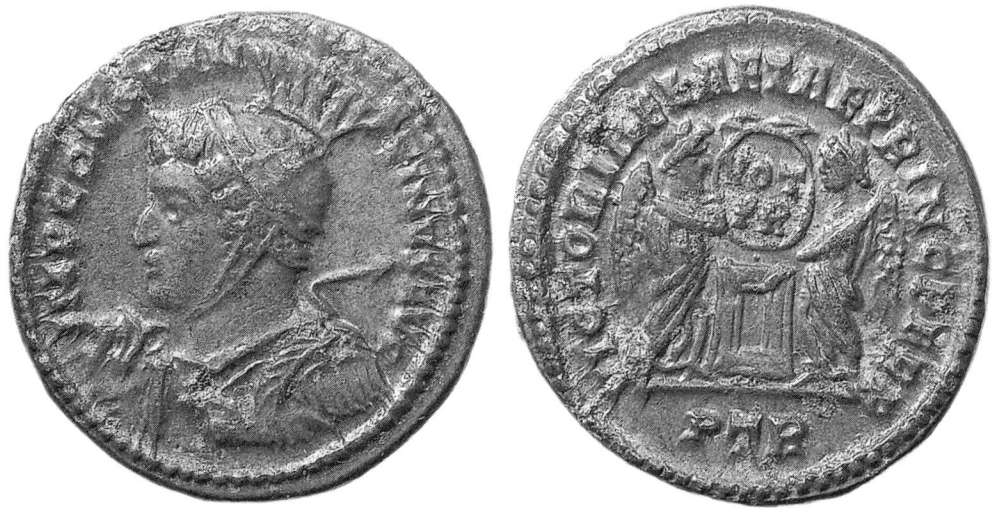

IV.24 Constantinian *aes*, ca. AD 318–319. *RIC* VII, Trier, no. 208A: *victoriae latae princ perp*.

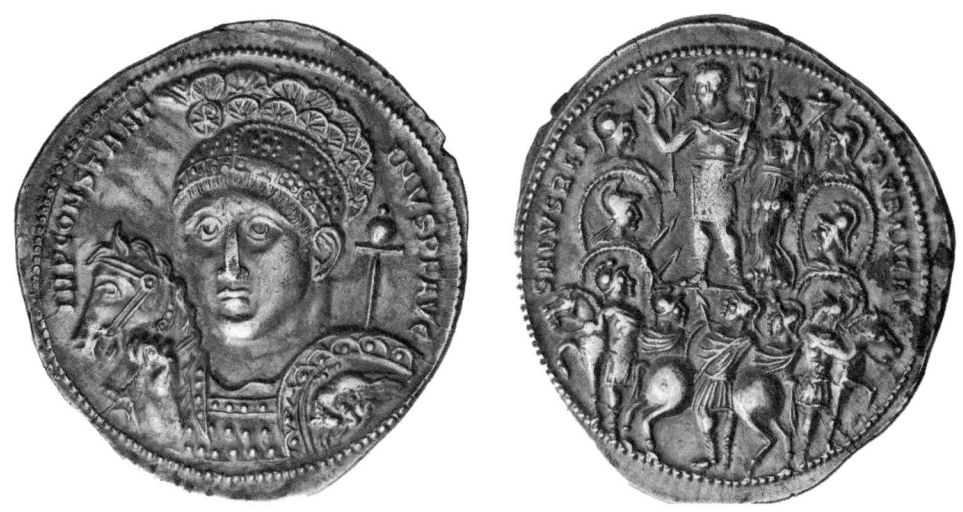

IV.25 Silver medallion of Constantine. *RIC* VII, Ticinum, no. 36.

CHAPTER 4

was equally effective when yoked to explicit reference to Christianity, both on coins and on the medallions (figures IV.24 and IV.25), and continued to dominate the coinage under Constantine's successors.[75]

☙

Across the Empire, such military imagery served as testimony to Constantine's claim to sole rule and as a reminder of the unequal relations between the senatorial class and their emperor. This was acutely felt at Rome, despite the privileged status of the *urbs* and its illustrious history. An expanded clarissimate, with many new senators drawn from the provincial elite, and many elevated from equestrian status, had minimized the roles of all but those from the fabled Roman *gens*, whose prestige endured as a source of influence and whose wealth continued to serve as a basis of power, whether they were pagan or Christian.[76] Constantine repeatedly professed his "restoration" of their status—but the effective scope of that status was nevertheless limited. Most relevant is the fact that senators no longer held military commands, for this had declined in the second half of the third century, after the limitations imposed by Gallienus, and it would eventually become law under Constantine II. Commands were no longer to be an *officium* of the senators; their *militia* was now administration.[77]

The display of honorific statues at Rome subtly reflected the new reality. Senators had long been so honored in the Forum of Trajan. But in the Constantinian period, only one is known to have been represented there in military garb; the commanders' statues stood, by contrast, in the Forum Romanum.[78]

---

[75] The material is readily surveyed in *RIC* VI and VII. The empire-wide role of militaristic imagery under Constantius II is examined in Wienand 2015c; cf. Grünewald 1990, 147–50.

[76] Expanded clarissimate: Salzman 2002, 31–35, and Clemente 2012, 321–22, both with bibliography. Favor toward the old *gens*: Salzman 2002, esp. 97–101; 2016, esp. 13.

[77] Restoration of senatorial status: Barnes 1981, 46; Van Dam 2007, 45–46, citing *CTh* 15.14.4 and with further bibliography; cf. Hekster 1999, 737, n. 72, on *Liberatori Urbis*. No senatorial military commands: Aur. Vict. 33; the fourth-century law apparently applied only to senators without military training: Lizzi Testa 2013, 354. Administration as *militia*: Salzman 2002, 41; cf. Chenault 2012, 108–9; Weisweiler 2015, 20–24.

[78] Forum of Trajan statues: Chenault 2012. Forum Romanum statues: Machado 2006; cf. Weisweiler 2012a and 2012b.

CONSTANTINE'S MILITARY IMAGE

The senatorial elite of Constantine's era was commemorated in Trajan's forum, all of whose statues would presumably have represented them as *togati*, and in many cases gilded, similar to others that survive.[79] Constantine stood amid them, as the recently discovered marble head suggests, *loricatus*[80]; its message was no doubt the same as it was on his arch's depiction of his appearance on the rostra. Constantine's representation on the two monuments, both erected by the senate, would have served as the Roman elite's recognition that the emperor's military might was to be reckoned with and as an acknowledgment of his ability to respond to the slightest threat of usurpation.

To conclude: Constantine's military image at Rome was consistent with what appeared on the coinage from all the imperial mints, both east and west; thus, given its widespread geographical appearance, this regularity cannot be attributed to independent design without Constantine's implicit, if not explicit, approval. The "triumphal" character of so much of this numismatic imagery found its most profound instantiation when set in the context of the Roman monumental arch, where its significance was enhanced both by the architectural form's long-accrued meaning and by the totality of the monument's decoration.

On the arch, the image of Constantine *paludatus* (figure IV.2) or *loricatus* (figure IV.15) took its place amid other images and monuments that publicly displayed such military scenes as taking place at Rome. The *adlocutio* scene on the arch of Constantine is also marked by specific reference to architectural monuments that set its scene of recent events in a recognizable Roman locale. This characteristic follows the precedent of earlier monuments in the city and is shared by several of the arch's reused Aurelian panels (*adventus, profectio*).[81] Such topographical specificity is readily distinguished from the generalized

---

[79] Cf. *ILS* 1273 = *CIL* III.19 (*statuam civili habitu*), *ILS* 1281 = *CIL* VI.1678 and *ILS* 1282 = *CIL* VI.1767 (*togatam statuam*).

[80] See n. 73 above.

[81] The same is true of two of the Aurelian reliefs in the Conservatori: the sacrifice on the Capitol and the triumph.

setting employed for other panels, as well as on the Hadrianic tondi, on which the setting remains vague and nondescript. A fundamental difference is to be grasped: one demonstrates the emperor's actual presence, while the other evokes his participation in an eternalizing mythos. This is a distinction that, *mutatis mutandis*, would eventually be enshrined by the Christian contrast of the temporal and the spiritual.

As has been suggested, the setting of the *adlocutio* in the Forum Romanum (figure IV.7) was a senatorial acknowledgment of Constantine's powers and a demonstration of his obligations, both *domi militiaeque*. The site of the arch, apparently alongside the *pomerium* at its northeast corner, may be seen to corroborate such an interpretation. According to Tacitus, the Romulean *pomerium* ran from the Forum Boarium, along the base of the Palatine, to the altar of Consus and then to the *Curiae Veteres*, the *Sacellum Larum*, and then to the forum—most likely describing the parameters of the city's original foundation centered on the Palatine, what Varro had called *Roma Quadrata*. The arch was set near what is held to be the site of the *Curiae Veteres*, which marked, at the northeast corner of the Palatine, at the very edge of the city, the archaic line of the *pomerium*.[82] The topographical setting was reaffirmed by the arrangement of the Aurelian panels' subjects on the arch's two sides in antithetical groupings—a matter of design that echoes that on earlier monuments, most notably the arch at Benevento—so that the arch's two main faces proclaimed differing collective messages to the city and to the Roman world beyond the *urbs*, messages that recall the religious and political distinction we have recognized between *domi* and *militiae* within the pomerial ideology.[83] This was still a living concept in the age of Constantine, even if predominantly the concern of antiquarians, whose understanding of ancient practices was clearly limited—as one sees from the *pomerium*'s appearance in the writings of

---

[82] Tac., *Ann.* 12.24; Varro *apud* Solinus 1.17. *Roma Quadrata*: discussion in Plattner-Ashby, 448–49, and Coarelli in *LTUR* IV:207–9. *Curia Veteres*: Plattner-Ashby, 147, and Torelli in *LTUR* I:336–37, all with sources, maps, and bibliography; cf. Bravi 2012, 459–62.

[83] Aurelian panels: Torelli in *LTUR* I:98–99, setting these in the context of the imagery on Trajan's Benevento arch. Pomerial ideology: sources, bibliography, and discussion in Andreussi in *LTUR* IV:96–105.

Sidonius and Macrobius.[84] Thus, one comprehends that, on the arch's *adlocutio* panel, Constantine's image in the forum, *paludatus*, signaled that it should be remembered by one and all that he too was willing to "cross the *pomerium*," if need arose, and assert his military might in the city. The message to potential usurpers was clear.

Finally, for the citizens of the *urbs*, Rome was not "where the emperor was"—to paraphrase Herodian. Despite his almost perpetual absence, they yearned for his "homecoming": *et iam reditum desideramus* (we long for your return), as the Panegyric relates. But the city's concern for the emperor's welfare was coupled traditionally to that of his troops. Constantine would write to the senate, as Cicero had done more than three hundred years before, *nos exercitusque nostri valemus* (we and our armies are well): his claim to legitimate rule was his military might, and this guaranteed stability in the old capital, something perhaps reinforced by his infrequent presence. And so the Constantinian age brought to realization, in paradoxical form, the prediction of Menander Rhetor: "The emperor's weapons are a safer fortress for us than our cities' walls."[85]

---

[84] Sid. Apoll. *Ep.* 1.5.9; Macrob. *Sat.* 1.7.15, 1.24.12; cf. S.H.A., *Aurel.* 21.9–10, with Syme 1978.

[85] "Rome is where the emperor is": Herodian. 1.6.3–5. "Homecoming": *Pan. Lat.* X (2), 14. "We and our armies are well": *CIL* VI.40776, lines 11–12, with commentary and contextualization in Weisweiler 2012b, 310–12; cf. Cic. *Fam.* 5.2.1, and how the topos was employed (albeit inappositely) by Valentinian in AD 450 (*Nov.* 1, 3). Menander Rhetor: *Peri Epideiktikon* 377, trans. Russell and Wilson; cited by Ando 2017, 405.

BIBLIOGRAPHY

Abaecherli Boyce 1942. A. Abaecherli Boyce, "The Origin of Ornamenta Triumphalia," *CP* 37 (1942): 130–41.

Albertoni 1993. M. Albertoni, "Le statue di Giulio Cesare e del Navarca," *BullComm* 95 (1993): 175–82.

Alföldi 1934. A. Alföldi, "Die Ausgestaltung des monarchischen Zeremoniells am römischn Kaiserhofe," *RM* 49 (1934): 1–118.

Alföldi 1948. A. Alföldi, *The Conversion of Constantine and Pagan Rome*. Oxford, 1948.

Alföldi 1959. A. Alföldi, "Hasta-Summa Imperii: The Spear as Embodiment of Sovereignty in Rome," *AJA* 63 (1959): 1–27.

Alföldi 1969. A. Alföldi, "Der früheste Denartypus des L. Buca mit CAESAR DICTATOR PERPETVO," *SchwMbll* 19 (1969): 1–8.

Alföldi 1970. A. Alföldi, *Die monarchische Repräsentation im römischen Kaiserreiche* [1935]. Darmstadt, 1970.

Alföldi 1976. A. Alföldi, *Oktavians Aufstieg zur Macht*. Bonn, 1976.

Ando 2011a. C. Ando, "Law and the Landscape of Empire," in S. Benoist, A. Daguet-Gagey, and C. Hoët-van Cauwenberghe, eds., *Figures d'empire, fragments de mémoire: Pouvoirs et identités dans le monde romain imperial (IIe s. av. n. è.– VIe s. de n. è)*, 25–47. Lille, 2011.

Ando 2011b. C. Ando, *Law, Language, and Empire in the Roman Tradition*. Philadelphia, 2011.

Ando 2017. C. Ando, "Triumph in the Decentralized Empire," in Goldbeck and Wienand 2017, 397–418.

Badian 1996. E. Badian, "Tribuni plebis and res publica," in J. Linderski, ed., *Imperium Sine Fine: T. Robert S. Broughton and the Roman Republic*, 187–213. Stuttgart, 1996.

Baker 2014. M. Baker, *The Marble Index: Roubiliac and Sculptural Portraiture in Eighteenth-Century Britain*. New Haven and London, 2014.

BIBLIOGRAPHY

Balsdon 1939. J. P. V. D. Balsdon, "Consular Provinces under the Late Republic, I, General Considerations," *JRS* 29 (1939): 57–73.

Bardill 2012. J. Bardill, *Constantine, Divine Emperor of the Christian Golden Age*. Cambridge, 2012.

Barnes 1974. T. D. Barnes, "The Victories of Augustus," *JRS* 64 (1974): 21–26.

Barnes 1981. T. D. Barnes, *Constantine and Eusebius*. Cambridge, MA, 1981.

Barnes 1982. T. D. Barnes, *The New Empire of Diocletian and Constantine*. Cambridge, MA, 1982.

Barnes 2014. T. D. Barnes, *Constantine: Dynasty, Religion, and Power in the Later Roman Empire* [2011]. Malden and Oxford, 2014.

Barrow 1973. R. H. Barrow, *Prefect and Emperor: The Relationes of Symmachus AD 384*. Oxford, 1973.

Bartocini 1932. R. Bartocini, "La statua di porfidio del Museo Arcivescovile in Ravenna," *FelRav* 40 (1932): 5–31.

Baudy 1998. D. Baudy, *Römische Umgangsriten: Eine ethologische Untersuchung der Funktion von Wiederholung für religiöses Verhalten*. Berlin and New York, 1998.

Beard 2007. M. Beard, *The Roman Triumph*. Cambridge, 2007.

Beard, North, and Price 1998. M. Beard, J. North, and S. Price, *Religions of Rome*, 2 vols. Cambridge, 1998.

Beckmann 2011. M. Beckmann, *The Column of Marcus Aurelius: The Genesis and Meaning of a Roman Imperial Monument*. Chapel Hill, 2011.

Behrends 1970. O. Behrends, "Ius und ius civile: Untersuchungen zur Herkunft des ius-Begriffs im römischen Zivilrecht," in *Sympotica Franz Wieacker: Sexagenario Sasbachwaldeni a suis libata*, 11–58. Göttingen, 1970.

Bellen 1985. H. Bellen, "Cicero und der Aufstieg Oktavians," *Gymnasium* 92 (1985): 161–89.

Bennett 2001. J. Bennett, *Trajan: Optimus Princeps*. Bloomington and Indianapolis, 2001.

Benoist 2005. S. Benoist, *Rome, le prince et la cité*. Paris, 2005.

Benoist 2012. S. Benoist, "*Princeps et Legati*, de la conception impériale de la délégation de pouvoir: Nature, function, devenir, d'Auguste au IVe siècle de notre ère," in *Hiérarchie des pouvoirs, delegation de pouvoir et responsabilité des administrateurs dans l'Antiquité et au Moyen Âge*, 135–59. Metz, 2012.

Béranger 1973. J. Béranger, "L'accession d'Auguste et l'idéologie du *privatus* [1958]," reprinted in Béranger, *Principatus: Études de notions et d'histoire politiques dans l'Antiquité gréco-romaine*, 243–58. Geneva, 1973.

BIBLIOGRAPHY

Bérenger 2009. A. Bérenger, "L'Adventus des gouverneurs de provence," in A. Bérenger and E. Perrin-Saminadayar, eds., *Les Entrées royales et impériale: Histoire, représentation et diffusion d'une cérémonie publique, de l'Orient ancien à Byzance*, 123–38. Paris, 2009.

Bergemann 1990. J. Bergemann, *Römische Reiterstatuen: Ehrendenkmäler im öffentlichen Bereich*. Mainz, 1990.

Bergmann 2018. M. Bergmann, "Zur Datierung und Deutung der Chlamysfiguren aus rotem Pophyr," *ActaArchArtiumPert* 30 (2018): 73–113.

Berthelet 2015. Y. Berthelet, *Gouverner avec les dieux: Autorité, auspices et pouvoir, sous la République romaine et sous Auguste*. Paris, 2015.

Bianchi 1997. E. Bianchi, *Fictio Iuris: Richerche sulla finzione in diritto romano dal period arcaico all'epoca augustea*. Padua, 1997.

Billows 1993. R. Billows, "The Religious Procession of the Ara Pacis Augustae: Augustus' *Supplicatio* in 13 BC," *JRA* 6 (1993): 80–92.

Binder 1991. G. Binder, ed., *Saeculum Augustum III: Kunst und Bildersprache*. Darmstadt, 1991.

Birley 1988. A. R. Birley, *Septimius Severus: The African Emperor* [1972]. New Haven and London, 1988.

Bispham 2006. E. Bispham, "COLONIAM DEDUCERE: How Roman Was Roman Colonization during the Middle Republic?" in G. Bradley and J.-P. Wilson, eds., *Greek and Roman Colonization: Origins, Ideologies, and Interactions*, 73–160. Lampeter, 2006.

Bleckmann 1991. B. Bleckmann, "Die Chronik des Johannes Zonaras und eine Pagane Quelle zur Geschichte Konstantins," *Historia* 40 (1991): 343–65.

Bleckmann 2014. B. Bleckmann, "Costantino dopo la battaglia presso il Ponte Milvio: Note sul medaglione di *Ticinum*," in Dal Covolo and Gasparro 2014, 197–220.

Bleicken 2016. J. Bleicken, *Augustus: The Biography* [1998], trans. A. Bell. London, 2016.

Blonce 2014. C. Blonce, "*Arcum cum statua*: Les dédicaces des arcs monumentaux dans leur contexte," in W. Eck, P. Funke, et al., eds., *Öffentlichkeit—Monument—Text: XIV Congressus Internationalis Epigraphiae Graecae et Latinae, Akten*, 698–701. Berlin, 2014.

Boak 1918. A. E. R. Boak, "The Extraordinary Commands from 80 to 48 BC: A Study in the Origins of the Principate," *AHR* 24 (1918): 1–25.

Boatwright 1986. M. T. Boatwright, "The Pomerial Extension of Augustus," *Historia* 35 (1986): 13–27.

Bodnaruk 2015. M. Bodnaruk, "Producing Distinction: Aristocratic and Imperial Representation in the Constantinian Age," in G. Greatrex, H. Elton, and L. McMahon, eds., *Shifting Genres in Late Antiquity*, 135–55. Farnham, 2015.

Boschung 1993. D. Boschung, *Die Bildnisse des Augustus*. Berlin, 1993.

Botsford 1909. G. W. Botsford, *The Roman Assemblies from Their Origin to the End of the Republic*. New York, 1909.

Bowden, Gutteridge, and Machado 2006. W. Bowden, A. Gutteridge, and C. Machado, eds., *Social and Political Life in Late Antiquity*, vol. 3.1, *Late Antique Archaeology*. Leiden, 2006.

Brandenburg 2005. H. Brandenburg, *Ancient Churches of Rome from the Fourth to the Seventh Centuries*. Turnhout, 2005.

Brandenburg 2005–2006. H. Brandenburg, "Die Architektur der Basilika San Paolo fuori le mura: Das Apostelgrab als Zentrum der Liturgie und des Märtyrkultes," *RM* 112 (2005–2006): 237–75.

Bravi 2012. A. Bravi, "L'arco di Costantino nel suo contesto topografico," in G. Bonamente, N. Lenski, and R. Lizzi Testa, eds., *Costantino prima e dopo Costantino* [*Constantine before and after Constantine*], 445–62. Bari, 2012.

Brenk 1987. B. Brenk, "Spolia from Constantine to Charlemagne: Aesthetics versus Ideology," *DOP* 41 (1987): 103–9.

Brennan 2000. T. C. Brennan, *The Praetorship in the Roman Republic*, 2 vols. Oxford, 2000.

Brennan 2004. T. C. Brennan, "Power and Process under the Republican 'Constitution,'" in H. Flower, ed., *The Cambridge Companion to the Roman Republic*, 31–65. Cambridge, 2004.

Brilliant 1967. R. Brilliant, *The Arch of Septimius Severus in Rome*. Rome, 1967.

Broggini 1966. G. Broggini, "Ius lexque esto" [1959], reprinted in Broggini, *Coniectanea: Studi di diritto romano*, 55–81. Milan, 1966.

Bruggisser 2002. P. Bruggisser, "Constantin aux rostres," in G. Bonamente and F. Paschoud, eds., *Historiae Augustae: Collquium Perusinum*, 73–91. Bari, 2002.

Brunt 1977. P. A. Brunt, "Lex de imperio Vespasiani," *JRS* 67 (1977): 95–116.

Brunt and Moore 1989. P. A. Brunt and P. Moore, eds., *Res Gestae Divi Augusti: The Achievements of the Divine Augustus* [1967]. Oxford, 1989.

Bruun 1976a. P. Bruun, "Notes on the Transmission of Imperial Images in Late Antiquity," in *Studia Romana in honorem Petri Krarup Septuagenarii*, 122–31. Odense, 1976.

Bruun 1976b. P. Bruun, "Portrait of a Conspirator: Constantine's Break with the Tetrarchy," *Arctos* 10 (1976): 5–23.

BIBLIOGRAPHY

Busch 2007. A. Busch, "*Militia in Urbe*: The Military Presence in Rome," in de Blois and Lo Cascio 2007, 315–41.

Busch 2011. A. Busch, *Militär in Rom: Militärische und paramilitärische Einheiten im kaiserzeitlichen Stadtbild*. Wiesbaden, 2011.

Buttrey 1983. T. V. Buttrey, "The Dates of the Arches of 'Diocletian' and Constantine," *Historia* 32 (1983): 375–83.

Campbell 2000. B. Campbell, ed., *The Writings of the Roman Land Surveyors: Introduction, Text, Translation, and Commentary*. London, 2000.

Campbell 2005. B. Campbell, "The Army," in *CAH* XII:110–30.

Cameron 2013. A. Cameron, "Il potere di Costantino: Dimensioni e limiti del potere imperiale," in *COSTANTINO I*, vol. I: 105–15.

Cameron and Hall 2010. A. Cameron and S. Hall, trans. and comm., *Eusebius: Life of Constantine* [1999]. Oxford, 2010.

Capogrossi Colognesi and Tassi Scandone 2009. L. Capogrossi Colognesi and E. Tassi Scandone, eds., *La Lex de Imperio Vespasiani e la Roma dei Flavi*. Rome, 2009.

Carlà 2015. F. Carlà, "*Pomerium, fines*, and *ager Romanus*: Understanding Rome's 'First Boundary,'" *Latomus* 74 (2015): 599–630.

Catalano 1960. P. Catalano, *Contributi allo studio del diritto augurale*, vol. I. Turin, 1960.

Catalano 1978. P. Catalano, "Aspetti spaziali del sistema giuridico-religioso romano: Mundus, templum, urbs, ager, Latium, Italia," *ANRW* 2.16 (1978): 440–553.

Cecamore 2002. C. Cecamore, "Le Curiae Veteres sulla Forma Urbis Marmorea e il pomerio romuleo secondo Tacito," *RM* 109 (2002): 43–58.

Champlin 1982 [= 1985]. E. Champlin, The *Suburbium* of Rome," *AJAH* 7 (1982 [= 1985]): 97–117.

Chastagnol 1960. A. Chastagnol, *La prefecture urbaine à Rome sous le bas-empire*. Paris, 1960.

Chastagnol 1966. A. Chastagnol, "Sur quelques documents rélatifs à la basilique de Saint-Paul-hors-les-murs," *Mélanges d'archéologie et d'histoire offerts à André Piganiol*, 3 vols., I:421–38. Paris, 1966.

Chastagnol 1988. A. Chastagnol, "Les inscriptions des monuments inaugurés lors des fêtes imperiales," *MEFRA* 100 (1988): 13–26.

Chenault 2012. R. Chenault, "Statues of Senators in the Forum of Trajan and the Roman Forum in Late Antiquity," *JRS* 102 (2012): 103–32.

Chioffi 1992–1993. L. Chioffi, "*Ferter Resius*: Tra *l'augurium* di Romolo e il *pomerium* di Claudio," *RendPontAccArch* 65 (1992–1993): 127–53.

BIBLIOGRAPHY

Chrissanthos 2001. S. G. Chrissanthos, "Caesar and the Mutiny of 47 BC," *JRS* 91 (2001): 63–75.

Clemente 2012. G. Clemente, "Il senato e il governo dell'impero tra IV e VI secolo: La religione e la politica," in G. Bonamente, N. Lenski, and R. Lizzi Testa, eds., *Costantino prima e dopo Constantino / Constantine before and after Constantine*, 321–31. Bari, 2012.

Coarelli 2000. F. Coarelli, *The Column of Trajan*. Rome, 2000.

Coarelli 2009. F. Coarelli, "Il pomerio di Vespasiano e Tito," in L. Capogrossi Colognesi and E. Tassi Scandone, eds., *La Lex de Imperio Vespasiani e la Roma dei Flavi* (Rome, 2009), 299–309.

Coleman-Norton 1966. P. R. Coleman-Norton, *Roman State and Christian Church: A Collection of Legal Documents to AD 535*, 2 vols. London, 1966.

Coles 2017. A. J. Coles, "Founding Colonies and Fostering Careers in the Middle Republic," *CJ* 112 (2017): 280–317.

Coli 1951. U. Coli, *Regnum*. Rome, 1951 = *SDHI* 17 (1951).

Combès 1966. R. Combès, *Imperator: Recherches sur l'emploi et la signification du titre d'Imperator dans la Rome républicaine*. Paris, 1966.

Conforto 2001. M. L. Conforto, "L'arco dedicato a Costantino: La sovrapposizione di due monumenti," in M. L. Conforto et al., *Adriano e Costantino: Le due fasi dell'arco nella valle del Colosseo*, 11–21. Milan, 2001.

Cooley 2009. A. Cooley, ed., tr., comm., *Res Gestae Divi Augusti*. Cambridge, 2009.

Corbier 1997. M. Corbier, "Pallas et la state de César: Affichage et espace public à Rome," *RN* 152 (1997): 11–40.

Corcoran 2000. S. Corcoran, *The Empire of the Tetrarchs: Imperial Pronouncements and Government AD 284–324* [1996]. Oxford, 2000.

Cotton and Yakobson 2002. H. M. Cotton and A. Yakobson, "Arcanum Imperii: The Powers of Augustus," in G. Clark and T. Rajak, eds., *Philosophy and Power in the Graeco-Roman World: Essays in Honour of Miriam Griffin*, 193–209. Oxford, 2002.

Coulston 2000. J. Coulston, "'Armed Men and Belted Men': The Soldiery in Imperial Rome," in J. Coulston and H. Dodge, eds., *Ancient Rome: The Archaeology of the Eternal City*, 76–118. Oxford, 2000.

Coulston 2007. J. Coulston, "Art, Culture, and Service: The Depiction of Soldiers on Funerary Monuments of the 3rd Century AD," in de Blois and Lo Cascio 2007, 529–61.

Cressendi 1950. G. Cressendi, "Caput Velatum e Cinctus Gabinus," *Rend Linc*, ser. 8, no. 5 (1950): 450–56.

BIBLIOGRAPHY

Cullhead 1994. M. Cullhead, *Conservator Urbis Suae: Studies in the Politics and Propaganda of the Emperor Maxentius*. Stockholm, 1994.

Curran 2000. J. Curran, *Pagan City and Christian Capital: Rome in the Fourth Century*. Oxford, 2000.

D'Accinni 1943–1945. A. D'Accinni, "Sull'ubicazione della statua loricate di Cesare," *BullComm* 71 (1943–1945): 113–15.

dal Covolo and Gasparro 2014. E. dal Covolo and G. Sfameni Gasarro, eds., *Costantino il Grande alle radici dell'Europa*. Vatican City, 2014.

Dalla Rosa 2011. A. Dalla Rosa, "Dominating the Auspices: Augustus, Augury, and the Proconsuls," in J. H. Richardson and F. Santangelo, eds., *Priests and State in the Roman World*, 243–69. Stuttgart, 2011.

Dalla Rosa 2014. A. Dalla Rosa, *Cura et tutela: Le origini del potere imperial sulle province proconsolari*. Stuttgart, 2014.

De Blois and Lo Cascio 2007. L. de Blois and E. Lo Cascio, eds., *The Impact of the Roman Army (200 BC–AD 476): Economic, Social, Political, Religious, and Cultural Aspects*. Leiden and Boston, 2007.

De Caprariis 2003. F. De Caprariis, "L'arco di Costantino: Due Problemi," *Rend Linc* 14 (2003): 467–91.

Delbrueck 2009. R. Delbrueck, *Dittici consolari tardoantichi*, ed. M. Abbatepaolo [1929]. Santo Spirito, 2009.

De Maria 1988. S. De Maria, *Gli archi onorari di Roma dell'Italia romana*. Rome, 1988.

De Sanctis 2007. G. De Sanctis, "Solco, muro, pomerio," *MEFRA* 119 (2007): 503–26.

Dirven 2007. L. Dirven, "The Julius Terentius Fresco and the Roman Imperial Cult," *Mediterraneo Antico* 10 (2007): 115–28.

Driediger-Murphy 2019. L. G. Driediger-Murphy, *Roman Republican Augury: Freedom and Control*. Oxford, 2019.

Drijvers 1976. H. J. W. Drijvers, *The Religion of Palmyra*. Leiden, 1976.

Drogula 2015. F. K. Drogula, *Commanders and Commands in the Roman Republic and Early Empire*. Chapel Hill, 2015.

Dubourdieu 1986. A. Dubourdieu, "Cinctus Gabinus," *Latomus* 45 (1986): 3–20.

Dubourdieu 1988. A. Dubourdieu, "Deux définitions du *cinctus Gabinus* chez Servius," in D. Porte and J.-P. Néraudau, eds., *Hommages à Henri le Bonniec: Res Sacrae*, 163–70. Brussels, 1988.

Eck 1984. W. Eck, "Senatorial Self-Representation: Developments in the Augustan Period," in F. Millar and E. Segal, eds., *Caesar Augustus: Seven Aspects*, 129–67. Oxford, 1984.

BIBLIOGRAPHY

Eck 1996. W. Eck, "I sistemi di trasmissione delle comuncazioni d'ufficio in età altoimperiale," in M. Pani, ed., *Epigrafia e territorio: Politica e società: Temi di antichità romane, IV*, 331–52. Bari, 1996.

Eck 1999. W. Eck, "Kaiserliche Imperatorenakklamation und ornamenta triumphalia," *ZPE* 124 (1999): 223–27.

Eckstein 1979. A. M. Eckstein, "The Foundation Day of Roman 'Coloniae,'" *CalifStClassAnt* 12 (1979): 85–97.

Eder 1990. W. Eder, "Augustus and the Power of Tradition: The Augustan Principate as Binding Link between Republic and Empire," in K. Raaflaub and M. Toher, eds., *Between Republic and Empire: Interpretations of Augustus and his Principate*, 71–122. Berkeley, 1990.

Elsner 2000. J. Elsner, "From the Culture of *Spolia* to the Cult of Relics: The Arch of Constantine and the Genesis of Late Antique Forms," *PBSR* 68 (2000): 149–84.

Elsner 2006. J. Elsner, "Perspectives in Art," in Lenski 2006b, 255–77.

Evers 1992. C. Evers, "Betrachtungen zur Ikonographie des Maxentius: Zu einer neuen Porträt-Replik im Kestner-Museum Hannover," *Niederdeutsche Beiträge zur Kunstgeschichte* 31 (1992): 9–22.

Ewald and Noreña 2010. B. C. Ewald and C. F. Noreña, eds., *The Emperor and Rome: Space, Representation, and Ritual*. Cambridge, 2010.

Fanizza 2014. L. Fanizza, "*Lex curiata, lex Cornelia, senatus consulta, imperium*: Palingenesi e mantriche ripetizioni," *Politica Antica* 4 (2014): 55–72.

Faust 2011. S. Faust, "Original und Spolie: Interaktive Strategien im Bildprogramm des Konstantinsbogen," *RM* 117 (2011): 377–408.

Fears 1981. J. R. Fears, "The Theology of Victory," *ANRW* II.17.2 (1981): 736–948.

Fejfer 2008. J. Fejfer, *Roman Portraits in Context*. Berlin and New York, 2008.

Feldherr 1998. A. Feldherr, *Spectacle and Society in Livy's History*. Berkeley, 1998.

Felletti Maj 1977. B. Felletti Maj, *La tradizione italica nell'arte romana*. Rome, 1977.

Felten 1971. F. Felten, "Römische Panzerstatue in München," *AA* 86 (1971): 233–46.

Ferrary 2001a. J.-L. Ferrary, "Les pouvoirs d'Auguste: L'affranchissement de la limite du pomerium," in N. Belayche, ed., *Rome, les Césars, et la Ville aux deux premiers siècles de notre ère*, 9–22. Rennes, 2001.

Ferrary 2001b. J.-L. Ferrary, "À propos des pouvoirs d'Auguste," *CCG* 12 (2001): 101–54.

Ferrary 2003. J.-L. Ferrary, "La législation romaine dans les liveres 21 à 45 de Tite-Live," in *Laurea Internationalis: Festschrift für Jochen Bleichen zum 75*, 107–41. Geburtstag, 2003.

BIBLIOGRAPHY

Fiori 2014a. R. Fiori, "La convocazione dei comizi centuriati: Diritto costituzionale e diritto augurale," *ZRG* 131 (2014): 60–176.

Fiori 2014b. R. Fiori, "Gli auspices e i confini," *Fundamina* 20 (2014): 301–11.

Fittschen 1970. K. Fittschen, review of Niemeyer 1968, *BJ* 170 (1970): 541–52.

Flory 1989. M. B. Flory, "Octavian and the Omen of the *Gallina Alba*," *CJ* 84 (1989): 343–56.

Fraschetti 1999. A. Fraschetti, *La conversion da Roma pagana à Roma christiana*. Rome and Bari, 1999.

Freier 1963. H. Freier, *Caput Velare*. Tubingen, 1963.

Frothingham 1912. A. L. Frothingham, "Who Built the Arch of Constantine? Its History from Domitian to Constantine," *AJA* 16 (1912): 668–86.

Galinier 2012. M. Galinier, "*Domi forisque*: Les vêtements romains de la vertu," in F. Gherchanoc and V. Huet, eds., *Vêtements antiques: S'habiller, se déshabiller dans les mondes anciens*, 189–208. Paris, 2012.

Gargola 1995. D. J. Gargola, *Lands, Laws, and Gods: Magistrates and Ceremony in the Regulation of Public Lands in Republican Rome*. Chapel Hill, 1995.

Gauer 1977. W. Gauer, *Untersuchungen zur Trajanssäule*, vol. I. Berlin, 1977.

Gehn 2012. U. Gehn, *Ehrenstatuen in der Spätantike: Chlamydati und Togati*. Wiesbaden, 2012.

Gelzer 1968. M. Gelzer, *Caesar: Politician and Statesman*, trans. P. Needham. Cambridge, 1968.

Ghedini 1986. F. Ghedini, "Riflessi della politica domizianea nei rilievi flavi di Palazzo della Cancelleria," *BullComm* 91 (1986): 291–309.

Giardina 1995. A. Giardina, "Seneca, Claudio e il pomerio," in *Alla signorina: Mélanges offerts à Noëlle de la Blanchandière*, 123–40. Rome, 1995.

Gildersleeve and Lodge 1895. B. L. Gildersleeve and G. Lodge, *Gildersleeve's Latin Grammar*, 3rd ed. London and New York, 1895.

Giovannini 1983. A. Giovannini, *Consulare Imperium*. Basel, 1983.

Girardet 1987. K. M. Girardet, "Die Lex Iulia de provinciis (46 v. Chr.): Vorgeschichte-Inhalt-Wirkungen," *RhM* 130 (1987): 291–329.

Girardet 1990a. K. M. Girardet, "Die Rechtstatus Oktavians im Jahre 32 v. Chr.," *RhM* 133 (1990): 322–50.

Girardet 1990b. K. M. Girardet, "Die Entmachtung des Konsulates im Übergang von der Republik zur Monarchie und die Rechtsgrundlagen des augusteischen Prinzipats," in W. Görler and S. Koster, eds., *Pratum Saraviense: Festgabe für Peter Steinmetz*, 89–126. Stuttgart, 1990.

BIBLIOGRAPHY

Girardet 1993. K. M. Girardet, "'Traditionalismus' in Politik des Oktavian/Augustus—mentalitäts-geschichtliche Aspekte," *Klio* 75 (1993): 202–18.

Girardet 1995. K. M. Girardet, "Per continuos annos decem (res gestae divi Augusti 7, 1): Zur Frage nach dem Endtermin des Triumvirats," *Chiron* 25 (1995): 147–61.

Giudetti 2013. F. Giudetti, "Iconografia di Costantino: L'invenzione di una nuova imagine imperiale," in COSTANTINO I, vol. I: 185–200.

Giuliani 2000. L. Giuliani, "Des Siegers Ansprache an das Volk: Zur politischen Brisanz der Frieserzählung am Constantinsbogen," in C. Neumeister and W. Raeck, eds., *Rede und Redner: Bewertung und Darstellung in den antiken Kulturen*, 269–87. Frankfurt, 2000.

Glinister 2009. F. Glinister, "Veiled and Unveiled: Uncovering Roman Influence in Hellenistic Italy," in M. Gleba and H. Becker, eds., *Votives, Places, and Rituals in Etruscan Religion: Studies in Honor of Jean MacIntosh Turfa*, 193–215. Leiden and Boston, 2009.

Goddard 2011. C. J. Goddard, "Au Coeur du dialogue entre païens et chrétiens: L'*adventus* des sénateurs dans les cites de l'Antiquité tardive," in P. Brown and R. Lizzi Testa, eds., *Pagans and Christians in the Roman Empire: The Breaking of a Dialogue (IVth–VIth Century AD)*, 371–400. Vienna, 2011.

Goethert 1931. F. Goethert, *Zur Kunst der römischen Republik*. Berlin, 1931.

Goette 1988. H. R. Goette, "Mulleus—Embas—Calceus: Ikonographische Studien zu römischem Schuwerk," *JdI* 103 (1988): 401–64.

Goette 1990. H. R. Goette, *Studien zu römischen Togadarstellungen*. Mainz, 1990.

Goldbeck and Wienand 2017. F. Goldbeck and J. Wienand, eds., *Der römische Triumph in Prinzipat und Spätantike*. Berlin, 2017.

Gordon 1952. A. E. Gordon, *Quintus Veranius Consul AD 49: A Study Based upon His Recently Identified Sepulchral Inscription*. Berkeley, 1952.

Grandazzi 2008. A. Grandazzi, *Alba Longa, histoire d'une légende: Recherches sur l'archéologie, la religion, les traditions de l'ancien Latium*, 2 vols. Rome, 2008.

Griebel 2013. J. Griebel, *Der Kaiser im Krieg: Die Bilder der Säule des Marc Aurel*. Berlin, 2013.

Gross 1940. W. H. Gross, *Bildnisse Trajans: Das Römische Herrscherbild II*, vol. 2. Berlin, 1940.

Gruen 1995. E. Gruen, *The Last Generation of the Roman Republic* [1974]. Berkeley, 1995.

Gruen 2005. E. Gruen, "Augustus and the Making of the Principate," in K. Galinsky, ed., *The Cambridge Companion to the Age of Augustus*, 33–51. Cambridge, 2005.

BIBLIOGRAPHY

Grünewald 1990. T. Grünewald, *Constantinus Maximus Augustus: Herrschaftspropaganda in der zeitgenössischen Überlieferung*. Stuttgart, 1990.

Grunow Sobocinski 2006. M. Grunow Sobocinski, "Visualizing Ceremony: The Design and Audience of the Ludi Saeculares Coinage of Domitian," *AJA* 110 (2006): 581–602.

Grunow Sobocinski and Thill 2018. M. Grunow Sobocinski and E. Wolfram Thill, "Dismembering a Sacred Cow: The Extispicium Relief in the Louvre," in B. Longfellow and E. Perry, eds., *Familiar Works Reconsidered*, 38–62. Ann Arbor, 2018.

Guittard 2002–2003. C. Guittard, "*Etrusca disciplina* et *regnum*: Actualité des signes rélatifs au pouvoir royal à la fin de la république," *ActaClDebre* 38–39 (2002–2003): 103–25.

Günther 1895. O. Günther, ed., *Epistulae imperatorum pontificum aliorum . . . Avellana quae dicitur collectio*. Prague, Vienna, Leipzig = *CSEL* 35.

Gurval 1998. R. Gurval, *Actium and Augustus: The Politics and Emotions of Civil War*. Ann Arbor, 1998.

Haack 2003. M.-L. Haack, *Les haruspices dans le monde romain*. Bordeaux, 2003.

Haake 2016. M. Haake, "Trophäen, die nicht vom äußeren Feinde gewonnen wurden, Triumphe, die der Ruhm mit Blut befleckt davon trug . . .' Der Sieg im imperialen Bürgerkrieg im 'langen dritten Jahrhundert' als ambivalentes Ereignis," in H. Börm, M. Mattheis, and J. Wienand, eds., *Civil War in Ancient Greece and Rome: Contexts of Disintegration and Reintegration*, 237–301. Stuttgart, 2016.

Haake 2017. M. Haake, "Zwischen Severus Alexanders Triumph über die Sāsāniden im Jahre 233 und den Triumphfeierlichkeiten Diocletians und Maximians im Jahre 303," in Goldbeck and Wienand 2017, 357–95.

Hall 1998. L. Jones Hall, "Cicero's *Instinctu Divino* and Constantine's *Instinctu Divinitatis*: The Evidence of the Arch of Constantine for the Senatorial View of the 'Vision' of Constantine," *JECS* 6 (1998): 647–71.

Hallett 2005. C. H. Hallett, *The Roman Nude: Heroic Portrait Statuary 200 BC–AD 300*. Oxford, 2005.

Hannestad 1988. N. Hannestad, *Roman Art and Imperial Policy*. Aarhus, 1988.

Harries 2012. J. Harries, *Imperial Rome: AD 284 to 363: The New Empire*. Edinburgh, 2012.

Hausmann 1981. U. Hausmann, "Zur Typologie und Ideologie des Augustusporträts," *ANRW* II.12.2 (1981): 513–98.

Havener 2014. W. Havener, "A Ritual against the Rule? The Representation of Civil War Victory in the Late Republican Triumph," in Lange and Vervaet 2104, 165–80.

Hekster 1999. O. Hekster, "The City of Rome in Late Imperial Ideology," *MedAnt* 2 (1999): 717–48.

Heller 2016. A. Heller, "The Religious Legitimation of War in the Reign of Antoninus Pius," in K. Ulanowski, ed., *The Religious Aspects of War in the Ancient Near East, Greece, and Rome*, 358–75. Leiden, 2016.

Héron de Villefosse 1899. A. Héron de Villefosse, *Le trésor de Boscoreale*. Paris, 1899.

Herz 2002. P. Herz, "Sacrifice and Sacrificial Ceremonies of the Roman Imperial Army," in A. I. Baumgarten, ed., *Sacrifice in Religious Experience*, 81–100. Leiden, Boston, and Köln, 2002.

Herzog 2001. H. Herzog, "Die Cancelleriareliefs," *BMonMusPont* 21 (2001): 103–47.

Hickson 1991. F. Hickson, "Augustus Triumphator: Manipulation of the Triumphal Theme in the Political Program of Augustus," *Latomus* 50 (1991): 124–38.

Hickson 1993. F. Hickson, *Roman Prayer Language: Livy and the Aeneid of Vergil*. Stuttgart, 1993.

Hickson Hahn 2007. F. Hickson Hahn, "Performing the Sacred: Prayers and Hymns," in J. Rüpke, ed., *A Companion to Roman Religion*, 235–48. Oxford and Malden, 2007.

Himmelmann 1989. N. Himmelmann, *Herrscher und Athlet: Die Bronzen vom Quirinal*. Milan, 1989.

Holliday 2002. P. Holliday, *The Origins of Roman Historical Commemoration in the Visual Arts*. Cambridge, 2002.

Holloway 2004. R. Ross Holloway, *Constantine and Rome*. New Haven, 2004.

Hölscher 1979. T. Hölscher, "Beobachtungen zu römischen historischen Denmälern," *AA* (1979): 337–48.

Hölscher 1980. T. Hölscher, "Die Geschichtsauffassung in der römischen Repräsentationskunst," *JdI* 95 (1980): 265–321.

Hölscher 2006. T. Hölscher, "The Transformation of Victory into Power: From Event to Structure," in S. Dillon and K. E. Welch, eds., *Representations of War in Ancient Rome*, 27–48. Cambridge and New York, 2006.

Hölscher, unpub. T. Hölscher, "Eine mehrfache Statuenehrung aus der Zeit der mittleren Republik?"

Huet 1992. V. Huet, "Le sacrifice romain sur les reliefs historiques en Italie," PhD diss., École des hautes études en sciences sociales (EHESS), Paris, 1992.

Huet 2005. V. Huet, "La mise à mort sacrificielle sur les reliefs romains: Une image banalisée et ritualisée de la violence?" in J.-M. Betrand, ed., *La violence dans les mondes Grec et Romain*, 91–119. Paris, 2005.

Huet 2008a. V. Huet, "L'encens sur les reliefs sacrificiels romains," in L. Bodiou, D. Frère, and V. Mehl, eds., *Parfums et odeurs dans l'antiquité*, 105–16. Rennes, 2008.

Huet 2008b. V. Huet, "Les images de sacrifice en Gaul romaine," in W. Van Andringa et al., eds., *Archéologie du sacrifice animal en Gaule romaine: Rituels et pratiques alimentaires*, 43–74. Montagnac, 2008.

Huet 2012. V. Huet, "Le voile du sacrifiant à Rome sur les reliefs romains: Une norme?" in F. Gherchanoc and V. Huet, eds., *Vêtements Antiques: S'habiller, se déshabiller dans les mondes anciens*, 47–62. Paris, 2012.

Huet et al. 2004. V. Huet et al., "Les sacrifices dans le monde romain," in *ThesCRA* 1 (2004): 183–235.

Humm 2011. M. Humm, "The Curiate Law and the Religious Nature of the Power of Roman Magistrates," in O. Tellegen-Coupers, ed., *Law and Religion in the Roman Republic*, 57–84. Boston, 2011.

Humm 2015. M. Humm, "La loi curiate et les auspices du peuple romain," *CCG* 26 (2015): 231–50.

Humphries 2003. M. Humphries, "Roman Senators and Absent Emperors in Late Antiquity," *ActaArchArtiumPert* 17 (2003): 27–45.

Humphries 2008. M. Humphries, "From Usurper to Emperor: The Politics of Legitimation in the Age of Constantine," *JLA* 1 (2008): 82–100.

Humphries 2009. M. Humphries, "From Emperor to Pope? Ceremonial, Space, and Authority at Rome from Constantine to Gregory the Great," in K. Cooper and J. Hillner, eds., *Religion, Dynasty, and Patronage in Early Christian Rome, 300–900*, 21–58. Cambridge, 2009.

Humphries 2015. M. Humphries, "Emperors, Usurpers, and the City of Rome," in Wienand 2015a, 151–68.

Hurlet 1993. F. Hurlet, "La *Lex de imperio Vespasiani* et la légimité augustéene," *Latomus* 52 (1993): 261–80.

Hurlet 1997. F. Hurlet, *Les collègues du prince sous Auguste et Tibère*. Rome, 1997.

Hurlet 2001. F. Hurlet, "Les auspices d'Octavien/Auguste," *CCG* 12 (2001): 155–80.

Hurlet 2006. F. Hurlet, *Le proconsul et le prince d'Auguste à Dioclétien*. Bordeaux, 2006.

Ingholt 1969. H. Ingholt, "The Prima Porta Statue of Augustus, II: The Location of the Original," *AJA* 22 (1969): 304–18.

Itgenshorst 2004. T. Itgenshorst, "Augustus und der republikanische Triumph: Triumphalfasten und summi viri-Galerie als Instrumente der imperialen Machsticherung," *Hermes* 132 (2004): 436–58.

BIBLIOGRAPHY

Jameson 1970. S. Jameson, "Pompey's Imperium in 67: Some Constitutional Fictions," *Historia* 19 (1970): 539–60.

Jashemski 1950. W. Jashemski, *The Origins and History of the Proconsular and the Propraetorian Imperium to 27 BC*. Chicago, 1950.

Jehne 1987. M. Jehne, *Der Staat des Dictators Caesar*. Cologne and Vienna, 1987.

Johnson 2006. M. J. Johnson, "Architecture of Empire," in N. Lenski, ed., *The Cambridge Companion to the Age of Constantine*, 278–97. Cambridge, 2006.

Jones 1951. A. M. H. Jones, "The Imperium of Augustus," = Jones 1960, 1–17.

Jones 1960. A. M. H. Jones, *Studies in Roman Government and Law*. New York, 1960.

Jones 1986. A. H. M. Jones, *The Later Roman Empire, 284–602*, 2 vols. [1964]. Baltimore, 1986.

Kähler 1964. H. Kähler, *Das Fünfsaulendenkmal für die Tetrarchen auf dem Forum Romanum*. Cologne, 1964.

Kähler 1958–1960. H. Kähler, *Rom und seine Welt: Bilder zu Geschichte und Kultur*. Munich, 1958–1960.

Kaiser Augustus 1988. *Kaiser Augustus und die verlorene Republik: Eine Ausstellung im Martin-Gropius-Bau, Berlin, 7. Juni–14. August 1988*. Mainz, 1988.

Kaizer 2006. T. Kaizer, "The Frescoes of Iulius Terentius," in R. Rollinger and B. Truschnegg, eds., *Altertum und Mittelmeerraum: Die antike Welt diesseits und jenseits der Levante*, 151–59. Stuttgart, 2006.

Kantorowicz 1961. E. Kantorowicz, "Gods in Uniform," *PAPhS* 105 (1961): 368–93.

Kaschnitz von Weinberg 1937. G. Kaschnitz von Weinberg, *Sculture del Magazzino del Museo Vaticano*. Rome, 1937.

Keller 1967. E. Keller, "Studien zu den Cancelleria-Reliefs: Zur Ikonographie der Personifikationen und Profectio-bzw: Adventus-Darstellungen," *Klio* 49 (1967): 193–215.

Kellum 1994. B. A. Kellum, "The Construction of Landscape in Augustan Rome: The Garden Room at the Villa *ad Gallinas*," *ArtBull* 76 (1994): 211–24.

Kempkes and Sarge 2009. M. Kempkes and C. Sarge, *Gesichter der Macht: Kaiserbilder in Rom und am Limes*. Baden-Wurttemberg, 2009.

Kent 1957. J. P. C. Kent, "The Pattern of Bronze Coinage under Constantine I," *Numismatic Chronicle*, 6th ser., 17 (1957): 16–77.

Keppie and Arnold 1984. L. J. F. Keppie and B. J. Arnold, *(CSIR)*. Oxford, 1984.

Kinney 2012. D. Kinney, "Hans-Peter L'Orange on Portraits and the Arch of Constantine: A Lasting Legacy," *ActaArchArtiumPert* (2012): 107–26.

BIBLIOGRAPHY

Kleiner 1983. F. S. Kleiner, "The Sacrifice in Armor in Roman Art," *Latomus* 42 (1983): 287–302.

Klose 2015. C. Klose, "A Farewell to Methods? Imperial 'Adventus-Scenes' and Interpretations of Roman Historical Reliefs," in C. Klose, L. C. Bossert, and W. Leveritt, eds., *Fresh Perspectives on Graeco-Roman Visual Culture*, 99–116. Published online, 2015.

Kockel 1993. V. Kockel, *Porträtreliefs stadtrömischer Grabbauten: Ein Beitrag zur Geschichte und zum Verständnis des spätrepublikanisch-frühkaiserzeitlichen Privatporträts*. Mainz, 1993.

Koeppel 1969. G. Koeppel, "Profectio und Adventus," *BJb* 169 (1969): 130–94.

Koeppel 1990. G. Koeppel, "Die historischen Reliefs der römischen Kaiserzeit 7: Der Bogen des Septimius Severus, die Decennalienbasis und der Konstantinsbogen," *BJb* 190 (1990): 1–64.

Kolb 1987. F. Kolb, *Diocletian und die erste Tetrarchie: Improvisation oder Experiment in der Organisation monarchischer Herrschaft?* Berlin, 1987.

Koortbojian 1995. M. Koortbojian, *Myth, Meaning, and Memory on Roman Sarcophagi*. Berkeley, 1995.

Koortbojian 2008. M. Koortbojian, "The Double Identity of Roman Portrait Statues: Costumes and Their Symbolism at Rome," in J. Edmondson and A. Keith, eds., *Roman Dress and the Fabrics of Roman Culture*, 71–93. Toronto.

Koortbojian 2010. M. Koortbojian, "Crossing the Pomerium: The Armed Ruler at Rome," in B. C. Ewald and C. Noreña, eds., *The Emperor and Rome: Space, Representation, and Ritual*, 247–74. Cambridge, 2010.

Koortbojian 2013. M. Koortbojian, *The Divinization of Caesar and Augustus: Precedents, Consequences, Implications*. Cambridge, 2013.

Koortbojian 2015. M. Koortbojian, "Roman Sarcophagi," in B. Borg, ed., *A Companion to Roman Art*, 286–300. Chichester, 2015.

Köves-Zulauf 2000. T. Köves-Zulauf, "Virtus und Pietas," *ActaArchHung* 40 (2000): 247–62.

Kuhoff 1991. W. Kuhoff, "Ein Mythos in der römischen Geschichte: Der Sieg Konstantins des Großen über Maxentius vor den Toren Roms am 28.Oktober 312 n. Chr." *Chiron* 21 (1991): 127–74.

Künzl 1988. E. Künzl, *Der römische Triumph: Siegesfeiern im antiken Rom*. Munich, 1988.

Küter 2014. A. Küter, *Zwischen Republik und Kaiserzeit: Die Münzmeisterprägung unter Augustus*. Berlin, 2014.

BIBLIOGRAPHY

Kuttner 1993. A. Kuttner, "Some New Grounds for Narrative: Marcus Antonius's Base (the *Ara Domitii Ahenobarbi Ahenobarbi*) and Republican Biographies," in P. J. Holliday, ed., *Narrative and Event in Ancient Art*, 198–229. Cambridge, 1993.

Kuttner 1995. A. Kuttner, *Dynasty and Empire: The Case of the Boscoreale Cups*. Berkeley, 1995.

Kuttner 2013. A. Kuttner, "Representing Hellenistic Numidia, in Africa and at Rome," in J. R. W. Prag and J. C. Quinn, eds., *The Hellenistic West: Rethinking the Ancient Mediterranean*, 216–72. Oxford, 2013.

Lachmann 1848. C. Lachmann, ed., *Gromatici Veteres* = F. Blume, K. Lachmann, and A. Rudorff, eds., *Die Schriften der römischen Feldmesser*, 2 vols., Berlin, 1848.

Laffranchi 1921. L. Laffranchi, *L'xi anno imperatorial di Constantino Magno*, Communicazione alla Pontificia Accademia Romana di Archeologia, 1. Rome, 1921.

Lahusen 1983. G. Lahusen, *Untersuchungen zur Ehrenstatue in Rom*. Rome, 1983.

Lahusen 1984. G. Lahusen, *Schriftquellen zum römischen Bildnis*, vol. 1, Bremen, 1984.

Lange 2012. C. Hjort Lange, "Constantine's Civil War Triumph of AD 312 and the Adaptability of Triumphal Tradition," *ARID* 37 (2012): 29–53.

Lange 2016. C. Hjort Lange, *Triumphs in the Age of Civil War: The Late Republic and the Adaptability of the Triumphal Tradition*. London, 2016.

Lange and Vervaet 2014. C. Hjort Lange and F. J. Vervaet, eds., *The Roman Republican Triumph: Beyond the Spectacle*. Rome, 2014.

La Rocca and Zanker 2007. E. La Rocca and P. Zanker, "Il ritratto colossale di Costantino dal Foro di Traiano," in Leone, Palombi, and Walker 2007, 145–68.

Laubscher 1975. H. P. Laubscher, *Der Reliefschmuck des Galeriusbogens in Thessaloniki*. Berlin, 1975.

Laubscher 1976. H. P. Laubscher, *Arcus Novus und Arcus Claudii, zwei Triumphbögen an der Via Lata in Rom*. Gottingen, 1976.

Lee 2016. A. D. Lee, *Pagans and Christians in Late Antiquity: A Sourcebook* [2000]. Abingdon and New York, 2016.

Lehmann-Hartleben 1926. K. Lehmann-Hartleben, *Die Trajanssäule: Ein römisches Kunstwerk am Beginn der Spätantike*. Berlin and Leipzig, 1926.

Lehnen 1997. J. Lehnen, ADVENTUS PRINCIPIS: *Untersuchungen zu Sinngehalt und Zeremoniell der Kaiserankunft in den Städten des Imperium Romanum*. Frankfurt, Berlin, and New York, 1997.

Lenski 2006a. N. Lenski, "The Reign of Constantine," in Lenski 2006b, 59–90.

BIBLIOGRAPHY

Lenski 2006b. N. Lenski, ed., *The Cambridge Companion to the Age of Constantine.* Cambridge, 2006.

Lenski 2008. N. Lenski, "Evoking the Pagan Past: *Instinctu Divinitatis* and Constantine's Capture of Rome," *JLA* 1 (2008): 204–57.

Lenski 2012. N. Lenski, "The Sun and the Senate: The Inspiration for the Arch of Constantine," in dal Covolo and Gasparo 2014, 155–96.

Lenski 2016. N. Lenski, *Constantine and the Cities: Imperial Authority and Civic Politics.* Philadelphia, 2016.

Leone, Palombi, and Walker 2007. A. Leone, D. Palombi, S. Walker, eds., *RES BENE GESTAE: Richerche di storia urbana su Roman antica in onore di Eva Margareta Steinby.* Rome, 2007.

Lepper and Frere 1988. F. Lepper and S. Frere, *Trajan's Column: A New Edition of the Chicoriuis Plates.* Gloucester, 1988.

Liegle 1941. J. Liegle, "Die Münzprägung Octavians nach dem Siege von Actium und die augusteische Kunst," *JdI* 56 (1941): 91–119 = Binder 1991, 308–47.

Linderski 1981. J. Linderski, review of Wistrand (1979) in *Gnomon* 52 (1981): 782–85 = Linderski 1995, 284–86.

Linderski 1984. J. Linderski, "Rome, Aphrodisias, and the *Res Gestae*: The *Genera Militiae* and the Status of Octavian," *JRS* 74 (1984): 74–80 = Linderski 1995, 147–53.

Linderski 1986. J. Linderski, "The Augural Law," *ANRW* II.16.3 (1986): 2146–2312.

Linderski 1993. J. Linderski, "Roman Religion in Livy," in W. Schuller, ed., *Livius: Aspekte seines Werkes*, 53–70. Konstaz, 1993 = Linderski 1995, 608–25.

Linderski 1995. J. Linderski, *Roman Questions: Selected Papers.* Stuttgart, 1995.

Linderski 1996. J. Linderski, "Q. Scipio Imperator," in J. Linderski, ed., *Imperium Sine Fine: T. Robert S. Broughton and the Roman Republic*, 145–85. Stuttgart, 1996 = Linderski 2007a, 130–74.

Linderski 2007a. J. Linderski, *Roman Questions II: Selected Papers.* Stuttgart, 2007.

Linderski 2007b. J. Linderski, "Founding the City: Ennius and Romulus on the Site of Rome," in Linderski 2007a, 3–19.

Lintott 2003. A. Lintott, *The Constitution of the Roman Republic* [1999]. Oxford, 2003.

Liou-Gille 1993. B. Liou-Gille, "Le pomerium," *MH* 50 (1993): 94–106.

Liverani 1989. P. Liverani, "San Paolo fuori le mura e l'iter vetus," *BMonMusPont* 9, no. 1 (1989): 79–84.

Liverani 2003a. P. Liverani, "Progetto architettonico e percezione commune in età tardoantica," *BABesch* 78 (2003): 205–19.

BIBLIOGRAPHY

Liverani 2003b. P. Liverani, "Basilica S. Paolo, *basilica nova, basilica Piniani*," *Boreas* 26 (2003): 73–81.

Liverani 2004. P. Liverani, "Reimpiego senza ideologia: La lettura degli spolia dall'arco di Costantino all'età carolingia," *RM* 111 (2004): 383–433.

Liverani 2005. P. Liverani, "L'arco di Costantino," in A. Donati and G. Gentili, eds., *Costantino il Grande: La civiltà antica al bivio tra Occidente e Oriente*, 64–69. Milan, 2005.

Liverani 2007. P. Livcrani, "Osservazioni sui rostri del Foro Romano in età tardoantica," in Leone, Palombi, and Walker 2007, 169–93.

Liverani 2011. P. Liverani, "Reading *Spolia* in Late Antiquity and Contemporary Perception," in R. Brilliant and D. Kinney, eds., *Reuse Value: Spolia and Appropriation in Art and Architecture from Constantine to Sherrie Levine*, 33–51. Farnham, 2011.

Liverani 2014. P. Liverani, "Chi parla a chi? Epigrafia monumentale e imagine publica in epoca tardoantica," in S. Birk, T. Myrup Kristensen, and B. Poulsen, eds., *Using Images in Late Antiquity*, 3–32. Oxford, 2014.

Liverani 2017. P. Liverani, "Roma tardoantica come spazio della rappresentazione trionfale," in F. Goldbeck and J. Wienand, eds., *Der römische Triumph in Prinzipat und Spätantike*, 487–510. Berlin, 2017.

Lizzi Testa 2013. R. Lizzi Testa, "Costantino e il Senato romano," in COSTANTINO I, vol. I: 351–67.

Lohmann 2009. H. Lohmann, "Die sogenannte Domitius-Ara," in R. Einicke, St. Lehmann, H. Löhr, et al., eds., *Zurück zum Gegenstand: Festschrift für A. E. Furtwàngler*, 109–22. Langenweißbach, 2009.

Lolli 1999. M. Lolli, "La 'celeritas principis' fra tattica militare e necessità politica nei *Panegyrici Latini*," *Latomus* 58 (1999): 620–25.

Long 1875. G. Long, "Fictio," in W. Smith, *A New Classical Dictionary of Greek and Roman Biography, Mythology, and Geography: Partly Based upon the Dictionary of Greek and Roman Biography and Mythology*. New York, 1875.

L'Orange and von Gerkan 1939. H. P. L'Orange and A. von Gerkan, *Der Spätantike Bildschmuck des Konstantinsbogens*. Berlin, 1939.

Lundgreen 2014. C. Lundgreen, "Rules for Obtaining a Triumph—The *Ius Triumphandi* Once More," in Lange and Vervaet 2014, 17–32.

Lusnia 2014. S. Lusnia, *Creating Severan Rome: The Architecture and Self-Image of L. Septimius Severus (AD 193–211)*. Brussels, 2014.

Lyasse 2005. E. Lyasse, "*Auctis finibus populi Romani*? Les raisons de l'extension du *pomerium* sous le principat," *Gerión* 23 (2005): 169–87.

BIBLIOGRAPHY

Maccari 2015. A. Maccari, "*Quid sit pomerium*: Appunti su Gellio, *Noctes Atticae* XIII, 14: Le fonti e il confronto con Fest. 294 L," *StClOr* 61 (2015): 313–33.

MacCormack 1981. S. MacCormack, *Art and Ceremony in Late Antiquity*. Berkeley, Los Angeles, and London, 1981.

Machado 2006. C. Machado, "Building the Past: Monuments and Memory in the *Forum Romanum*," in Bowden, Gutteridge, and Machado 2006, 157–92.

Magdelain 1968. A. Magdelain, *Recherches sur l' "imperium": La loi curiate et les auspices d'investiture*. Paris, 1968.

Magdelain 2015. A. Magdelain, *Jus Imperium Auctoritas: Études de droit romain* [1990], Rome, 2015.

Maggi 1993. S. Maggi, "La figura di *Victoria* nelle rappresentazioni di *profectio* e di *adventus* di età imperiale," *Ostraka* 2 (1993): 81–91.

Magi 1956–1957. F. Magi, "Il coronamento dell'Arco di Costantino," *RendPontAccArch* 29 (1956–1957): 83–110.

Mannsperger 1982. D. Mannsperger, "Annos undeviginti natus: Das Münzsymbol für Octavians Eintritt in die Politik," in B. von Freytag et al., eds., *Praestant Interna: Festschrift U. Hausmann*, 331–37. Tubingen, 1982.

Mantovani 2008. D. Mantovani, "*Leges et Iura P(opuli) R(omani) Restituit*: Principe e diritto in un aureo di Ottaviano," *Athenaeum* 96 (2008): 5–54.

Marcattili 2015. F. Marcattili, "L'altare del vicus Sandaliarius agli Uffizi: Culto compitale e politiche dinastiche nel 2 a.C.," *BABesch* 90 (2015): 125–37.

Marcone 1987. A. Marcone, *Commento storico al Libro IV dell'epistolario di Q. Aurelio Simmaco: Introduzione, commento storico, testo, traduzione, indici*. Pisa, 1987.

Marco Simon 2011. F. Marco Simon, "The *Feriae Latinae* as Religious Legitimation of the Consuls' *Imperium*," in H. Beck, ed., *Consuls and* Res Publica: *Holding High Office in the Roman Republic*, 116–32. Cambridge, 2011.

Marlowe 2004. E. Marlowe, "'That Customary Magnificence Which Is Your Due': Constantine and the Symbolic Capital of Rome," PhD diss., Columbia University, 2004.

Marlowe 2010. E. Marlowe, "*Liberator Urbis suae*: Constantine and the Ghost of Maxentius," in Ewald and Noreña 2010, 199–219.

Marlowe 2016. E. Marlowe, "The Multivalence of Memory: The Tetrarchs, the Senate, and the Vicennalia Monument in the Roman Forum," in K. Galinsky and K. Lapatin, eds., *Cultural Memories in the Roman Empire*, 240–62. Los Angeles, 2016.

Marshall 1972. A. J. Marshall, "The Lex Pompeia de provinciis (52 BC) and Cicero's Imperium in 51–50 BC: Constitutional Aspects," *ANRW* I.1 (1972): 887–921.

BIBLIOGRAPHY

Maschek 2018. D. Maschek, "Not *Census* but *Deductio*: Reconsidering the *"Ara* of Domitius Ahenobarbus,'" *JRS* 108 (2018): 27–52.

Mayer 2002. E. Mayer, *Rom ist dort, wo der Kaiser ist: Untersuchungen zu den Staatsdenkmälern des dezentralisierten Reiches von Diocletian bis zu Theodosius II*. Mainz, 2002.

Mayer 2006. E. Mayer, "Civil War and Public Dissent: The State Monuments of the Decentralised Roman Empire," in Bowden, Gutteridge, and Machado 2006, 141–55.

McCormick 1990. M. McCormick, *Eternal Victory: Triumphal Rulership in Late Antiquity, Byzantium and the Early Medieval West*. Cambridge and Paris, 1990.

McLynn 1994. N. McLynn, *Ambrose of Milan: Church and Court in a Christian Capital*. Berkeley, Los Angeles, and London, 1994.

Meier 1996. C. Meier, *Caesar*, trans. D. McLintock. London, 1996.

Melucco Vaccaro 2001. A. Melucco Vaccaro, "L'arco di Adriano e il riuso di Costantino," in M. L. Conforto et al., *Adriano e Costnatino: Le due fasi dell'arco nella valle del Colosseo*, 22–57. Milan, 2001.

Michels 1967. A. Kirsopp Michels, *The Calendar of the Roman Republic*. Princeton, 1967.

Millar 1973. F. Millar, "Triumvirate and Principate," *JRS* 63 (1973): 50–67 = Millar 2002, 241–70.

Millar 1989. F. Millar, "Political Power in Mid-Republican Rome: Curia or Comitium?" *JRS* 79 (1989): 138–50 = Millar 2002, 85–108.

Millar 1992. F. Millar, *The Emperor in the Roman World* [1977]. Ithaca, 1992.

Millar 2002. F. Millar, *The Roman Republic and the Augustan Revolution: Rome, the Greek World, and the East*, vol. 1, ed. H. M. Cotton and G. M. Rogers. Chapel Hill, 2002.

Mittag 2017. P. F. Mittag, "Die Triumphatordarstellung auf Münzen und Medallions in Prinzipat und Spätantike," in F. Goldbeck and J. Wienand, eds., *Der römische Triumph in Prinzipat und Spätantike*, 419–52. Berlin, 2017.

Mitthof and Schörner 2017. F. Mitthof and G. Schörner, eds., *Columna Traiani: Traianssäule—Siegesmonument und Kriegsbericht in Bildern*. Vienna, 2017.

Moatti 2007. C. Moatti, "La communication publique écrite à Rome, sous la République et le haut empire," in J.-P. Genet, ed., *Rome et l'état modern européen*, 217–50. Rome, 2007.

Momigliano 1969. A. Momigliano, "*Praetor Maximus* e questioni affini" [1968], in *Quarto contributo alla storia degli studi classici e del mondo antico*, 403–17. Roma, 1969.

BIBLIOGRAPHY

Mommsen 1887–1888. Th. Mommsen, *Römisches Staatsrecht*, 3rd ed., 3 vols. Leipzig, 1887–1888.

Mommsen 1889–1896. Th. Mommsen, *Le droit public romain*, 2nd ed., tr. P. Girard, 7 vols., Paris, 1889–1896.

Newman 1990. R. Newman, "A Dialogue of Power in the Coinage of Antony and Octavian (44–30 BC)," *AJN* 2 (1990): 37–63.

Nicholls 1967. J. J. Nicholls, "The Content of the Lex Curiata," *AJP* 88 (1967): 257–78.

Nicolet 1988. C. Nicolet, *The World of the Citizen in Republican Rome* [1976], trans. P. S. Falla. Berkeley, 1988.

Nicolet 2004. C. Nicolet, "Dictatorship in Rome," in P. Baehr and M. Richter, eds., *Dictatorship in History and Theory*, 263–78. Cambridge, 2004.

Niemeyer 1968. H. G. Niemeyer, *Studien zur statuarischen Darstellung der römischen Kaiser*. Berlin, 1968.

Oakley 1997. S. Oakley, *A Commentary on Livy, Books VI–X*. Oxford, 1997.

Ogilvie 1961. R. M. Ogilvie, "Lustrum Condere," *JRS* 51 (1961): 31–39.

Oppermann 1985. M. Oppermann, *Römische Kaiserreliefs*. Leipzig, 1985.

Orlin 2002. E. Orlin, "Foreign Cults in Republican Rome: Rethinking the Pomerial Rule," *MAAR* 47: 1–18.

Panciera 1999. S. Panciera, "Dove finisce la città," in *La Forma dell Città e del Territorio: Esperienze metodologiche e risultati a confront*, 3 vols., Rome, 1999, I:9–15.

Parisi Presicce 2005. C. Parisi Presicce, "L'abbandono della moderazione: I ritratti di Costantino e della sua progenie," in A. Donati and G. Gentili, eds., *Costantino il Grande: La civiltà antica al bivio tra Occidente e Oriente*, 138–55. Cinisello Balsamo, 2005.

Parisi Presicce 2012. C. Parisi Presicce, "Costantino e i suoi figli: Il nuovo volto dei potenti," in P. Biscottini and G. Sena Chiesa, eds., *Costantino 313 d. C. L'editto di Milano e il tempo della tolleranza*, 109–19. Milan, 2012.

Parisi Presicce 2013. C. Parisi Presicce, "Arte, imprese e propaganda: L'Augusto di Prima Porta 150 anni dopo la scoperta," in E. La Rocca, C. Parisi Presicce, et al., eds., *Augusto*, 118–29. Milan, 2013.

Pekáry 1985. T. Pekáry, *Das römische Kaiserbildnis in Staat, Kult, und Gesellschaft: Dargestellt anhand der Schriftquellen*. Berlin, 1985.

Pensabene 2006. P. Pensabene, "Arco di Costantino: Tra continuità e innovazione," *ActaArchArtiumPert* 20 (2006): 131–41.

Pensabene and Panella 1999. P. Pensabene and C. Panella, eds., *Arco di Costantino tra archeologia e archeometria*. Rome, 1999.

BIBLIOGRAPHY

Perea Yebenes 1997. S. Perea Yebenes, "Un aspecto militar de la religión romana: Los 'ritos de purificación' de la Marina de guerra," *Revista de Historia Naval* 15 (1997): 39–53.

Petruccioli 2014. G. Petruccioli, "The Cancelleria Reliefs, Vespasian the Younger, and Domitian's Dynastic Program," *BABesch* 89 (2014): 109–27.

Pfanner 1989. M. Pfanner, "Über das Herstellen von Porträts: Ein Beigrag zu Rationalisierungsmassnahmen und Produktionsmechanismen von Massenware im späten Hellenismus und in der römischen Kaiserzeit," *JdI* 104 (1989): 157–257.

Phillips 1972–1974. E. J. Phillips, "The Roman Distance Slab from Bridgeness," *PSAS* 105 (1972–1974): 171–81.

Pighi 1965. G.-B. Pighi, *De ludis saecularibus*, 2nd ed. Amsterdam, 1965.

Polacco 1955. L. Polacco, "Il trionfo di Tiberio nella tazza Rothschild da Boscoreale," in *AttiMemAccPat* 67, no. 3 (1955): 253–70.

Pollini 1978. J. Pollini, "Studies in Augustan Historical Reliefs," PhD diss., University of California at Berkeley, 1978.

Pollini 1995. J. Pollini, "The Augustus from Prima Porta and the Transformation of the Polykleitan Heroic Ideal: The Rhetoric of Art," in W. Moon, ed., *Polykleitos, the Doryphoros, and Tradition*, 262–82. Madison, 1995.

Pollini 1999. J. Pollini, review of Boschung 1993. *Art Bull* 81 (1999): 723–35.

Pollini 2012. J. Pollini, *From Republic to Empire: Rhetoric, Religion, and Power in the Visual Culture of Ancient Rome*. Norman, 2012.

Pollini 2017. J. Pollini, "The 'Lost' Nollekens Relief of an Imperial Sacrifice from Domitian's Palace on the Palatine: Its History, Iconography, and Date," *JRA* 30 (2017): 97–126.

Popkin 2016. M. L. Popkin, "Symbiosis and Civil War: The Audacity of the Arch of Constantine," *JLA* 9 (2016): 42–88.

Prescendi 2007. F. Prescendi, *Décrire et comprendre le sacrifice: Les réflexions des Romains sur leur proper religion à partir de la littérature antiquaire*. Stuttgart, 2007.

Prückner 2008. H. Prückner, "Kaiser Konstantins Bilderbogen oder: Die Botschaft der Spolien," *Thetis* 15 (2008): 59–75.

Prusac 2012. M. Prusac, "The Arch of Constantine: Continuity and Commemoration through Reuse," *ActaArchArtiumPert* 25 (2012): 127–57.

Raeck 1998. W. Raeck, "Ankunft an der Milvischen Brücke: Wort, Bild und Botschaft am Konstantinsbogen in Rom," in J. Holzhausen, ed., *Ψυχή-Seele—anima: Festschrift für Karin Alt zum 7. Mai 1998*, 345–54. Stuttgart and Leipzig, 1998.

Raubitschek 1954. A. Raubitschek, "Epigraphical Notes on Julius Caesar," *JRS* 44 (1954): 65–75.

BIBLIOGRAPHY

Rawson 1978. E. Rawson, "Caesar, Etruria, and the *Disciplina Etrusca*," *JRS* 68 (1978): 132–52 = Rawson 1991, 289–323.

Rawson 1991. E. Rawson, *Roman Culture and Society: Collected Papers*. Oxford, 1991.

Reifferscheid 1863. A. Reifferscheid, "De Ara Veneris Genetricis," *AdI* (1863): 361–72.

Reinsberg 2006. C. Reinsberg, *Die Sarkophage mit Darstellungen aus dem Menschenleben*, vol. III, *Vita Romana* [= *Die antiken Sarkophagreliefs*, vol. I, 3]. Berlin, 2006.

Reynolds 1982. J. M. Reynolds, *Aphrodisias and Rome*. London, 1982.

Rich 1990. J. W. Rich, ed., *Cassius Dio: The Augustan Settlement (Roman History 53–55.9)*. Warminster, 1990.

Rich 1996. J. W. Rich, "Augustus and the *Spolia Opima*," *Chiron* 26 (1996): 85–127.

Rich 1998. J. W. Rich, "Augustus's Parthian Honours, the Temple of Mars Ultor, and the Arch in the Forum Romanum," *PBSR* 66 (1998): 71–128.

Rich 2010. J. W. Rich, "Deception, Lies, and Economy with the Truth: Augustus and the Establishment of the Principate," in Turner, Chong-Gossard, and Vervaet, *Private and Public Lies*, 167–91.

Rich 2011. J. Rich, "The *Fetiales* and Roman International Relations," in J. H. Richardson and F. Santangelo, eds., *Priests and State in the Roman World*, 187–242. Stuttgart, 2011.

Rich 2014. J. W. Rich, "The Triumph in the Roman Republic: Frequency, Fluctuation, and Policy," in C. Hjort Lange and F. J. Vervaet, eds., *The Roman Republican Triumph: Beyond the Spectacle*, 197–258. Rome, 2014.

Richardson 1975. J. S. Richardson, "The Triumph, the Praetors, and the Senate in the Early Second Century BC," *JRS* 65 (1975): 50–63.

Richardson 1991. J. S. Richardson, "Imperium Romanum: Empire and the Language of Power," *JRS* 81 (1991): 1–9.

Richardson 1995. J. S. Richardson, "The Roman Mind and the Power of Fiction," in L. Ayres, ed., *The Passionate Intellect: Essays on the Transformation of Classical Traditions Presented to Professor I. G. Kidd*, 117–30. New Brunswick and London, 1995.

Ridley 1981. R. T. Ridley, "The Extraordinary Commands of the Late Republic: A Matter of Definition," *Historia* 30 (1981): 280–97.

Ridley 1982. R. T. Ridley, trans. and comm., *Zosimus: A New History*. Melbourne, 1982.

Rinaldi Tufi 1981. S. Rinaldi Tufi, "Frammenti delle statue dei *summi viri* nel foro di Augusto," *DialArch* 1, n.s. 3 (1981): 69–84.

BIBLIOGRAPHY

Rist 1920. W. Rist, *Die Opfer des römischen Heeres*. Tubingen, 1920.

Ritter 1995. St. Ritter, *Hercules in der römischen Kunst von den Anfängen bis Augustus*. Heidelberg, 1995.

Rodenwaldt 1935. G. Rodenwaldt, "Über den Stilwandel in der antoninischen Kunst," *AbhBerlin* 3 (1935): 1–27.

Rodríguez-Almeida 1978–1979/1979–1980. E. Rodríguez-Almeida, "Il Campo Marzio settentrionale: *Solarium* e *pomerium*," *RendPontAccArch* 51–52 (1978–1979/1979–1980): 195–212.

Roller 2004. M. Roller, "Exemplarity in Roman Culture: The Cases of Horatius Cocles and Cloelia," *CP* 99 (2004): 1–56.

Rose 1997. C. B. Rose, *Dynastic Commemoration and Imperial Portraiture in the Julio-Claudian Period*. Cambridge, 1997.

Rose 2005. C. B. Rose, "The Parthians in Augustan Rome," *AJA* 109 (2005): 21–75.

Rosenstein 1995. N. Rosenstein, "Sorting Out the Lot in Republican Rome," *AJP* 116 (1995): 43–75.

Rowan 2012. C. Rowan, *Under Divine Auspices: Divine Ideology and the Visualisation of Imperial Power in the Severan Period*. Cambridge, 2012.

Rüpke 1990. J. Rüpke, *Domi militiae*. Stuttgart, 1990.

Ruysschaert 1963. J. Ruysschaert, "Essai d'interpétation synthétique de l'arc de Constantin," *RendPontAccArch* 35 (1963): 79–100.

Ryberg 1955. I. Scott Ryberg, *Rites of the State Religion in Roman Art = MAAR supplement*, 22.

Ryberg 1976. I. Scott Ryberg, *The Panel Reliefs of Marcus Aurelius*. New York, 1976.

Salzman 1990. M. R. Salzman, *On Roman Time: The Codex-Calendar of 354 and the Rhythms of Urban Life in Late Antiquity*. Berkeley, Los Angeles, and Oxford, 1990.

Salzman 2002. M. R. Salzman, *The Making of a Christian Aristocracy: Social and Religious Change in the Western Roman Empire*. Cambridge, MA, 2002.

Salzman 2016. M. R. Salzman, "Constantine and the Roman Senate: Conflict, Cooperation, and Concealed Resistance," in M. R. Salzman, M. Sághy, and R. Lizzi Testa, eds., *Pagans and Christians in Late Antique Rome: Conflict, Competition, and Coexistence in the Fourth Century*, 11–45. Cambridge, 2016.

Sánchez 2014. P. Sánchez, "Le fragment de L. Cincius (Festus p. 276L) et le commandement des armées du Latium," *CCG* 25 (2014): 7–48.

Schäfer 1989. T. Schäfer, *Imperii insignia: Sella curulis und fasces: Zur Repräsentation römischer Magistrate*. Mainz, 1989.

BIBLIOGRAPHY

Scheid 1990. J. Scheid, *Romulus et ses Frères: Le college des Frères Arvales, modèle du culte public dans la Rome des empereurs.* Rome, 1990.

Scheid 1992. J. Scheid, "L'investiture imperial d'après les commentaires des arvales," *CCG* 3 (1992): 221–37.

Scheid 1994. J. Scheid, "Attalus Noni M(arci) S(ervvs) [Un Trévire à Aesernia]," *Métis* 9/10 (1994): 245–56.

Scheid 1995. J. Scheid, "*Graeco Ritu*: A Typically Roman Way of Honoring the Gods," *HSCP* 97 (1995): 15–31.

Scheid 1996. J. Scheid, "Les sens des rites: L'exemple Romain," in J. Scheid, ed., *Rites et Croyances dans les Religions du Monde Romain*, 39–71. Geneva, 1996.

Scheid 1998a. J. Scheid, "Nouveau rite et nouvelle piété: Réflections sur le *ritus Graecus*," in F. Graf, ed., *Ansichten griechischer Rituale: Geburtstag-Symposium für Walter Burkert*, 168–82. Stuttgart and Leipzig, 1998.

Scheid 1998b. J. Scheid, "Déchiffrer des monnaies: Réflexions sur la representation figure des Jeux Séculaires," in C. Auvray-Assayas, ed., *Images Romaines*, 13–35. Paris, 1998.

Scheid 1998c. J. Scheid, "Les annals des pontifes: Une hypothèse de plus," in *Convegno per Santo Mazzarino*, 199–220. Rome, 1998.

Scheid 2000. J. Scheid, "Sujets religieux et gestes rituels sur la colonne Aurélienne: Questions sur la religion à l'époque de Marc Aurèle," in J. Scheid and V. Huet, eds., *Autour de la Colonne Aurélienne: Geste et image sur la colonne de Marc Aurèle à Rome*, 227–42. Turnhout, 2000.

Scheid 2005. J. Scheid, *Quand faire, c'est croire: Les rites sacrificiels des Romains.* Aubier, 2005.

Scheid 2007. J. Scheid, ed., *Res Gestae Divi Augusti.* Paris, 2007.

Scheid 2012a. J. Scheid, "Le rite des auspices à Rome: Quelle evolution? Réflexions sur la transformation de la divination publique des Romains entre le IIIe et le Ier siècle avant notre ère," in S. Georgoudi, R. Koch Piettre, and F. Schmidt, eds., *La Raison des signes: Présages, rites, destin dans les sociétés de la Méditerranée ancienne*, 109–28. Leiden, 2012.

Scheid 2012b. J. Scheid, "Roman Animal Sacrifice and the System of Being," in C. A. Faraone and F. S. Naiden, eds., *Greek and Roman Animal Sacrifice: Ancient Victims, Modern Observers*, 84–95. Cambridge, 2012.

Scheid 2015. J. Scheid, "Auspices et autres pratiques divinatoires des magistrats romains à l'époque medio-républicaine," *CCG* 26 (2015): 251–60.

Scheid 2016. J. Scheid, "Le lustrum et la lustratio: En finir avec la 'purification,'" in V. Gasparini, ed., *Vestigia: Miscellanea di studi storico-religiosi in onore di Filippo*

Coarelli nel suo 80° anniversario [= Potsdamer Altertumswissenschaftliche Beiträge, vol. 55], 203–9. Stuttgart, 2016.

Schmauder 2007. M. Schmauder, "Die Bewaffnung des spätantiken Heeres," in A. Demandt and J. Engemann, eds., *Imperator Caesar Flavius Constantinus / Konstantin der Grosse*, 147–53. Trier and Mainz, 2007.

Schmid 2007/2008. St. G. Schmid, "*Et in consulatu sexto censum populi conlega M. Agrippa egi*: Ein neuer Vorschlag zum Kontext der Santocroce-Reliefs," *Boreas* 30/31 (2007/2008): 41–71.

Schmidt Heidenreich 2013. C. Schmidt Heidenreich, *Glaive et l'autel: Camps et piété militaires sous le Haut-Empire romain*. Rennes, 2013.

Schnegg-Köhler 2002. B. Schnegg-Köhler, *Die augusteischen Säkularspiele = ARG* 4.

Schultz 2014. C. Schultz, *Commentary on Cicero: De Divinatione I*. Ann Arbor, 2014.

Schumacher 1985. L. Schumacher, "Die imperatorischen Akklamationen der Triumvirn und die auspicia des Augustus," *Historia* 34 (1985): 191–222.

Schwegler 1868–1872. A. Schwegler, *Römische Geschichte*, 3 vols. Tübingen, 1868–1872.

Sehlmeyer 1999. M. Sehlmeyer, *Stadtrömische Ehrenstatuen der republikanischen Zeit: Historizität und Kontext von Symbolen nobilitären Standesbewußtseins*. Stuttgart, 1999.

Sette 2000. G. Sette, *L'abbigliameno* [= Vita e costume dei Romani antichi, 22]. Rome, 2000.

Settis 1988. S. Settis, *La Colonna Traiana*. Turin, 1988.

Sewell 2014. J. Sewell, "Gellius, Philip II, and a Proposed End to the 'Model-Replica' Debate," in Stek and Pelgrom 2014, 125–39.

Shackleton-Bailey 1980. D. R. Shackleton Bailey, *Cicero Epistulae ad Quintum Fratrem et M. Brutum* [= Cambridge Classical Texts and Commentaries, vol. 22. Cambridge, 1980.

Shaw 1997. B. Shaw, "Ritual Brotherhood in Roman and Post-Roman Societies," *Traditio* 52 (1997): 327–55.

Sherk 1988. R. Sherk, ed., *The Roman Empire: Augustus to Hadrian*. Cambridge, 1988.

Simon 1985. E. Simon, "Virtus und Pietas: Zu den Friesen A. u. B. von der Cancelleria," *JdI* 100 (1985): 543–55.

Simon 1991. E. Simon, "Altes und Neues zur Statue des Augustus von Primaporta," in Binder 1991: 204–33.

Simon 1993. B. Simon, *Die Selbstdarstellung des Augustus in der Münzprägung und in den Res Gestae*. Hamburg, 1993.

BIBLIOGRAPHY

Simonelli 2001. A. Simonelli, "Considerazioni sull'origine, la natura, e l'evoluzione del *pomerium*," *Aevum* 75 (2001), 119–62.

Simpson 1998. C. J. Simpson, "IMP. CAESAR DIVI FILIUS: His Second Imperatorial Acclamation and the Evolution of an Allegedly 'Exorbitant' Name," *Athenaeum* 86 (1998): 419–37.

Simpson 2005. C. J. Simpson, "Where Is the Parthian? The Prima Porta Statue of Augustus Revisited," *Latomus* 64 (2005): 82–90.

Sisani 2016. S. Sisani, "Il concetto di *pomerium*: Valenza giuridico-sacrale e realtà topografica dei *fines urbis*," in V. Gasparini, ed., *Vestigia: Miscellanea di studi storico-religiosi in onore di Filippo Coarellil nel suo 80° anniversario*, 65–80. Stuttgart, 2016.

Smith 1996. R.R.R. Smith, "Typology and Diversity in the Portraits of Augustus," *JRA* 9 (1996): 31–47.

Smith 1997. R.R.R. Smith, "The Public Image of Licinius I: Portrait Sculpture and Imperial Ideology in the Early Fourth Century," *JRS* 87 (1997): 170–202.

Smith 2012. C. J. Smith, "The *Feriae Latinae*," in J. Rasmus Brandt and J. W. Iddeng, eds., *Greek and Roman Festivals: Content, Meaning, and Practice*, 267–88. Oxford, 2012.

Spannagel 1999. M. Spannagel, *Exemplaria Principis: Untersuchungen zu Entstellung und Ausstattung des Augustusforums*. Heidelberg, 1999.

Spannagel 2009. M. Spannagel, "*Annos undeviginti natus* . . . Die Rückführung von Augustus' Principat auf die Jahre 44/43 v. Chr," in F. Hurlet and B. Mineo, eds., *Le Principat d'Auguste: Réalités et representations du pouvoir: Autour de la* Res publica restituta, 25–47. Rennes, 2009.

Stasse 2005. B. Stasse, "La loi curiate des magistrats," *RIDA* 52 (2005): 375–400.

Staveley 1956. E. S. Staveley, "The Constitution of the Roman Republic, 1940–1954," *Historia* 5 (1956): 74–119.

Staveley 1963. E. S. Staveley, "The Fasces and Imperium Maius," *Historia* 12 (1963): 458–84.

Stefan and Chew 2015. A. Simon Stefan and H. Chew, eds., *La Colonne Trajane*. Paris, 2015.

Stein 1930. P. Stein, "Die Senatssitzungen der ciceronischen Zeit" (diss.). Münster, 1930.

Stek and Pelgrom 2014. T. D. Stek and J. Pelgrom, eds., *Roman Republican Colonization: New Perspectives from Archaeology and Ancient History* (= Papers of the Royal Netherlands Institute in Rome, vol. 62). Rome, 2014.

Stemmer 1978. K. Stemmer, *Untersuchungen zur Typologie, Chronologie und Ikonographie der Panzerstatuen*. Berlin, 1978.

BIBLIOGRAPHY

Stephenson 2009. P. Stephenson, *Constantine: Roman Emperor, Christian Victor.* New York, 2009.

Stewart 1998. R. Stewart, *Public Office in Early Rome: Ritual Procedure and Political Practice.* Ann Arbor, 1998.

Stoll 2001. O. Stoll, *Zwischen Integration und Abgrenzung: Die Religion des Römischen Heeres im Nahen Osten: Studien zum Verhältnis von Armee und Zivilbevölkerung im römischen Syrien und den Nachargebieten.* St. Katherinen, 2001.

Straub 1955. J. A. Straub, "Konstantins Verzicht auf den Gang zum Kapitol," *Historia* 4 (1955): 297–313.

Strong 1907. Mrs. A. Strong, *Roman Sculpture from Augustus to Constantine.* London, 1907.

Sumi 2015. G. Sumi, *Ceremony and Power: Performing Politics in Rome between Republic and Empire.* Ann Arbor, 2015.

Syme 1939. R. Syme, *The Roman Revolution.* Oxford.

Syme 1978. R. Syme, "The *Pomerium* in the Historia Augusta," *Bonner HAC* 1975–1976 (= 1978), 217ff., as reprinted in Syme, *Historia Augusta Papers*, 130–45. Oxford, 1978.

Syme 1979. R. Syme, "Imperator Caesar: A Study in Nomenclature," *Historia* 7 (1979): 172–88.

Tarpin 2003. M. Tarpin, "M. Licinius Crassus, *Imperator*, et les dépouilles opimes de la république," *Revue Philologique* 77 (2003): 275–311.

Thomas 1995. Y. Thomas, "*Ficto Legis*: L'empire de la fiction romaine et ses limites médiévales," *Droits* 21 (1995): 17–63.

Thomas 2017. E. Thomas, "The Cult Statues of the Pantheon," *JRS* 107 (2017): 146–212.

Toher 2004. M. Toher, "Octavian's Arrival in Rome, 44 BC," *CQ* 54 (2004): 174–84.

Torelli 1982. M. Torelli, *Typology and Structure of Roman Historical Reliefs.* Ann Arbor, 1982.

Torelli 2011. M. Torelli, "The *Haruspices* of the Emperor: Tarquitius Priscus and Sejanus," in J. H. Richardson and F. Santangelo, eds., *Priests and State in the Roman World*, 137–59. Stuttgart, 2011.

Torelli 2014. M. Torelli, "*Effigies parvae simulacraque Romae*: La fortuna di un modello teorico repubblicano: Leptis Magna colonia romana," in Stek and Pelgrom 2014, 335–55.

Tortorella 1985. S. Tortorella, in *Archéologie et Projet Urbain*, 42–45. Rome, 1985.

BIBLIOGRAPHY

Tortorella 1988. S. Tortorella, "Il rilievo dell'*extispicium* del Museo del Louvre," *ScAnt* 2 (1988): 475–95.

Tortorella 2013. S. Tortorella, "Archi di Costantino," *ArchCl* 64 (2013): 637–55.

Turner, Chong-Gossard, Vervaet 2010. A. J. Turner, J. H. Kim On Chong-Gossard, and F. J. Vervaet. *Private and Public Lies: The Discourse of Despotism and Deceit in the Graeco-Roman World.* Leiden and Boston, 2010.

Ungaro and Milella 1995. L. Ungaro and M. Milella, eds., *I luoghi del consenso: Il Foro di Augusto, il Foro di Traiano*, 2 vols. Rome, 1995.

Vaahtera 1993. J. Vaahtera, "On the Religious Nature of the Place of Assembly," in U. Pannen, K. Heikkila, et al., eds., *Senatus Populusque Romanus: Studies in Roman Republican Legislation*, 97–116. Rome, 1993.

Vaahtera 2001. J. Vaahtera, *Roman Augural Lore in Greek Historiography.* Stuttgart, 2001.

Van Dam 2007. R. Van Dam, *The Roman Revolution of Constantine.* Cambridge, 2007.

Van Dam 2011. R. Van Dam, *Remembering Constantine at the Milvian Bridge.* Cambridge, 2011.

Van Dam 2018. R. Van Dam, "Constantine's First Visit to Rome with Diocletian in 303," *JLA* 11 (2018): 6–41.

Van Haeperen 2007. F. Van Haeperen, "Les rites d'accession au pouvoir des consuls romains: Une part intégrante de leur entrée en charge," in J.-M. Cauchies and F. Van Haeperen, eds., *Le pouvoir et ses rites d'accession et de confirmation*, 31–45. Brussels, 2007.

Van Haeperen 2012. F. Van Haeperen, "Auspices d'investiture, loi curiate et légitimité des magistrates romains," *CCG* 23 (2012): 71–112.

Van Haeperen 2015. F. Van Haeperen, "De la nécessité d'une loi curiate pour les magistrats sans *imperium*," *CCG* 26(2015): 225–30.

Van Haeperen 2017. F. Van Haeperen, "Les comices curiates, une assemblée garante de la norme?" in T. Itgenshorst and P. Le Doze, eds., *La norme sous la République romaine et le Haut-Empire: Élaboration, diffusion et contournements*, 389–97. Bordeaux, 2017.

Vermeule 1959–1960. C. C. Vermeule, "Hellenistic and Roman Cuirassed Statues: The Evidence of Paintings and Reliefs in the Chronological Development of Cuirass Types," *Berytus* 13 (1959–1960): 1–82.

Versnel 1970. H. S. Versnel, *Triumphus: An Inquiry into the Origin, Development, and Meaning of the Roman Triumph.* Leiden, 1970.

Versnel 1975. H. Versnel, "Sacrificium Lustrale: The Death of Mettius Fufetius (Livy I, 28): Studies in Roman Lustration—Ritual I," *MededRome* 37 (1975): 97–115.

BIBLIOGRAPHY

Vervaet 2006. F. J. Vervaet, "The Scope of the *Lex Sempronia* Concerning the Assignment of the Consular Provinces (123 BCE)," *Athenaeum* 94 (2006): 625–54.

Vervaet 2009. F. J. Vervaet, "Pompeius' Career from 79 to 70 BCE: Constitutional, Political, and Historical Considerations," *Klio* 91 (2009): 406–34.

Vervaet 2010. F. J. Vervaet, "Arrogating Despotic Power through Deceit: The Pompeian Model for Augustan *Dissimulatio*," in Turner, Chong-Gossard, and Vervaet 2010, 133–66.

Vervaet 2014. F. J. Vervaet, *The High Command in the Roman Republic: The Principle of the* Summum Imperium Auspiumque *from 509 to 19 BCE*. Stuttgart, 2014.

Vervaet 2015. F. J. Vervaet, "The Lex Curiata and the Patrician Auspices," *CCG* 26 (2015): 201–24.

Wace 1907. A.J.B. Wace, "Studies in Roman Historical Reliefs," *PBSR* 4 (1907): 229–57.

Wallace-Hadrill 1982. A. Wallace-Hadrill, "Civilis Princeps: Between Citizen and King," *JRS* 72 (1982): 32–48.

Wallace-Hadrill 1986. A. Wallace-Hadrill, "Image and Authority in the Coinage of Augustus," *JRS* 76 (1986): 66–87.

Wallace-Hadrill 1990. A. Wallace-Hadrill, "Roman Arches and Greek Honors: The Language of Power at Rome," *PCPhS* 216 (1990): 143–81.

Wallmann 1977. P. Wallmann, *Münzpropaganda in den Anfängen des Zweiten Triumvirats (43/42 v. Chr.)*. Bochum, 1977.

Wardle 2014. D. Wardle, ed., trans., comm., *Suetonius: Life of Augustus*. Oxford, 2014.

Weinstock 1971. S. Weinstock, *Divus Julius*. Oxford, 1971.

Weisseborn and Müller 1887–1912. G. Weisseborn and M. Müller, eds., *Titi Livi Ab Urbe Condita Libri*. Leipzig, 1887–1912.

Weisweiler 2012a. J. Weisweiler, "From Equality to Asymmetry: Honorific Statues, Imperial Power, and Senatorial Identity in Late-Antique Rome," *JRA* 25 (2012): 319–50.

Weisweiler 2012b. J. Weisweiler, "Inscribing Imperial Power: Letters from Emperors in Late Antique Rome," in R. Behrwald and C. Witschel, eds., *Rom in der Spätantike: Historische Erinnerung im städtischen Raum*, 309–29. Stuttgart, 2012.

Weisweiler 2015. J. Weisweiler, "Domesticating the Senatorial Elite: Universal Monarchy and Transregional Aristocracy in the Fourth Century AD," in J. Wienand, ed., *Contested Monarchy: Integrating the Roman Empire in the Fourth Century AD*, 17–41. Oxford, 2015.

BIBLIOGRAPHY

Wellesley 2000. K. Wellesley, *The Year of the Four Emperors*, 3rd ed. London, 2000.

Wheeler 2008. E. L. Wheeler, "Pullarii, Marsi, Haruspices, and Sacerdotes in the Roman Imperial Army," in V. E. Hirschmann et al., *A Roman Miscellany: Essays in Honour of Anthony R. Birley on His Seventieth Birthday*, 185–201. Gdańsk, 2008.

Wienand 2012. J. Wienand, *Der Kaiser als Sieger: Metamorphosen triumphaler Herrschaft unter Constantin I*. Berlin, 2012.

Wienand 2015a. J. Wienand, ed., *Contested Monarchy: Integrating the Roman Empire in the Fourth Century AD*. Oxford.

Wienand 2015b. J. Wienand, "O tandem felix civili, Roma, Victoria! Civil-War Triumphs from Honorius to Constantine and Back," in Wienand 2015a, 167–97.

Wienand 2015c. J. Wienand, "The Empire's Golden Shade: Icons of Sovereignty in an Age of Transition," in Wienand 2015a, 423–51.

Wilson Jones 2000. M. Wilson Jones, "Genesis and Mimesis: The Design of the Arch of Constantine in Rome," *JSAH* 59 (2000): 50–77.

Winkler 1991. L. Winkler, "Die Opferszenen der Trajanssäule: Bedeutung innerhalb der narrative Systematik," in L. Baumer, T. Hölscher, and L. Winkler, "Narrative Systematik und politisches Konzept in den Reliefs der Traianssäle: Drei Fallstudien," *JdI* 106 (1001): 261–95, at 267–77.

Wissowa 1912. G. Wissowa, *Religion und Kultus der Römer*. Munich, 1912.

Woytek 2003. B. Woytek, *Arma et Nummi: Forschungen zur römischen Finanzgeschichte und Münzprägung der Jahre 49 bis 42 v. Chr.* Vienna, 2003.

Wrede 1981. H. Wrede, "Der genius populi Romani und das Fünfsäulendenkmal der Tetrarchen auf dem Forum Romanum," *BjB* 181 (1981): 111–42.

Wright 1987. D. H. Wright, "The True Face of Constantine the Great," *DOP* 41 (1987): 493–507.

Zanker 1973. P. Zanker, *Studien zu den Augustus-Porträts I: Der Actium-Typus*. Göttingen, 1973.

Zanker 1979. P. Zanker, "Prinzipat und Herrscherbild," *Gymnasium* 86 (1979): 353–68.

Zanker 1981. P. Zanker, "Das Bildnis des M. Holconius Rufus," *AA* (1981): 349–61.

Zanker 1988. P. Zanker, *The Power of Images in the Age of Augustus*, trans. A. Shapiro. Ann Arbor, 1988.

Zanker 2010. P. Zanker, "By the Emperor, for the People: "Popular" Architecture in Rome" [1997], in Ewald and Noreña 2010, 45–87.

Zanker 2012. P. Zanker, "Der Konstantinsbogen als Monument des Senates," *ActaArchArtiumPert* 25 (2012): 77–105.

BIBLIOGRAPHY

Zanker and Ewald 2012. P. Zanker and B. Ewald, *Living with Myths: The Imagery of Roman Sarcophagi*. Oxford, 2012.

Ziolkowsi 1992. A. Ziolkowski, *The Temples of Mid-Republican Rome and Their Historical and Topographical Context*. Rome, 1992.

Ziolkowsi 2011. A. Ziolkowski, "The Capitol and the 'Auspices of Departure,'" in S. Ruciński, K. Balbuza, and K. Króczky, eds., *Studia Lesco Mrozewicz ab amicis et discipulis dedicata*, 465–71. Poznań, 2011.

INDEX OF ANCIENT TEXTS

Ad Herr. 4.68	44 n.5
Amm. Marc. 16.10.6	147 n.60
App. *BCiv.*	
1.14	44 n.5
1.100	23 n.28
2.2.8	22 n.23
2.106	23 n.25
4.2–3	76 n.104
4.6–7	76 n.104
App. *Mith.* 94	57 n.50
Aug. *Civ.D.* 2.24	54 n.40
Aur. Vict.	
33	164 n.77
40	146 n.58, 158 n74
Aus. *Grat. Act.* 11	147 n.62
Caes. *BCiv*	
1.6.5–7	49 n.22
2.21.5	22 n.23
3.2	46 n.10
Caes. *BGall.* 1.52.5	70 n.84
Cassiod. *Chron.* 576	32 n.47
Cato, *Agr., pass.*	116
Cato, *FRH.* F132	6 n.15
Cato, *Orig.* 77	79 n.5
Censor. 23.4	69 n.81
Cic. *ad Brut.*	
1.12.1	73 n.96
1.15.9	73 n.96

INDEX OF ANCIENT TEXTS

Cic. *Att.*
- 4.15 — 64 n.67
- 4.16 — 64 n.67
- 4.17 — 64 n.67
- 4.17.2 — 36 n.59, 51 n.29
- 4.18 — 64 n.67
- 4.18.4 — 36 n.59, 65 n.68
- 6.3.3 — 36 n.59, 48 n.19
- 7.7.4 — 48 n.19
- 8.9(a) — 25 n.33
- 8.13.1 — 25 n.33
- 9.15 — 22 n.23
- 9.16.1 — 25 n.33
- 10.4 — 25 n.33

Cic. *Balb.* 17 — 63 n.65

Cic. *Div.*
- 1.3 — 10 n.1, 66 n.73
- 1.18 — 45 n.10
- 1.27–28 — 6 n.15
- 1.33 — 11 n.4, 39 n.68, 42 n.78
- 1.72 — 54 n.40
- 1.77 — 60 n.59
- 1.95 — 54 n.38, 66 n.73
- 1.102 — 97 n.48
- 1.107 — 6 n.15
- 1.119 — 54 n.40
- 2.21 — 60 n.59
- 2.53 — 55 n.40
- 2.67 — 60 n.59
- 2.71 — 60 n.59
- 2.73 — 6 n.15
- 2.75 — 42 n.78
- 2.76 — 35 n.56, 36 n.59, 56 n.44

Cic. *Dom.* 39 — 51 n.31

Cic. *Fam.*
- 1.9.25 — 11 n.5, 36 n.59, 65 n.68
- 2.7.4 — 48 n.19
- 3.2.1 — 36 n.58, 48–9 n.22
- 5.2.1 — 167 n.85
- 10.30 — 71 n.89

INDEX OF ANCIENT TEXTS

15.9.2	48 n.19
15.14.5	48 n.19
Cic. *Leg.*	
2.21	51 n.31
2.31	10 n.1
3.6	10 n.1
Cic. *Leg. Agr.*	
2.26	45 n.7
2.26–28	48 n.22
2.34	10 n.1
2.86	97 n.49
Cic. *Mur.* 1	44 n.5
Cic. *Nat. D.*	
2.3	35 n.56
2.8	60 n.59
2.9	56 n.44, 66 n.73
2.10	79 n.4
2.10–11	42 n.78
2.11	11 n.4, 51 n.31
Cic. *Off.* 1.61	18, 19 n.18
Cic. *Phil.*	
2.40	3 n.8
2.82	44 n.5
2.102	97 n.47 and 49
3.5	44 n.3, 47 n.14
3.27	75 n.103
5.21	75 n.103
5.27	99 n.51
5.40–41	73 n.96
5.45	43–44 and n.3, 46 n.13
5.46	47 n.14
6.2	74 n.98
9.13	73 n.95
9.16	73 n.95
11.20	44 n.3, 47 n.14
13.8–9	73 n.96
14.11	57 n.49, 71 n.90
14.28	44 n.3
14.29	71 n.90
14.37	71 n.90

INDEX OF ANCIENT TEXTS

Cic. *Pis.*
   50   11 n.5
   73   138 n.40, 148 n.62
Cic. *QFr.*
   3.1.15   64 n.67
   3.1.24   64 n.67
   3.2.2–3   64 n.67
   3.2.3   36 n.59, 65 n.68
   3.3.2   64 n.67
Cic. *Rep.*
   1.63   10 n.1
Cic. *Sen.* 12   51 n.31
Cic. *Sull.* 34.7   45 n.8
Cic. *Ver.*
   2.1.51.133   63 n.65
   2.2.10   54 n.38, 54 n.40
   2.3.11   54 n.40
   2.3.60   54 n.38
   2.5.34   12 n.5, 45 n.8, 67 n.75
Const. Porphr. *De Caer.*   132 n.28
CTh
   14.101   158 n.74
   15.14.4   164 n.77
De Viris Illust. 11.2   19 n.18
Digest
   1.2.2.43   73 n.95
   35.1.24   93 n.33
   35.2.1   93 n.33
   50.16.87   5 n.13
   50.17.161   93 n.33
Dio Cass.
   36.23.4   57 n.50
   37.1.2   57 n.50
   39.63.4   12 n.5
   40.30.1   46 n.12
   40.56.1–3   35 n.56
   41.36.1–2   22 n.23
   42.19.3   23 n.26
   42.20.1–3   22 n.24, 23 n.26

INDEX OF ANCIENT TEXTS

42.23–24	24 n.29
42.27.2	24 n.30
42.29.3	24 n.30
43.14.6	23 n.26
43.21.1–2	23 n.26
43.43.1	23 n.25
43.44.2	22 n.23
44.41.3	22 n.23
45.5.3–4	49 n.22
46.2.1–2	46 n.12
46.29.5	74 n.98
46.33.4	49 n.23
46.35.4	46 n.13, 53 n.36
46.38.1	71 n.90
46.55–56	76 n.104
46.56.1	46 n.12
47.38.4	97 n.49
50.24	30 n.41
50.33.4–5	94 n.38
51.19.6	8 n.18
53.13.1	33 n.49
53.13.1–8	57 n.50
53.14.2	35 n.57
53.16.2	33 n.49
53.18.4	41 n.76
53.27.2–3	29 n.38
53.32.5	33 n.50
54.1.1	29 n.39
54.8.2	32 n.47
54.8.3	32 n.47
54.10.3–4	32 n.47
54.10.5	34 n.52
54.24.7	32 n.47
72.33.3	94 n.39
75.1.3–5	148 n.64
Dion. Hal.	
2.4	70 n.84
2.5.1	45 n.8
2.6.2–3	51 n.29
4.13.4	5

INDEX OF ANCIENT TEXTS

4.22	96 n.43
5.25.2	19 n.18
5.70.1	24 n.32
5.70.4	24 n.32
5.73.1	24 n.32
7.59.2	44 n.5
8.69.3–4	8 n.17
8.87.3–6	8
10.24.2	23 n.28
12.16.2–4	79 n.4

Ennius, *Ann.*
81V	6
92V	69 n.81
157V	3 n.5
Epit. *De Caes.* 41.16	146 n.58

Eusebius, *VC*
3.31.2–32.2	129 n.19
4.1	146 n.58

Festus
15	67 n.75
30	94 n.39
228	19 n.19
276–77	68 n.77
294	3 n.7,
298	19 n.18, 87 n.16
310	2, 3 n.5
439	87 n.16
474	69 n.81

Florus
1.33.7	63 n.65
2.15.2–3	49 n.22
2.54	38 n.65
Front. *De Controv.*	4

Gaius, *Inst.*
2.5–7	94 n.36
4.37	93 n.33
4.104	8 n.18

INDEX OF ANCIENT TEXTS

Gell. *NA*
  3.2.10 — 69 n.81
  4.5.1 — 19 n.18
  13.14.1–3 — 3 n.8, 11 n.4
  14.7.9 — 45 n.8
  15.27.5 — 4 n.10, 42 n.79
  16.13.9 — 99 n.51

Herodian
  1.6.3–5 — 167 n.85
  2.14.1 — 148 n.64
  5.5–6 — 148 n.64

Jul. *Caes.* 335B — *146 n.58*

Lact. *De Mort. Pers.*
  25 — 132 n.28
  44.11 — 148 n.63

Livy
  1.7.3 — 82 n.7
  1.8.2 — 23 n.28
  1.17.6 — 23 n.28
  1.44.1–2 — 96 n.43
  1.44.4 — 3 n.7
  2.1.5–7 — 67 n.75
  2.7.7 — 23 n.28
  2.10.12 — 19 n.18
  2.18.8–9 — 24 n.32
  2.42.6–9 — 8 n.17
  3.20.6 — 59 nn.55–56
  3.20.7 — 8 n.18
  3.31.1 — 10 n.1
  3.64.9–10 — 44 n.5
  4.22.7 — 96 n.43
  4.41.11 — 23 n.28
  5.41.2 — 19 n.19, 139 n.44
  5.52.15 — 3 n. 8, 67 n.73
  5.52.15–16 — 63 n.66
  6.11.1 — 10 n.1
  6.16.3 — 24 n.32
  6.16.5 — 24 n.32

INDEX OF ANCIENT TEXTS

6.38.3	24 n.32
7.3.5	69 n.79
7.12.9	99 n.52
7.16.7	59 n.55
7.21.9	99 n.52
8.9.5	79 n.4
8.23.10–12	48 n.18, 48 n.20
8.23.15	69 n.81
8.26.7	48 n.18
8.32.3	52 n.32
8.32.4	58 n.54
9.42.2	48 n.18
10.3.3–8	58 n.54
10.7.10	79 n.4
10.8.9	10 n.1
10.16.1	48 n.18
10.22.9	48 n.18
10.40.2	69 n.81
10.46.2–3	139 n.44
21.63.1–2	46 n.11
21.63.5–9	67 n.75
21.63.5–12	61 n.60
21.63.7	45 n.8
21.63.8	46 n.11
21.63.9	67 n.75
1.63.11–12	62 n.63
21.63.14–15	45 n.8
21.63.39	67 n.75
22.1.5–7	46 n.11, 67 n.75
22.1.6	62 n.64, 67 n.75
22.1.6–7	61 n.62
22.9.7	45 n.8, 60 n.59
23.19.3–5	58 n.54
23.19.18	107 n.65, 110, 115
23.36.9–10	58 n.54
23.36.10	54 n.39
24.9.9	58 n.52
24.43.5	58 n.52
24.43.9	58 n.52
26.2.1	47 n.17

INDEX OF ANCIENT TEXTS

26.2.2–3	61 n.61
26.9.6–10.10	12 n.7
26.18.6–10	48 n.18
26.21.1–13	34 n.53
28.38.1	49 n.23
29.13.6	49 n.23
30.45.2	19 n.18
31.3.2–3	55 n.42
31.5.1–2	46 n.11
31.5.4–5	45 n.8
31.14	88 n.18
31.50.6–8	45 n.9
31.50.11	55 n.42
32.1–9	46 n.10
33.44.2	45 n.8
34.14.1	67 n.73
36.1.2	45 n.8
36.1.2–3	54 n.37
38.20.6–7	106 n.61
38.56.12	19 n.18
40.45.8	96 n.43
41.10	67 n.75, 88 n.18
41.14.7–15.1	45 n.8, 54 n.39
41.16.1	46 n.10
42.28.7	45 n.8
42.28.9	45 n.8
42.30.8	45 n.8, 54 n.37, 54 n.39
42.30.8–31.9	105 n.59
42.35.3	46 n.10, 106 n.60
42.49.1	67 n.75
44.19.4	46 nn.10–11
44.37.13	107 n.62
44.39.4	99 nn.51–52
45.35.3–4	34 n.53
45.39.1	67 n.75, 88 n.18
45.46.15	96 n.43, 97 n.49
Liv. *Per.*	
47	46 n.11
120	76 n. 104

INDEX OF ANCIENT TEXTS

Macrob. *Sat.*
    1.7.15   167 n.84
    1.24.12   167 n.84
Men. Rhet., *Peri Ep.* 377   167 n.85

Obseq.
    56b   54 n.40
    69   53 n.36
Ov. *Fast.*
    1.79–81   45 n.8
    1.83–84   45 n.8
    4.673–76   71 n.90
    6.205–8   94 n.39
    6.363   31 n.46
Ov. *Pont.*
    4.4.30   45 n.8
    4.4.31   45 n.8
    4.4.35–36   45 n.10
Pan. Lat.
    IV (10).29.5   147 n.60
    VII (6).6.2   147 n.60
    X (2).6.4–5   136 n.35
    X (2).14   167 n.85
    XII (9). 2.4   55 n.40
    XII (9).17.3   134 n.32
    XII (9).20   133 n.30
Plaut. *Cas.* 626   63 n.65
Plin. *HN*
    5.36   37 n.60
    7.19   138 n.40
    11.190   53 n.35
    11.195   55 n.40
    34.18   14, 18
    34.22   19 n.18
    34.27   141 n.51
Plin. Min. *Ep.* 8.6.13–14   14
Plin. Min. *Paneg.* 64   45 n.9
Plut. *Brut.* 39   97 n.49
Plut. *Caes.* 29.5   149 n.66

INDEX OF ANCIENT TEXTS

Plut. *Fab.*	
2.3–3.1	60 n.59
4.2	23 n.28
Plut. *Pobl.* 16.7	19 n.18
Plut. *Pomp.*	
16.2	55 n.42
17.4	55 n.42
25.2–3	57 n.50
58.2	149 n.66
Plut. *Quaest. Rom.* 10	79 n.4
Plut. *Rom.* 11.1–3	1–2
Polyb.	
3.87	23 n.28
6.15.6	48 n.20
6.19–21	7 n.16
6.53.7	31 n.46
16.23	19 n.18
Rufinus, *HE* 9.9.11	133 n.30
Sall. Cat.	
29	10 n.1
52.21	10 n.1
Sall. *Jug.*	
8.5.3	10 n.1
41.7	144 n.56
Serv. *Aen.*	
2.178	60 n.58
2.187	95 n.40
9.52	95 n.40
S. H. A., *Aurel.* 21.9–10	167 n.84
S. H. A., *Hadr.* 3.5–6	88 n.20
S. H. A., *Pesc. Nig.* 6.10.3	144 n.56
S. H. A., *Max. and Balb.* 6.1.3	144 n.56
S. H. A., *Div. Claud.* 2.6.2	144 n.56
S. H. A., *Tac.* 16.6.2	144 n.56
Sid. Apoll. *Ep.* 1.5.9	167 n.84
Solinus 1.17	166 n.82
Strabo	5.3.8 27 n.34
Suet. *Aug.*	
31.5	19 n.20, 31 n.46

36.1	35 n.57
73	32 n.47
90–92	55 n.40
95	53 n.36
96.2	55 n.40
Suet. *Jul.*	
76.1	22 n.23
81	54 n.40
Suet. *Dom.* 13.2	139 n.44
Suet. *Galb.* 8.2	136 n.35
Suet. *Tib.* 9.2	32 n.47
Suet. *Vit.*	
10.2	40 n.72
11.1	40 n.70, 148 n.64
Symm. *Ep.*	
IV.70	129 n.20
Symm. *Rel.*	
9.4	131 n.25
25–26	129 n.20
Tac. *Ann.*	
1.7.5	13 n.10
12.24	3 n.6, 166 n.82
Tac. *Hist.*	
1.56.2	41 n.73
2.55	41 n.74
2.89	40 n.70, 148 n.64
Val. *Max.*	
1.6.4	107 n.62
1.6.6	61 n.60
2.8	127 n.16
2.8.6	35 n.54
4.1.6	19 n.18
8.11.2r	55 n.40
9.7 *mil. Rom.* 2	107 n.62
Varro, *Ling.*	
5.33	58 n.53
5.87	56 n.47
5.143	3 nn. 4 and 7, 39 n.68, 96 n.45
6.91	44 n.5, 45 n.8

INDEX OF ANCIENT TEXTS

6.93	97 n.47, 97 n.49
7.37	88 n.18
Varro, *Rust.*	
2.1.10	96 n.43
3.2.4–5	96 n.43
Vell.	
2.22.2	45 n.8
2.51.3	35 n.57, 37 n.60
2.61.3	72 n.91
2.115.3	37 n.60
Verg. *Aen.* 3.403–7	79 n.4
Zosimus	
2.9.2	132 n.28
2.17	134 n.32
2.34	148 n.64
2.38	146 n.58

INDEX OF INSCRIPTIONS

AE
   1948, 2   139 n.45
   1948, 6 a and b   144 n.55
   1953, 85   144 n.55
   1985, 879   139 n.45
   2002, 796   139 n.45

CIL
   I, p. 230   44 n.3
   III.19   165 n.79
   VI.959   144 n.55
   VI.1033   144 n.54
   VI.1139   136 n.36, 141 n.49
   VI.1196   139 n.43
   VI.1318   58 n.54
   VI.1678   165 n.79
   VI.1741   144 n.55
   VI.1767   165 n.79
   VI.31245   141 n.49
   VI.36953   158 n.74
   VI.40776   167 n.85
   VIII.24   139 n.45
   VIII.210   138 n.40
   VIII.10999   139 n.45
   VIII.22670   139 n.45
   IX.2563   22 n.23
   XII.4333   44 n.3, 52 n.34
   XIII.11810   139 n.45
CSEL 35   130 nn.21 and 23

INDEX OF INSCRIPTIONS

EJ
- 44   44 n.3
- 53   44 n.3

ILLRP   406   22 n.23

ILS
- 53   58 n.54
- 70   22 n.23
- 108   44 n.3
- 112   44 n.3, 52 n.34
- 292   144 n.55
- 425   144 n.54
- 694   136 n.34, 141 n.49
- 798   139 n.43
- 1273   165 n.79
- 1281   165 n.79
- 1282   165 n.79
- 1886   51 n.29
- 1907   51 n.29
- 5570   138 n.40

Inscr. Ital.
- XIII.1, 77   19 n.18
- XIII.1, 79   19 n.18
- XIII.2, 113   44 n.3
- XIII.2, 257   135 n.34
- XIII.2, 392   44 n.3
- XIII.2, 527   135 n.34
- XIII.3, 17   20 n 20
- XIII.3, 83   20 n.20

IRT
- 562   144 n.55
- 563   144 n.55

RGDA
- 1.1   43 n.1
- 4.1   32 n.47
- 6.1   42 n.80
- 29

RS
- I, no. 24, 20   8 n.18
- I, no. 25, 62, 12–40   54 n.39
- II, no. 66, 3–4   51 n.31

INDEX OF PERSONS

Aemilius Lepidus, Marcus. *Cos. 46* BC; *IIIvir*	55, 73
Aemilius Paullus, Lucius. *Cos. 182* BC	46 n.11
Afranius, Lucius. *Cos. 60* BC	57 n.48
Agrippa (*see* Vipsanius)	
Albinius, Lucius. *fl.* 390 (cf. *ILS* 51)	20 n.20
Alfenus (jurist, 1st c. BC)	5
Ampius Balbus, Titus. *Pr. 59*	57 n.48
Anicius, Marcus.	107, 110–11, 115
Antonius, Lucius. *Cos. 41* BC	73
Antonius, Marcus. *Cos. 44* BC	23–24, 71, 75, 77, 94
Appuleius, Sextus. *Cos. 29* BC	37
Arcadius. Emp: 395–408	129–31, 139 n.43
Attalus Nonius	107
Attius Varus, Publius. *Pr. 53* (?)	57 n.48
Augustus (*see* also, Octavian)	chapter 1 passim, 43, 53, 57 n.50, 72, 119 n.77, 127, 137, 141, 143 n.53, 148
Caesar (*see* Julius)	
Cassius, Spurius. *Cos. 486* BC	8 n.17
Cicero (*see* Tullius)	
Cincius, Lucius	67–70
Claudius. Emp: 41–54	6
Claudius Caecus, Appius	20 n.20
Claudius Marcellus, Gaius. *Cos. 49* BC	24 n.31
Claudius Marcellus, Marcus. *Cos. 222* BC	18, 19 n.18, 34 n.53, 67
Claudius Pulcher, Appius. *Cos. 54* BC	36 n.59, 64
Constantine. Emp: 312–37	55 n.40, chapter 4 passim
Cornelius Balbus, Lucius. *Procos.* (?)	35 n.57, 37 n.60
Cornelius Blasio, Gnaeus. *Procos. 199* BC	55 n.42
Cornelius Cossus, Aulus. *Trib. Mil. 437* BC	24 n.32

INDEX OF PERSONS

Cornelius Lentulus, Lucius. *Procos.* 206 BC	49
Cornelius Lentulus Gaetulicus, Cossus. *Cos.* 1 BC	37 n.60
Cornelius Lentulus Crus, Lucius. *Cos.* 49 BC	24 n.51, 49
Cornelius Scipio Asina, Cn. *Cos.* 260 BC	19 n.18
Cornelius Scipio Africanus, Publius. *Cos.* 205 BC	19 n.18, 23 n.25, 36 n.59, 37, 47–49
Cornelius Sulla Felix, Lucius. *Cos.* 88 BC	23 n.27, 24, 46, 54, 72–74
Decius Mus, Publius. *Cos.* 340 BC	68–69
Domitius Ahenobarbus, Lucius. *Cos.* 64 BC	64
Fabius, Marcus. *Cos.* 483 BC	7
Fabius Maximus, Quintus. *Leg.* 45 BC	57 n.48, 58
Fabius Maximus Verrucosus, Quintus. *Cos.* 233 BC	54
Flaminius, Gaius. *Cos.* 233 BC	60–62, 64, 66–67
Flavius Eusignius. *Procos.* AD 383	129
Flavius Felix, Titus. *Praef. Coh.*	107
Fufius Calenus, Quintus.	*Pr.* 59 57 n.48
Gabinius, Aulus. *Cos.* 58 BC	57 n.48, 64
Gaius Caesar	102
Galerius. Emp: 305–11	89, 132
Gratian. Emp: 367–83	126 n.10, 129
Hannibal	12
Hirtius, Aulus. *Cos.* 43 BC	43, 49, 57
Horatius Cocles	18–19
Holconius Rufus, Marcus.	18 n.16, 19 n.18, 20 n.21
Iunius Pera, Marcus. *Cos.* 245 BC	58
Julius Caesar, C.	chapter 1 passim, 46 n.10, 54, 70 n.84, 75–76, 134, 149 n.66
Julius, Gaius. *Dict.* 352 BC	99 n.52
Licinius. Emp: 308–24	132 n.29, 137, 148
Licinius Crassus, Publius. *Cos.* 171 BC	106
Considius Longus, Gaius. *Pr.* 58 BC	57 n.48
Lucretius Gallus, Gaius. *Pr.* 171 BC	106
Maenius, Gaius. *Trib. Pl.* 483 BC	7
Manlius Vulso, Gnaeus. *Cos.* 189 BC	59, 106

INDEX OF PERSONS

Manlius Acidinus, Lucius. *Procos.* 206 BC	49
Marcellus (jurist, 2c AD)	5
Marius, Gaius. *Cos.* 82 BC	20 n.20
Maxentius. Emp: 306–12	133, 134 n.32, 141, 145, 154
Maximianus. Emp: 286–305	132
Caecilius Metellus Pius Scipio Nasica, Quintus. *Cos.* 52 BC	57
Octavian	30 nn.41–42, chapter 2 passim, 94, 134
Pansa (*see* Vibius)	
Passienus Rufus, L. *Cos.* 4 BC	37 n.60
Pedius, Quintus. *Leg.* 45 BC	57 n.48
Petreius, Marcus. *Pr.* 64 BC	57 n.48
Pompeius Magnus, Gnaeus. *Cos.* 70 BC	12 n.5, 23–24, 35–36, 48–49, 55, 57, 72
Pomptinus, Gaius. *Pr.* 63 BC	36 n.59
Postumius, Gaius. *Haruspex*	54
Quintius, Titus Flamininus	46 n.11, 49
Sempronius Atratinus, Lucius. *Leg.*	35 n.57, 37
Sempronius Gracchus, Tiberius. *Tr. pl.* 133 BC	39 n.68
Servilius Isauricus, Publius. *Cos.* 48 BC	24 n.31
Servius Tullius. *Rex*	4
Spurinna. *Haruspex*	54 n.40
Stertinus, Lucius. *Procos.* 199 BC	55 n.42
Sulla (*see* Cornelius Sulla)	
Sulpicius Galba, Servius	71, 73
Sulpicius Peticus, Gaius. *Dict.* 358	99 n.52
Theodosius. Emp: 392–5	126 n.10, 129–31
Tiberius. Emp: 14–37	13, 41, 42, 90–92
Tullius Cicero, Marcus. *Cos.* 63 BC	6, 12 n.5, 18, 19 n.18, 35 nn.56–57, 36 nn.58–59, 43, 45–54, 56–57, 60, 62, 64–66, 71, 73–75, 167
Tullus Hostilius. *Rex*	67–69
Valentinian II. Emp: 375–92	126 n.10, 129–30, 132
Valentinian III. Emp: 424–55	167 n.85
Valerius, L. *Cos.* 483	7
Valerius Laevinus, Marcus. *Cos.* 220 BC (?)	55 n.42

INDEX OF PERSONS

Valerius Maximus Corvus, Marcus. *Cos.* 348 BC	58
Varus (*see* Attius Varus)	
Vatinius, Publius. *Cos.* 47 BC	24 n.31
Verres, Gaius. *Pr.* 74 BC	12 n.5, 54, 67 n.75
Vespasian. Emp: 69–79	6, 41
Vibius Pansa Caetronianus, Gaius. *Cos.* 43 BC	43–44, 49, 57
Vipsanius Agrippa, Marcus. *Cos.* 37 BC	29, 37
Vitellius. Emp: 69	40–42, 148
Volusius. *Haruspex*	54
Volusius Saturninus, Lucius. *Cos. suff.* AD 3	30, 31 n.43

INDEX OF WORKS OF ART

Coins

BM
Inv. B2142   fig. IV.21

RIC
    I², Augustus (Spain) no. 99   19 n.19
    I², Augustus (Spain) no. 131   37
    I², Augustus (Spain) no. 138   119 n.77
    I², Augustus (uncertain mint) no. 262   74 n.101
    II, Domitian (Rome) no. 381   81–82
    II, Trajan (Rome) no. 294   142 n.52
    II, Trajan (Rome) no. 295   142 n.52
    IV.1, Septimius (Rome) no. 761   117
    VI, Constantine (Rome) no. 151   159
    VI, Constantine (Rome) no. 284 add.   159
    VI, Constantine (Rome) nos. 345–52   141 n.52
    VI, Constantine (Alexandria) no. 63   152
    VI, Constantine (Trier) no. 627   159
    VI, Constantine (Trier) no. 636   159
    VI, Constantine (Trier) no. 638   159
    VI, Constantine (Trier) no. 815   141
    VII, Constantine (Trier) no. 208a   159, 164
    VII, Constantine (Trier) no. 469   137
    VII, Constantine (Ticinum) no. 36   147, 159, 164

RRC
    291   75 n.102
    293   75 n.102

INDEX OF WORKS OF ART

381	23 n. 27, 74 n.101
425	74 n.101
429	74 n.101
454	74 n.101, 75 n.102
456/1a	25 n.33
480/6	25 n.33
490/1	30 n.42, 72
490/2	76–77
494/3a	30 n.42
494/25	30 n.42
497/1	76 n.106, 77
518	30 n.42
518/2	75 n.102
526	30 n.42

Statues

Berlin, Staatliche Museen: Tetrarchic statue	154
Chieti: "General" from Foruli	20–21
Munich, Glyptotek: Cuirassed statue	16
Naples: Statue of Marcus Holconius Rufus	20 n.21
Rome	
Palazzo Massimo: "general" from Tivoli	20, 22 n. 22
Palazzo Senatorio: statue of Julius Caesar	14
Capitoline balustrade: Statue of Constantine	
Equestrian statue of M. Aemilius Lepidus	73
Equestrian statue of L. Antonius	73
Equestrian statue of Octavian	71–74, 77
Equestrian statue of Philippus	74
Equestrian statue of Pompeius	72
Equestrian statue of Sulla	72, 74 n.101
Statue of Servilius Sulpicius	73
Vatican Museum	
Augustus from Prima Porta statue	20
Four Tetrarchs	149
Venice, San Marco: Four Tetrarchs	149

INDEX OF WORKS OF ART

Portraits

Lucus Feroniae, Antiquarium: Portrait of Augustus	27–28, 30 n.42
Rome, Forum of Trajan: Constantine portrait (colossal)	157

Reliefs, Altars

Aesernia: Monument of Attalus Nonius	107
Berlin, Staatliche Museen: Rinuccini sarcophagus	113
Chatsworth: Trajanic relief	13
Edinburgh, National Museum: Bridgeness slab	112–13, 115
Eining: Altar of T. Flavius Felix	107–108, 112
Florence, Uffizi: Altar from the Vicus Sandaliarius	102–103, 106
Narbo (Narbonne): Augustan altar	52
Paris	
Census/Lustratio relief ("Altar of Domitius Ahenobarbus")	39, 95–100
Extispicium relief	103–105
Poggio a Caiano, Villa Medici: General's sarcophagus	112, 117
Rome	
Anaglypha Triani	13 n.11, 146
Cancelleria reliefs	13
Galleria Borghese, Hercules Altar	116–17
Museo Capitolino: M. Aurelius sacrificing	79–80
Palazzo Massimo: Via Cassia relief	23 n.26
Vatican Museum	
Belvedere Altar	18 n.17, 22 n.22
Galleria Lapidaria relief	88
Sacrifice relief	14, 101

Architectural Monuments

Rome	
Arch of Augustus (Parthian Arch)	37, 141

INDEX OF WORKS OF ART

Arch of Constantine	13, 117, 119, Ch. 4, passim
Arch of Septimius Severus	126, 139, 141, 143, 145, 147 n.61
Bocchus Monument	39
Column of Marcus Aurelius	86, 90, 97, 115–16, 117
Column of Trajan	82 n.9, 83–85, 87–88, 88 n.19, 89 n.22, 90, 97–100, 135, 136 n.35, 142 n.52, 144, 147
Caesar's monument on the Capitol	23 n.26
Vulci: François Tomb	19 n.19

Varia

Paris, Louvre	
Augustan tripod base	79–80
Boscoreale cup	13 n.9, 90–95, 100, 102
Piazza Armerina: Small Hunt Mosaic	119
Vatican Library: Calendar of 354	127 n.14, 135 n.34, 149

GENERAL INDEX

acerra, 83
acclamations, 22 n.23, 38, 41–42, 71–72, 74
adlocutio, 143, 147, 149, 154, 165–67
adventus, 41, 88, 104 n.57, 105, 134 n.32, 135, 136 n.35, 147 n.61, 165
Aeneas, 22 n.22, 92
Ariminum, 61–62
Augury, 4, 6, 51, 58, 70 n.84, 87 n.16; *Auguraculum*, 67 n.75; Augural College, 76–77; Augural law, 10, 39 n.68, 42, 51; *inauguratio*, 3, 10, 45, 54, 58–59, 61, 64, 69; *locus inauguratus*, 3, 58 n.53
Auspicia, 3, 5–6, 10–11, 19, 23 n.28, 34–36, 37 n.60, 38–39, 42, chapter 2 passim, 102; *auspicia habere*, 56; *auspicia militiae*, 33, 36 n.59, 42, 55, 63, 66, 70–71, 77; *auspicia ponere*, 56; *auspicia publica*, 44–45, 55; *auspicia repetendorum causa*, 58; *repetitio auspiciorum* 58, 60 n.57, 62; *auspicia urbana*, 11 nn.2–3, 39 n.68, 56, 71

castra, 99–100, 106 n.61
cinctus Gabinus, 81, 82 n.7, 96
civil war, 24, 35, 46 n.12, 56, 73, 127, 134, 137, 141
civilis princeps, 42, 124, 145, 146 n.58
clementia, 24–25
coercitio, 8, 10 n.1
colonia, 3 n.8, 51 n.29, 54, 96–99
coloniae deductio, 96–97

comitia: *centuriata*, 4, 48, 58, 64; *curiata*, 45, 48, 51, 58, 63 n.66, 64; *tributa*, 39, 41, 59
comparatio, 69
concordia, 25, 147
continentia aedificia, 4–5
cuirass, 14–20, 22 nn.21–22, 23, 27–32, 37–38, 75 n.102, 83, 85 n.12, 89, 107, 110, 159
cultores, 79
cursus honorum, 22, 30, 47

decennalia, 141
Diana, 119–20
domi et militiae, 10–12, 24–25, 34, 40, 42, 70, 75, 95, 101, 148, 166

Entmachtung, 24
Entritualisierung, 119
exempla, 67
exercitus, 46, 88, 94, 97, 99–100, 107, 124, 167
extispicium, 53–54, 85 n.12, 103–6

fas, 50, 70
fasces, 12, 23, 25, 34, 44, 52, 104 n.57
Fasti/Feriale: Cumanum, 44; Praenestini, 44
Feriae Latinae, 45, 49, 58 n.53, 61
fibula, 85 n.12, 87
fiction, 6, 32, 57, 62, 93–95, 99, 101, 141
Forum Gallorum, 71

GENERAL INDEX

Gabinus, *cinctus*, 81–82, 96
Gaul, 32 n.47, 61, 106

habitus, 97, 115, 117, 149 n.66
haruspices, 54, 82, 105
Hercules, 3, 85 n.12, 116–17
hostiae, 45 n.8, 85 n.12, 105, 116,

immolatio, 79, 83
imperator, 13, 22 n.23, 23 n.26, 25, 31, 34, 38, 40–41, 71, 74, 124, 146, 148
imperium, passim; *imperium consulare*, 39; delegated, 56–57; *domi*, 11 n.3, 12 n.8, 39 n.67; *extra ordinem*, 24, 37, 47- 49, 55, 58; *maius*, 33; *militiae*, 4, 8, 11–12, 24, 35 n.56, 39, 49, 55; *pro consule*, 33 n.50, 52, 55 n.42, 67; *pro praetore*, 46, 52, 55 n.42, 57, 67
iursidictio, 10 n.1, 25 n.33, 34
ius: *ius augurum*, 51; *ius auspicii*, 62; *auspicandi*, 52, 71; *auspiciorum*, 52, 62; *imperii*, 55 n.41; *publicum*, 51
iustus, 45, 50–51, 62–63
Iuventas, 116

Jupiter, 3, 6, 11, 23 n.25, 50, 85 n.12, 90, 92, 101 n.54, 112, 135, 136 n.35

Lake Regillus, 59
Lake Trasimene, 60
Latin League, 68–70
legatus, 36 n.59, 37 n.60, 56–57
lex: 11, 24 n.31, 35–36, 39, 41, 45–52, 54, 55 n.43, 58, 61–67, 75; *lex curiata*, 36, 39, 45, 47–52, 55 n.43, 58, 61- 66; *lex de imperio Vespasiani*, 41; *leges fictio Corneliae*, 93; *lex Pompeia de provinciis*, 24 n.31, 35, 46; *lex Titia*, 75, 76 n.104
libation, 79, 83, 85–86, 119
lictor, 23, 34, 63, 87–88

lituus, 76
locus inauguratus, 59
Ludi Saeculares, 79, 81, 117, 119 n.77, 145 n.57
lustratio, 87, 95–97, 99–100, 107, 112, 117, 136; *lustratio exercitus*, 97, 99–100

magistrates, 11, 23, 35 n.57, 36, 40, chapter 2 passim, 93, 96, 105–6, 128, 133
magistratus iustus, 50, 62–63
Mars, 4, 29, 85 n.12, 96–97, 101
ministri, 79, 112
Mons Albanus, 92, 58 n.53, 68
mos Etruscus, 82
mos maiorum, 42, 56
mutatio vestis, 40, 42, 74 n.99, 148
Mutina, 47, 49, 71–72

Narbo, altar, 52, 55
negligentia, 56, 60 n.59
nova et integra, 61, 63
nuncupatio votorum, 14, 61, 67, 90, 92–95, 99, 100–106, 112–13

optimo lege et iure, 50–51, 66
ornatus, 18–19; *provinciae ornatus*, 66; *triumphali ornatus*, 19 nn.18–19
ornithoskopoi, 51
ovatio, 27, 32

paenula, 83, 87–88
paludamentum, 40, 83, 85 n.12, 86–87, 90, 107, 110, 146–47, 149 n.66, 154,
paludatus, 13, 18–19, 87–88, 106, 110, 112, 149, 165,
Pannonia, 90
parapetasma, 113
patres, 47, 59, 105
Pharsalus, 23, 73
Piazza Armerina, 119
pietas, 111, 113

GENERAL INDEX

pomerium, passim; expansion of, 5–6
pontiff, 4
populus Romanus, 40, 44, 48 n.19, 74, 94 n.35, 134, 145–47, 158
praefatio, 83
Praeneste, 44, 107
prayer, 44–45, 54, 105
privatus, 33, 35 n. 57, 36 n.59, 39, 48, 55, 56 n.43, 61–62; *privatus cum imperio*, 46–47, 49, 66
pro magistratu, 63–64
profectio, 105, 165
prorogatio, 48, 64
provincia, 36, 46, 48 n.19, 55–56, 57 n.50, 60, 62–71, 76, 94, 100, 105, 135
pullarius, 51

quadriga, 127, 135, 146

recte, 45, 51
recusatio, 32
Reisekostüm, 83 n.11, 87, 90, 146, 147 n.61, 154
religio, religiosus, 60 n.59, 94, 127 n.17
Remus, 70 n.83
res: *res civiles*, 8, 101; *res militares*, 8, 46, 90, 101; *res publica*, 33 n.50, 74
ritus, chapter 3, passim; *ritus Albanus*, 81–82; *Etruscus*, 82; *Gabinus* (see Cinctus Gabinus); *ritus Graecus*, 79, 101, 117; *militaris*, chapter 3 passim; *Romanus*, 78–79, 89–90, 97, 101, 117, 119
Roma Quadrata, 2 n.2, 3, 166
Rome (Sites/Monuments): Altar of Consus, 3, 166; Ara Maxima, 116–17; Arco di Portogallo, 126; Arcus Novus, 126; Basilica Nova, 145; Campus Martius, 4, 95–96, 100, 137; Capitol, 6, 14, 23 nn. 25–26, 38 n.65, 45–6, 58, 61, 67–71, 86 n.12, 90–92, 96 n.43, 100, 103, 106–7, 111, 113, 135–36, 154, 157n.71, 165 n.81; Comitium, 1–2, 45; Curiae Veteres, 3, 166 n.82; Five-Column Monument, 147, 148 n.63; Forum Augustum, 18 n.17, 19–20 n.20, 22 n.22, 31 n.46; Forum Boarium, 3, 117, 166; Forum Iulium, 14, 23 n.26; Forum Romanum, 3, 13, 18, 146, 154, 164, 166–67; Mausoleum, 27 n.35; Milvian Bridge, 40, 124, 146; *Mundus*, 1–3; Palatine, 2–4, 166; Pantheon, 29–32; *Sacellum Larum*, 3, 166
Romulus, 1, 6, 18, 22 n.22, 70 n.83

sacrifice, *sacrificium*, 45, 54, 55 n.40, 58, 61, chapter 3 passim, 136, 165; *capite aperto*, chapter 3 passim, 136; *capite velato*, 31 n.45, chapter 3 passim
sarcophagus, 92, 112–14, 117, 132
sedes imperatoriae, 154
sella curulis, 23 n.28, 34
senatus consulta, 41, 47–48, 52, 55, 65, 69, 105
Serdica, 154
sine magistratu, 36, 46, 48–49, 52
Sirmium, 154
sortitio, 63, 65, 69
sparsio, 149
Spoleto, 30, 47, 53, 54, 58
spolia, 123, 126–27, 143
SPQR, 52, 55, 123, 125, 140–41, 148 n.63
standards, Parthian, 27, 32–33, 37, 39
statua: statua loricata, chapter 1 passim, 75, 87, 107 n.65, 146, 149, 154–57, 165; *statua honoraria*, 14, 18, 19–20, 27, 30, 71, 72 n.91, 73, 110–11, 127, 131, 133, 164–65
sulcus primigenius, 2, 10
suovetaurilia, 83, 89 n.22, 96–97, 106–7, 112–13, 115, 117
supplicationes, 38, 57, 71

GENERAL INDEX

temple, 4, 23 n.25, 29, 90, 92, 94–95, 103, 105, 107, 110, 112–13, 135; Temple of Bellona, 94–95; Temple of Jupiter Capitolinus, 23 n.25, 90, 112, 135
Tetrarchs, 147, 149, 154 n.66, 158–59
Thessalonica, 63 n.66, 89, 132 n.29, 154
toga: 41, 74, 83, 90, 96–97, 102, 104, 107, 110, 112–13, 115, 116 n.75, 119, 138 n.40, 147, 148 n.62, 154, 158n.74, 165; *toga picta*, 19–20, 22, 146, 147 n.60; *praetexta*, 23, 40; *triumphalis (vestis triumphalis)*, 18–19, 111; *virilis*, 44 n.3

tripudium, 60, 62
triumph, 18–20, 22–4, 27 n.35, 31–40, 57 n.48, 66 n.70, 90, 92, 111, 123, 127, 134–41, 146, 147 n.60, 165
tunica, 83, 86–87, 107, 146–47

victimarius, 83, 85
Victoria, 104–5, 113, 116, 146, 149
victoriola, 149
virtus, 111, 159
vota, 14, 45 n.8, 61, 67, 90, 92, 95, 101, 103, 106, 110, 113, 141, 145 n.57; *vota soluta*, 141; *suscepta*, 74, 145